"The greatest way to influence tl
cards and letters—but by praying for them. This prayer is py
ing, and I believe it is from the heart of our wonderful and merciful God.
May the Lord cause many to catch the vision of this book."

> —DR. BILL BRIGHT, founder and president,
> Campus Crusade for Christ International

"I've seen it with my own eyes—God is in the business of changing people's
lives! It doesn't matter who they are. Ask the Lord to change the world as you
pray for each person profiled in this interesting, informative, and provocative new book."

> —LUIS PALAU, international evangelist; author of *Where Is
> God When Bad Things Happen?*

"Praying for leaders is a God-given privilege and, indeed, His command.
Here in one volume is information to help us carry out that privilege and
command."

> —DR. BRANDT GUSTAVSON, president,
> National Religious Broadcasters

"The effective prayer of a righteous man *does* accomplish much! You can
truly make a difference in this world by praying faithfully for spiritual, cultural, and political leaders. And this book is a resource that can help you be
more informed and effective as you pray."

> —JOSH MCDOWELL, author,
> founder & president, Josh McDowell Ministries

"We all need prayer, and the affirmation and courage loving prayer gives us.
As we pray for others, so we count on our communities praying for us."

> —MADELEINE L'ENGLE, Newbery Award-winning author,
> *A Wrinkle in Time*

"How do we Christians treat the prominent people of today? Often we ignore
those we should listen to, idolize those we should beware of, and demonize
those who have something to teach us. This book leads us to a better stance:
praying wisely for those who influence our world."

> —MARSHALL SHELLEY, editor, *Leadership*;
> vice president of editorial, Christianity Today, Inc.

"I can't think of a more powerful way to influence someone's life than to pray
for them! This book could be one of the most powerful tools for people to
make an impact on our nation's future."

> —GARY SMALLEY

"I think that *Praying for the World's 365 Most Influential People* is one of the most exciting challenges to come before us in a long time. It is an intentional and positive call to all of us to join together in prayer for peace and harmony in our time."

—THE RIGHT REVEREND EDMOND L. BROWNING,
Presiding Bishop (retired), the Episcopal Church in the U.S.A.

"Working as I do among the most influential 'unreached people group' on the planet—the leaders of American media in Hollywood and New York—I see one *sine qua non* for success—prayer. Where prayer ascends, power descends. The Pray 365 Project may well be the pivotal factor in stirring the Wind of the Spirit to fan the existing flames of revival in media into an inferno of spiritual awakening."

—LARRY W. POLAND, Ph.D.,
Chairman and CEO, MasterMedia International

"How do you change the world? One heart at a time. How do you change a heart? One prayer at a time. Why pray for people of influence? Paul told Timothy with absolute clarity, 'That all might be saved and come to a knowledge of the Truth!' May you and I use this book as a catalyst for the most profound and lasting influence of all in the lives of those who influence us."

—JANET PARSHALL, **Host of the nationally syndicated talk show, "Janet Parshall's America"**

"Spiritual awakening has always been preceded by an awakening among Christians regarding the power of prayer. Praise God for a book that challenges us to widen our horizons to pray for those who influence the currents of our culture. I believe God will respond in ways beyond all expectations."

—REV. WALTER GERBER, **senior pastor, Menlo Park Presbyterian Church, Menlo Park, California**

"In my 12 years experience with the Green Bay Packers, I've seen how much others are impacted by sports icons. But I've also witnessed the power of Christ through prayer to change my life and the lives of my fellow teammates. Please join me in praying for the men and women on the pages of this book—for their protection and salvation, so that our mighty God can impact our world through them."

—KEN RUETTGERS, **12 year veteran (retired), the Green Bay Packers; Author of *The Homefield Advantage***

"I think this is a splendid project. We are commanded to pray for those in authority. Leaders around the world are subject to terrible distractions and temptations. Every Christian should pray for those in positions of influence, as the Bible tells us, so that we might live peaceable lives. This is a wonderful effort.

—CHARLES W. COLSON, author; president,
Prison Fellowship Ministries

"The Pray 365 Project is a vision that could change the world! I can only imagine the awesome good that will come forth as thousands of intercessors join together in one accord to pray for the individuals who control the ways and means to make changes for good in our global village!"

—C. PETER WAGNER, president, Global Harvest Ministries &
World Prayer Center; author; professor of
Church Growth (retired), Fuller Seminary

"I can't tell you how much this book touches our hearts. Our experience in the television and film industry has shown us how much prayer changes things—hearts, plans, priorities . . . the world! *Praying for the World's 365 Most Influential People* is brilliantly conceived to help us meet and pray for those in positions of leadership and influence. The Pray 365 Project clearly has the power to change our world in the 21st century.

—KEN WALES, executive producer, the CBS "Christy" series
—SUSAN WALES, author, *A Match Made in Heaven*

"Just think what God could do if Christians are inspired and mobilized to earnestly pray for these 365 influential people! This is a great resource for families, churches, and individuals who want to make a difference in our world."

—CHERI FULLER, author, *When Mothers Pray*

"The Pray 365 Project is a unique instrument for focusing collective prayer on points of leverage for the love of God to be manifested in the world."

—HARVILLE HENDRIX, Ph.D., author,
Getting the Love You Want; marriage and relationship mentor

"Any level of God-given influence carries responsibility that only His enablement can fulfill. Pray for any leader you know, as you pray for these."

—JACK HAYFORD, senior pastor,
The Church on the Way, Van Nuys, California

"What I appreciate about *Praying for the World's 365 Most Influential People* is being offered portraits which are human and accessible. The authors have put real faces on these persons, described with clarity the tough issues with which they live, and invited the reader to be as genuine with prayer as the text is with these personal profiles."

—THE RT. REV. RUSTIN R. KIMSEY,
Episcopal Bishop of Eastern Oregon

"I would urge Christians to pray earnestly for the people in this book as an addition to their regular prayers for family and church leaders. We never know when a Christian leader needs encouragement. And we never know when a person who is "on the other side" is searching for answers in their own lives."

—MICHAEL P. FARRIS, president,
Home School League Defense Fund

"The money. The arrogance. The loose living. The trash talk. Too often these elements of the sports world cause us to criticize the men and women in that arena. Instead of criticizing them, though, we need to do something positive—something that can guide them toward the light of Christ. This book provides that way by suggesting a godly, results-oriented mechanism: Prayer."

—DAVE BRANON, managing editor,
Sports Spectrum magazine

"You are to be commended for catching the vision to urge God's people to pray for God's servants everywhere. These are enormous days of soul harvest opportunity and we need to pray millions into the kingdom before Christ returns."

—TIM LAHAYE, author of *Jesus, Who Is He?*
and coauthor of the "Left Behind" fiction series

"The Pray 365 Project is a powerful way to exercise and strengthen the muscles in the body of Christ. Thank heavens for heartfelt intercessions!"

—JONI EARECKSON TADA, author;
founder & president, JAF Ministries

"You and I may not have made the list as 'the World's 365 Most Influential People,' but this book provides practical ways for each of us to be influential through our prayers."

—JAMES WATKINS, newspaper columnist; pastor,
LaOtta Free Methodist Church,
Indiana; adjunct professor at Taylor University

"Prayer is the one sure way we can affect the hearts and decisions of the world's powerful people. In fact, it's the only method of influence for most of us. Thank you for providing a constructive and positive way to think about and pray for those who have such an impact on society."

—RON JENSON, author; president,
Future Achievement International and High/Ground

"American culture today has polarized the 'right' and 'left' to the point of gridlock. I believe this book is a message from God to the 'right' to reach out to the world. Christians should be praying for the world in love, instead of hurling insults from their closets."

—JAMES LLOYD, president and CEO,
Versatile Systems, Seattle, Washington

"There is nothing God cannot do when His people pray. What better way to change our world for the better than to sincerely seek God's will in the lives of the people who shape our culture. I hope everyone who reads this book will do just that."

—SAM MOORE, CEO and president,
Thomas Nelson Publishers/Word

"What a great way to influence the influencers in our world! If we believe in a God who gives grace, peace, wisdom and joy to those who ask, then this is a very worthwhile effort. May the love of God go forth as a result."

—BRIAN PETERSON, editor, *New Man* magazine

"God's Word tells us that He wants everyone to come to the knowldge of the truth....Through our faithful prayers, we can accomplish spiritually what we'll probably never get a chance to do personally—change our world by asking God to change our world leaders' hearts. I recommend this book."

—GREG LAURIE, author of *The Upside Down Church*;
senior pastor, Harvest Christian Fellowship, Riverside, California

"You need look no further than a school yard near you to know that gun violence is piercing America's soul. As president of Mothers Against Violence in America, I recognize that our communities must come together at a deeper level than what politics or personal rights will allow. That's why I applaud the objectives of this book, and value the support and spiritual unity it promotes.

—PAMELA EAKES, founder and president,
Mothers Against Violence in America

PRAYING
FOR THE WORLD'S
365 MOST
INFLUENTIAL
PEOPLE

David Kopp
Heather Harpham Kopp,
and Larry Wilson,

editors

HARVEST HOUSE PUBLISHERS
Eugene, Oregon 97402

Cover by David Uttley Design, Sisters, Oregon

Every attempt has been made to secure and cite permission for use of the photographs reproduced in this book. Where accuracy or completeness of credit is in error, corrections will gladly be reflected in future editions. Please direct queries to:

 Pray 365 Project
PO Box 723
Sisters, OR 97759

PRAYING FOR THE WORLD'S 365 MOST INFLUENTIAL PEOPLE
Copyright © 1999 by David and Heather Kopp
Published by Harvest House Publishers
Eugene, Oregon 97402

Library of Congress Cataloging-in-Publication Data

Kopp, David, 1949–
    Praying for the world's 365 most influential people / David and Heather Kopp.
        p.   cm.
    ISBN 0-7369-0047-0
    1. Prayer—Christianity.   2. Celebrities Miscellanea.   I. Kopp, Heather Harpham,
1964–   . II. Title. III. Title: Praying for the world's three hundred sixty five most
influential people.
    BV215.K66   1999
    248.3'2—dc21   99-20323
                                                                                    CIP

Printed in the United States of America.

        99   00   01   02   03   04   / BP /   10   9   8   7   6   5   4   3   2   1

ACKNOWLEDGMENTS

We owe a tremendous debt of gratitude to Katherine Mosby, our project coordinator, for her endless hours gathering photos and permissions and providing valuable editorial assistance.

This book would not have been possible without the research and writing help of Holly Halverson, Suzanne Woods Fisher, Kris Ingram, Katherine Jones, Kim Hayes, Melody Carlson, Ruth Nygren Keller, and Linda Claire.

We received valuable input and guidance from the following specialists: Marshall Shelley, editor, *Leadership* magazine; Dave Branon, managing editor, *Sports Spectrum* magazine; Ken Ruettgers, defensive tackle (retired) for the Green Bay Packers; Derek Wesley Selby, free-lance music reviewer; Mary Manz Simon, D.Ed., children's author and parenting columnist; Craig Morton, MarketKnowledge; Hugh Ross, Ph.D., physicist and president of Reason to Believe; Dr. Buster Holmes, vice president, MasterMedia; Ken Wales, television producer; Susan Wales, author and speaker; Dr. Bill Pannel, professor of homiletics, Fuller Theological Seminary; Kris Ingram, author of *Blessing Your Enemies, Forgiving Your Friends* (Liguori); and Terry Dirks, director of International Renewal Ministries.

Special thanks to Deborah Hedstrom, English professor, and her team of student reporters at Western Baptist College (Salem, Oregon): Leigha Cranston, Anndee Beatty, Steele Bailey, Cassie Doyle, Crystal Brown, Jill Jackson, Jarod King, Jason Merrel, Machelle Briggs, Beau Batsell, Heather Lewis, Dusty Dexter, Betsy Thomas, Rebecca Hill, Perry Steinbrook, Katie Frasier, Jeff Tollison, David Clinton, Ryan Watkins, Alicia Philbrook, Ronda Martin, Eric Doran, Grace Doebler, Stacey Durbin, Tifanie Lumm, Jared Slyh, Jackie Norris, Mandy Holt, Amanda Kirkelie, Holly Cozby, Jason Tompkins, Anthony Trail, Mike Franke, Kristin Larrabee, Kristine Wood, Darren Banek, Jessica Sarver, Jenelle Wilson, Matt Miller, Marcella McIntyre, Andrew Crawmer, Kurt Palmer, Kevin Turner, Heidi Potter, Miriam Palmer, Ryan Watkins, Jeremy Rainbow, and David Burke.

We appreciated the generous assistance of photographer Rick Reinhard, and the help of all those who provided photographs.

As always, we value the incredible support and perseverance of the entire publishing team at Harvest House Publishers, especially Carolyn McCready, Terry Glaspey, and Betty Fletcher in editorial, Ty Pauls in design, and Bill Jensen and Christy Curtis in sales.

We're deeply grateful for our supportive family at Episcopal Church of the Transfiguration, Sisters, Oregon, and especially for the personal enthusiasm of Pastor Larry Harrelson, Craig and Rebecca Morton, and Penny Buttke.

Finally we'd like to thank our wonderful children for their love and prayers: Neil, Taylor, Noah, Jana, and Nathan.

—*David Kopp, Heather Harpham Kopp, and Larry Wilson, editors*

HAVE YOU CHANGED YOUR WORLD TODAY?

The book you're holding is the result of a simple and irrefutable spiritual premise: Prayer changes things. And together, God's people can dramatically change the world by praying for those who impact it most.

Think of the possibilities:

Imagine the power of thousands of people praying and agreeing together on the same day for the same world figure.

Imagine the love of Christ pouring out in prayers for people who on any day are capable of accomplishing good or harm for millions.

Imagine a nonbeliever hearing, instead of judgment and rejection, a beautiful refrain from Christ's people: "You are loved! We bless you in Jesus' name today!"

An important goal for The Pray 365 Project has been to bring together believers from many denominations, promoting unity and love as we enter God's presence in prayer together. This book is only a small part of a growing prayer and renewal movement that is making itself felt around the world. Like virtually all of these groups, our goal is simple—we want to change the world through the power of prayer. With this in mind, we approach a daily prayer commitment like this humbly, gratefully, and expectantly.

But first, we thought you might have some questions:

How does this book work?

Praying for the World's 365 Most Influential People is presented in a daily format so that you can read about and pray for one influential person each day (knowing that thousands of other Christians are joining you). Each entry includes information about the person's point of impact, an insightful quote, and a behind the scenes look at his or her personal life.

The prayer starters which follow suggest—but aren't intended to limit—your prayer responses. Sometimes you may not agree with our tips, or the person's circumstances may have changed. We hope you will let the Holy Spirit guide you in your prayers.

What do you mean by influential?

An influencer, as we mean it in this book, is a living person whose life and work has a far-reaching impact—whether for good or ill—in the world today.

One criterion we favored was active influence versus potential influence. That would mean, for example, that the man who uses his millions to champion literacy around the world is more influential than the one who leaves his tens of millions in a Swiss bank. For similar reasons, fame doesn't always equal influence. You'll notice that some celebrities and public figures of the moment are missing. You'll also notice that some world-changers are not listed because we deemed their influence to be more a historically accomplished fact than on the leading edge of change now.

Ultimately, we recognize that influence is always a judgment call. And who but God really knows who the key influencers of our generation are? Somewhere a Sunday school teacher is shaping the president of the future, a little-known researcher is toiling on an entirely new way of treating cancer, a starving writer is putting the finishing touches on the next *Pilgrim's Progress*.

Besides, influence can be expressed in a variety of ways: for example, by personal sacrifice, use of power, spending or investing money, dynamic personal example, use of authority or position, service or generosity, influencing trends or setting new standards, or by a far-reaching faith or vision that mobilizes millions.

How did you decide whom to include?

Our team of researchers went to primary sources, talked with "gatekeepers" and knowledgeable resources in each category, combed published lists, and worked closely with a group of advisers, at least one for each category, who were experts in their area. Because this edition of the book is being distributed primarily in North America, you may notice a somewhat greater emphasis on U.S. and Canadian world-changers.

For the most part, the world influencers you'll encounter here—Christians and nonChristians alike—have welcomed our invitation for prayer on their behalf, including: Barbara Walters; David Geffen, DreamWorks partner; Jack Welch, CEO of General Electric (the world's most valuable company); Dan Rather; Irv Rubin, president of the Jewish Defense League; Kathie Lee Gifford; Harville Hendrix, author of *Getting the Love You Want;* famed scientist Ian Wilmut (he cloned a sheep); Jill Barad, CEO of Mattel; Rabbi Harold Kushner; Adam Werbach, president of the Sierra Club; famed geneticist, Dr. Craig Venter; Lutheran Presiding Bishop George Anderson; and Betty Beene, president of the United Way.

An overwhelming number of people we contacted also gave us detailed, helpful feedback, as well as providing photographs. Many endorsed this venture with great enthusiasm.

Why should I pray for influential people more than anyone else?

Of course we're never meant to limit our prayers to the movers and shakers of the world. But the Bible makes a special point of asking God's people to pray for them. The apostle Paul recognized that by praying for those who have power to affect many, we pray strategically. He told young Pastor Timothy: "I urge you then, first of all, that requests, prayers, intercession and thanksgiving be made for everyone—for kings and all those in authority—that we may live peaceful and quiet lives in all godliness and holiness" (1 Timothy 2:1-2).

In New Testament times power rested with the Caesars, the Roman governors and government officials, and the religious leaders of the Jews. In our time, the mantle of influence has spread far and wide—to sports figures, media personalities, research scientists, global investors, and writers, among many others. These change-makers help to determine cultural trends, legislation, the economy, politics, personal values, and social movements.

How can I pray effectively for the spiritual life of someone I don't know?

You'll notice we've tried not to make prejudgments or exclusionary assumptions about others' spiritual lives. For all of us, only God knows the heart (1 Samuel 16:7). We encourage you to trust that He will use even your incomplete knowledge of persons and situations to accomplish His perfect will.

Here are some prayers we can offer sincerely for everyone in this book:

- that each person will know Jesus Christ as Lord and Savior,
- that each person will desire and experience God's loving best for their life,
- that each one will be protected form life's dangers, upheld in life's trials, and grateful and generous in life's blessings, and
- that by the Spirit's power, each person will use their life and gifts to honor God and benefit others.

Why should I care about—much less pray for— people who seem to do nothing but harm?

Jesus called us to love and pray for all people—"I tell you: love your enemies, and pray for those who persecute you" (Matthew

5:44). However, it can take a lot of courage to pray for someone you dislike, disrespect, or fear. No wonder the disciples reacted with so much amazement when Jesus told them to intercede for their persecutors. "If you love those who love you," He asked, "what reward will you get? . . . Do not even pagans do that?" (Mattew 5:46-47).

Perhaps praying for our enemies is so hard because this kind of praying is nearly synonymous with forgiving. And forgiveness costs. Indifference at least feels safe, and even an attitude of goodwill leaves us feeling faintly superior. But to love and to pray for? There's just no room to hide in those words!

When we pray for those who seem to be doing everything in their power to take our world further from God, or to make it more dangerous for us and those we love, something amazing happens. We begin to love and forgive the world as God does. Paul says that Christ came to win us through love *while we were still sinners and enemies of God* (Romans 5:8,10).

Praying for those who seem opposed to the gospel allows us to see the world as God does, and to release His power to redeem even His sworn enemies.

How do you pray for a person whose life is offensive or destructive without being judgmental?

You'll notice that the profiles focus on the person's point of impact, not our opinion of them. The information is presented journalistically. Our goal in this case is not to endorse or condemn, but to allow facts and informed opinion to assist our praying.

In their little book, *31 Days of Prayer*, Warren and Ruth Myers have some good advice for praying without judging: "Especially when we're asking God to overcome negative qualities [of others], we must be on guard against the sin of a critical, proud spirit cloaked in prayer," write the Myerses. "When we're concerned about a person's negative qualities, it helps to think through to the corresponding positive qualities we hope for, and pray for those. We personally find it easier to have faith for the positives than against the negatives."

What are some ways I can put this prayer book to work?

This book lends itself to personal devotional use or to family reading around the house. You might consider leaving it on the kitchen table or in the car as a conversation and prayer starter for each day's date. Churches and other ministries will find it an encouraging and helpful tool for group use.

Finally, don't forget to make use of www.pray365.com, our website. There you'll find updates on the person of the day (what's happened since we went to press), a place to post prayers and to read the prayers of others, postings on "influencers in the news," and an invitation to suggest new influential people for inclusion in the next edition of this book. You'll also be able to order copies of the book direct for family, friends, or groups.

Now to him who is able to do immeasurably more
than all we ask or imagine, according to his power
that is at work within us, to him be glory
in the church and in Christ Jesus
throughout all generations.

Ephesians 3:20-21

The Pray 365 Project
David Kopp, Heather Harpham Kopp,
and Larry Wilson, editors

Maya Angelou
Author, Poet, Speaker

Archive Photo

POINT OF IMPACT: When she was eight, Maya Angelou was raped by her mother's boyfriend—an event which shaped her life as well as her acclaimed autobiographical novel *I Know Why the Caged Bird Sings.* Through this book and her other poetry and writings, Angelou has become a symbol of courage and a leading spokesperson for the oppressed, African-Americans, and women worldwide. Her books have sold in the millions and are required reading in most American colleges. The poem she read at Clinton's inauguration, "On the Pulse of Morning," now hangs in the White House. In 1996, Angelou— who has more than 50 honorary degrees and a Pulitzer Prize nomination—was named an ambassador for UNICEF. Now 71, she has one son and currently serves as a professor at Wake Forest University in North Carolina.

She gives courage to the oppressed.

QUOTABLE: "To be angry is very good. It burns out things and leaves nutrients in the soil. You should always be ready to be angry at injustice and cruelty."

BEHIND THE SCENES: Three days after Angelou reported she'd been raped, her attacker was found beaten to death. In her young mind, Angelou believed that it was her voice that killed the man, and for the next seven years she refused to speak. Instead, she read poetry and memorized it. It was during that period that she developed an ear for the lyricism that is the hallmark of her work.

PRAYER STARTERS:

- Give thanks for Maya Angelou's contributions to suffering people everywhere, and for the richness of her literary contributions.
- Pray for her well-being; ask God to reveal Himself to her in new ways today—"The Lord is near to all who call on him" (Psalm 145:18).
- Ask God to show you one thing you could do today to help a suffering child.

> *Rescue the weak and needy; deliver them from the hand of the wicked.*
> Psalm 82:4

CONTACT: Random House, 201 E. 50th St., New York, NY 10022-7703

Photo by Russ Busby

Billy Graham
Evangelist, Author

POINT OF IMPACT: In his 60 years of ministry, Billy Graham has preached to more people—over 200 million—than anyone else in history. Close to 3 million people in 185 countries have responded to his simple gospel message. He founded the Billy Graham Evangelistic Association in 1950, which now includes radio and television programs, two magazines, and a film company. The Gallup organization has listed Graham, now 80, as one of the Ten Most Admired Men in the World an unparalleled 39 times. He's written 18 bestselling books, including his autobiography, *Just As I Am*, and been the confidante and advisor of American presidents since Eisenhower.

He's preached to more people than anyone in history.

QUOTABLE: On his accomplishments: "I have in many ways failed. I haven't lived a life of devotion, meditation and prayer. I've allowed the world to creep into my life way too much." *USA Today*

BEHIND THE SCENES: Despite being afflicted with Parkinson's disease, Billy Graham continues to preach. He walks with a cane, his preaching is slower, but just as certain as ever. "I'm not a judge, I'm a shepherd," he says. Married to Ruth Bell Graham and the father of five grown children, in his spare time, Graham lounges in comfy blue jeans at home in Montreat, North Carolina. He likes to go for walks "praying every step of the way."

PRAYER STARTERS:

- Praise God for the millions who have met Christ through Graham's ministry, and give thanks for his enduring example of integrity.
- Pray for Graham's health, safety and strength, and for the continuing impact of the Billy Graham Evangelistic Association.
- Pray that Graham's legacy would continue to encourage unity among Christians around the world.

> *I am not ashamed of the gospel, because it is the power of God for the salvation of everyone who believes. Romans 1:16*

CONTACT: Billy Graham Evangelistic Association, 1300 Harmon Pl., Box 779, Minneapolis, MN 55440-0779

J. Dennis "Denny" Hastert III

Speaker of the House

POINT OF IMPACT: Today he holds the second most powerful position in America. But until he was named Speaker of the House of Representatives, J. Dennis "Denny" Hastert III was unknown to most outside of Washington and his home district in Illinois. In the wake of Clinton's impeachment hearings and Gingrich's resignation, Hastert has been charged not only with running the House but also with restoring public faith in Congress. While neither an idealogue or lawmaker, he's deeply respected by both parties for his integrity, listening skills, and his ability to build bridges across the ideological spectrum. Supporters say the low-key Hastert, 58, will be a "healing agent" in a body that needs one. Hastert's voting record recently earned him a 100-percent approval rating from the Christian Coalition. House majority leader Dick Armey calls Hastert "the best-kept secret in the House."

He holds the second most powerful political position in America.

QUOTABLE: "The American people want us to earn respect and win the recognition back for this U.S. Congress so they can be proud of what we do."

BEHIND THE SCENES: Hastert, an evangelical Christian, graduated from Wheaton College (Illinois) in 1964. Friends say it's not unusual to find a Bible open in his Capitol Hill apartment or to see him thumbing through Scripture before important votes. "Religion is in his heart and mind, and not on his sleeve," one GOP insider says. "We need a little more of that kind of religion." He and his wife, Jean, have two sons, Joshua and Ethan.

PRAYER STARTERS:

- Give thanks for Hastert's positive impact. Pray for wisdom and perseverance for Denny Hastert in his leadership role today.
- Pray for greater moral strength and leadership vision for Congress.
- Ask for provision and peace for the Hastert family today; pray that their relationships will flourish despite the pressures of public life.

Serve wholeheartedly, as if you were serving the Lord, not men. Ephesians 6:7

CONTACT: 2453 Rayburn House Office Building, Washington, DC 20515; e-mail: dhastert@hr.house.gov

Ted Turner

Vice Chairman,Time Warner, Inc.

POINT OF IMPACT: In the sixties, Ted Turner took the merest blip of a UHF station in Atlanta and created the satellite broadcast empire that now includes CNN, TBS, and TNT. Some say that the news station CNN, seen in more than 210 countries, has done more to close the gaps of misunderstanding between the world's people than any other enterprise. In 1996, Turner's reach grew when he merged his empire with Time Warner, creating the world's largest media company. In 1997, he donated $1 billion to the United Nations— and challenged others of the world's super-rich to match him. The grant (targeted for use with refugees, women's health, the environment, and land-mine clearance) was at the time the biggest single act of personal charity in history. *Time* magazine named him Man of the Year in 1992.

His CNN brings the world home.

QUOTABLE: "It takes all of us. We have to win over the vast majority of the world's people to win this fight for the survival of humanity. That's why I support the United Nations. . . . We cannot save the United States in the long haul without saving the whole world."

BEHIND THE SCENES: In the seventies and eighties, Turner earned a reputation as a hard-drinking womanizer. Since his marriage to his third wife, Jane Fonda, Turner—the father of five grown children—has mellowed and found happiness. "I want to be one of the good guys," he says. Turner, 62, resides in Atlanta.

PRAYER STARTERS:

- Give thanks for Ted Turner's bold example of generosity. Ask for other large-scale donors to take up his challenge.

- Pray that Turner's far-reaching influence in media and sports will be for good; pray that he will seek God's guidance today in his decisions.

- Ask for health and peace for the Turner family. Pray for spiritual wealth for Turner today—personally, and in his family relationships.

Command [those who are wealthy] to do good, to be rich in good deeds, and to be generous and willing to share. 1 Timothy 6:18

CONTACT: 1 CNN Center, Atlanta, GA 30303

Christie Hefner

CEO, Playboy Enterprises

Archive Photo

POINT OF IMPACT: Credited with "teaching an old rabbit new tricks," Christie Hefner has turned her father's notorious and long-lived magazine company back toward profitability. Hugh Hefner started *Playboy* with $600 in 1953; three decades and millions of dollars later, the company was losing revenue and popularity. In stepped the next of kin, and reform followed—financial reform, that is: Christie sold off the failing Playboy casinos and skinned the Bunnies, but she kept and extended the company's trademark naked girls and sex appeal. *Playboy* moved to television, offered videos and compact discs in a merchandise catalog, and went online. The magazine now has a circulation of 3.5 million. It's been a battle, partly because readers have wanted racier material, and partly because the antipornography movement has cost the company major advertising dollars.

She runs the most famous skin magazine for men.

QUOTABLE: About speculation that she may move into politics: "After spending all this time turning the company around, I'd have to be a masochist to leave and let someone else take all the credit and have all the fun."

BEHIND THE SCENES: Playboy has been part of Hefner's background nearly all her life; she was just a year old when her father launched the business. Now 48, the "softly spoken heiress," who has a degree in English and American literature, is single and lives in Chicago.

PRAYER STARTERS:

- Ask the Lord to draw Christie Hefner to Himself with His unfailing love. Pray that she will use her power and skills for morally uplifting purposes.
- Pray for her health and safety, and a growing awareness of spiritual realities.
- Pray for a renewed understanding of God's beautiful intentions in human sexuality and a renewed commitment in society to protect it from exploitation and degradation.

> *Temptation comes from the lure of our own evil desires. These evil desires lead to evil actions, and evil actions lead to death. So don't be misled, my dear brothers and sisters. James 1:14-16*

CONTACT: Playboy, 680 North Lakeshore Dr., Chicago, IL 60611

Archive Photo

Larry King
Talk-Show Host, Author

POINT OF IMPACT: Larry King, in his trademark suspenders and bow tie, works his vast media audience like a seasoned ringleader. His success as a host is reaffirmed every time a politician chooses *Larry King Live* to make a major announcement. Since 1985, his highly rated TV show has become a platform for key political and social debates. He wins his audience by being blunt, provocative, and genuinely curious. Considering his range of knowledge, it's hard to believe King (born Lawrence Harvey Zeiger) barely squeaked through high school, and his first job at a radio station was as a janitor. These days, his all-night radio call-in show is heard on more than 400 stations. Since 1985, he's hosted figures ranging from President Clinton to Michael Jordan. Taken together, his daily radio and television shows affect more than 170 million people in 210 countries. King also writes a weekly column for *USA Today*.

His show is a platform for key debates.

QUOTABLE: "All the other kids were going to college, and I was working at the United Parcel Service. I was always telling everyone, 'I want to be a broadcaster.' My best friend's father would put his arms around me and say, 'What, are you crazy? Get a job with a future!'"

BEHIND THE SCENES: He grew up in Brooklyn, where his mother went on welfare to support the family after his father died. King has had a history of heart problems, including bypass surgery in 1987. At 67, he's married to Shawn Southwick and has four children from six previous marriages.

PRAYER STARTERS:

- Pray that Larry King would use his tremendous television, radio, and newspaper influence in ways that benefit his audience and the world.
- In His 1998 book, *Powerful Prayers,* King wrote: "My parents prayed, my wife, Shawn, prays and many of my close friends pray. Me? I don't know to what or to whom I'd be praying so I have always left it alone." Pray for a spiritual breakthrough for King, that he might know God personally.
- Pray that his relationship with his wife will be blessed and enduring.

The joy of the LORD is your strength. Nehemiah 8:10

CONTACT: ICM, 8942 Wilshire Blvd., Beverly Hills, CA 90211

Kevin Williamson

Screenwriter, Director, Producer

AP/Wide World Photos

POINT OF IMPACT: Kevin Williamson's reign as the new king of teenage horror films keeps audiences everywhere wondering just what he'll come up with next. The 32-year-old screenwriter from North Carolina is credited with reviving the genre with *Scream* and *I Know What You Did Last Summer. Scream,* which Williamson wrote and directed, grossed more than $100 million at the box office and in 1997 was named Movie of the Year by MTV. His TV series on WB network, *Dawson's Creek,* is also a favorite among teen viewers. As a child Williamson was fascinated and "almost obsessed," he says, with horror movies. He also has a penchant for plots that involve revenge upon teachers, such as the forthcoming *Killing Mrs. Tingle* and the recent release, *The Faculty.* Many parents object to the violence, sex, and profanity that lace his movies, but the handsome young man with the soft Southern accent says he is simply a storyteller like his mother.

He revived the genre of teen horror films.

QUOTABLE: "Kids are smart today, they always have been, and I just sort of seek to compliment the teenage experience rather than insult it."

BEHIND THE SCENES: A high school English teacher once told Williamson he would never be a writer because he couldn't write a proper English sentence. These days Williamson recruits his friends to use as sounding boards for his ideas. He tells the whole story, he says, and "if it keeps their attention, it's time to write."

PRAYER STARTERS:

- Pray that Kevin Williamson will seek ways to attract teen audiences with less gratuitous violence, sex, and profanity.
- Pray that the exposure to evil and fear will instill in teenagers a desire to know the Lord of goodness and love.
- Pray for protection, peace, and health for Williamson and his loved ones.

Say to those with fearful hearts, "Be strong, do not fear." Isaiah 35:4

CONTACT: ICM, 8942 Wilshire Blvd., Beverly Hills, CA 90211

UN Photo 178716/J. Isaac

Sadako Ogata

United Nations High Commissioner
for Refugees (UNHCR)

POINT OF IMPACT: Soft-spoken Sadako Ogata is "Mother" to millions. She cares for families where chaos often reigns—the dirty, often disheartening refugee camps around the globe where 22 million reside. She's overseen multiple postwar resettlement projects in places like Vietnam and Ethiopia. She's brought help to 2 million refugees in Yugoslavia and personally encouraged thousands of children whose parents had been executed by political rebels. Her goals are to increase awareness of health epidemics and to improve policies regarding the protection of refugees. Upon awarding Ogata the Liberty Medal it was said: "To be devoted to refugees and to overcoming their deprivations is to be devoted to human liberties. No one has played a greater humanitarian role in this regard, or is a more significant symbol of future aspirations, than Sadako Ogata." With unrest and instability rampant, Ogata's success will continue to be critical for millions in the next decade.

She is "Mother" to millions of refugees.

QUOTABLE: "We have seen some progress in finding solutions to refugee problems. But much more needs to be done. Today, one in every 120 people on earth has been forced to flee because of violence or persecution."

BEHIND THE SCENES: Sadako Ogata was born into a Roman Catholic family of ministers and scholars, many of whom have served Japanese emperors. In her spare time, Ogata likes to travel with her husband, a Tokyo banker. She lives in New York, Geneva and Tokyo and has two grown children.

PRAYER STARTERS:

- Give thanks for Sadako Ogata's heart for helping the world's homeless.
- Pray for families struggling to survive and stay intact in refugee camps today. Give thanks for the food and shelter we so often take for granted.
- Pray that Ogata and her coworkers meet Christ in the face of the poor.
- Ask God to bless her family and marriage today with His grace and plenty.

The LORD is a refuge for the oppressed, a stronghold in times of trouble.
Psalm 9:9

CONTACT: www.unhcr.com

Amy Grant
Pop Singer

Courtesy of Blanton Harrell, Inc.

POINT OF IMPACT: More than any other artist, Amy Grant has been a forerunner of the "crossover" trend among today's Christian musicians. She scored her biggest mainstream hit in 1991 with the catchy "Baby, Baby." She cut her first album at 17, and at 32, she's sold more than 20 million records, won 17 Dove Awards and five Grammys, and performed at the White House. "Parents encourage their kids to see Amy because her lyrics are clean and her venues are wholesome," explains an industry executive. Grant told *Entertainment Weekly Online* that the emergence of Christian musicians on mainstream charts is simply a reflection of listeners' needs. "This music feeds people who are spiritually malnourished."

Her music changed the landscape of pop.

QUOTABLE: "There is always that cycle that brings us back around to just throwing ourselves on Jesus' breast."

BEHIND THE SCENES: In March 1999, Grant filed for a divorce from her husband of 16 years, Gary Chapman, recording artist and host of *Prime Time Country*. When the two announced their separation in December 1998, Gospel Music Association President Frank Breeden said, "The message that Amy and Gary have sung and will sing isn't changed or lessened by their personal experience. Truth doesn't get more true, or less true. It's not a victim of a family event like this." The couple have three children: Matthew, Millie, and Sarah.

PRAYER STARTERS:

- Praise God for the impact of quality Christian pop music among youth.
- Give thanks for Amy Grant's legacy of music that honors God and encourages others to pursue a relationship with Him.
- Pray for Grant's children—for comfort, security, and restored hope. Pray for healing and reconciliation in the family.
- Ask God to favor Grant with continued success and positive impact.

> *It is good . . . to sing praises to Thy name, O Most High; to declare Thy lovingkindness in the morning, and Thy faithfulness by night.*
> *Psalm 92:1-2* NASB

CONTACT: Blanton/Harrell, 2910 Poston Avenue, Nashville, TN 37203

Photo by Rick Reinhard, Washington, DC

Louis Farrakhan
Leader, Nation of Islam

POINT OF IMPACT: Since 1996's Million Man March in Washington, DC, Minister Louis Farrakhan (born Louis Eugene Walcott) is familiar to most Americans. Yet for 30 years he's led the country's most influential black rights movement, the Nation of Islam. Farrakhan's mentors, Elijah Mohammed and Malcolm X, both called for separate black development. Farrakhan, 62, has been called a hate monger and anti-Semite. Many blacks accuse his group of complicity in the 1965 assassination of Malcolm X. But since the mid-1980s, Farrakhan has tried to lead his sect into the political mainstream, running rehabilitation programs for prisoners and addicts, and providing jobs and training through its businesses. His speeches attract huge crowds, and political leaders court support from him and his Muslim movement.

He leads the country's most influential black rights movement.

QUOTABLE: "White history is written in the blood of the human family. It comes out of you like a web comes out of a spider."

BEHIND THE SCENES: In early 1999 Farrakhan had surgery for a life-threatening recurrence of prostate cancer. As a member of the Nation of Islam, he lives by a strict personal code: no drugs, alcohol, tobacco, movies, or sexual relations outside of marriage. He's been married to his childhood sweetheart since 1953; they have nine children and 23 grandchildren and live in Chicago.

PRAYER STARTERS:

- Give thanks for Louis Farrakhan's work for the poor and disadvantaged. Ask God to heal him of bitterness and racist attitudes, and to bring widespread responsiveness to the gospel among the Nation of Islam.
- Thank God for African-Americans and their contributions to America and the world. Pray for an end to racial and religious strife.
- Pray for Farrakhan's health and that the Farrakhan family would be aware of God's presence and blessings in their lives today.

Love your enemies, do good to those who hate you, bless those who curse you, pray for those who mistreat you. Luke 6:27-28

CONTACT: Nation of Islam, 7351 South Stoney Island Avenue, Chicago, IL 60649

Marcy Carsey

*Co-director of Carsey-
Werner Productions*

AP/Wide World Photos

POINT OF IMPACT: Marcy Carsey is half of the heavyweight Hollywood production house Carsey-Werner, built by Carsey and longtime partners Caryn Mandabach and Tom Werner. The company, one of the last remaining independent producers, sells its programming in Asia, Europe, and the Middle East. The leading force and shaper of television situation comedies, the studio is responsible for such sitcoms as *The Cosby Show, Roseanne, Grace Under Fire, 3rd Rock from the Sun,* and *That '70s Show.* Recently Carsey teamed up with Geraldine Laybourne, former president of Disney, to create a new channel for women and children called "Oxygen Media." It's the first general-interest channel for women run and owned by women.

Her sitcoms generate a world of interest.

QUOTABLE: "We look for what's not on the air and what ought to be. We don't do a lot of wasted development. By the time we shoot a pilot, we really think the thing ought to be on the air. And it usually is."

BEHIND THE SCENES: According to *Time* magazine, Carsey, 55, is one of Hollywood's most unassuming moguls. She tries to keep her family out of the limelight, drives a modest Mustang convertible, and doesn't even have an answering machine on her home phone. She lives in Los Angeles with her husband, John, and two children.

PRAYER STARTERS:

- Carsey's is one of the few companies that has networks clamoring for its services. Pray that she will seek God's wisdom in her programming choices today. Ask for God's blessings for her and her family.
- Pray also for Carsey's partner, Tom Werner, and his wife, Jill, and their three kids.
- Pray that Carsey's new channel for women and children will set a high standard for moral content and genuine encouragement.

> *A happy heart makes the face cheerful, but heartache crushes the spirit.*
> *Proverbs 15:13*

CONTACT: Carsey-Werner, 4024 Radford Ave., Los Angeles, CA 91604

John Gray
Author, Speaker

POINT OF IMPACT: Offering self-help advice to couples who want to improve their relationships, Dr. John Gray has created a virtual empire based on his phenomenally bestselling *Men Are from Mars, Women Are from Venus* book series. The original book has remained on both the *New York Times* and the *Publishers Weekly* bestseller lists more than five years, making it the top-selling hardcover book of the last decade. Gray's other eight books have been translated into 40 languages. A favorite Oprah guest, he also conducts seminars and infomercials, and has an online store, a newspaper column, a magazine, and even a board game.

He helps men and women get along.

QUOTABLE: "Men and women are supposed to be different. When you remember that your partner is as different from you as someone from another planet, you can relax and cooperate with the differences instead of trying to change them. Relationships do not have to be such a struggle."

BEHIND THE SCENES: For nine years, Gray traveled as a celibate monk, picking up along the way a master's in the Science of Creative Intelligence at Maharishi International University. Later he earned a Ph.D. in psychology. He and his wife, Bonnie, have three children and live in Mill Valley, California.

PRAYER STARTERS:

- Give thanks for the insights and helps that John Gray has brought to readers about men and women in relationship.
- Pray that the Holy Spirit would guide Gray into a deeper understanding of God's designs and to an encounter with Jesus Christ.
- Ask God to bless John and Bonnie Gray in their own marriage and family, surrounding them with grace and health.

He who finds a wife finds what is good and receives favor from the LORD.
Proverbs 18:22

CONTACT: Mars Venus Institute, 20 Sunnyside Ave. A-130, Mill Valley, CA 94941; www.marsvenus.com

Nicholas Negroponte

Founder, Director, Massachusetts Institute of Technology's Media Laboratory

AP/Wide World Photos

POINT OF IMPACT: To describe the genius of "Future Doc" Nicholas Negroponte, one colleague had to reach for three others geniuses—"He's a combination of Walt Disney, Buckminster Fuller and Joseph Campbell all rolled into one!" Negroponte, an MIT professor, has been credited with envisioning, more than any other individual, how the digital age of computers and electronic information would transform society. He pioneered computer-aided design for engineers and architects. As director of the Institute's future think tank, The Media Lab, Negroponte's goals have always been to make the computer more human. An unwavering optimist, he envisions a day soon when computers will possess an almost emotional awareness—recognizing speech, tracking eyes, and acknowledging fatigue or lack of interest.

His goal is to "humanize" computers.

QUOTABLE: "The first entertainment atoms to be displaced . . . will be those of videocassettes in the rental business, where consumers have the added inconvenience of having to return the atoms and being fined if they are forgotten under a couch."

BEHIND THE SCENES: Negroponte's philanthropic organization, called 2B1, helps children around the world receive access to computers and ideas. He lives in Massachusetts with his wife, Elaine, and their bulldog, Clara Bow.

PRAYER STARTERS:

- Thank God for Nicholas Negroponte's achievements, and for the gifts of creativity and problem-solving He so generously bestows.

- Pray for results today in Negroponte's efforts to close the gap between the "digital haves" and the "digital have-nots."

- Ask God to bring the Negropontes into the place of His greatest blessings today; pray that futurists in all professions will seek God's will in their work.

"I know the plans I have for you," declares the LORD, "plans to prosper you and not to harm you, plans to give you hope and a future." Jeremiah 29:11

CONTACT: www.media.mit.edu/~nicholas

Archive Photo

Jodie Foster

Actress, Director, Producer

POINT OF IMPACT: Jodie Foster is one of the few child film stars (her first Oscar nomination came at age 14 for her performance in *Taxi Driver*) who has found success as an adult. To many she epitomizes "pretty-but-powerful." The *Hollywood Reporter* lists Foster, 36, as the most "globally bankable" female star. And yet, wanting full control of the movies she makes, Foster established her own production company, Egg Pictures. Now a Hollywood veteran, Foster has appeared in 34 films. A *Vanity Fair* writer, speaking of Foster's turns in *Silence of the Lambs* (which won her a Best Actress Oscar) and *Nell*, says, "What she [Foster] becomes, by quelling her fears and confronting her enemies, is something no other American actress of our time has embodied with such consistency and aplomb: a hero."

She's the most globally bankable female star.

QUOTABLE: "One of the reasons I've survived . . . is that when people do business with me they know that I'm going to show up on time, that when I say something I don't lie about it, that I can be trusted not to repeat something that's none of my business . . . and that I'll do the honorable thing."

BEHIND THE SCENES: As valedictorian of her prep school, Foster delivered her speech in flawless French. She graduated from Yale University with honors in literature. In 1998, she chose to have a baby—alone (she declines to name the father). Her next project was the appropriately titled film *The Baby Dance*.

PRAYER STARTERS:

- Ask God to bring Foster fulfillment in her mothering role and to bless her in her creative work. Pray for safety and health for her son, Charles.
- Pray for high-achieving young women you know—that they will find positive mentors and role models.
- Ask God to bring Christian friends and influences into Foster's life.

The advantage of knowledge is this: that wisdom preserves the life of its possessor. Ecclesiastes 7:12

CONTACT: ICM, 8942 Wilshire Blvd., Beverly Hills, CA 90211

Phil Knight

Chairman and CEO, Nike

Courtesy of Nike Corp.

POINT OF IMPACT: In 1964 Phil Knight began selling shoes from the back of a station wagon. Today he heads Nike, whose "swoosh" is the most recognizable business logo on earth. Nike owns around half of the U.S. athletic shoe market, dominates the sports apparel market, and has promotion deals with the planet's most recognizable athletes. Many credit Knight with revolutionizing the business by making breakthroughs in technology (air cushions in running shoes), retailing (Niketown), and marketing strategies (creating an entire culture in which Nike is synonymous with a can-do attitude). Knight, 61, was named The Most Powerful Man in Sports by the *Sporting News,* and *Forbes* listed him as one of the country's most generous for his $25 million gift to the University of Oregon.

He revolutionized the business of sports apparel.

QUOTABLE: "I listen to my colleagues define Nike's business challenges during the day but the answers and ideas come when I least expect them—out on a trail run, riding in an airplane."

BEHIND THE SCENES: The Asian economic crisis contributed to Nike's posting a loss in 1998 for the first time in 13 years. In addition, Nike was charged with using children and cheap overseas laborers to make their products. In response, Knight has promised to raise the minimum age for workers in Asia to 18, improve factory air quality, allow independent monitoring, and provide free education for workers.

PRAYER STARTERS:

- Pray for wisdom and integrity for Phil Knight and his management team.
- Ask God to bless him with insight and guidance about the course ahead, especially given the impact of Nike on the global economy.
- Remember Phil Knight and his family in your prayers today whenever you see the swoosh, or as you walk, jog, or exercise.

> *Stand at the crossroads and look; ask for the ancient paths, ask where the good way is, and walk in it, and you will find rest for your souls.*
> *Jeremiah 6:16*

CONTACT: One Bowerman Dr., Beaverton, OR 97005; www.nikeair.com

AP\Wide World Photos

Gordon Bitner Hinckley

*President, The Church of Jesus Christ
of Latter-day Saints*

POINT OF IMPACT: To Mormons, Gordon Hinckley is more than president of the church administrators; he is a living prophet, one who can pronounce a revelation from God. He was ordained as the fifteenth president of the church on March 12, 1995, after serving 24 years in the organization's inner circle. Millions of Mormons love and revere President Hinckley, believing he received his appointment from God through revelation to the church. Mormonism (at 10 million members) is experiencing rapid growth worldwide, especially in South America and nations of the former Soviet Union.

His followers believe that he can speak for God.

QUOTABLE: "If our society is coming apart at the seams, it is because the tailor and the seamstress in the home are not producing the kind of stitching that will hold together under stress."

BEHIND THE SCENES: Except for a short period during World War II, Hinckley has worked as an employee or General Authority of the Mormon church on a full-time basis since 1935. For 20 years he was responsible for all the church's public communications. Hinckley, 89, and his wife, Marjorie, have five grown children.

PRAYER STARTERS:

- Ask God to bless Gordon Hinckley and his family with health and harmony.
- Pray that wisdom from God will direct Hinckley's decisions today, that God's sovereign will would be done.
- Pray that God would speak through the Bible to bring truth and freedom to Latter-day Saints throughout the world.

> *God . . . wants all men to be saved and to come to a knowledge of the truth. For there is one God and one mediator between God and men, the man Christ Jesus. 1 Timothy 2:3-5*

CONTACT: Church of Jesus Christ of Latter-day Saints, 50 W. South Temple Street, Salt Lake City, UT 84103

Coretta Scott King

Civil Rights/Human Rights Activist

Archive Photo

POINT OF IMPACT: For years a young Coretta Scott King worked side-by-side with her husband, Martin Luther King, Jr., helping to organize boycotts, giving speeches, and marching on behalf of civil rights. Together they dreamed a dream. And together they faced death threats. After Martin's assassination, King continued to work for civil rights, equal rights and economic justice for women, and in the peace movement. She served as president of the Martin Luther King, Jr. Center for Social Change until her youngest son, Dexter, took over in 1995. Says one colleague, "She is the heartbeat, she carried on his legacy. She has helped make it live. She has been an exemplary wife, a widow, a mother. She is just a supreme role model for all women to follow and continues to be on the list of the most admired women of the world."

She keeps a legacy—and its impact—alive.

QUOTABLE: "From the first, I had been determined to get ahead, not just for myself, but to do something for my people and for all people. I took to my heart the words of Horace Mann, 'Be ashamed to die until you have won some victory for humanity.'"

BEHIND THE SCENES: King, 71, has four grown children: Dexter, Yolanda, Martin III, and Bernice. "I hope that the world would remember me as a champion for women and a protector of children. . . . But if I had to choose one thing . . . I would want to be called a good, loving, and caring mother. There would be no greater honor."

PRAYER STARTERS:

- Give thanks for the strength and dedication of Coretta Scott King, and others like her who carry on the battle for racial equality.
- Pray that her impact in the civil rights arena would be one that is lasting— that the things she has accomplished would keep a hold on the nation.
- Pray for God's favor, protection, and peace upon Mrs. King and her family.

> *Over all these virtues put on love, which binds them all together in perfect unity. Colossians 3:14*

CONTACT: The King Center, 449 Auburn Avenue N.E., Atlanta, GA 30312

Tom Wolfe
Novelist and Cultural Journalist

POINT OF IMPACT: The originator of such phrases as "the me decade," no writer over the past 35 years has better captured America's obsession with sex, greed, racial conflicts, power, class, and status better than Wolfe. In the sixties he defined a generation with his book *The Electric Kool-Aid Acid Test.* In the seventies, he did it again with *The Right Stuff,* and in the eighties his *Bonfire of the Vanities* became a "cultural phenomenon," chronicling the material excesses of the Reagan era. Many critics say that Wolfe's *A Man in Full,* published in 1998, will become the definitive novel of the nineties. "Right now, no writer—reporter or novelist—is getting [America] on paper better than Tom Wolfe," says *Newsweek.*

He's helped to define American culture for generations.

QUOTABLE: "We like to consider ourselves free spirits, but here is my Theory of Everything: we're all motivated, and I certainly include myself here, far more than we want to admit, by group expectations. How other people view us has an important effect on how we view ourselves."

BEHIND THE SCENES: Wolfe was a baseball pitcher for his college team and says if he could have reached the major leagues, he'd never have become a writer. He loves shopping; he owns 30 or 40 suits and rewards himself for a good day's work by visiting his tailor to discuss new possibilities. Wolfe, in his late sixties, lives in New York City with his wife. They have two children.

PRAYER STARTERS:

- Give thanks for Wolfe's acute insights about the boomer generation. Pray that Wolfe's influence will continue to inspire others to acknowledge and counteract social sins like racism, greed, and arrogance.
- Ask God to bring respected Christians into Wolfe's inner circle today.
- Pray for grace and peace for Wolfe, his wife, and their children.

> *Get rid of all bitterness, rage and anger, brawling and slander, along with every form of malice. Be kind and compassionate to one another. Ephesians 4:31-32*

CONTACT: www.tomwolfe.com

Catherine Bertini

*Executive Director, United Nations
World Food Program (WFP)*

Courtesy of World Food Programme

POINT OF IMPACT: As a high schooler, Cathy Bertini volunteered with her church youth group each week at a homeless shelter. In the eighties, as Assistant Secretary for Agriculture, she made sure that 25 million schoolkids got lunch every day. Today, as Executive Director of the largest food-aid organization in the world, Bertini takes care of hungry women and children in 80 countries. The WFP has a budget of $1.2 billion (largest in the United Nations) and 4,000 workers around the globe. Bertini is a self-proclaimed conservative, yet she has strong convictions about the need for handouts for the world's 830 million hungry. "It is next to impossible for chronically hungry people to take the first important steps on the path out of poverty," she says. "The man who sleeps with his family on the streets of Calcutta and the woman who must spend four hours a day gathering firewood in Mali do not have the energy to do anything more than barely survive."

She cares for hungry children in 80 countries.

QUOTABLE: "Hunger should not exist. Globally, we produce more than enough food for everyone."

BEHIND THE SCENES: Bertini, 50, was born in New York State and went on to study at Harvard. She is married to freelance photographer Thomas Haskell, who has donated many of his photographs to WFP. They live in Rome.

PRAYER STARTERS:

- Pray that Bertini will be guided by God's wisdom and strengthened by His Spirit in her work today.
- Worldwide, 11,000 children die each day from illnesses stemming from chronic hunger. Pray for those who work in hunger relief today. Ask God to show your family one step you could take to be part of the solution.
- Ask for harmony and abundance in Bertini's home and family today.

He who is full loathes honey, but to the hungry even what is bitter tastes sweet. Proverbs 27:7

CONTACT: Viale delle Terme di Caracalla, 001000 Rome, Italy; www.wfp.org

AP/Wide World Photos

Stephen King
Bestselling Author

POINT OF IMPACT: America's bogeyman, Stephen King, is the world's leading author of horror fiction. In his 40-plus books and eight films, King explores almost every terror-producing theme from vampires, rabid dogs, deranged killers, and pyromania to ghosts, demons, extrasensory perception, telekinesis, and biological warfare. According to reviewer David Ulin, King's purpose is to "articulate a moral of vision of the world," evoking Old Testament themes of good and evil. His books, ranging from *Carrie* in the early seventies to the recent *Bag of Bones,* have sold more than 250 million copies—one book for every American—making King the richest writer in history. Many U.S. educators use his books to interest reluctant readers.

He's the world's leading author of horror.

QUOTABLE: "If you're going to talk about the power of evil, you have to talk about the power of God, the power of good, to combat evil. By doing that, you make the evil a lot more real."

BEHIND THE SCENES: The "gentle, cheery" husband and father of three enjoys bowling, poker, and playing in a band called The Rock Bottom Remainders with fellow authors Dave Barry, Amy Tan, Robert Fulghum, Matt Groening, and Roy Blount, Jr. As for fears, King himself is reportedly terrified of flying.

PRAYER STARTERS:

- Pray for God's tender lovingkindness to be experienced by Stephen King and his wife and family today.
- Pray that King would be wise about the spiritual impact of his writing; pray his work will be seasoned by the life-giving fear of God (Proverbs 3:7-8).
- Pray for the millions of readers of horror fiction today, that their curiosity about evil and fear will lead them to an encounter with the Lord: "God is light; in him there is no darkness at all" (1 John 1:5).

Whoever listens to me will live in safety and be at ease, without fear of harm.
Proverbs 1:33

CONTACT: Creative Artists Agency, 9830 Wilshire Blvd., Beverly Hills, CA 90212; www.stephenkinghome.com

Madeleine Albright

U.S. Secretary of State

Photo by Rick Reinhard, Washington, DC

POINT OF IMPACT: As the president's top advisor on foreign affairs, Madeleine Albright—the person and the professional—has captured the public's imagination. She's the most powerful woman in American politics and the highest-ranking woman in the history of American government. She's established herself as an outspoken advocate of human rights and was the point person for the U.S. response to the Kosovo crisis. As the new millennium dawns, she's charged with negotiating the expansion of NATO, keeping peace in the Middle East, fighting world terrorism, and selling U.S. foreign policy to average Americans. Albright is regarded as a brilliant communicator, feisty and hard-nosed, bringing a disarming directness to the usual diplomatic double-talk.

She's the most powerful woman in American politics.

QUOTABLE: "Women often are [the ones] most interested in sustainable development, family health, and education—the kinds of issues that help create stable societies."

BEHIND THE SCENES: Madeleine Albright was born into a prominent diplomatic family in 1937 in Prague, Czechoslovakia. But when she was two, her family fled to the United States to escape the growing Nazi threat. Her parents raised her as a Catholic and rarely talked about their past in Europe. Later, Albright learned that all four of her grandparents were Jewish. Three died in concentration camps. She is the divorced mother of three adult daughters.

PRAYER STARTERS:

- Pray that Madeleine Albright and all those representing the United States to world governments will be successful in their efforts to promote peace and justice. Remember especially those working in global trouble spots.
- Ask God to bless Albright and her family with strength, safety, and hope.

God of our fathers . . . you rule over all the kingdoms of the nations. Power and might are in your hand, and no one can withstand you. 2 Chronicles 20:6

CONTACT: Department of State, 2201 C Street N.W., Washington, DC 20520; e-mail: secretary@state.gov

Courtesy of Flip Benham

Philip L. Benham

Director, Operation Rescue National

POINT OF IMPACT: Philip "Flip" Benham is America's most visible antiabortion protester, articulating the pro-life cause from a conservative Christian point of view. His Operation Rescue, which he founded in 1988, organizes clinic protests and pro-life marches and brings influence to bear in legislative bodies. For his cause, Benham, 52, has gone to jail numerous times. He preaches Jesus Christ, not politics, as the answer to the practice of abortion. He shrinks from violence (he condemned the shooting of abortion provider Dr. Barnett Slepian), but never controversy. "Christians are winning," he says, citing recent steady declines in rates of abortions, a declining number of abortion providers, and medical breakthroughs that support pro-life convictions about the humanity of life in the womb.

He's frequently jailed for his pro-life activities.

QUOTABLE: Benham calls his jail time his "ministry behind bars." But before a recent six-month sentence, he said, "No matter what kind of veteran you are, it tears your heart knowing you'll be separated this long from your family."

BEHIND THE SCENES: Once a saloon owner, after his conversion in 1976, Benham became a Methodist minister. He and his wife, Faye, have three grown children and two—Abigail and Jonathan—still at home. They live in Dallas.

PRAYER STARTERS

- Give thanks for the heightened awareness among voters about right-to-life issues. Pray that progress continues in ways that honor Christ.
- Today is the anniversary of the *Roe vs. Wade* court decision which legalized abortion. The three individuals most instrumental in that case, including Norma McCorvey (Jane Roe), have all become Christians who reject the pro-choice position, Benham reports. Pray for more changes of heart among pro-abortion advocates.
- Ask for discretion, strength, and God's grace for Benham and his family.

> *You created my inmost being; you knit me together in my mother's womb.*
> *Psalm 139:13*

CONTACT: O.R.N., P.O. Box 740066, Dallas, TX 75374; e-mail: orn@airmail.net

David (Paul) Yonggi Cho

Pastor

AP/Wide World Photos

POINT OF IMPACT: He started his first church in a tent next to a city dump. Today, Dr. David Yonggi Cho pastors the world's largest church, which has more than 750,000 members and is located in Seoul, Korea. Founded in 1958, Yoido Full Gospel church takes up an 11-story building, has 650 pastors, and has sent 700 missionaries all over the world. A pioneer in the "cell church" movement, Cho lectures around the globe on the principles of church growth. His church also runs a major national newspaper, a university, and four seminaries. Cho has been criticized by some for his teachings on the power of the spoken word (e.g. in *The Fourth Dimension,* "You create the presence of Jesus with your mouth. . . . He is bound by your lips and by your words"). At 64, he prays about eight hours daily.

He pastors the largest church in the world.

QUOTABLE: "I pray and I obey."

BEHIND THE SCENES: At 19 Cho was diagnosed with incurable tuberculosis and expected to die. When after prayer he wasn't healed, he denounced his Buddhist faith. A few days later, a young Christian girl told him about Jesus; he decided that since he was dying, he would confess Christ and read the Bible. Cho came to know Jesus as Savior and miraculously returned to health.

PRAYER STARTERS:

- Thank God for the spread of Christianity in Korea, and for the generations of faithful missionaries who have worked there planting seeds.
- Half of the world's 50 largest churches are in Korea. Pray for believers in Korea, Japan, China and Mongolia—many face isolation, want, and persecution.
- Pray for mega-churches worldwide—that their leaders will seek God's wisdom and discover new ways to multiply and mature believers.
- Give thanks for Pastor David Cho's ministry; ask God to bless him and his family today with protection, strong friendships, and spiritual renewal.

> *The message of the cross is foolishness to those who are perishing, but to us who are being saved it is the power of God. 1 Corinthians 1:18*

CONTACT: Church Growth International, Yoido P.O. Box 7, Seoul 150-600, Korea

Archive Photo

Shaquille O'Neal

Professional Basketball Player, Rapper, Actor

POINT OF IMPACT: With Michael Jordan retired, the number one force in pro basketball is the 7'-1", 320-pound center for Los Angeles Lakers, Shaquille O'Neal. And the big man is proving that his size 22 EEE feet are plenty ample to fill Mike's shoes. At only 27, O'Neal has already been named one of the 50 greatest players in the history of the NBA. "Shaq" is a global brand for the likes of Reebok, Pepsi, and Taco Bell; a mega rap star with with one platinum album and another gold; and an actor, with at least two movies to his credit. O'Neal directs programs for the children's network Nickelodeon, and hosts his own TV sports show. In annual polls conducted by *Sports Illustrated for Kids*, O'Neal is frequently named the most popular athlete in the world.

In pro basketball, he dominates the courts.

QUOTABLE: "The whole world is looking for me to do something crazy. And I won't. No drinking and driving. No drugs here. I want to be the perfect big brother. Controversy sells, but I don't need to do that."

BEHIND THE SCENES: O'Neal devotes substantial time and money to charities like Athletes & Entertainers for Kids, City of Hope, Boys & Girls Clubs, and the Elizabeth Glaser Pediatric AIDS Foundation. He started an apparel and marketing business in south L.A. with the "hope of creating jobs and keeping kids out of trouble." He's unmarried and has one daughter.

PRAYER POINTS:

- Give thanks for O'Neal's vigorous charitable commitments.
- Pray that O'Neal's choices on and off the court would inspire a generation of youth to excell physically and morally.
- "As long as my mother's smiling, I'm successful," says O'Neal. Pray that the Lord would bless and preserve O'Neal's family relationships, especially his role as father. Pray that he would encounter God the Father's love today.

He gives strength to the weary and increases the power of the weak.
Isaiah 40:29

CONTACT: William Morris, 151 El Camino Dr., Beverly Hills, CA 90212

Mike Judge

Creator, Beavis and Butthead,
King of the Hill

AP/Wide World Photos

POINT OF IMPACT: Cartoon and TV writer Mike Judge is the creator of the world's most famous teen slacker, Beavis, and his dopey, monotone laugh: "Heh-heh, heh-heh." Beavis, along with buddy Butthead—always irresponsible and sometimes violent—became favorite teens on MTV and then through their movie *Beavis and Butthead Do America.* Given the 'round-the-world reach of MTV, the duo's influence has been enormous—especially, as some parents and critics fear, for fans who take their negative and destructive lifestyle as an endorsement. Writes one observer, "You can find children in Kuala Lumpur wearing Beavis T-shirts and stockbrokers in London sipping tea from Butthead mugs." Judge says his latest hit TV series, *King of the Hill,* is meant to be taken as a funny and irreverent satire on America.

His irreverent cartoons make some laugh, and some nervous.

QUOTABLE: On his infamous cartoon adolescents: "They don't know who their dads are. They're the bastard children of the sexual revolution. Maybe that's one of the reasons they've upset so many people."

BEHIND THE SCENES: Judge, 36, writes and draws his characters and even delivers most of the voices himself. He majored in physics at UC-San Diego, but when his entry at a Festival of Animation caught the eye of a *Saturday Night Live* producer, his cartoon career was launched. He lives in Austin, Texas, with his wife, Francesca, and their two daughters.

PRAYER STARTERS:

- Pray that young viewers around the world would learn positive lessons from the negative example of Mike Judge's fictional characters.
- Pray that media programmers would choose to use their tremendous influence on teen attitudes in ways that are both fun and uplifting.
- Ask God to bless the Judge family today with harmony, health, and knowledge of His love.

The sluggard craves and gets nothing, but the desires of the diligent are fully satisfied. Proverbs 13:4

CONTACT: MTV, 1515 Broadway, New York, NY 10036

Archive Photo

Joan Kroc
Philanthropist

POINT OF IMPACT: Joan B. Kroc, the widow of McDonald's restaurant magnate Ray Kroc, is the richest woman in California—and probably the most generous. Two years after her husband died, she founded Ronald McDonald House Charities, to which she has given more than $100 million. Kroc favors children's causes and relief organizations such as the Salvation Army, to whom she has donated $80 million. In past years, she has given away millions to groups working to prevent nuclear war, world famine, and drug and alcohol abuse. The *San Diego Union-Tribune* says that Kroc "has a big heart and a sort of Cinderella sense. She likes to surprise people with the golden slippers." No one is certain just how much Kroc has actually given away because she shuns publicity at all costs.

She covertly gives millions to charity.

QUOTABLE: Kroc likes to tell about the time a friend of her husband's asked him why he gave so much of his money away. He replied: "Well, I've never seen a Brinks truck follow a hearse, have you?" "I loved that!" says Kroc.

BEHIND THE SCENES: Kroc enjoys traveling around the country in her 36-foot motor home with her four granddaughters and a Labrador retriever. "I'm in the prime of my golden years and loving it," she says.

PRAYER STARTERS:

- Give thanks to God for Joan Kroc's generosity and for all the help and comfort she and her late husband have brought to thousands of children.
- Pray that many others, wealthy or not, will be inspired by her example.
- Ask for God's blessing on Joan Kroc's life, her finances, her spiritual growth, and her family. Pray He would surround her with love and favor.
- Every time you see the golden arches today, remember to pray for those who benefit from the Ronald McDonald House Charities.

> *He who is kind to the poor lends to the* LORD, *and he will reward him for what he has done. Proverbs 19:17*

CONTACT: McDonald's Corporation, 1 McDonald's Plaza, Oak Brook, IL 60523

Mel Gibson

Actor, Director, Producer

Archive Photo

POINT OF IMPACT: Mel Gibson, born in the United States and raised in Australia, originally dreamed of becoming a journalist or a chef, but he found himself in drama school after his sister applied for him. His big break came in the form of post-apocalyptic character Mad Max. The film grossed more than any other Australian movie before it and led to two sequels. From there, movies like *Gallipoli, Mrs. Soffel,* and *The Year of Living Dangerously* showcased his talent and charm. After starring in *Hamlet, Maverick,* and *Lethal Weapon,* Gibson won Best Director and Best Picture Oscars for *Braveheart.* But ultimately, he's proved more than just a handsome face (*People* magazine named him its first "Sexiest Man Alive"). Since marrying Robyn Moore in 1980, Gibson has set a new standard in Hollywood for "success" by investing the majority of his time in the lives of his seven children. Their large but close family attends a Catholic church in Southern California.

His devotion to family defies Hollywood stereotypes.

QUOTABLE: On his favorite role: "Dad. I'm far from being an expert on child rearing. I make mistakes. I'm human. I just do the very best I can and pray I'm not doing any permanent damage."

BEHIND THE SCENES: Known on movie sets as an avid practical joker, Gibson is also involved in many educational and charitable foundations, including Rabbit Ears Radio (a children's programming show), the American Library Association, and the American Paralysis Association.

PRAYER STARTERS:

- Give thanks for the example of Mel Gibson's devotion to his wife and children, and for his work with charitable groups.
- Pray that the Lord would continually reveal Himself to Gibson and his family through their faithful participation in their church.
- Pray that Gibson will find ways to impact lives for good through his work.

Trust in the LORD and do good; dwell in the land and enjoy safe pasture.
Psalm 37:3

CONTACT: ICM, 8942 Wilshire Blvd., Beverly Hills, CA 90211

John "Jack" Welch

CEO, General Electric

POINT OF IMPACT: As chairman and CEO of the world's most valuable company (worth more than $300 billion), Jack Welch has been called "the gold standard" by which all CEOs are measured. In addition to building GE into America's greatest generator of wealth, he is credited with introducing a corporate management model for the twenty-first century—emphasizing quality, creativity, and informality. In addition to electrical appliances, GE builds power plants, jet engines, and locomotives, produces medical supplies, offers financial services, and runs the NBC television network. Under Welch's leadership, GE staff have pledged 1 million hours of volunteer service for young people in the United States. Around the world, they operate numerous charitable projects. "If leadership is an art," says *Business Week,* "then surely Welch has proved himself a master painter."

He runs the most valuable corporation in the world.

QUOTABLE: "The idea flow from the human spirit is absolutely unlimited. All you have to do is tap into that well. I don't like to use the word *efficiency.* It's creativity. It's a belief that every person counts."

BEHIND THE SCENES: Welch's late mother, Grace, gave him the confidence to succeed. Now 63, he fondly remembers how she honed his competitive skills playing games like gin rummy at the kitchen table. "I had a pal in my mom, you know," he says. "It was a powerful, unique, reinforcing experience."

PRAYER STARTERS:

- Ask God to work powerfully for good through Jack Welch today—his decisions, his personal impact, his words. Pray for guidance for Welch as he contemplates retirement in 2000.

- Give thanks for the charitable efforts of GE, as well as for the many jobs and livelihoods provided through GE around the world.

- Ask for spiritual blessings and health for Welch, his wife, Jane, and their four children. (Let GE products or advertising prompt your prayers.)

The plans of the diligent lead to profit as surely as haste leads to poverty.
Proverbs 21:5

CONTACT: General Electric, 3135 Easton Tpke., Fairfield, CT 06431-0001

Oprah Winfrey

Talk-Show Host, Actress, Producer

Archive Photo

POINT OF IMPACT: Called every woman's best friend, and "therapist to the nation," Oprah Winfrey is arguably the most influential woman in America. She started hosting talk shows in 1978, and just eight years later, *The Oprah Winfrey Show* had become TV's number-one daytime talk show (more than 33 million viewers weekly). She's received countless awards, including 32 Daytime Emmys. Her viewers find her compassionate and authentic. But it's her higher standard of talk fare (she is critical of Jerry Springer) and ability to motivate listeners (her charitable Angel Network and "change your life" theme) that set her apart. Says *Redbook,* "She demonstrates through her life and her daily hour on the air that the journey within is the most important journey of all." Winfrey recently joined forces with the Carsey-Werner-Mandabach team and their new network, called Oxygen Media. She has also acted in and produced several TV and feature films. She's known for her on-air book club (every selection becomes a best-seller), her drive for fitness, and her enormous wealth: At 46, she may become America's first African-American billionaire.

She wants to change your life.

QUOTABLE: "I've survived because of my faith in a power that is greater than me."

BEHIND THE SCENES: Born to an unmarried teenaged couple, Winfrey was raised by her grandmother. She had a baby at 14 that died soon after birth. She moved in with her father, who supplied the discipline she craved. She lives in Chicago with businessman Stedman Graham.

PRAYER STARTERS:

- Give thanks for Oprah's positive example and heart for people. Pray that God will use her show to encourage many today, for His glory.
- Ask God to bless Oprah Winfrey in her personal relationships and business ventures. Pray that her spiritual sensitivities will grow to include a personal relationship with Jesus Christ.
- Pray that the viewers of her show will find the truth they seek.

Blessed are the merciful, for they will be shown mercy. Matthew 5:7

CONTACT: Harpo Productions, P.O. Box 909715, Chicago, IL 60607

Courtesy of Franciscan University

Cardinal John O'Connor
Roman Catholic Archbishop of New York

POINT OF IMPACT: One of the most quoted and powerful of Catholic voices, Cardinal O'Connor was once considered a candidate for the papacy. Now 80, he is no longer eligible to run or vote, but his influence remains strong. An O'Connor sermon often gets reported and discussed around the globe. (For example, his objection to the Clintons having taken communion while visiting a Catholic church in South Africa made headlines.) When the Cardinal protested Sunday morning soccer, parents filled a *New York Times* page with both outrage and support. He has a special passion for helping the poor and homeless. O'Connor's legacy has been one of warmth, energy, and orthodoxy in the face of rapid, often painful change in his 60-million-member family of U.S. Catholics.

His sermons echo around the globe.

QUOTABLE: To candidates for the priesthood: "As a priest I can promise you sorrow, suffering, sacrifice and loneliness. If you're good priests, I can promise, as well, the greatest joy that any human being can experience."

BEHIND THE SCENES: John O'Connor grew up in Philadelphia, fourth of five children. During the first seven years of his ministry, while O'Connor served as a parish priest and educator, he also worked heavily with mentally disabled children. Ever since, he's championed programs for those with handicaps.

PRAYER STARTERS:

- Pray for John Cardinal O'Connor's good health, safety, and peace.
- "Christ came for everybody. His was a ministry of reconciliation, to pick up the pieces," O'Connor says. Pray for unity and healing in the church.
- Pray that the world's 1 billion Catholics "may have power, together with all the saints," to grasp the depths of God's love (Ephesians 3:17).
- Pray that O'Connor's life will inspire many to enter full-time Christian service.

> *Those who have served well gain an excellent standing and great assurance in their faith in Christ Jesus. 1 Timothy 3:13*

CONTACT: Archdiocese of New York, 1011 First Avenue, New York, NY 10022

Jack Kevorkian

Assisted Suicide Advocate

AP/Wide World Photos

POINT OF IMPACT: His detractors call him "Dr. Death" and describe him as a lunatic. His supporters call him merciful and herald him as a freedom fighter. Jack Kevorkian's clearly stated mission is to pioneer radical change in the way human beings die. He advocates a society that allows euthanasia not only for the terminally ill, but also for the disabled, the mentally ill, infants with birth defects, and comatose adults. He built his first "suicide machine" in the summer of 1989, and his physician's license was revoked in 1991. He has since assisted in at least 45 deaths. Autopsies on several of his clients revealed no physical ailments. In 1998, Kevorkian himself administered a lethal injection to Thomas Youk, 52, taking the debate further: from doctor-assisted suicide to mercy killing. To prompt his arrest, he asked *60 Minutes* to air a videotape of the death. In March 1999 he was convicted of second degree murder and could face 10-25 years in prison.

If you want to die, he's happy to help.

QUOTABLE: On doctors manipulating deaths for scientific gain: "It would be a unique privilege in the most emphatic sense to be able to experiment on a doomed human being. . . . No aim could be too remote, too silly, too simple, too absurd; and no experiment too outlandish."

BEHIND THE SCENES: When Mike Wallace asked Kevorkian if there isn't something "ghoulish" about his approach, he responded, "I can't argue with that—maybe it is ghoulish." Kevorkian doesn't believe in an afterlife.

PRAYER STARTERS:

- Pray that Kevorkian's crusade will be stopped by the courts.
- Pray for those whom Kevorkian is trying to help, that they will find healing, comfort, and peace with God in their time of suffering.
- Kevorkian has said that his "god" is Johann Sebastian Bach—"I mean, why not? At least he's not invented." Pray that Kevorkian will come to know Jesus as Lord.

Man is destined to die once, and after that to face judgment. Hebrews 9:27

CONTACT: Dr. Jack Kevorkian, 4870 Lockhart, West Bloomfield, MI 48323

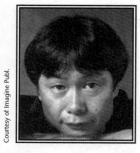

Courtesy of Imagine Publ.

Shigeru Miyamoto
Video Game Creator, Nintendo

POINT OF IMPACT: Shigeru Miyamoto heads the world's most celebrated team of video game designers. Both Steven Spielberg and George Lucas have made pilgrimages to Japan to spend time with him. Revered by industry experts as a visionary, Miyamoto has consistently created hot-selling games, including Donkey Kong and Super Mario Brothers for Nintendo Inc., which has sold more than 1 billion games worldwide. In December 1998, 46-year-old Miyamoto revolutionized interactive entertainment with a new Legend of Zelda game, Ocarina of Time. A video game writer for *Disney Adventure* says, "It is the first game to be very close to an interactive movie." A *Time* writer reported, "In some ways Zelda is every bit as compelling as the best painting I've ever seen, or even the best movie."

He imagined your kid's favorite video game.

QUOTABLE: "I come up with ideas only after I've devoted myself to a day of hard work. If we've been relaxing all throughout the day, we [the team of designers he heads] hardly ever come up with any new ideas."

BEHIND THE SCENES: Miyamoto sports a Beatles hairstyle and loves to play banjo. He lives simply, commuting to work on a mountain bike. He and his wife and two children reside in a small, five-room home in Kyoto. He doesn't, however, keep a Mario game (a family favorite) at home because he says his kids might neglect their studies or chores.

PRAYER STARTERS:

• Thank God for His amazing gifts of creativity and imagination.

• Ask God to bless Shigeru Miyamoto and his team with insight and integrity as they develop games that will affect the imaginations and values of millions.

• Pray that Miyamoto and his family will be drawn closer to the Author and Genius of all Creation.

• Pray for children (and adults) who play video games regularly—that they will not neglect other responsibilities or relationships.

Test everything. Hold on to the good. Avoid every kind of evil.
1 Thessalonians 5:21-22

CONTACT: www.nintendo.com

> *"If we truly love people, we will desire for them far more than it is within our power to give them, and this will lead us to prayer. Intercession is a way of loving others."*
>
> —RICHARD FOSTER

ABC Photo

Peggy Wehmeyer

Religion Correspondent,
ABC World News Tonight

POINT OF IMPACT: Religion outdraws sports as America's main "leisure" activity, but you wouldn't know it by the news coverage. In 1994, ABC news anchor Peter Jennings hired Peggy Wehmeyer to fix the problem. She became the first full-time network religion correspondent. According to Wehmeyer, newsroom apathy about the role of religion indicates media aren't focusing on the facts (eight in ten Americans pray regularly and nearly 60 percent say religion is very important to their lives), or else they're discounting people of faith altogether. A producer once asked her, "Wehmeyer, how come no matter what we send you out on, you come back with God?" She replied, "How come you keep missing Him?" Wehmeyer has proved her case in a series of high-profile scoops: interviewing the pastors who counseled Clinton post-Monica, an award-winning series on Mormons, and exclusive coverage of the McCaughey septuplets.

She investigates how faith moves the world.

QUOTABLE: "What you can do in religion reporting is take an issue about seven babies being born and deal with some profound questions about life, meaning, transcendence, and belief."

BEHIND THE SCENES: Peggy Wehmeyer, 45, was raised with no religious orientation, although after she converted to evangelical Christianity in college, she discovered that her family were Jews who had suffered under the Nazis. She and her husband Mark Woods, a psychologist, live in Dallas and have two daughters, Lauren and Hannah.

PRAYER STARTERS:

- "People are looking for spiritual connections to their faith traditions," says Wehmeyer. Pray for a worldwide renewal and hunger for the gospel.
- Pray that persons of faith will make a significant impact for Christ in the nation's leading institutions.
- Pray that Wehmeyer will continue to make significant new breakthroughs in her religion reporting.
- Ask God to bless the Wehmeyer/Woods household with peace and plenty.

> *That . . . which we have looked at and our hands have touched—this we proclaim concerning the Word of life. 1 John 1:1*

CONTACT: ABC, 77 W 66th St., New York, NY 10023-6298; www.abc.com

George Tenet

Director, Central Intelligence Agency (CIA)

Archive Photo

POINT OF IMPACT: You might call George Tenet the boss of the good-guy spies. As the leader of America's foreign intelligence agencies, including the Central Intelligence Agency, he's responsible for all the information the government uses to control arms proliferation, terrorism, and narcotics. In addition he is responsible for governing U.S. responses to Iraq, Kosovo, Russia, and China, and improving relations with Iran and Cuba. The son of Greek immigrants, Tenet now oversees a $30 billion budget and 80,000 employees. At 47, he also faces the daunting challenge of refining the CIA's mission in a complicated era in international relations. When he was named CIA Director in 1998, both Democrats and Republicans called him the perfect man for the role because of his smarts, loyalty, reputation for truth telling, and commitment to reform.

It's his job to keep America's secrets safe.

QUOTABLE: "The CIA should be able to see what others could not, dare what others would not, and refuse to give up in the face of overwhelming odds."

BEHIND THE SCENES: Tenet, who grew up in Queens, often chomps an unlit cigar (he doesn't smoke them due to heart problems). Ironically, a family friend remembers that Tenet could never keep a secret. "We called George 'the mouthpiece,'" says Sol Winder, owner of the Scobee Grill in Queens. Tenet and his wife Stephanie have a son, John Michael.

PRAYER STARTERS:

- The CIA has gone through three leadership changes in six years, suffering a number of scandals and dismal morale. Pray for George Tenet's difficult task of creating a proficient and ethical intelligence force.
- The CIA is feared and distrusted in many quarters. Pray that Tenet can lead the agency in ways that don't compromise America's foundational values.
- Ask for safety and an awareness of God's loving presence for the Tenets.

> *Because the hand of the* LORD *my God was on me, I took courage and gathered leading men. Ezra 7:28*

CONTACT: Central Intelligence Agency, Washington, DC 20505; www.odci.gov/cia

Archive Photo

David Letterman
Late-Night Talk-Show Host

POINT OF IMPACT: David Letterman is the host of the *CBS Late Show with David Letterman,* one of the most talked-about, acclaimed, and imitated talk-show programs in history. Letterman won a George Foster Peabody Award for taking "one of TV's most conventional and least inventive forms—the talk show—and infusing it with freshness and imagination." His concepts have been copied all around the world, including in Germany and Sweden. Letterman, who is beginning his sixteenth year on late-night network television, has consistently delivered comedy that is edgy, inventive, and sometimes controversial (e.g., his segments featuring a probation-violating drug user named Manny the Hippie, who was subsequently incarcerated). The gap-toothed New Yorker is especially beloved by the college crowd, who enjoy his absurdist skits, celebrity baiting, and off-the-news Top Ten lists.

He makes his living making millions laugh.

QUOTABLE: On where he gets his adrenaline: "Way too much coffee. But if it weren't for the coffee, I'd have no identifiable personality whatsoever."

BEHIND THE SCENES: Letterman's angst—about life and himself—is legendary. Bill Zehme, a reporter for *Esquire,* once put it this way: "I have known him for a dozen years. I have watched him become the most powerful man in all of television and derive enjoyment from almost no aspect of it, save perhaps the good seats at Indy." Letterman grew up in Indiana; he is a divorced bachelor with no children.

PRAYER STARTERS:

- Ask God to bless David Letterman with the joy and peace of Jesus Christ.
- Pray that Letterman will use his gifts of humor and commentary in positive ways.
- Pray for spiritual discernment for the millions of young people who watch his show.
- Ask God to send credible Christians into Letterman's life—believers who can encourage him about spiritual matters.

Even in laughter the heart may ache. Proverbs 14:13

CONTACT: CBS Mailbag, The Late Show, 1697 Broadway, New York, NY 10019

Ernesto Zedillo Ponce de Leon

President of Mexico

UN/DPI photo by Evan Schneider

POINT OF IMPACT: Mexican President Ernesto Zedillo's leadership is like a breath of optimism after years of gloom, reports *Time* magazine. He's the first reform-minded leader of the Institutional Revolutionary Party, which has ruled Mexico unchallenged since 1929. The relationship between Mexico and the United States is "one of the handful of relationships that profoundly and directly affect the welfare of the American people," says Deputy National Security Director Jim Steinberg. Our shared border, history, and peoples create a myriad of challenges. But Zedillo, 49, is cooperating with the United States to fight drug trafficking, illegal border crossings, and organized crime. Though change can bring hardship, Zedillo's approval ratings have remained strong. "Mexico seems transformed . . . from the perfect dictatorship to a pluralistic society, thanks in large part to Zedillo's own sweeping electoral reform," says *Time*.

His leadership is transforming Mexico.

QUOTABLE: "Mexico is getting ready not only for a new era of economic growth, but also of greater productivity, justice, and democracy."

BEHIND THE SCENES: As a child Zedillo collected and sold scrap metal to a nearby foundry in Tijuana to help his family. He also shared his extra earnings with the local Catholic church. Today he has a Ph.D. in economics from Yale. He and his wife, Nilda Patricia Velasco, live in Mexico City, and have five children: Ernesto, Emiliano, Carlos, Nilda Patricia, and Rodrigo.

PRAYER STARTERS:

- Give thanks for the promise of economic and political reforms under Ernesto Zedillo. Pray for his courage, integrity, and safety as he pursues a risky course, and ask that he and his advisers will be led by God's wisdom.
- Pray for the Mexican people, the majority of whom have yet to benefit from change or prosperity.
- Pray that the United States and Mexican governments find workable solutions to their shared problems.

Do two walk together unless they have agreed to do so? Amos 3:3

CONTACT: Mexican Consulate, 2401 West 6th Street, Los Angeles, CA 90057

Steve Largent
U.S. Congressman

POINT OF IMPACT: Steve Largent may not hold the most powerful position in the House of Representatives, but he has something others don't: star quality. A Hall of Fame football player, *People* has twice named him one of its 50 Most Beautiful People in the World, and he's been named one of the Ten Outstanding Men of America. Since being elected to Congress in 1994, Largent has wielded his influence to help craft the Republican party's pro-family agenda. He was a major sponsor of the Defense of Marriage Act (passed in 1996), and supports the Parental Rights and Responsibilities Act, which gives parents more say on what their children are taught. He opposes abortion, gay rights, gun control, and the National Endowment for the Arts. The *New York Times* has called him "the class member most likely to succeed."

He uses star power to promote family values.

QUOTABLE: "Learning to ask, 'Is it right?' speaking the truth from our hearts, doing what is honorable, and promoting a message of reconciliation—those are things that need to be applied in the halls of Congress . . . at the White House, at my house, and at your house."

BEHIND THE SCENES: Largent, 46, and four fellow Congressmen get together every Tuesday night to pray. Largent organized the group in an attempt to build a spiritual firewall between them and the dominant culture of Capitol Hill, which he describes as lonely, workaholic, and full of temptation. He and his wife, Terry, have four children: Casie, Kyle, Kelly, and Kramer.

PRAYER STARTERS:

- Give thanks for Steve Largent's powerful example to Christian men.
- Ask God to help Largent nurture his spiritual growth and protect his priorities, choices, and reputation.
- Largent's youngest child was born with spina bifida. Pray for health and well-being for the Largent family today.

> *A wicked man puts up a bold front, but an upright man gives thought to his ways. Proverbs 21:29*

CONTACT: 426 Cannon, Washington, DC 20515-3601; www.house.gov/largent

Edward Fugger

Reproductive Biologist, Gender Engineer

Digital Stock

POINT OF IMPACT: Edward Fugger is the leading researcher behind MicroSort, a sperm-sorting procedure that is being used to help prevent gender-based diseases. It also boasts an 85-percent success rate for ensuring couples of having a girl. Producing males has proved trickier; MicroSort raises the odds to 65 percent. No one argues the merit of using the technology to prevent gender-based diseases, but some are concerned about the ethical implications of gender selection. "We're well on our way to designer children," says Lori Knowledge of the Hastings Institute, a bioethics think tank. "If we don't say there's something wrong about choosing the gender of a baby, how can we say there's anything wrong with choosing its hair or eye color or height?" Fugger, a lanky Texan, grew up as an only child wishing for a brother, and he's unapologetic about giving families the option of gender selection.

He wants you to be able to choose your baby's sex.

QUOTABLE: "I believe that using a sex selector will tend to balance the ratio of boys and girls in families. It shouldn't be an ethical issue."

BEHIND THE SCENES: Fugger, 58, says more than 400 animals have been born through "sperm sifting," none with defects. All of the human babies have been born healthy as well. "That doesn't mean all of the risk has been excluded," admits Fugger. He and his wife, Betty, have two grown children.

PRAYER STARTERS:

- Pray that God will guide Fugger as he pioneers procedures that could benefit those who could inherit sex-linked disorders, such as hemophilia.
- Ask God to bless Dr. Fugger and his family today with a renewing encounter with His sovereignty and redeeming love.
- Pray that authorities will set wise safeguards for sex selection, especially in cultures that set a high priority on male children.
- Pray for a couple you know today who struggles with infertility.

> *God created man in his own image . . . male and female he created them.*
> *Genesis 1:27*

CONTACT: Genetics & IVF Institute, Department of Obstetrics and Gynecology, 3020 Javier Road, Fairfax, VA 22031

Madonna
Singer, Actress, Icon of Pop Culture

Archive Photo

POINT OF IMPACT: Madonna's rise to superstardom began in the eighties with her controversial video and song, "Like a Prayer." It featured Madonna dancing in her slip before burning crosses and kissing an African-American saint (she was raised Catholic). To date, the singer has sold at least 115 million albums worldwide and now runs her own label, Maverick. In 1996 Madonna won a Golden Globe for her starring role in the film *Evita.* Idolized and imitated around the world, Madonna, 41, has built her career on controversy, sex appeal, and rebellion. In recent years, however, the singer's public image has been that of a devoted single mother (to daughter Lourdes Maria, whom she had with her ex-boyfriend and trainer), serious artist, and keen manager of her business empire.

She's one of the most recognized stars on earth.

QUOTABLE: On how motherhood has impacted her career: "I now have absolutely no free time. But on the other hand, I'm a lot happier and a lot more grounded and focused."

BEHIND THE SCENES: Madonna (born Madonna Louise Veronica Ciccone), was five when she lost her own mother to cancer. These days she often takes her daughter to work with her, joking that she won't share the stage with her because "she would steal the show." She lives in New York.

PRAYER STARTERS:

- Madonna says, "I'm very frightened of death the more I think about it, but also very intrigued by it: I believe in reincarnation and I wonder what will happen next." Pray that she will discover the truth about eternal life.

- Thank God for Madonna's creative and performing gifts; pray that she would use them to influence her fans for good.

- Pray that God would bring her closer to Him through her experiences as a mother. Ask that God will bless her and her family.

> *Sing to the LORD a new song, his praise from the ends of the earth.*
> *Isaiah 42:10*

CONTACT: Creative Artists Agency, 9830 Wilshire Blvd., Beverly Hills, CA 90212

Bill Gates
Chairman, CEO, Microsoft

Archive Photo

POINT OF IMPACT: Some call William Henry Gates III the Henry Ford and Thomas Edison of our age. A few call him a modern-day robber baron. Love him or hate him, as owner of Microsoft, Bill Gates has become the embodiment of the communications revolution, the most famous business celebrity in the world (*Time's* Man of the Year in 1996), the world's richest private individual (his Microsoft stocks are worth nearly 100 billion), and one of the most powerful men on earth. Microsoft, the world's second most valuable corporation, is the leading provider worldwide of software for the personal computer and exerts more power over the technology business than any other company. At the prompting of competitors like Sun Systems and Netscape, the Department of Justice undertook litigation against Microsoft's alleged monopolistic practices (a verdict was expected in late 1999).

He's the Thomas Edison of our age.

QUOTABLE: "Even though I'm not religious, the amazement and wonder I have about the human mind is closer to religious awe than dispassionate analysis."

BEHIND THE SCENES: Gates, 45, is among the nation's charitable elites. In February 1999, he and his wife donated $3.34 billion for educational, environmental, and health causes. Gates also is donating the proceeds from his bestseller, *The Road Ahead*, to help teachers worldwide incorporate computers into their classrooms. He and his wife, the former Melinda French, have one daughter and live near Seattle.

PRAYER STARTERS:

- Give thanks for the inspiration Gates has been to young entrepreneurs and students of technology. Ask for continued impact for good.
- Pray that he will seek God's guidance in his corporate decisions, which affect so many.
- Pray for Bill Gates, his marriage and his family—ask God for spiritual breakthroughs for him.
- Pray especially for teachers and managers today, that they will nurture the God-given curiosity of learners.

Show me your ways, O LORD, teach me your paths. Psalm 25:4

CONTACT: Microsoft Corporation, One Microsoft Way, Redmond, WA 98052

Brent Andrew Marshall, Calgary-Canada

Wesley Chu
Pianist, Composer

POINT OF IMPACT: Wesley Chu may be a pint-sized pianist, but his talent has him standing above the crowd. At seven, he's reminding the world that childhood genius at the keyboard didn't end with Mozart (whom Chu has mastered). He's played in the Philharmonic Orchestra to a standing ovation, and performed an original composition for the Queen of England. At age four years and nine months, he made his mark in the world of music by becoming the youngest person to achieve all nine grades in one year in the 100-year history of the Royal Conservatory of Music. Chu recently recorded a CD of five original songs, but more important, he is inspiring others. "I was amazed at the impact Chu had on my TV-addicted son," says one mom. "Suddenly his world is bigger and he's dead-serious about his music lessons."

He's mastered Mozart and played for the queen—at age seven.

QUOTABLE: "God tells me everything I need to know about music, like notes, dynamics—and not to read books while I'm practicing."

BEHIND THE SCENES: Wesley Chu, like other kids, has a collection of trucks, loves Legos, and is very serious about his crayons—his other passion being drawing. He was born to Lucia and Simon Chu, both talented musicians themselves. Wesley has two sisters, Sharon and Esther, ages one and three.

PRAYER STARTERS:

- Give thanks for God's amazing creative gifts, and for the inspiration that unusually talented young performers like Wesley Chu are to children and parents alike.
- Pray that Chu will use his opportunity for influence in positive ways.
- Pray that Lucia and Simon Chu will seek God's wisdom in raising Wesley, and for success as they try to guide him into a fulfilling, well-rounded life.
- Ask God to surround the Chu family with protection and grace.

I will praise God's name in song and glorify him with thanksgiving.
Psalm 69:30

CONTACT: Jeff Parry Promotions P.O Box 1234, Station M, Calgary, Alberta, Canada T2P 2L2

Nelson Mandela

President of South Africa

Photo by Rick Reinhard, Washington, D.C.

POINT OF IMPACT: Nelson Mandela has led the South African crusade against racial segregation for nearly half a century. Born in a Zulu village in 1918, Mandela dreamed of one day helping his people in their struggle for freedom. In the fifties, he became the leader of the African National Congress, a grassroots mass movement against apartheid, the "separate but equal" law set in place by the white government. He was charged, tried, and imprisoned on several occasions for his activities. On February 11 (this day) 1990, he left prison for the last time, having served 27 years. He accepted the 1993 Nobel Peace Prize on behalf of the South Africans who suffered in the struggle for peace and was elected President of South Africa in 1994. When Mandela's term ends in December 1999, the country will face a difficult transition, and as elder statesman, Mandela will play an influential role in its outcome.

He led South Africa's fight against apartheid.

QUOTABLE: "I detest racism because I regard it as a barbaric thing, whether it comes from a black man or a white man."

BEHIND THE SCENES: Mandela loves to watch the sun set while listening to Handel or Tchaikovsky; he was denied music and sunlight for much of his imprisonment. He also missed his children: "My daughter Zinzi says that she grew up without a father, who, when he returned, became the father of a nation." Today he lives in Pretoria with wife Graca Machala.

PRAYER STARTERS:

- Give thanks for Nelson Mandela and his commitment to democracy and freedom against great odds. Ask for his health and safety.
- Pray that Mandela and those who follow him in power will seek God's wisdom as they guide the nation through challenging times.
- The message of Christ often suffers in South Africa because of its previous association with white supremacists. Pray for the churches there.

You will know the truth, and the truth will set you free. John 8:32

CONTACT: South African Consulate, 50 N. La Cienega Blvd, Ste. 300, Beverly Hills, CA 90211

Archive Photo

Howard Stern
Radio & TV Personality

POINT OF IMPACT: Howard Stern is a highly controversial syndicated radio deejay (or "shock jock") renowned for his vulgarity and obscene humor. Every day, around 3 million people, many of them young, tune in to his program. In 1998 he launched a late-night TV show, "The Howard Stern Radio Show." The premiere episode included kissing lesbians and a body-builder of questionable gender. One conservative media watchdog group called the show "one of the raunchiest, [most] tasteless and lewd shows" ever aired, and kicked off a campaign against advertisers. Stern has also written two autobiographical books, *Miss America* and *Private Parts*. The latter was the fastest-moving book in its publisher's history, and the movie by the same name, and in which he starred, was a hit for Paramount.

He aims to shock listeners.

QUOTABLE: "It's crazy to attach a lot of significance to what I do. Whether it's sarcastic commentary or passing wind into the microphone, the purpose is to make people laugh. . . . If you find me funny, great. If not, don't listen."

BEHIND THE SCENES: Stern has said that he doesn't drink, smoke, or take drugs. He's been married to the same woman, Alison, for 20 years and has three daughters: Emily, Debra, and Ashley Jade. Many insist that in person Howard Stern is a perfect gentleman. The Sterns live in New York.

PRAYER STARTERS:

- Pray that Stern's vulgar brand of humor would appeal to audiences less and less, and that Stern himself would choose to put his remarkable abilities to more positive, constructive use.

- Ask that God's kindness surrounding Stern's family would be so apparent to them that they would be drawn to Him (Romans 2:4).

- Pray for those in our world who are exposed to destructive influences and wrong moral choices. Ask God to open people's eyes to discern what is true and what is beneficial.

> *The mocker seeks wisdom and finds none, but knowledge comes easily to the discerning. Proverbs 14:6*

CONTACT: CBS Radio, 40 West 57th Street FL 14, New York, NY 10019

Anthony Campolo

Sociologist, Professor, Pastor

Courtesy of Tony Campolo

POINT OF IMPACT: Dr. Anthony "Tony" Campolo's convictions are reflected in his accomplishments: he's developed a school for inner-city children, helped to establish Christian hospices for AIDS victims, and created the Evangelical Association for the Promotion of Education to promote educational, medical, and economic development in Third World countries. Both provocative and engaging, he's an academic as well as a pastor with an international ministry. Recently he made the news for serving, along with Gordon MacDonald, as pastor to President Clinton during the Lewinsky scandal. Sometimes controversial among evangelicals for his theology and social activism, Campolo sees himself as an old-fashioned preacher with an abiding concern for the poor, the uneducated, and the at-risk.

He urges Christians to take the lead in social activism.

QUOTABLE: Campolo's gift to evangelicals has been to "afflict the comfortable, and comfort the afflicted." For example, at a Jesus festival in the seventies he declared: "Tonight thousands of people on this earth will die of starvation. Most of you will not give a s—t. And most of you will be more upset with the fact that I said 's—t' than that thousands of people will die tonight."

BEHIND THE SCENES: Cable viewers can watch Campolo Monday mornings on *Hashing It Out*. His books include *Is God a Democrat or a Republican?* He teaches at Eastern College and pastors a Baptist church in Philadelphia. He and his wife, Margaret, have two grown children, Lisa and Bart.

PRAYER STARTERS:

- Thank God for Tony Campolo's forthright defense of the poor and powerless, and for his example of social action and an integrous lifestyle.
- Pray for his teaching and preaching effectiveness, and for the future impact of his students.
- Ask God to bless Campolo and his family with peace, health and plenty.

> *Religion that God our Father accepts as pure and faultless is this: to look after orphans and widows in their distress and to keep oneself from being polluted by the world. James 1:27*

CONTACT: Anthony Campolo, 1300 Eagle Rd., St. Davids, PA 19087

Courtesy of Smalley Relationship Center

Gary Smalley
Marriage Consultant, Author

POINT OF IMPACT: He's given marriage advice to some of America's top celebrities, but author Gary Smalley is best known as the marriage fixer for the average couple. His late-night program, *Keys to Loving Relationships,* is the longest-running infomercial in broadcast history. The videos Smalley markets feature well-known celebrities like Dick Clark, John Tesh and Connie Sellecca, and Kathie Lee and Frank Gifford. "I learned that I could reach a different audience," Smalley says. "These people wouldn't be reached through the usual means of bookstores or seminars." Smalley's video series, *Keys to Loving Relationships,* has been viewed by more than 3 million. His dozen bestselling books include *If Only He Knew* and *Language of Love.*

He helps millions of couples learn how to love.

QUOTABLE: "I'm still making mistakes in my marriage but there aren't as many funny, disastrous experiences to write about. After three years, it adds up to enough for a new book. Before, it could be two books a year because I was messing up that often."

BEHIND THE SCENES: Smalley, 59, once asked 63,000 men at a conference to take off one shoe, hold it up, then drop it. Then he asked them to drop one strand of hair. "When we're angry," he told them, "we think we're dropping a strand of hair on our wives, our friends, and our kids. But they feel it like a shoe." Smalley and his wife, Norma, have three children and six grandchildren.

PRAYER STARTERS:

- Smalley says that anger is a "plague damaging families." Pray for healing and reconciliation in homes around the world.

- Pray that husbands and wives in your community will invest in strong marriages; pray especially for Christian couples in this regard.

- Give thanks for Gary Smalley's impact on millions of homes. Ask God to favor him and his wife with joy, health, and long lives.

> *The Lord is faithful, and he will strengthen and protect you from the evil one.*
> 2 Thessalonians 3:3

CONTACT: Smalley Relationship Center, 1482 Lakeshore Dr., Branson, MO; www.garysmalley.com

Lauryn Hill

Singer, Actress, Songwriter

Archive Photo

POINT OF IMPACT: In 1993 Lauryn Hill burst upon the music scene with a rap trio called the Fugees. After her gritty alto voice helped make the Fugees the biggest-selling rap group of all time, the 25-year old from South Orange, New Jersey went solo. The songs she writes range from deeply personal to sociopolitical, and her remarkable talent has not gone unnoticed. The *New York Times* called her "visionary," and by 1999 she had garnered an extraordinary ten Grammy Award nominations and won five for her debut solo album, *The Miseducation of Lauryn Hill.* Between writing and producing her own albums, she also writes songs for other artists including CeCe Winans and Aretha Franklin. As part of her acceptance speech during the 1999 Grammy Awards Hill read from Psalm 40.

Her hip-hop wows the music world.

QUOTABLE: "I want my music to touch real people. I'm still trying to figure myself out, like most people, because I'm still living and learning."

BEHIND THE SCENES: Hill is the founder of the Refugee Camp Project, a program for inner-city youth. She has one son, Zion, and was expecting her second child in late 1999. Hill says that she and her children's father, Rohan Marley, have plans to marry but have not set a date. "I don't consider myself a single parent," she says, "because my son's father is very involved."

PRAYER STARTERS:

- Give thanks for Hill's creative gifts and charitable activities.
- Pray that Hill will make motherhood a priority along with the blessings of marriage. Pray that her mothering experience will draw her closer to God and His loving plans for her life.
- Pray that she will have a growing desire to influence her young listeners for good.

> *Our mouths were filled with laughter, our tongues with songs of joy.*
> Psalm 126:2

CONTACT: www.laurynhill.com

Roberto Benigni
Actor, Director

Archive Photo

POINT OF IMPACT: The Holocaust usually doesn't inspire comic possibilities, but when Italian director Roberto Benigni wrote and directed a poignant film about a father's love for his son set in a concentration camp, he made tragedy and humor coexist—beautifully. *Life Is Beautiful* won myriad awards, including a 1999 Oscar for best foreign film. When Benigni went on to win the Oscar for best actor—beating out opponents like Tom Hanks and Nick Nolte—he set the film industry back on its heels (it was the first time in 40 years for a foreign film star to win best actor). Benigni says he does not view his work as a comedy, but rather as a comedian's exploration of tragedy.

His daring film moved us to laughter, and to tears.

QUOTABLE: While Russian nationalist Leon Trotsky was trapped and waiting for Stalin's hit men to assassinate him, he wrote down, "Life is beautiful." Says Benigni, "I fell in love with this simple phrase. Even with darkness all around us, we can still find beauty. That is true strength."

BEHIND THE SCENES: Benigni's father, an Italian soldier, was imprisoned in a German labor camp for two years. "He was obsessed for years by his stay in the camp," says Benigni. "Each evening, he would tell stories about it to me and my sisters. My mother made him understand that he was scaring us, so he stopped. Then he started telling the stories in a lighter way. He started to smile again and he stopped having nightmares. He found funny things to say, even when dealing with these painful circumstances. The way he was telling the stories is exactly what I have done in my story." Benigni 46, is married to actress Nicoletta Braschi, who starred in the film—as his wife.

PRAYER STARTERS:

- Give thanks for the redemptive themes portrayed in Benigni's work.
- Pray that Benigni will use his widening influence for great good; that he will seek God's guidance in his choices of projects and talent.
- Ask God to bless Benigni and his wife with His best gifts.

He has made everything beautiful in its time. Ecclesiastes 3:11

CONTACT: None available.

Martha Stewart

*Chairman, CEO,
Martha Stewart Living Omnimedia*

Archive Photo

POINT OF IMPACT: Dubbed "the grande dame of much-better living" and "the queen of domesticity," Stewart is credited with encouraging women's domestic impulses. *Time* magazine has named her one of the 25 Most Influential People in America. And *Harper's Bazaar* says, "The persona she has developed and branded to the hilt—attractive but serious, intelligent but accessible, domestic but dignified—has won her the gratitude of millions of women for restoring their right to take pleasure and pride in the household arts." Yet Stewart has detractors. Observed one columnist, "She's become the woman other women love to resent. She has a knack for making us feel guilty—reminding us that we never have enough time to bake lemon squares." Her latest project is a children's interactive show called *Every Day After School.* Her highly profitable company, Martha Stewart Living Omnimedia, now includes magazines, television and radio shows, a newspaper column, a web site, books, a mail-order catalog, and a product line with Kmart.

She's been dubbed "the queen of domesticity."

QUOTABLE: "Yummm."

BEHIND THE SCENES: Martha Stewart, 59, hosted a Democratic fund-raiser lunch at her Connecticut headquarters for President Clinton (helping to pull in $1.6 million). "There's no telling how much she's broadened my base today by giving me the chance to come here," said Clinton. Stewart is divorced and lives in Connecticut and New York; she has a daughter, Alexis.

PRAYER STARTERS:

- Give thanks for Martha Stewart's ability to appreciate beauty and bring beauty into the world in so many creative ways. Pray for her welfare.
- Pray that as she encounters beauty, she would come to know better "the beauty of the Lord" (Psalm 27:4).
- Pray for women today who long to find ways to make their homes more simple, organized, and beautiful for their families to enjoy.

She watches over the affairs of her household. Proverbs 31:27

CONTACT: www.marthastewart.com

Photo credit: Ginger Gamage

Frederick Buechner
Author, Minister

POINT OF IMPACT: Writing fiction and nonfiction books considered "too secular for church people, yet too churchy for secular people," Frederick Buechner has nonetheless become one of America's best-loved writers. A Presbyterian minister and evangelist, he considers his congregation to be the many thousands of people worldwide who read his books. He has written 14 novels (including the Pulitzer Prize-nominated *Godric*) and 15 nonfiction books (including *A Room Called Remember,* and *The Alphabet of Grace*). His skill at communicating the Gospel in fresh ways has won readers from the antireligious elite to conservative evangelicals. Philip Yancey calls him "the most quoted living writer among Christians of influence."

He writes in the alphabet of grace.

QUOTABLE: "There are all different kinds of voices calling you to all different kinds of work. The challenge is to find which is the voice of God rather than society, ego, or self-interest. The place God calls you to is where your deep gladness and the world's deep hunger meet."

BEHIND THE SCENES: When Buechner was ten, he and his younger brother Jamie watched from their upstairs bedroom window as their mother and grandmother tried to revive a motionless body lying on the driveway. It was their father, dead of carbon monoxide poisoning. Out of consideration for his mother, Buechner didn't write directly of his father's suicide for decades, though scenes of suicide haunt his novels. A resident of Rupert, Vermont, Buechner, 73, and his wife Judith have three grown children.

PRAYER STARTERS:

- Buechner says, "Christ is an enormously moving figure. I never cease to be moved to the roots of my being. It is only His friends who make Him boring." Pray that Christian writers will never make Christ "boring."
- Pray for a growing audience for Buechner's works.
- Ask the Lord to bless the Buechners and their family with health, nurturing friendships and contentment.

    Pleasant words are ... sweet to the soul and healing to the bones.
    Proverbs 16:24

CONTACT: HarperSanFrancisco, 1160 Battery St., San Francisco, CA 94111-9197

Saddam Hussein

President of Iraq

Archive Photo

POINT OF IMPACT: Hussein is infamous as a terrorist and warmonger who has used chemical weapons to quell an uprising inside Iraq. After he invaded Kuwait in 1990, Arab and Western forces defeated Saddam Hussein in Operation Desert Storm. When he continued to breach peace terms, President Clinton declared in 1998 that Hussein presented a threat to world peace and ordered another military strike. "Saddam must not be allowed to threaten his neighbors or the world with nuclear arms, poison gas or biological weapons," said Clinton. American and British forces continued to carry out air strikes into 1999. Under Hussein's leadership, Iraq remains a regional threat, especially to Israel, to minorities inside its own borders, and indirectly to the nations to which it supplies oil.

He's the Middle East's biggest bully.

QUOTABLE: Hussein, addressing his people during the 1998 military strike: "Fight the enemies of God, enemies of the nation and enemies of humanity. God will be on your side and disgrace will be theirs, now and on the day of the judgment."

BEHIND THE SCENES: Hussein was born into poverty. At ten, he left his mother and abusive stepfather to live with his uncle, a devout Sunni Muslim. The uncle later become governor of Baghdad, and wrote the pamphlet *Three Whom God Should Not Have Created: Persians, Jews and Flies.* Hussein has been married twice and has five children; he maintains luxurious homes in Baghdad and many other Iraqi cities.

PRAYER STARTERS:

- Pray that Saddam Hussein will govern justly and be restrained from violence.
- Pray for healing, safety, and comfort for the thousands who have been displaced or oppressed by Saddam Hussein's forces. Pray for relief for the people of Iraq who suffer daily deprivations, and for the survivors of the Gulf War who still suffer aftereffects.
- Saddam's first name can be translated, "He who confronts." Pray that he will encounter, confront, and submit to the one true God, and be changed by a personal spiritual renewal.

   I tell you: Love your enemies and pray for those who persecute you. Matthew 5:44

CONTACT: Embassy of Iraq, 1801 P Street NW, Washington, DC 20036

Katie Couric
Coanchor, NBC News' Today

AP/Wide World Photos

POINT OF IMPACT: When in 1991 Katherine Couric first joined NBC's *Today*, many considered her just too cute to take seriously. These days Couric, once called a "perky prop," has transformed herself into one of the most respected journalists on television—a "fist in a velvet glove," says NBC News president Andy Lack. Considered the "driving ratings force" of *Today's* popularity, 42-year-old Couric is a favorite among viewers who want to, as one viewer put it, "trust and like the person who tells me the good or bad news each morning." Among Couric's coups was obtaining the first interview with Hillary Rodham Clinton after she had become First Lady.

She wakes up more people with a smile than anyone.

QUOTABLE: "It is disconcerting to see the dumbing down of America. Some news coverages have become more salacious, more sensationalistic, less intelligent. I would like to think of us as communicators who elevate people and enlighten them, and not go to the lowest common denominator."

BEHIND THE SCENES: Couric's husband, Jay Monahan, a lawyer and highly respected NBC News legal analyst, was diagnosed with colon cancer in the summer of 1997. After battling the disease for eight months, he died in January 1998. Couric has bravely maintained her cheery and professional persona on camera. Friends say since then her focus has been almost entirely on her young daughters, Elinore and Caroline. They live in New York.

PRAYER STARTERS:

- Give thanks for Katie Couric's life and work, for her pursuit of integrity in journalism, and for her dedication to her family.
- Ask God for encouragement for Couric today as she encourages others. Pray for comfort and healing for Couric's daughters.
- Remember someone you know who is facing cancer today or grieving the loss of a loved one.

And now these three remain: faith, hope and love. But the greatest of these is love. 1 Corinthians 13:12-13

CONTACT: NBC Studios, 30 Rockefeller Plaza, New York, NY 10112

William Jefferson Clinton
President of the United States

Photo by Rick Reinhard, Washington, DC

POINT OF IMPACT: During President Bill Clinton's two terms in office, he has presided over one of the most prosperous peacetime economies of the past 100 years. His administration saw the lowest combination of unemployment and inflation since 1968, passage of the Crime Bill, the Brady Bill (handgun control), the Family and Medical Leave Act, a Justice Department crackdown on deadbeat parents, and efforts in foreign policy to balance trade and solve problems in the Middle East. Yet Clinton's presidency has been blighted by his extramarital dalliances with White House intern Monica Lewinsky and charges that he lied about the affair under oath. Though Clinton survived a Senate trial, the crisis left Americans deeply divided about the place of personal morality in public life.

His presidency brought both prosperity and scandel.

QUOTABLE: On NATO airstrikes in Kosovo: "We can't respond to every tragedy in every corner of the world. But just because we can't do everything for everyone doesn't mean . . . we should do nothing for no one."

BEHIND THE SCENES: President Clinton, 55, often attributes his achievements to lessons learned during a tough childhood. His stepfather was an alcoholic who abused his mother. Clinton is a Southern Baptist. He and First Lady Hillary Rodham Clinton have one daughter, Chelsea, a student at Stanford.

PRAYER STARTERS:

- Give thanks for the public service of President and Mrs. Clinton. Ask for God's presence, peace, and protection to surround them today.
- Pray for wisdom and integrity in Clinton's choices and actions.
- After the disclosure of the Lewinsky affair, Clinton turned to his spiritual advisors. Pray that their impact will continue to bear fruit in Clinton's life.
- Pray that those who come next to the office of the U.S. presidency will restore a reputation for sound moral leadership.

> *You kings, be wise; be warned, you rulers of the earth. Serve the Lord with fear and rejoice with trembling. Psalm 2:10-11*

CONTACT: The White House, 1600 Pennsylvania Ave. NW, Washington, DC

Archive Photo

John Travolta
Actor

POINT OF IMPACT: John Travolta first became a cultural phenomenon in the seventies, defining tastes in music and fashion through such movies as *Saturday Night Fever* and *Grease.* During the eighties, however, he had a hard time coming up with a hit, and producers wrote him off as a "has-been." In the nineties Travolta made a dramatic comeback with hits such as *Pulp Fiction, Phenomenon, Primary Colors,* and *A Civil Action.* One of Hollywood's elite circle of $20-million-per-movie actors, Travolta is among a growing number of celebrities who practice and promote the religion of Scientology. "As a Scientologist," says Travolta, "I have the technology to handle life's problems and I have used this to help others in life as well."

He's king of Hollywood comebacks.

QUOTABLE: On how being a father has affected his life: "I became more selfless. I knew what it was like to be willing to give my life for someone—and I would, hands down."

BEHIND THE SCENES: Travolta, 46, and his wife, Kelly Preston, have one son, Jett. Travolta was born in "late life" to Catholic parents, who considered him a miracle and indulged his creative aspirations. When Travolta was 16, his parents gave him permission to drop out of school to pursue acting full time.

PRAYER STARTERS:

- Travolta once said, "I think there's a God. But I don't know much more than that at this point." Pray that he would seek God and that God would reveal Himself to Travolta, as He has promised (Psalm 145:18). Ask God to bring Christians across Travolta's path who can gain his respect.
- Ask God to bless and protect John Travolta's marriage and family.
- Pray that the many followers of Scientology would be drawn to the life-changing truths of the Bible.

> *We have not received the spirit of the world but the Spirit who is from God, that we may understand what God has freely given us. 1 Corinthians 2:12*

CONTACT: John Travolta, P.O. Box 20029-790, Encino, CA 91416

George Soros
Investment Banker and Philanthropist

Archive Photo

POINT OF IMPACT: Widely regarded as one of the most successful investment managers in history, George Soros has accumulated a fortune through management of a private mutual fund, Quantum, which today has more than $11 billion in assets. Soros' reputation is such that the very disclosure of his investments can sway the market as other investors rush to imitate his choices. Through his Open Society Institute, he promotes a vision that *Forbes* magazine calls "a sort of borderless, multicultural world, where people respect one another and the well-to-do take care of the less-well-off." Soros has already given away more than $1.5 billion and established his foundation in 30 countries. He's been described as the only man in the United States who has his own foreign policy—and can afford to implement it. Among his books are *Underwriting Democracy* and *Soros on Soros: Staying Ahead of the Curve.*

His money moves sway Wall Street.

QUOTABLE: "The archenemy of an open society is no longer the communist threat but the capitalist one."

BEHIND THE SCENES: Born to upper-middle-class Jews in Hungary, Soros posed as the godson of a Hungarian government official to avoid the Nazis in World War II. In spite of the constant threat of discovery, he describes this time as "dangerous and exciting. It made me a bit of a risk-taker." Soros emigrated to America in 1956. Now 69, he's married to his second wife, Susan. He has five children, and homes in London, New York City, and Long Island.

PRAYER STARTERS:

- Give thanks for George Soros' remarkable generosity, which has benefitted thousands of people around the world.
- Pray for wisdom and discernment for Soros as he makes financial decisions that impact entire nations.
- Pray for protection and blessing for Soros' marriage and family.

> *A generous man will prosper; he who refreshes others will himself be refreshed.*
> Proverbs 11:25

CONTACT: Soros Fund Management, 888 7th Ave., #3300, New York, NY 10106

Sandra Day O'Connor
Supreme Court Justice

Archive Photo

POINT OF IMPACT: Sandra Day O'Connor was the first woman to break the ultimate glass ceiling when in 1981 she took a seat as Justice on the U.S. Supreme Court. Since then she has often held the balance of power on the nine-member bench. O'Connor is a conservative who has stressed the importance of lessening the gap between church and state. She supports prayer in schools and questions "whether our country is doing all it can to avoid any further deterioration in values." Her grandmotherly presence is particularly influential in the Supreme Court on important issues such as state rights, reproductive rights, and affirmative action.

Her conservative voice is heard in the highest court.

QUOTABLE: On being the first woman justice on the Supreme Court O'Connnor said: "I tend to think that probably at the end of the day, a wise old woman and a wise old man are going to reach the same decision."

BEHIND THE SCENES: Sandra Day O'Connor, 70, grew up on a cattle ranch in Arizona and New Mexico where she used to "get up at 3:00 A.M. and be in the saddle by sunup." Highly influenced by her father's work ethic, she graduated from Stanford University and Stanford Law School. She and husband John O'Connor have three sons: Scott, Brian, and Jay.

PRAYER STARTERS:

- Give thanks for Sandra Day O'Connor's support of appropriate expressions of religion in public schools and for her strong voice for values education.
- Pray that God will give her discernment in the difficult decisions she continues to face on the Supreme Court.
- Ask the Lord to give her mental and spiritual strength, and blessing at home.

Preserve sound judgment and discernment, do not let them out of your sight.
Proverbs 3:21

CONTACT: U.S. Supreme Court, 1 First St. N.E., Washington, DC 20543

Bill Maher

Host, Politically Incorrect

Archive Photo

POINT OF IMPACT: As host of ABC's late-night talk show *Politically Incorrect,* Bill Maher is considered the highest-impact political entertainer in America. *George* magazine says of the show's hybrid of humor and politics, "Maher has done for the talk show what Jerry Seinfeld did for the sitcom. *Incorrect* may change the way America watches politics, and it will almost certainly affect how younger Americans get their information." The Emmy-nominated host delights in pairing unlikely guests, ranging from movie stars to preachers, politicians to musicians. The goal is a political, religious or social debate that's heated, humorous, and controversial. He is critical of America's "culture of entitlement"—"Farmers depend on subsidies, industries on bailouts, minorities on Affirmative Action and wrestlers on steroids. OK, not all wrestlers. But definitely the bad guys."

He orchestrates pivotal discussions.

QUOTABLE: "The Washington media hate me, and I'm not that fond of them. They think that I have no business interloping on their area. They think, 'We're the ones who sit around and talk about national affairs; not you, Comedy Boy.'" *U.S. News & World Report*

BEHIND THE SCENES: According to Maher, 44, the fact that his mother was Jewish and his father Catholic has been a great source of easy stand-up material. Maher was always more likely to make the teacher laugh than the students. For the most part Maher's own politics are liberal: pro-animal rights, pro-drug legalization, and pro-choice. However, Maher is also pro-death penalty and anti-porn on the internet. He is single.

PRAYER STARTERS:

- Ask God to bring Bill Maher trusted Christian friends and a growing sensitivy to spiritual issues.
- Maher hopes to "make an interest in current affairs cool." Pray that he'll be part of boosting civic involvement, especially among Gen Xers.
- Pray that Christian guests on the show will be articulate and influential.

> *Live as free men, but do not use your freedom as a cover-up for evil; live as servants of God. 1 Peter 2:16*

CONTACT: P.I., CBS Television City, 7800 Beverly Blvd., Los Angeles, CA 90046

Prince Alwaleed bin Talal bin Abdulaziz al Saud

Billionaire Investor

AP/Wide World Photos

POINT OF IMPACT: *Forbes* magazine calls him the shrewdest entrepreneur in the world next to Bill Gates. Prince Alwaleed bin Talal bin Abdulaziz al Saud (pictured on right with Michael Jackson) obtained his vast fortune ($13 billion) the old-fashioned way: he earned it. He took a $15,000 loan from his father in the early eighties and turned it into an empire consisting of investments in Citicorp, Rupert Murdoch's News Corp., Netscape, Apple Computer, and dozens of other companies in communications, technology, and entertainment on four continents. He's the chairman and sole shareholder of Kingdom Holding Co., which manages his investments, and has increasing political influence in troubled Saudi Arabia, where he runs several Arabic satellite TV and radio networks and operates an elaborate aid program that dispenses $200 million a year to needy families. Oh, yes, he's also pop star Michael Jackson's business manager.

He turned a $15,000 loan into a $13 *billion* dollar fortune.

QUOTABLE: Jokes his Saudi adviser, Mustafa al Hejailan: "With the prince, it is like playing Monopoly with real money."

BEHIND THE SCENES: The grandson of Saudi Arabia's founding father, Alwaleed lives in a new, $100 million palace adorned with 1,500 tons of Italian marble, 250 TV sets, and five kitchens (one just for desserts). The prince and his two children (he is twice-divorced) can swim in a lagoon-shaped pool or catch a movie in their own cinema.

PRAYER STARTERS:

- Pray that Prince Alwaleed will experience a deep hunger for the spiritual truth fround in Christ.
- Pray that he will increasingly find ways to invest his fortune on ventures and causes that better humanity and bring long-term prosperity to the less advantaged of the Middle East.
- Ask God to surround the prince and his family with His tender mercies.

> *When God gives any man wealth and possessions, and enables him to enjoy them, to accept his lot and be happy in his work—this is a gift of God.*
> *Ecclesiastes 5:19*

CONTACT: none available

Kirk Franklin

Gospel Recording Artist

Courtesy of Gospo Centric

POINT OF IMPACT: Called the "Garth of gospel," Kirk Franklin and his impressive backup singers have been widely credited with reviving the genre of contemporary gospel music. By adding elements of modern R&B, rap and hip-hop, and joining forces with secular stars like U2's Bono, he gains credibility with the unchurched teens he wants to reach while sparking some controversy in Christian circles. His lyrics are unabashedly Christian. As the *Washington Times* put it, "Mr. Franklin manages to make you want to dance while keeping in mind what the message is all about." Franklin says, "I hope we've tapped into something kids can listen to that's not going to destroy their minds and their souls." His first two albums each sold more than 1 million copies. His third, *Nu Nation*, won a 1999 Grammy for best contemporary gospel album and became the biggest-selling gospel album ever.

He mixed things up, and revived gospel music.

QUOTABLE: "See, I know the Kirk that ya'll don't know. I know the Kirk with all his screw-ups and mistakes, and all the things he's done in his past that should've stopped him from having all that God has given him. When you know yourself like that, you are so humbled, worthy only of praising Him."

BEHIND THE SCENES: Franklin, 29, abandoned by first his father, then mother, was raised by his great aunt, who was a Baptist. Using money he had collected from recycling cans, she started him on piano lessons at age four. At seven, he wrote his own "sacred" lyrics to Elton John's "Bennie and the Jets." At age 11, he led the church choir. His autobiography is *Church Boy*. He lives in Arlington, Texas with his wife, Tammy, and their three children.

PRAYER STARTERS:

- Give thanks for the influence of gospel music on millions of listeners.
- Ask God to protect Kirk Franklin and his family amid the pressures of success. Pray that his marriage will be a source of strength to him.
- Pray for the impact of Franklin and other Christian musicians like him, who are winning a new audience among pop music buyers.

Clap your hands, all you nations; shout to God with cries of joy. Psalm 47:1

CONTACT: Word Records, 3319 West End, Suite 600, Nashville, TN 37203

Courtesy of Cambridge University

Stephen Hawking

Scientist

POINT OF IMPACT: "The greatest genius in the twentieth century." "The finest mind alive." "Master of the universe." Each moniker belongs to Stephen Hawking, 58, Lucasian Professor of Mathematics at Cambridge University, a post once held by Isaac Newton. Hawking did nothing less than revolutionize modern thought about the origins of life and the nature of time. Applying Einstein's theory of relativity, he discovered that black holes radiate energy (correcting the assumption that nothing escapes from a black hole). "My goal is simple," Hawking says. "It is the complete understanding of the universe." His research reveals the startling possibilities of time running backward and an 11-dimensional universe. His bestselling book *A Brief History of Time* helps nonscientists understand questions being asked by scientists today.

He's the most famous living scientist.

QUOTABLE: "The reward of understanding the universe may be a glimpse of the 'mind of God.'"

BEHIND THE SCENES: Since college days Hawking has suffered from Lou Gehrig's disease, a slow deterioration of the muscles in the body. He was told he had only two years to live—but that was 35 years ago. Now he's confined to a wheelchair and uses technological aids to communicate. Hawking is married to the former Elaine Mason; he has three children by a previous wife.

PRAYER STARTERS:

- Thank God for giving Stephen Hawking an extended life of scientific productivity. Ask God to bless him and his family with peace and joy.
- Pray for his relief from physical symptoms that continue to impair him, and the fortitude to endure. Pray for others who suffer in similar ways.
- Pray that Hawking's work will lead others to evidence of a loving, intelligent Designer who set the laws of science in motion.

> *Do not take me away, O my God, in the midst of my days; your years go on through all generations. In the beginning you laid the foundations of the earth, and the heavens are the work of your hands. Psalm 102:24-25*

CONTACT: Department of Applied Math and Theoretical Physics, Silver Street, Cambridge CB3 9EW England; e-mail: S.W.Hawking@damtp.cam.ac.uk

Fidel Castro
President of Cuba

UN/DPI photo by E. Schneider

POINT OF IMPACT: Fidel Castro, leader of the Cuban revolution, is the dictator of one of the world's last communist regimes. Since the sixties, tens of thousands of Cubans who have opposed Castro have been arrested or imprisoned; hundreds of thousands more have fled the country. In recent years, Castro has softened some of his hard-line communist doctrine. In 1998, the Pope visited Cuba at Castro's invitation. During the Pope's stay, Castro attended mass, some say for the first time in 40 years. Cubans still suffer daily from the effects of government mismanagement and a 35-year U.S. economic embargo. Fidel's brother, Raul, is in line to be Castro's successor.

He's one of the world's last Communist dictators.

QUOTABLE: After an interview with Castro, journalist Dan Rather commented: "In addition to being a consummate politician and an intelligent person, Castro's also a consummate actor. What's always difficult is to determine where the actor leaves off, if ever, and where the real man takes up."

BEHIND THE SCENES: Castro's father was a prosperous farmer who emigrated from Spain to Cuba. Castro was the second of his father's five illegitimate children by his cook. At 73, Castro is tall and still sports the trademark beard he grew in the mountains. He has a son, Fidel, Jr., from a six-year marriage in the fifties and a daughter, Alina, by a mistress during that same period.

PRAYER STARTERS:

- During his visit, Pope John Paul II urged Castro to allow Cubans broader religious freedom and human rights. Pray for progress in these areas.
- Some sources say that 500 prisoners of conscience remain in Cuban jails. Pray for their release, and for comfort for their families.
- Pray for the leaders who will take power after Castro is off the scene.
- Castro has said he has never believed in God. Ask for God to break through his unbelief. Pray for his health and well-being in body and spirit.

> *Be still, and know that I am God; I will be exalted among the nations.*
> Psalm 46:10

CONTACT: Palacio del Gobierno, Havana, Cuba

Kenneth "Babyface" Edmonds

Songwriter, Producer

Photo credit: Randee St. Nicholas

POINT OF IMPACT: Kenneth Edmonds (stage name, "Babyface") dominated the pop and R&B sounds of African-American music in the nineties. He's won a Grammy for producer of the year three years in a row, and has been nominated for more non-classical Grammys than any other person in the decade (12 in 1997 alone). Like the Motown era that preceded him, Edmons' lyrics and music both express and define the dreams and the values of millions of urban listeners. His melodies have been recorded by Toni Braxton, Mariah Carey, Celine Dion, and Madonna, among others. Songs he wrote and produced for Boyz II Men and Whitney Houston both established records for the longest stay at No. 1 on the Billboard charts. "I'm a writer, then a producer, then an artist," he has said. He has his own recording label (LaFace), and is branching into film and television.

The stars sing his songs.

QUOTABLE: "Initially I wanted to be Muhammed Ali. But then I got into a fight and I figured I should choose something else."

BEHIND THE SCENES: Edmonds, 41, and his five brothers were raised in Indianapolis by their mother after their father died. Today he supports The Boarder Baby Project, which cares for abandoned children until they're adopted. He and his wife, Tracey, and their preschooler Brandon live in Los Angeles.

PRAYER STARTERS:

- Pray that Kenneth "Babyface" Edmonds will express the longings of urban listeners in ways that draw them toward God's best in their lives.
- Pray that the Edmonds will grow in his knowledge of God's saving love.
- Ask God to bless Babyface and his family with health, peace, and joy.

By day the LORD directs his love, at night his song is with me. Psalm 42:8

CONTACT: The Edmonds Companies, 1635 North Cahuenga Blvd., Los Angeles, CA 90028

Boris Yeltsin
President of Russia

UN Photo 179200/M. Grant

POINT OF IMPACT: Boris Yeltsin trained as a construction engineer before launching into politics. His political work has seemed to run a parallel course—out of rubble, he tried to reconstruct a new Russia. In the mid-eighties, as mayor of Moscow, he was eager to reform the party's dysfunctions, arrested hundreds of corrupt authorities, and openly criticized bureaucrats enjoying luxury—like chauffeured limousines—while the common people struggled. Suddenly, in the late eighties Yeltsin resigned, announcing that, under Gorbachev, economic recovery was lagging. His move precipitated Gorbachev's downfall and sped up the dissolution of the Soviet Union. Yeltsin has been president of the Russian Federation for ten turbulent years. He's been described as "hardworking and incorruptible." But his plan for a market economy failed, and his military handling of a revolt in the Chechin Republic proved disastrous. Yeltsin's health, and the deterioration of the Russian economy, make his future uncertain.

Russia's future weighs heavy on him.

QUOTABLE: "We don't appreciate what we have until it's gone. Freedom is like that. It's like air. When you have it, you don't notice it."

BEHIND THE SCENES: Yeltsin, 69, was born in the Ukraine and grew up in a working family. In 1956 he married Naina Iosifovna Girina, a student he knew in college. They have two daughters, Yelena and Tatiana. Tatiana now serves her father as adviser, helping him with personal matters and watching over his health.

PRAYER STARTERS:

- Pray that Boris Yeltsin will exercise wisdom in personal and public decisions. Pray for the spiritual and physical welfare of the Russian people during difficult times.
- Ask for blessings of hope, faith and love for Boris Yeltsin and his family.
- Pray that Yeltsin will permit and even endorse the revival of Christianity among his people.

> *I pray that you may enjoy good health and that all may go well with you, even as your soul is getting along well. 3 John 2*

CONTACT: Embassy of Russia in the United States, 2650 Wisconsin Ave. N.W., Washington, DC 20007

Steven Spielberg

Director, Writer, Producer

Archive Photo

POINT OF IMPACT: *Time* magazine once hailed Steven Spielberg, 52, as "the most successful movie maker ever." Novelist Michael Crichton calls him "the most influential popular entertainer of the twentieth century." Spielberg's movies—including *E.T.* and the *Indiana Jones* series—rank among the top moneymakers of all time and have to date grossed over $2 billion. While Spielberg's commercial talent was becoming obvious, his artistic talents were little recognized by the Academy Awards until *Schindler's List* (1993), which won seven Oscars, including best picture, best director, and best adapted screenplay. Next came Spielberg's *Jurassic Park*, whose $1 billion worldwide receipts shattered all previous records. But increasingly, Hollywood's premiere power broker is more interested in historical fare. Thus he gave us *Amistad* (about a slave ship crossing the Middle Passage) and most recently, *Saving Private Ryan*, credited with altering young people's attitudes toward veterans.

He's the most successful movie maker in history.

QUOTABLE: On *Saving Private Ryan:* "Everybody asks that question at one time or another: 'Have I been a good person?' It's a question we should want to ask ourselves now, not when we're old and standing in a cemetery but every day of our lives."

BEHIND THE SCENES: Married to his second wife, actress Kate Capshaw, he's the proud father of a blended family of five children. He makes breakfast for them and drives carpool every day. He describes himself as "a nice Jewish boy from Phoenix, Arizona." Of his motivation for making *Schindler's List* (half of the movie's proceeds went to Jewish philanthropic groups) he says, "I wanted my children to be proud that they are members of the best tribe in history."

PRAYER STARTERS:

- Give thanks for Spielberg's remarkable imagination and sensitivities.
- He says, "I love history and want to do things my kids want to know about." Pray that his work will have a positive influence on people of all ages.
- Pray for a growing spiritual sensitivity. Ask God to bless Spielberg's marriage and family with joy today.

> *I will utter hidden things, things from of old . . . what our fathers have told us. . . . We will tell the next generation the praiseworthy deeds of the LORD, his power, and the wonders he has done. Psalm 78:2-4*

CONTACT: DreamWorks SKG, P.O. Box 8520, Universal City, CA 91608

Aung San Suu Kyi

*General Secretary, National League
for Democracy (NLD)*

Courtesy of Free Burma

POINT OF IMPACT: Aung San Suu Kyi is a slim, 54-year-old mother of two who loves to wear fresh flowers in her hair. She's also an international symbol of heroic and peaceful resistance in the face of oppression. She won the 1991 Nobel Prize for Peace for leading Burma—an Asian country of 46 million—in a nonviolent struggle for democracy. From 1989 to 1995, Suu Kyi (pronounced Soo Chee) was kept in isolation under house arrest for speaking out against Burma's government. The brutal military dictatorship has used torture and forced labor to hold power, and refuses to hand over rule even though it lost a national election. Despite her official release from house arrest, she still faces restrictions on her movement and speech. Aided by the National League for Democracy, Suu Kyi continues her inspiring campaign while Burma's human rights record remains one of the worst in the world.

She's a wife, she's a mother, she's a freedom fighter.

QUOTABLE: "I do believe in the spiritual nature of human beings. To some it's a strange or outdated idea, but I do believe there is such a thing as a human spirit. There is a spiritual dimension to man which should be nurtured."

BEHIND THE SCENES: Aung San Suu Kyi married Michael Aris, a British scholar specializing in Tibetan studies. He is now a don at Oxford. Prior to their marriage, she wrote these words to him: "I only ask one thing, that should my people need me, you would help me to do my duty by them." While under house arrest, Suu Kyi did not see her children for two and a half years.

PRAYER STARTERS:

- Pray for Suu Kyi's health, safety, and spiritual well-being. Ask God to help her and Michael find ways to nurture family relationships under severe strain.
- Give thanks for the sacrifices Suu Kyi has made on behalf of her country.
- Ask God for an end to repression and political violence in Burma.

> *This is what the Lord says: "Administer justice every morning; rescue from the hand of the oppressor the one who has been robbed." Jeremiah 22:12*

CONTACT: FreeBurma@POBox.com

Courtesy of T.D. Jakes Ministry

Thomas "T.D." Jakes, Sr.

Pastor, TV Preacher

POINT OF IMPACT: Bishop T.D. Jakes has rapidly become one of the world's dominant preachers with his fiery style and compassionate Bible teaching. Jakes' program, *The Potter's House,* broadcasts four times weekly on Trinity Broadcasting Network and Black Entertainment Television. His book, *Woman, Thou Art Loosed,* one of nine bestsellers, has sold nearly 1.5 million copies. Since moving his ministry to Dallas in 1996, Jakes' church, The Potter's House, has mushroomed into a multiracial congregation of 21,000. The church is active in ministries to the homeless, prostitutes, drug and alcohol abusers, AIDS victims, and prisoners. No wonder Jakes has been described as "the Shepherd of the Shattered." According to *Charisma* magazine, Jakes' message "is about God's supernatural ability, bestowed by a Lord who is color-blind and cares about each person."

He's been called "The Shepherd of the Shattered."

QUOTABLE: "There are prisoners outside in society as well as inside prison gates. I tell them all that God is the best friend they're ever going to have—the only one who is always there to hear you. He comes in and doesn't need to wait for visiting hours. He sits with you whether you're in the penitentiary or on a yacht."

BEHIND THE SCENES: Jakes, 43, grew up in rural West Virginia. His parents taught him a strong work ethic (his father, Ernest, started a janitorial service with a mop and bucket that grew to 42 employees). In 1980 Jakes opened his first church in a storefront. He's married to Serita Ann Jamison, who plays an active role as a speaker and leader in the church. They have five children.

PRAYER STARTERS:

- Give thanks for Bishop T.D. Jakes' ministries to the needy and hurting.
- Jakes has said, "My struggle is the scheduling, stress, busyness, weariness—the loss of normalcy and privacy." Pray for his peace, wisdom, and refreshment.
- Ask God to protect the Jakes' marriage and family. Pray that they will keep love and faithfulness at the top of their priorities.

> *Direct me in the path of your commands, for there I find delight.*
> Psalm 119:35

Contact: T.D. Jakes Ministries, P.O. Box 5390, 6777 W. Kiest Boulevard, Dallas, Texas 75236

Kathie Lee Gifford

Cohost, Live with Regis & Kathie Lee;
Singer, Actress

Courtesy of Kathie Lee Gifford

POINT OF IMPACT: Her welcoming presence and upbeat attitude set the day's tone for millions of women. Says one viewer, "She radiates something special. It's like having morning coffee with a close friend." *Live with Regis & Kathie Lee* debuted in 1988; the hosts' sassy interplay, along with Gifford's tales of life with husband Frank and their children, won high ratings and shot Gifford's popularity to an all-time high. The late nineties, however, brought personal traumas. First it was revealed that clothes for her Wal-Mart clothing collection were made at sweatshops. Then her husband was caught—on film—in a tryst with another woman. On both counts, Gifford responded with courage. She lobbied for improved conditions for garment workers worldwide. Then she and her husband entered marital counseling to try to find healing.

She's one of TV's classiest acts.

QUOTABLE: "I am a successful person if I am living a godly life."

BEHIND THE SCENES: Gifford, 47, graduated from Oral Roberts University. She has always been outspoken about her Christian faith. Of her husband's infidelity she says, "A rocky time in your marriage comes out of the blue for no reason and throws you for a loop and makes you reexamine everything, but love without forgiveness is never love to begin with." The Giffords donate time to charities, including two they started which care for HIV-positive and crack-addicted kids. They live in Connecticut with their children, Cody and Cassidy.

PRAYER STARTERS:

- Give thanks for the courage, kindness, and tenacity that Kathie Lee Gifford has embodied to millions of viewers.
- Pray that Gifford will be a strong influence inside ABC today for quality programs, especially ones that encourage women toward right living.
- Ask the Lord to bless the Gifford family today with health, friendship, and renewing joy. Pray, too, for God's best for Regis and Joy Philbin.

> *You are forgiving and good, O LORD, abounding in love to all who call to you.*
> Psalm 86:5

CONTACT: ABC-TV, 77 West 66th St., New York, NY 10023

Walter H. Annenberg

Former Publisher, Broadcaster, Diplomat

Archive Photo

POINT OF IMPACT: Walter H. Annenberg used to be the man behind such popular magazines as *Seventeen* and *TV Guide.* But that was billions of dollars ago. By the time he'd sold off his family's company (Triangle Publications, which also operated TV and radio stations) in the eighties, he'd raised his corporation's assets from $25 million to an estimated $200 million. He went on to pioneer the concept of education via television. But his greatest gifts to education came when he turned to philanthropy. He and his wife Lenore established the Annenberg Foundation, which now boasts assets of more than $5.5 billion—much of which benefits schools. Among his many awards, he's received the National Medal of Arts and the Medal of Freedom.

He donates millions to education.

QUOTABLE: On his office wall, Annenberg keeps this quotation from Winston Churchill: "Look not for reward from others but hope that you have done your best."

BEHIND THE SCENES: Walter's father and predecessor was once charged with bribery, evasion of taxes, and other crimes. Annenberg found his father's tragedy "a great source of inspiration for constructive endeavor." He and his wife live outside of Philadelphia.

PRAYER STARTERS:

- Give thanks for Walter Annenberg's willingness to dedicate his later years to giving selflessly to others. Pray for his continued strength and influence.
- Pray that the enormous resources of the Annenberg Foundation will be applied in positive ways.
- Pray for the health of Walter and Lenore Annenberg, for their peace and safety, and for a growing responsiveness to God's redeeming love.

> *He will be the sure foundation for your times, a rich store of salvation and wisdom and knowledge; the fear of the LORD is the key to this treasure.*
> *Isaiah 33:6*

CONTACT: The Annenberg Foundation, St. Davids Center, Suite A-200, 150 Radnor-Chester Road, St. Davids, PA 19087

Jill Elikann Barad

Chairman and CEO, Mattel, Inc.

Courtesy of Mattel, Inc.

POINT OF IMPACT: Mattel CEO Jill Barad is the highest-ranking woman in a Fortune 500 company. Barad, who favors high heels and tailored Chanel suits, has been described as "more Hollywood than corporate." But don't be fooled. Demonstrating an amazing intuition for consumer tastes, she helped build Mattel into a $4.8 billion company and upped the annual Barbie brand revenue from $200 million in the eighties to almost $2 billion in 1998. "If Barbie is the symbol of success," writes *Business Week,* "then surely Jill Barad herself is an equally powerful icon for corporate women." Intel Chairman Andrew S. Grove invited her to give a presentation on branding to his senior executives, and Pixar CEO Steven Jobs, whose board she sits on, calls her "a dynamo." Since Barbie was first released in 1959, the doll's anatomically exaggerated features have been criticized for instilling unrealistic expectations of beauty. Worldwide, two Barbie dolls are sold every second.

She's the dynamo behind Barbie.

QUOTABLE: "When Barbie is in a little girl's hands, she is a vehicle for dreaming, for imagining what girls can be."

BEHIND THE SCENES: How does Barad measure her success? "After my son watched me give a speech on my career," she says, "he turned to me and said, 'Wow, Mom, did you really do all that? I'm so proud of you!' That's when I knew I'd made it." Barad says she couldn't have done it without her husband, Tom, a Hollywood producer who cut back on work when their two boys were young.

PRAYER STARTERS:

- Pray for peace, health and spiritual blessing for Jill Barad and her family today.
- Ask that she will seek God's wisdom in all her decisions at Mattel.
- The average American girl owns nine Barbie dolls. For a young girl you know today, pray for joy in her play and a growing confidence that she is cherished. Ask that she'll grow to treasure the beauty that lasts.

From the lips of children and infants you have ordained praise. Psalm 8:2

CONTACT: Mattel, Inc., 333 Continental Blvd., El Segundo, CA 90245-5012

Archive Photo

Tom Cruise
Actor, Director, Producer

POINT OF IMPACT: Tom Cruise is the most success-ful, bankable, and influential film star of his genera-tion. He's able to green-light $100 million projects with a single phone call, and at age 36, makes $20 million per picture. He has racked up well over $1.5 billion in domestic box-office receipts during his career, and seen few misses in the 20 movies he's released in the last 18 years—including *The Firm, Rain Man,* and *Jerry Maguire.* As *Entertainment Weekly* put it, Cruise is "big-ger than Arnold, bigger than Brad, bigger than Bruce—in a town full of 800-pound gorillas, he's King Kong." For the movie *Eyes Wide Shut* (July '99), Cruise teamed with his wife, Nicole Kidman, and the legendary late British director Stanley Kubrick. Meanwhile, his Cruise/Wagner Productions has been acquiring the film rights to a number of new novels.

He's the definition of star power.

QUOTABLE: Cruise has often been the target of rumors about his sexual prefer-ences, his marriage, his controversial religion (Scientology), even his virility. "I think people must sit in a room and make it up," he says. "I know they do. They sit there and wonder, 'Okay, what can we say next?'"

BEHIND THE SCENES: After Cruise dropped out of high school, he spent a year in a monastery, hoping to become a Franciscan priest. Today, "He forgets he's a star," says director Rob Reiner. "He just goes along like a normal person." His wife agrees. "He assumes people don't talk to him because they aren't interested. I'll have to explain that it's because they're too nervous to come over." They have an adopted son and daughter and live in Syracuse, New York.

PRAYER STARTERS:

- Ask God to bless and protect Tom Cruise, his wife Nicole, and their two children. Pray that the Cruises' marriage will be strengthened by mutual commitment in the face of many pressures.

- Pray that Cruise's influence in creative projects and on fellow professionals in the film industry will be a positive one.

- Ask God to draw Cruise's spiritual hunger toward knowledge of Himself.

> *The LORD is near to all who call upon him, to all who call upon him in truth.*
> Psalm 145:18

CONTACT: Creative Artists Agency, 9830 Wilshire Blvd., Beverly Hills, CA 90212

Nora Roberts

Novelist

POINT OF IMPACT: Romance queen Nora Roberts helps shape the attitudes of millions of women toward men and romance. "When Roberts puts her expert fingers on the pulse of romance," writes *Publishers Weekly,* "legions of fans feel the heartbeat." In all Nora Roberts has written more than 130 novels and has more than 42 million copies of her books in print. She sold 7 million books and had six *New York Times* bestsellers in 1997 alone. She's best known for combining romance, suspense, mystery, and adventure in titles like *True Betrayals, Sacred Sins,* and *Carnal Innocence.* It all started in a blizzard in 1979, when Roberts was snowed in with two young sons. "We couldn't even get out to buy Oreos," she recalls. Roberts decided to escape the boredom by starting a novel. Three years and six rejected manuscripts later, she struck pay dirt with Silhouette Books. Roberts says she works up to eight hours a day fueled by chocolate and diet soda. "If I'm stuck, I hammer away until I unstick."

She has her finger on the pulse of romance.

QUOTABLE: "I like men. I'd better, as I have four older brothers. I grew up outnumbered, then had two sons and continued to be in the minority. It was either like them . . . and do my best to understand them, or run screaming."

BEHIND THE SCENES: Nora Roberts grew up in Maryland. And believe it or not, she also writes futuristic romantic suspense under the pen name of J.D. Robb. She has two sons and lives in Keedysville, Maryland, with her second husband, Bruce Wilder, a carpenter she met when he remodeled her bedroom.

PRAYER STARTERS:

- Pray that Nora Roberts would know God as her first love, and weave the truth of redeeming love into her stories.
- Forty percent of all fiction bought in the U.S. falls into the romance genre; the average reader is a married woman of 33. Pray that romance readers would be motivated to invest in their marriage relationships.
- Ask the Lord to bless Roberts with love and good health.

> *Many waters cannot quench love; rivers cannot wash it away. If one were to give all the wealth of his house for love, it would be utterly scorned.*
> *Song of Songs 8:7*

CONTACT: www.romance.net

Jeff Bezos

Founder and Owner, Amazon.com

POINT OF IMPACT: In 1994 Jeff Bezos built Amazon.com, now the largest bookstore on the internet, with a database of more than 2.5 million titles (that's five times bigger than the largest Barnes & Noble). He instantly became the poster child of internet commerce, which could add up to $920 billion by 2002, reports *USA Today*. Of all the web upstarts, Bezos' is the most watched. Already Amazon.com has 3 million customers from 160 countries. Some half-million visitors go to Amazon every day, making it the most heavily trafficked retail site on the web. And now Bezos, 35, is creating a kind of virtual supermall—"the Wal-Mart of online." In 1998 *Time, Vanity Fair,* and *Entertainment Weekly* all named Bezos one of the most powerful men in the communications industry.

He's the poster child of internet commerce.

QUOTABLE: On buying books at regular bookstores: "I've been doing that all of my life, and I'm not about to give that up. People . . . shop for books because it's fun. When you go into a bookstore, you can smell the books and hear the bindings creak. All those tactile sensations are very enjoyable."

BEHIND THE SCENES: In 1994 Bezos quit his job on Wall Street, packed up, and moved to Seattle. Even before the furniture caught up, Bezos had set up computers in the garage and he and four employees started writing the software that would make Amazon.com work. "I decided that when I was 80 I wouldn't regret quitting Wall Street when I was 30," he says, "but . . . I might really regret missing a great opportunity." He lives with his wife, MacKenzie, in Bellevue.

PRAYER STARTERS:

- Ask that Bezos and his team will seek the Lord's guidance today, and that his family will experience many spiritual blessings.
- Pray that those on the leading edge of online commerce will be blessed with both creativity and sound judgment.
- Ask that God will use online bookstores to bring the gospel to many who would never find it otherwise.

> *Wisdom is a shelter as money is a shelter, but the advantage of knowledge is this: that wisdom preserves the life of its possessor. Ecclesiastes 7:12*

CONTACT: www.amazon.com/exec/obidos/thebookstore03A

Luis Palau

Evangelist, Author

POINT OF IMPACT: Since his first evangelistic campaign in 1966, Luis Palau has spoken through radio and TV broadcasts to hundreds of millions of people in more than 100 countries, and in person to 13 million in 67 nations. Featured in a *Wall Street Journal* article in November 1995 as "the Billy Graham of everywhere," Dr. Palau, 64, has also written several books, including *Calling America and the Nations to Christ,* and *Where Is God When Bad Things Happen?* He's been a guest on CNN, MSNBC, and *The News Hour with Jim Lehrer.* The Archbishop of Canterbury describes Palau as "an evangelist of integrity, relevance and compassion." Palau and his evangelistic team's ministry has led to at least a million conversions. In 1998 the ministry launched Next Generation Alliance, a partnership to encourage and equip a new generation of evangelists.

He's taking Jesus to the world.

QUOTABLE: The Palau team sees the internet as a promising tool for spreading the gospel. Says Palau, "It's fitting that the internet should be used to communicate what still remains to be one of the most relevant debates for our world today: Was Jesus Christ who He said He was? And did He rise from the dead?"

BEHIND THE SCENES: Palau accepted Jesus Christ at a summer camp in his native Argentina. "That night I could hardly sleep," he remembers. "Back in my tent, by the light of my flashlight, I wrote in my Bible: 'February 12, 1947, I received Jesus Christ.'" He and his wife, Pat, have four sons and live near Portland, Oregon.

PRAYER STARTERS:

- Give thanks for Luis Palau's impact around the world. Ask God to bless him and his family with strength, stimina, peace, and plenty.
- Pray that God will continue to empower Palau's preaching.
- Pray that those who respond to Palau's message will quickly become established in a fellowship, and that they too will become His ambassadors.

> *God was in Christ, reconciling the world to himself, no longer counting people's sins against them. This is the wonderful message he has given us to tell others. We are Christ's ambassadors. 2 Corinthians 5:19-20* NLT

CONTACT: Luis Palau Evangelistic Association, P.O. Box 1173, Portland, OR 97207; www.lpea.org

T. Berry Brazelton
Child Development Expert, Author

POINT OF IMPACT: In the past few decades, Dr. Brazelton has become a household name, friend, and mentor to millions of parents. Widely respected in the United States and abroad as an expert on pediatrics and child development, he's spent more than 40 years in clinical practice, teaching, and academic research. He's described as "a soft-spoken Southern gentleman with a smile that warms up the room and the heart." Fellow expert Dr. Benjamin Spock once told *USA Today*, "Brazelton's greatest legacy may be training pediatricians coming along to look with great sensitivity at the emotional development of children." He's authored 27 books, including the highly acclaimed *Touchpoints*. He hosts the Lifetime television series,*What Every Baby Knows*, and writes a weekly column syndicated by the *New York Times*. As chair of the Pampers Parenting Institute, he provides families around the globe with information, guidance, and support.

To many, his books are a parent's best friend.

QUOTABLE: "I first wanted to be a missionary, but my decision was also a guilty reaction to my jealousy of my younger brother, a terribly engaging child. I hated him so much that I felt I should save the rest of the children in the world. I know the exact night I decided. An evangelist . . . asked for anybody who wanted to be saved to walk up to the podium, and I did. Everybody was singing, 'Waiting not to rid my soul of one dark blot.' My blot was my feeling about my brother."

BEHIND THE SCENES: Brazelton admits his penchant has been for babies. He claims that his four children, now 34 to 46, drove him a little crazy as teens. Brazelton and his wife of 50 years, Christina, live in Cambridge, Massachusetts.

PRAYER STARTERS:

- Give thanks for Brazelton's help and encouragement to millions.
- Pray that Dr. Brazelton will seek the Lord's wisdom even as he dispenses it to others. Ask for the Holy Spirit to bring his family closer to God today.
- Brazelton reports that most young mothers feel alone, cut off from traditional sources of support. Pray for a young or expectant mom you know.

> *Whoever welcomes one of these little children in my name welcomes me.*
> Mark 9:37

CONTACT: www.pampers.com.

Osama bin Laden
Sunni Islamic Terrorist

Archive Photo

POINT OF IMPACT: Osama bin Laden, the world's wealthiest and perhaps most feared terrorist, has been implicated in worldwide attacks on Americans ranging from the 1992 bombing of U.S. soldiers in Yemen to the tragic bombings of the U.S. embassies in Kenya and Tanzania. The youngest of 20 sons of a Saudi construction magnate, bin Laden first used his wealth and influence during the 1979 invasion of Afghanistan by the Soviet Union. Since then, however, his goals have become more violent. The Saudi government revoked his citizenship in 1994 and his family officially disowned him. He moved to the Sudan but eventually was forced to a remote mountain hideout in Afghanistan, where he faxes to the outside world religious edicts he calls *"fatwas."* In February 1996 bin Laden vowed to kill Americans, his goal being to unite the Muslim population of 1 billion and run the United States out of the Middle East. President Bill Clinton called him "America's Public Enemy Number One."

He tops the world's "most wanted" list of criminals.

QUOTABLE: "Resistance against America will be spread in many, many countries. . . . We must drive out the Americans."

BEHIND THE SCENES: Before his foray into religious terrorism, bin Laden was described as a free-spending, fun-loving youth in flashy nightclubs and bars. Today the 41-year-old, with his piercing eyes and graying beard, is much more serious and lives as a recluse somewhere in Afghanistan with three of his wives and their children.

PRAYER STARTERS:

- Pray that Osama bin Laden will be restrained from further violence. Pray that he will see the truth: "These men lie in wait for their own blood; they waylay only themselves!" (Proverbs 1:18).
- Ask that God will miraculously deliver bin Laden from his prison of hatred.
- Pray for Muslims all over the world, especially those who feel oppressed by Western cultural values and economic dominance.
- Pray for Islamic leaders who call for an end to religious hatred and violence.

Turn from evil and do good; seek peace and pursue it. Psalm 34:14

CONTACT: none available

Trent Lott
Senator, Mississippi

AP/Wide World Photos

POINT OF IMPACT: As the Senate Majority Leader, Trent Lott is responsible for a great deal: setting the Republican agenda of the Senate, making sure that it reflects both the public's will and the nation's needs, and asserting the interests of the Republican party in advancing its policy initiatives. Over the past 24 years, he has forged a reputation as one of the more ambitious and conservative Republicans on the Hill, hawkish on military matters, in favor of a balanced budget amendment, and strongly opposed to abortion and gay rights. According to *All Politics,* an online political magazine, "Lott is the most powerful man in Congress," and any success that President Clinton enjoys will depend on his ability to get along with him. Many speculate that Lott's ambition will eventually move him toward a run at the White House.

He wields power where it counts.

QUOTABLE: On the Lewinsky scandal: "I think bad conduct is enough, frankly, for impeachment. If you have brought disrepute on the office, that is sufficient."

BEHIND THE SCENES: A man of strong opinions, Lott has opposed homosexuality, calling it a sin. On the other hand, his alleged pro-tobacco stance has reportedly derailed much of Congress' attempts at controlling the tobacco industry. Lott, 59, is married to Patricia. They have two children.

PRAYER STARTERS:

- Pray that Lott will seek God's wisdom, both for his positions and his public statements.
- Ask God to give Trent Lott and his family health and protection.
- Pray for the Congress that develops in 2000 and beyond, that it will become distinguished for its integrity, teamwork, and vision.

> *This is my prayer: . . . that you may be able to discern what is best and may be pure and blameless until the day of Christ. Philippians 1:9-10*

CONTACT: 487 Russell Senate Office Building, Washington, DC 20510-2403; www.senate.gov/~lott/

Sherry Lansing

Chairman, Motion Picture Group,
Paramount Pictures

Archive Photo

POINT OF IMPACT: The "most powerful woman in Hollywood" began her career reading scripts for five dollars an hour. Today, as chairman of Paramount Pictures, Lansing is the preeminent studio boss with a stream of hits (*Titanic, The Truman Show, Saving Private Ryan*) unmatched in recent history. She had the foresight to pick up *Forrest Gump* when Warner Brothers threw it out. Since Lansing took over in 1992, Paramount has experienced top market shares in the industry, record-breaking profits, and has won the Oscar for Best Picture three times. Lansing's success has paved the way for more female exectives in the industry—and, many hope, better representation of women in movies. *Fortune* magazine listed her as the fifth most powerful female executive in the nation.

She's Hollywood's supreme studio boss.

QUOTABLE: "My mother and stepfather wanted me to quit college and study to be a nurse's aide so I could work in my husband's office. I was sobbing. I wanted to work in the movie business, but how could I tell them? That was like saying I wanted to go to the moon."

BEHIND THE SCENES: Lansing grew up in Chicago, the eldest daughter of a woman who escaped Nazi Germany and was widowed at 32. Lansing has said that her passion, besides making movies, is raising money for cancer research (her mother died of cancer). Once a model, Lansing, 55, has both "looks and brains." But she also has a reputation for being one of the most gracious executives in the business. She is married to director Billy Friedkin and has two grown stepsons.

PRAYER STARTERS:

- Pray that Sherry Lansing will seek God's guidance in her decisions.
- Ask God to show her and her family His care and redemption.
- Pray that Lansing and her colleagues will favor film projects, like *Saving Private Ryan*, that will make a lasting impact for the next generation.

Grace and peace be yours in abundance. 1 Timothy 1:2

CONTACT: www.paramount.com

Archive Photo

Gerard "Gerry" Adams

Irish Politician

POINT OF IMPACT: Gerry Adams has been at the center of the clash between Irish Republicans and the British since 1969 when the current phase of "the Troubles" began. More than any other leader, Adams, President of Sinn Fein—the political arm of the Provisional Irish Republican Army (IRA)—will influence Ireland's immediate future. During most of the seventies, he was either on the run or imprisoned without trial, all for the cause of a united Ireland free from British rule. Some regard Adams as a terrorist. They cite his link with the IRA, which has killed 1,800 people, roughly a third of them civilians, in its 28-year attempt to end British rule in Northern Ireland. Others note that Adams helped persuade the IRA to abandon violence for politics. Sinn Fein is now involved in peace negotiations with the British government.

He leads the IRA—and is key to peace.

QUOTABLE: "Peace is more than a cessation of violence. Peace is the process of justice, peace is people having ownership in their daily lives, having a place in society." BBC interview, 1998.

BEHIND THE SCENES: Gerry Adams was one of 13 children born into a strongly activist family. Now 50, he and his wife, Colette, have three children. Adams is tall, lean, well-groomed, and bespectacled—"reminiscent of Clint Eastwood," one journalist says. His wardrobe includes a bulletproof vest. His friends say he has as much interest in talking about literature as politics. Since a 1984 assassination attempt in which he was severely wounded, he's been a virtual security prisoner.

PRAYER STARTERS:

- Pray for healing and comfort for all those in the United Kingdom and Ireland who have been injured or personally affected by terrorist attacks.
- Pray that the IRA will permanently abandon terrorism as a strategy. Ask that peacemakers will prevail on all sides.
- Ask God to bless and protect Gerry Adams' whole family. Pray that he will pursue peace in Ireland and a personal relationship with a forgiving God.

He has sent me to proclaim freedom for the prisoners and recovery of sight for the blind, to release the oppressed. Luke 4:18

CONTACT: Sinn Fein, 55 Falls Road, Belfast, BT12 4PD, Northern Ireland

Dee Jepsen

Founding President, Enough Is Enough!

POINT OF IMPACT: Dee Jepsen is leading a crusade. Her organization wants to restore an environment where parents are free to raise children without the intrusion of offensive sexual material. Toward this end, she travels extensively to educate the public about the existence, availability, and dangers of illegal pornography. Some of her objectives: to make pornographic material unavailable to children; to make illegal pornography unavailable in the marketplace; and to encourage community efforts to guard against illegal pornography and treat its victims. Enough Is Enough! activists come from varied backgrounds, professions, and religious affiliations. Jepsen has taken her battle to Senate Judiciary hearings in 1995 and 1996. A major ongoing arena of concern is pornography peddled through the internet.

Courtesy of Enough Is Enough

She battles illegal pornography.

QUOTABLE: Jepsen says that as things stand now, "Bringing a computer into your home for your child's use . . . is like having them bring home a rabid dog for the kids to play with, sitting him in a corner, and then having to watch them constantly so the dog won't bite them."

BEHIND THE SCENES: Jepsen is also the award-winning author of four books, including *Women Beyond Equal Rights*. She and her husband, former Senator Roger Jepsen, have six children and nine grandchildren.

PRAYER STARTERS:

- Praise God for the gift of sexuality. Ask for forgiveness for how much our culture has allowed its beauty to be spoiled by lust and selfishness.
- Give thanks for the efforts of Dee Jepsen and many others who are crusading to protect familes from the intrusions of pornography.
- Ask God to bless and strengthen Jepsen and her family today.
- Pray today for deliverance for the victims of pornography: users, producers, those in affected marriages and relationships, and children.

> *Do not lust. . . . Can a man scoop fire into his lap without his clothes being burned? Proverbs 6:25,27*

CONTACT: Enough is Enough!, P.O. Box 888, Fairfax, VA 22030

Azizah al-Hibri

Muslim Feminist, Lawyer, Law Professor

POINT OF IMPACT: Dr. Azizah al-Hibri, a spokeswoman for Muslim women all over the world, insists that in the Quran (the Muslim scripture), Mohammed the Prophet never intended for women to be oppressed, veiled, hidden, or given fewer privileges than men. Her desire for women to read and understand the Quran, and her openness to the truth of Christianity, have made her the target of angry fundamentalist Muslims in Iran and other Shiite countries. Al-Hibri is also an American lawyer who finds no contradiction between Islamic values and the basic values in the U.S. Constitution, and she has shared her views with President Clinton. In 1996 al-Hibri was a favorite panelist on the celebrated *Genesis* series facilitated by Bill Moyers on PBS. Currently she teaches at the University of Richmond in Virginia.

She wants to liberate Muslim women.

QUOTABLE: "Many observant, often veiled, American Muslim women are doctors, lawyers and professors. This should not come as a surprise to anyone, because Islam does not oppress women, patriarchy does."

BEHIND THE SCENES: Al-Hibri was born in Beirut, Lebanon. Raised a Muslim, al-Hibri was also taught Christianity in a missionary school. In 1966 she came to the United States for her graduate education. She and her husband, Ahmad al-Haidar, a computer engineer, make their home in Richmond, Virginia. "We have been blessed with a very caring and close relationship," she says.

PRAYER STARTERS:

- Pray that God would use the work of Azizah al-Hibri and others to bring spiritual as well as cultural well-being to Muslim women around the world.
- Pray that God's truths about inherent value of womanhood—whether single or married—would prevail in all cultures, especially where women face oppression.
- Ask God to bless al-Hibri and her family with a growing awareness of His grace and good purposes for their lives.

If the Son sets you free, you will be free indeed. John 8:36

CONTACT: Williams School of Law, University of Richmond, Richmond, VA 23173

Jimmy Carter

Former U.S. President. Peacemaker,
Humanitarian

Rosalynn Carter

Former First Lady,
Advocate for the Mentally Ill

Photo credit: Rick Diamond

POINT OF IMPACT: President from 1976-1980, Jimmy Carter is best remembered for his commitment to morality in government and his strong Baptist faith (he continued to teach Sunday school during most of his administration). Many saw his integrity, humility, and broad smile as a welcome relief after the Vietnam and Watergate years. After losing a bid for reelection, Carter became instrumental as a global negotiater. Today the silver-haired Carter heads the nonprofit, Atlanta-based Carter Center, which promotes peace and humanitarian causes worldwide. Rosalynn Carter remains a leading activist for the mentally ill all over the world. She was responsible for the Mental Health Systems Act of 1980, which advocated health insurance coverage and protection from discrimination for the mentally ill. Mrs. Carter's fourth and latest book is *Helping Someone with Mental Illness,* written with Susan K. Golant.

Together they do the world good.

QUOTABLE: "The proper function of a government is to make it easy for people to do good and difficult for them to do evil."

BEHIND THE SCENES: Last year Carter traveled to 13 countries to monitor elections and to promote health and human rights. The Rosalynn Carter Fellowship, awarded to five journalists annually, supports study of mental-health issues. The Carters have four children and nine grandchildren.

PRAYER STARTERS:

- Praise God for the work Jimmy and Rosalynn Carter have done and continue to do in the interest of human welfare around the world.
- Ask God to bless the former President and First Lady with health, joy and family fulfillment in their later years.
- Pray that their Christian testimony will influence many to live out the gospel in practical, lifelong ways.

> *God is not unjust; he will not forget your work and the love you have shown*
> *him as you have helped his people and continue to help them. Hebrews 6:10*

CONTACT: The Carter Center, 453 Freedom Parkway, Atlanta, GA 30307; www.cartercenter.org

AP/Wide World Photos

Judy McGrath
President, MTV/M2

POINT OF IMPACT: As president of Music Television (MTV) and its spin-off channel, M2, Judy McGrath heads both the business and creative sides of MTV. The channels now reach 265.8 million households in 85 countries on five continents. *Fortune* magazine calls McGrath "the most important music maven for any record exec to meet," and notes that she "rules youth culture." One reporter says, "You could say that Judy McGrath is Beavis and Butthead's mother. Without her maternal nod, Mike Judge's teenage dudes-from-hell would not have made it onto the tube." McGrath is credited with developing programs such as *MTV Unplugged* and *Real World*. Under her leadership MTV's ratings and revenues have been rising. In addition to expanding MTV viewership into Russia and Asia, she's moved into filmmaking—MTV's first success was *Dead Man on Campus*. Five more feature films are in the works.

QUOTABLE: On graphic videos: "I think that music is inherently sexual and emotional, and that's what's great about it. Within the broadest limits that I can, I want to show it all."

She rules youth culture.

BEHIND THE SCENES: McGrath, 46 and single, works in a poster-plastered office high above Times Square. She has been described as surprisingly "girlish"—she's watched MTV every day for more than a decade. Growing up, she dreamed of writing for *Rolling Stone*.

PRAYER STARTERS:

- Pray that McGrath and her colleagues who program music, TV, and movies for young and impressionable consumers will take risks for quality entertainment of high moral content.
- Ask for God's unfailing goodness and surpassing peace to surround Judy McGrath today.
- Pray for creative Christians to rise to positions of influence within MTV management.

> *I will walk in my house with blameless heart. I will set before my eyes no vile thing. Psalm 101:2-3*

CONTACT: www.mtv.com

Dario Fo

Author, Playwright

Agenzia Fotografica

POINT OF IMPACT: Dario Fo, who won the Nobel Prize for Literature in 1997, is one of the world's most controversial literary figures. For the past 40 years, the leftist Italian playwright has used farce and slapstick to ridicule government authority, the rich, religion (most notably the Catholic church), and to fight oppression and uphold the dignity of the downtrodden. He has been jailed for his work, the Italian government routinely censors him, and the United States has denied him visas twice. Fo, now in his seventies, is one of the most-produced playwrights in the world. His best-known works include *Can't Pay, Won't Pay; Accidental Death of an Anarchist;* and *Mistero Buffo,* which has played to more than 50 million people worldwide (the Catholic church calls it "the most blasphemous show in the history of television"). One Italian critic likened Fo's body language to that of Jerry Lewis, his irreverent tongue to that of the late Lenny Bruce.

His words make waves.

QUOTABLE: "We continue doing what we set out to do from the start: to attack, with laughter and reason, in song and in mime, every form of oppression and injustice."

BEHIND THE SCENES: After winning the Nobel Prize, Fo donated his award (about $950,000) to the disabled. His wife said they would also try to raise more funds to build houses and establish scientific laboratories for disabled people. Fo and his wife live in Milan, Italy.

PRAYER STARTERS:

- Pray for health, strength, and peace for Dario Fo and his wife.
- Give thanks for Fo's generosity to the disabled and his sensitivity to the needs of the less fortunate. Pray that God will bless his efforts on their behalf.
- Pray that Fo will receive the insight of spiritual rebirth, seeing past religion or organization to God Himself.

> *It is better to heed a wise man's rebuke than to listen to the song of fools.*
> *Ecclesiastes 7:5*

CONTACT: Theatre Communications Group, publicity@routledge-ny.com

Michael Eisner

CEO, Walt Disney Productions

POINT OF IMPACT: Michael Eisner's career reads like a Disney story—one of repeated come-from-behind victories. As vice president of ABC, then as president/CEO of Paramount Pictures, and finally CEO of Walt Disney, Eisner took weak or flailing companies and made them the most successful in their league. Upon arriving at Disney, which had lost its way since Walt Disney's death in 1966, Eisner oversaw animated features such as *The Little Mermaid, Beauty and the Beast,* and *The Lion King*—all blockbusters. As Disney stock soared, market watchers called Eisner "the prince who awakened Sleeping Beauty and revived the Magic Kingdom." At the same time, Disney acquired Miramax and launched Touchstone Pictures to produce more diversified films. Some, including James Dobson of Focus on the Family, have been highly critical of Disney's move away from "safe family fare." In the mid-nineties, a merger with Capital Cities/ABC made Eisner the single most powerful figure in the industry.

He's king of Disney's empire.

QUOTABLE: "I always went into an area that was in last place, with a philosophy, 'You can't fall off the floor,'" says Eisner.

BEHIND THE SCENES: Eisner grew up in a Jewish family in Manhattan. "I was extremely lucky," he says of his wife. "Jane was interested in what I was doing, but didn't believe any of my baloney. She delivered for me three sons who became the center of my life. . . . Whenever the heady experience of achievement and reward is presented," he says in jest, "I have three children and a wife who could care less."

PRAYER STARTERS:

- Give thanks for the delight Disney has brought children through the years; pray that only what is good will penetrate the minds of today's viewers.
- Pray for joy, health, and spiritual blessings for Eisner and his family.
- Ask God to show Michael Eisner and his creative team breakthrough projects that will positively influence youth in the next generation.

> *Even a child is known by his actions, by whether his conduct is pure and right.*
> Proverbs 20:11

CONTACT: The Disney Company, 500 S. Buena Vista St., Burbank, CA 91521

Andrew Grove
Founder, Intel Corporation

AP/Wide World Photos

POINT OF IMPACT: Computer technology begins and ends with a little chip. And under Andrew Grove's leadership, Intel has grown to dominate the market for these, called computer microprocessors—arguably the world's most important product. Producing 90 percent of the little chips worldwide, Intel has done more than any other company to make the microprocessor the dominant technology of our times. In 1997 when *Time* named Grove Man of the Year, it called him "a brilliant mind on the front line of a revolution." In 1998 Grove stepped down as CEO of Intel but continues to serve as its chairman, focusing on broad strategic issues. He writes for *Fortune,* the *Wall Street Journal,* and the *New York Times.*

His little chip packs a lot of power.

QUOTABLE: "If competition is chasing you, you only get out of the valley of death by outrunning the people who are after you. And you can only outrun them if you commit yourself to a particular direction and go as fast as you can."

BEHIND THE SCENES: Andrew Grove, who is Jewish, was born Andras Grof in Budapest, Hungary, in 1936. His family was able to elude the Nazis with the aid of a local Christian family. During the Hungarian uprising against the Soviet Union in 1956, when he was labeled "an enemy of the classes," Grove escaped to the United States, where he arrived penniless. He helped found Intel in 1968 and emerged a billionaire. He now lives in San Francisco with his wife.

PRAYER STARTERS:

- Pray that Andrew Grove's remarkable leadership qualities will influence for good many in the computer-related industry.
- Ask for God's blessing on Grove's health, his spirit, and his personal life.
- Grove has said, "Technology happens. It's not good or bad." Pray that Intel and other leading-edge corporations will wield power wisely and make social and moral responsibility a high priority.

Though your riches increase, do not set your heart on them. Psalm 62:10

CONTACT: Intel Corporation, 2200 Mission College Blvd., Santa Clara, CA 95052

Nancy Dickey

President,
American Medical Association (AMA)

POINT OF IMPACT: She lived in a house without indoor plumbing until she was 9, and was once told by a high school counselor that she couldn't be a successful physician if she was a wife and mother. Yet today Dr. Nancy Dickey—wife and involved mother—has been called "the most powerful woman in medicine in the free world." She's the first woman president of the American Medical Association, representing 700,000 physicians whose powerful lobbying, teaching, and publishing activities shape national opinions and policies. Dickey also chairs the AMA board of trustees, a more influential but less visible role than the presidency. Her one-year tenure as president comes at time when medical care is being dramatically reshaped. AMA policies on prickly topics such as health insurance, euthanasia, and late-term abortions are under enormous pressure.

She defied the odds to become a power player in medicine.

QUOTABLE: "There's a part of you that says, 'You know, I'm just a little farm girl from South Dakota. What am I doing here? What have I got to say they could possibly want to hear?'"

BEHIND THE SCENES: When she was 9, her near-penniless parents moved with their five children in a '54 Ford from their South Dakota farm to California. Dickey and her husband of 27 years have three children, all of whom have been heavily involved in sports. "She has missed few contests," says her husband, who sometimes jokingly refers to himself as "Mr. Dr. Dickey."

PRAYER STARTERS:

- Critics charge that the AMA does more to look out for the health of doctors' pocketbooks than of the patients they treat. Pray that Nancy Dickey would leave a legacy of wisdom, justice, and integrity.

- Pray for a health provider you know to be strengthened today to fulfill the Hippocratic oath to care for the sick and protect the living.

- Ask God to bless the Dickey family with health and harmony.

Pray for each other so that you may be healed. James 5:16

CONTACT: www. ama-assn.org

Tokunboh Adeyemo

Evangelist, Preacher

POINT OF IMPACT: Tokunboh Adeyemo likes to begin his addresses by shouting, "The Lord is good" and waiting for his audiences to respond, "All the time!" A powerful and popular evangelist and preacher, Adeyemo is helping to convert Africa. As a leader in both World Evangelism Fellowship and the Association of Evangelicals in Africa, he is well placed to effect change. Adeyemo believes that the last frontier of his continent is the 16 states of North Africa with Muslim populations of up to 90 percent. He says that for too long, evangelists accepted the Sahara Desert as a great barrier. No longer, he says: "Now we can cross it. We can fly over it. We can go around it. . . . The Sahara is no longer an excuse!"

His heart is set on North Africa.

QUOTABLE: On there being only one missionary for every 1 million Muslims: "We must be ashamed of ourselves. Jesus wants us to go to the unreached. I challenge you . . . don't pray for an easy life. Pray God will burden you with passion for the Muslim world. I've made up my mind, and I pray 'Lord give me the continent of Africa, or else, I die.'"

BEHIND THE SCENES: Born into a wealthy Muslim family, daily he prayed, "There is no God but Allah." But inside he says he was empty. A friend invited him to church, where he saw people adoring God with joy despite their poverty. Soon after, he chose to follow "Yeshua, the giver of life." Today his whole family—once devout Muslims—follows Jesus. He's married and has two sons.

PRAYER STARTERS:

- Join Tokunboh Adeyemo in praying for widespread conversions among the non-Christian populations of Africa.
- Pray that Adeyemo will seek and follow God's wisdom for his ministry.
- Ask God to protect Adeyemo and his family from spiritual and physical harm.

> *He turned the desert into pools of water and the parched ground into flowing springs; there he brought the hungry to live. Psalm 107:35-36*

CONTACT: Association of Evangelicals of Africa, P.O. Box 49332, Nairobi, Kenya, East Africa; e-mail: AEA@MAF.org

Archive Photo

George Lucas
Producer, Director, Screenwriter

POINT OF IMPACT: George Lucas is the famed creator of the record-shattering *Star Wars* saga, as well as (with Steven Spielberg) the *Indiana Jones* series. Lucas' ability to marry entertainment and technology have revolutionized the art of motion pictures. In the words of the American Academy of Achievement, "Twenty years later, its [*Star Wars*'] impact on American culture—film and otherwise—is undisputed, and creator George Lucas has been canonized as a genius." In recent years, Lucas has devoted himself to helping other young filmmakers and to making improvements in special-effects technology. His company, LucasFilm Ltd., now includes LucasArts Entertainment Company, and Lucas Digital, credited with countless technical breakthroughs. In May of 1999, Lucas released the prequel to his *Star Wars* saga, *The Phantom Menace*.

He revolutionized the art of motion pictures.

QUOTABLE: "A talent is a combination of something you love a great deal—something you can lose yourself in, something that you can start at nine in the morning, look up from your work and it's ten o'clock at night—and something that you have a natural ability to do very well. "

BEHIND THE SCENES: Lucas, 55, had trouble getting anyone interested in *Star Wars*. His script was turned down by two studios before 20th Century Fox took it on. Years ago, Lucas survived a horrific car crash and realized, "There must be some purpose for me to be here and I'd better figure out what it is." Lucas' ex-wife, the former Marcia Griffin, helped him edit *Star Wars*. They have three children.

PRAYER STARTERS:

- Ask for God to bless and protect George Lucas and his children. Pray that their hearts would be open to His love and His care today.
- Pray for the new generation of filmmakers who will benefit from Lucas' advances and will make decisions about how to apply them in art and entertainment.
- Pray that Lucas will use his creative gifts to bring good to the world.

Who laid [the earth's] cornerstone—while the morning stars sang together and all the angels shouted for joy? Job 38:6-7

CONTACT: Industrial Light and Magic, P.O. Box 2459, San Rafael, CA 94912

Sean "Puff Daddy" Combs

Hip-Hop Singer, Producer

Archive Photo

POINT OF IMPACT: "Puff Daddy" Combs started out as a young African-American in Harlem with no connections and very little education. Yet he's gone on in just a few years to revolutionize the entire music industry through his hard work and creative genius. Today Combs is known as the Father of Hip-hop, the musical style that dominates contemporary youth culture. In fact, at only 29, Combs is considered a major influence on the way this generation dances, dresses, rhymes, sings, and walks. *People* magazine placed Combs on the 1998 Best-Dressed List, calling him a "hip-hop version of GQ." His company, Bad Boy Entertainment, can be likened to Motown or Def Jam—recording studios that shaped and defined youth culture from the sixties through the eighties.

Fans imitate his style, and his hip-hop.

QUOTABLE: "What has made me more grounded over the years is my belief in God. I always believed in God. I just started speaking about it more because I've had more success and I owe him."

BEHIND THE SCENES: Despite his prosperity, controversy dogs Combs. Many question his role in the death of his partner, Notorious B.I.G., in the mid-nineties. In January, 1999, a claims court ruled that he shared responsibility for a stampede at a 1991 celebrity basketball AIDS charity event that left nine people dead. "Not a day passes that I do not regret the fact that I was a promoter of this tragic event," he says. He's single and has one son.

PRAYER STARTERS:

- Ask God to bless and influence "Puff Daddy" Combs and his endeavors today. Ask for God's grace and leading to surround his family.
- Combs has worked on a gospel album called *Thank You* so he can "help make God cool with kids." Pray that he will positively influence this generation and become a role model of integrity and faith.
- Pray for the success of Daddy's House Social Programs, a Combs endeavor which helps inner-city homeless and foster kids.

> *Guard my life and rescue me; let me not be put to shame, for I take refuge in you. Psalm 25:20*

CONTACT: Bad Boy Entertainment, Philadelphia, PA; bad.boy@bmge.com

Ann Landers
Syndicated Columnist

POINT OF IMPACT: Seven days a week for 40 years, Ann Landers (born Esther Pauline Friedman) has dispensed down-to-earth advice to readers seeking help on topics ranging from family to manners to sex to ethics. Her column, which runs in 1,200 newspapers, is popular with children and teenagers as well as adults. Landers has authored five books and many public service booklets, such as *Sex and the Teenager* and *The Lowdown on Dope.* Landers has received honorary degrees from 33 universities. A World Almanac poll once listed her as the most influential woman in the United States. Her mail (2,000 letters a day) has been called "an index of American sociology, a glossary of our discontent—leavened with occasional words of wisdom and recipes for curing hiccups."

She shoots from the hip, and her aim is still good.

QUOTABLE: "I think people who aren't positive don't succeed. . . . I am open to positive thinking; I am going to make it, it is going to be good, things are going to be better. That is my signature, that is the way I have lived my life. I don't look back, I don't care what was—I care what is."

BEHIND THE SCENES: Ann Landers and her twin sister, Abigail Van Buren (advice columnist "Dear Abby"), grew up in Sioux City, Iowa, children of a Russian immigrant. They dressed alike until they married—on the same day, in matching gowns, to men who were best friends. Now 80, Landers is divorced, has one daughter, three grandchildren, and three great-grandchildren.

PRAYER STARTERS:

- Pray for Ann Landers as she counsels millions, that her words would be "full of knowledge and every wise insight . . ." (Philippians 1:9-10 Phillips).
- Pray that God would draw her to Him in a new way, and that she would base her advice on biblical principles.
- Ask God to bless her with health, strength, and contentment.

> *The wisdom that comes from heaven is first of all pure; then peace-loving, considerate, submissive, full of mercy and good fruit, impartial and sincere. James 3:17*

CONTACT: *The Chicago Tribune,* 435 N. Michigan Ave., Chicago, IL 60611; annlanders@creators.com

David Satcher
Surgeon General of the United States

POINT OF IMPACT: David Satcher has always been a health servant—first as a family physician in low-income neighborhoods, now as "America's family doctor." As Surgeon General, Satcher makes far-reaching decisions on issues ranging from smoking, AIDS, pornography, child abuse, and domestic abuse to breast cancer and environmental toxins. Though he's come under fire for his pro-choice stance, Satcher says his Christian faith is a major influence in his life and profession. He cites as a favorite the story of the woman caught in adultery and Jesus' response to her. It helped shape his goal "not to judge other people, but to do everything I can to help people move toward a better life." That attitude spreads to his profession: "I believe that if people have illnesses that can be treated, our job is not to blame them or to judge them, but to help them achieve real help." Says Satcher, "I want to take the best science in the world and place it firmly within the grasp of all Americans."

He's America's family doctor.

QUOTABLE: "I have come to know over and over again just how powerful hope can be, even in the direst of situations. Hope is infectious. Hope is strong."

BEHIND THE SCENES: Satcher, 59, was one of ten children raised in rural Alabama. At age two Satcher became gravely ill with the whooping cough. The family doctor, an African-American, took young David to his own home to better care for him. This physician became Satcher's inspiration. Satcher, an avid jogger, and his wife, Nola, have four children and reside in Bethesda, Maryland.

PRAYER STARTERS:

- Pray for the work of David Satcher and the Surgeon General's office. Pray that he will earnestly seek God's guidance and wisdom.
- Pray for new initiatives to bring medical care to the poor and underserved.
- Ask God to give strength and peace to the Satcher family.
- Pray for someone you know who suffers from a substance addiction or chronic illness.

> *When you enter a town and are welcomed . . . heal the sick who are there and tell them, "The kingdom of God is near you." Luke 10:8-9*

CONTACT: U.S. Department of Health and Human Services, Washington, DC 20036

Archive Photo

Rosie O'Donnell
Host, The Rosie O'Donnell Show,
Comedian, Actress

POINT OF IMPACT: Talented variety show host Rosie O'Donnell could be considered Oprah without the issues and Roseanne without the brass. And as such, she's become a good friend to daytime TV watchers who identify with her—a few pounds overweight, in need of a laugh, and looking forward to a trip to Kmart (She's been featured in their ads). She began hitting the club circuits at 20, and then Penny Marshall cast her as Madonna's best friend in *A League of Their Own.* Film roles in *Sleepless in Seattle* and *The Flintstones* followed, and Hollywood took notice. By then O'Donnell, who is single, had adopted a son, Parker, and wanted the stability of a TV career. (She has since adopted a daughter, Chelsea.) The success of her Emmy-winning *Rosie O'Donnell Show* prompted *Newsweek* to deem her "The Queen of Nice." Merv Griffin (whose show she'd like to emulate) told her, "You are born for a talk show." It helps some that she and Oprah share the same distributor, meaning they never compete in the same time slot. She recently inked a deal with Warner for $3 million to write her memoirs.

In daytime talk shows, she's the "Queen of Nice."

QUOTABLE: "I see myself as Rhoda, not Mary Tyler Moore."

BEHIND THE SCENES: Rosie O'Donnell, 38, won the *Star Search* competition five times. She takes her children to work, where the network built a nursery adjoining her office. They live, without a nanny, in New York.

PRAYER STARTERS:

- Pray that Rosie O'Donnell and her guests will encourage and empower the show's viewers to reach for God's best in their lives.

- Pray that O'Donnell's success would motivate the networks to move away from salacious programs that pander to viewers' base impulses.

- Ask the Lord to surround O'Donnell and her children with Christian friends and draw her family to Himself.

A kindhearted woman gains respect . . . Proverbs 11:16

CONTACT: ICM, 8942 Wilshire Blvd., Beverly Hills, CA 90211

Matt Groening

Writer, Cartoonist, Animator, Producer,
Screenwriter

Archive Photo

POINT OF IMPACT: Making television history, Matt Groening (rhymes with raining) created the first cartoon series in 20 years to be on prime time—*The Simpsons*. The regular series first debuted on Fox in 1990. The wildly creative story lines revolve around a blue-collar family who often treat each other terribly—but stick together and love each other, too. There's the goofy dad whose frailties get him into trouble; a loving, sensible mom; two adorable but cloying little girls; and one ten-year-old trickster. In spite of the many parents who object to the show's irreverent flavor, for kids under 17, it is the number-one Fox show, and for adults 18 to 34, it's number four. The show has received a Peabody Award and 15 Emmys, among other awards. Says Groening, 46 (who also draws the *Life Is Hell* comic strip), "Overall, I've always said it is a celebration of the American family at its wildest."

He's the mind behind Bart Simpson's.

QUOTABLE: On parents' complaints that Bart Simpson is a terrible role model: "I now have a 7-year-old boy and a 9-year-old boy, so all I can say is, I apologize. Now I know what you guys were talking about."

BEHIND THE SCENES: Groening's own father and son are named Homer, his mother is Marge ("My mom is long-suffering like Marge, and she did have tall hair when I was a kid. She always denied it, but we have photos."), and his two sisters are Lisa and Maggie. (The name Bart is an anagram of "brat.") He's married to Deborah Caplan and has two sons, Homer and Abraham.

PRAYER STARTERS:

- Pray that the sometimes harsh presentations in the Simpson family would motivate families to treat each other well and value respect and integrity.
- Pray that Groening would be influenced in his own life and creative work by the truths of Scripture and a growing awareness of God's loving presence.
- Ask God to surround the Groening family with love, laughter, and safety.

> *No eye has seen, no ear has heard, no mind has conceived what God has prepared for those who love him. 1 Corinthians 2:9*

CONTACT: The Simpsons, Fox TV, P.O. Box 900, Beverly Hills, CA 90213-0900

Madeleine L'Engle

Author

Courtesy of Madeleine L'Engle

POINT OF IMPACT: How many Christian writers can speak from the pages of both *Ms.* magazine and *Today's Christian Woman*, are invited to speak by both the Library of Congress and the Gaithers' Praise Gathering, and serve as writer-in-residence for *Victoria* magazine and Regent University? Over the past 40 years, Madeleine L'Engle has earned the respect of Christian and non-Christian, young and old readers alike. The author of more than 50 books, spanning science fiction, suspense, and mystery novels, L'Engle is considered one of the foremost American creators of fantasy and science fiction. She's perhaps best known for her Newbery Award-winning *A Wrinkle in Time*. Although some Christians accuse her of new age influences, L'Engle has often been likened to C.S. Lewis for her ability to weave fascinating, biblically informed fantasies. Her children's books are required reading in many school districts. At 80, she still receives up to 100 letters a week from fans telling her how her books have changed their lives.

Her books captivate young and old.

QUOTABLE: "Let your imagination inform your intellect. Instead of letting them fight each other, as we so often do, let them make love. That's how art is born."

BEHIND THE SCENES: After college, she worked briefly in theater, where she met her husband, the late actor Hugh Franklin, who later became a soap opera star (he played Dr. Charles Tyler in *All My Children*). Together they raised three children. L'Engle, who recently became a great grandmother, lives in Goshen, Connecticut.

PRAYER STARTERS:

- Offer thanks for the positive impact of Madeleine L'Engle's fiction and devotional writing, and for the respect she has won for Christian literature. Pray for younger writers to carry on her literary tradition.

- Pray that L'Engle's audience will grow in their understanding of God and desire to know Him better through reading the Bible.

- Pray that L'Engle will be blessed with health and contentment. "Pray that God will give me the strength to do the work of love in my writing, speaking, and living," she asks.

> *Those who are wise will shine like the brightness of the heavens, and those who lead many to righteousness, like the stars for ever and ever. Daniel 12:3*

CONTACT: Farrar, Straus & Giroux, 19 Union Square West, New York, NY 10003

"We must not conceive of prayer as an overcoming of God's reluctance, but as a laying hold of His highest willingness."

—R. C. TRENCH

"Pray the largest prayers. You cannot think a prayer so large that God, in answering it, will not wish you had made it larger. Pray not for crutches but for wings."

—PHILLIPS BROOKS

Judah Folkman
Cancer Researcher

AP/Wide World Photos

POINT OF IMPACT: Dr. Judah Folkman, a Harvard Medical School professor, won international acclaim in 1998 for his discoveries of two experimental cancer drugs that effectively eliminated tumors in mice. The drugs, angiostatin and endostatin, are naturally occurring proteins that block the growth of blood, or "starve" the vessels that feed tumors. Clinical trials on humans are hoped to begin soon. Richard Claussner, director of the National Cancer Institute, calls the breakthough "the single most exciting thing on the horizon." Folkman, however, counsels caution, pointing out that it's a long leap from mice to men. In spite of skepticism from some in the science community, Folkman has been pursuing this line of research for more than 30 years. Says one observer, "He has had the vision and the perseverance and the passion to work at what he believes in, and that dedication has had a profound effect on the lives of all of us. He represents all that is the very best in science and scientists."

His research may someday halt cancer.

QUOTABLE: Folkman tells his students, "If your idea succeeds, everybody says you're persistent. If it doesn't, they say you're obstinate."

BEHIND THE SCENES: He once tackled a school science project by using his sister's toy refrigerator and his brother's bicycle pump to keep a rat's heart beating outside its body for more than 30 minutes. When he turned 13, he turned down his grandfather's offer of a Jeep as a bar mitzvah gift—no one was too surprised when Folkman requested a powerful microscope instead.

PRAYER STARTERS:

- Thank God for Dr. Folkman's example of dedication and for his contributions to medical research. Ask God to bless Dr. Folkman and his family with health and spiritual well-being.

- Cancer kills half a million people a year in the United States alone. Pray that Folkman's research would take medicine closer to a cure for cancer in humans.

- Pray for healing and comfort for a person you know who is suffering from cancer today, or for a family that has been touched by the disease recently.

Heal me, O LORD, and I will be healed; save me and I will be saved, for you are the one I praise. Jeremiah 17:14

CONTACT: Harvard Medical School, 25 Shattuck Street, Boston, MA 02115

Barbara Walters

Reporter, Producer, TV Personality

ABC Photo

POINT OF IMPACT: When Barbara Walters joined *ABC News* in 1976, she became the first woman ever to cohost network news and the first million-dollar-a-year newscaster. Since then her ground-breaking exclusive interviews with world figures (including the first joint interview with Egypt's President Anwar Sadat and Israel's Prime Minister Menachem Begin) have made her one of the most acclaimed journalists in television history. She's interviewed every president since Richard Nixon, and has shared private conversations with some of the most important names in history. (Once, after Walters interviewed Fidel Castro for six hours in 1978, he took her and her crew into the kitchen at 3:00 A.M. and made them all grilled cheese sandwiches. "As I remember," she says, "they weren't bad.") These days, Walters interviews subjects on the weekly ABC newsmagazine *20/20*, *The View*, and on *The Barbara Walters Special* for an estimated 20 million viewers. She's famous in the industry for landing the most sought-after subjects, including Monica Lewinsky in March 1999.

She's famous for landing the big ones.

QUOTABLE: Walters was married briefly in the fifties. She says with some regret, "I'm convinced that you stay married when the days are bad only because you really want to be. But I always had an out. I had this job, and this life, and enough money. I didn't have to fight the bad days."

BEHIND THE SCENES: Growing up, Walters' sister suffered from what Walters has described as borderline retardation. She died about 11 years ago of ovarian cancer. "She never married, never lived independently," explains Walter. "She was a great influence on my life. I think she made me more understanding and compassionate." Now in her late sixties, Walters lives alone in New York; she has one grown daughter.

PRAYER STARTERS:

- Pray today for God's blessings of peace, health, and a growing awareness of His presence for Barbara Walters and her family.
- Ask that God will continue to use Walters' skills to ferret out truth and insight.
- Pray that she and her colleagues will use their influence for significant purposes.

> *It is the glory of God to conceal a matter; to search out a matter is the glory of kings.* Proverbs 25:2

CONTACT: PMK, 955 S. Carillo Dr., Suite 200, Los Angeles, CA 90048

Rupert Murdoch

CEO, NewsCorp

Archive Photo

POINT OF IMPACT: If information is the power that controls politics and culture, then NewsCorp easily ranks as one of the most powerful entities on the planet. And that makes often-reviled CEO Rupert Murdoch one of the world's most influential people. Murdoch's empire includes newspapers (the *New York Post*, four national papers in Great Britain, and 60 percent of Australia's newspapers, for example), movies (20th Century Fox), television (Fox Broadcasting and dozens of stations), books (HarperCollins), the internet (LineOne, positioned to become the AOL of Europe), sports (L.A. Dodgers), magazines, and satellite broadcasting. Murdoch's media (which have been accused of perfecting "sleaze journalism" and "vulgarizing culture on a global scale") reach about 75 percent of the world's population. Viacom CEO Sumner Redstone once said, "Rupert wants to rule the world, and he seems to be doing it."

He rules over a vast media empire.

QUOTABLE: The night of the 1987 stock market crash, Murdoch sat down to dinner with some colleagues and quipped, "I hope one of you is picking up the check because I lost $1.2 billion today."

BEHIND THE SCENES: Murdoch was 21 when his father died, bequeathing him a small newspaper in South Australia. Ironically, his mother has said that his father doubted Rupert had it in him to take over the company. In 1998, Pope John Paul II awarded Murdoch a papal knighthood. Murdoch is not Catholic, but he and his ex-wife, Anna, have supported Catholic education causes, Israel, and child causes worldwide. The Murdochs have three grown children.

PRAYER STARTERS:

- Ask God to bless Rupert Murdoch and his family today with health, contentment, and an awareness of His presence.
- Murdoch has said, "For better or for worse, our company is a reflection of my thinking, my character, my values." Pray for his personal and spiritual renewal.
- Ask that integrity and compassion will infuse decisions today throughout NewsCorp holdings.

> *Turn my heart toward your statutes and not toward selfish gain. Turn my eyes away from worthless things; preserve my life according to your word. Psalm 119:36-37*

CONTACT: NewsCorp, 2 Holt Street, Sydney, New South Wales, Australia

Chris Rock

Comedian, Actor

Archive Photo

POINT OF IMPACT: Chris Rock's rise as a popular comedian is almost ironic considering that during his school years in Brooklyn he suffered dead-serious racism, beatings, and insecurity. But Rock found as mentors funny guys like Eddie Murphy and Steve Martin—and humor gave him a hand up. Now *he's* the one looked up to by millions of black youth. He's laughed his way to three seasons on *Saturday Night Live*, roles in feature films such as *New Jack City*, his own cable series *The Chris Rock Show,* and the comedy special *Chris Rock: Bring the Pain!* which won two Emmys. He's also become known for his tart tongue; the *Today* show dropped an interview with him after he repeatedly used language "inappropriate for morning television." His jokes are often harsh and always equal-opportunity—no subject or person is sacred. He has roles in forthcoming films, *High Boys and Low Boys, Dogma,* and *Superman Lives.*

His humor is no holds barred.

QUOTABLE: "I'm not a superstar. Jim Carrey makes $20 million a movie. I make a weird face when they tell me I have to pay $8.50 to see one."

BEHIND THE SCENES: Even before his discovery by Eddie Murphy, Rock seemed to know he'd be famous one day. Friends recall him as a teen telling people repeatedly, "I'm Chris Rock. I'm Chris Rock"—as if practicing at being famous. Rock, 33, is married to Malaak Compton-Rock, a publicist. They live in Brooklyn.

PRAYER STARTERS:

- Pray that God would bring strong Christian friends around Chris Rock who can affirm his talents and encourage him to use them in positive ways.
- Pray for a new generation of African-American comedians and entertainers who can be powerful and positive role models for urban youth.
- Ask God to bless Rock in his marriage, and personal and spiritual life.

> *He who loves a pure heart and whose speech is gracious will have the king for his friend. Proverbs 22:11*

CONTACT: ICM, 8942 Wilshire Blvd., Beverly Hills, CA 90210

Leigh Steinberg

Sports Agent, Author

Courtesy of Steinberg & Moorad

POINT OF IMPACT: Mega-sports agent Leigh Steinberg has set a new standard for what's expected of professional athletes both on and off the field. He is best known as the inspiration for the movie *Jerry Maguire* and for the philosophies outlined in his book *Winning with Integrity: Getting What You're Worth Without Selling Your Soul* (Villard, 1998). In the last 25 years he has negotiated deals totaling more than $2 billion for the likes of Steve Young, Warren Moon, Kordell Stewart, and Drew Bledsoe—all starting quarterbacks with multimillion-dollar contracts. Steinberg, 49, who firmly believes that professional athletes must be good role models, takes only clients who give back to their communities. As a result, his clients are some of the most widely recognized philanthropists in pro sports. Steinberg spends 40 percent of his own time working for charities and has given away more than $2 million.

He's a sports agent for the good guys.

QUOTABLE: "We have a pretty strict requirement in our law practice that we take athletes who understand the tremendous power of a role model and that they trigger imitative behavior, whether they want to or not."

BEHIND THE SCENES: Steinberg attributes some of his strong convictions to his father. "I grew up with my father talking every night about values. My father was the head of the city's (Los Angeles) human relations commission. I was raised to . . . make a positive change in the world." Steinberg is married to Lucy Semeniuk, also a lawyer; their children are Jon, Matt, and Katie. They live in Newport Beach, California.

PRAYER STARTERS:

- Give thanks for Leigh Steinberg's positive influence on athletes and youth.
- Ask God to deepen Steinberg's spiritual hunger today, and to bless his humanitarian work, his relationships, his business, and especially his family.
- Pray that more professional athletes worldwide will be influenced by Steinberg's convictions about their tremendous power as role models, and aspire to use their impact for good.

> *How much better to get wisdom than gold, to choose understanding rather than silver! Proverbs 16:16*

CONTACT: Steinberg & Moorad, www.leighsteinberg.com

Tenzin Gyatso

Dalai Lama, Leader of Tibetan Buddhists

Archive Photo

POINT OF IMPACT: Tenzin Gyatso was born in a tiny village in northeastern Tibet in 1935. At the age of two his people recognized him as the reincarnation of the thirteenth Dalai Lama (Mongolian for "Ocean of Wisdom") and groomed him to become head of both Tibetan Buddhism and the country's government. Gyatso is a monk and an international spokesman for peace, nonviolence, and understanding among varying cultures and religions. He's particularly influential among university students and the media elite. He's resided in exile in India since 1959, when China forcibly occupied Tibet and he was forced to flee. His life and the predicament of his people have been the subject of two recent films, *Kundun* and *7 Years in Tibet*. He has established educational, cultural, and religious institutions to preserve the Tibetan culture, and worked to free Tibet from Chinese rule. More than 130,000 Tibetans live in exile, many in India and Nepal and more than 33 countries in the West.

He works to free Tibet from China.

QUOTABLE: "Compassion can be put into practice if one recognizes the fact that every human being is a member of humanity and the human family regardless of differences in religion, culture, color, and creed. Deep down there is no difference."

BEHIND THE SCENES: When he received the Nobel Peace Prize, the awards committee said, "He has . . . advocated peaceful solutions based upon tolerance and mutual respect in order to preserve the historical and cultural heritage of his people."

PRAYER STARTERS:

- Ask God for increased influence of the Christian message in Tibet, and in the inner circles of the Dalai Lama, and on the leader himself.
- Give thanks for the Dalai Lama's role as peacemaker—"there is a future for a man of peace" (Psalm 37:37).
- Pray for a peaceful settlement to the claims of the Tibetan people for freedom.

> *I will grant peace in the land, and you will lie down and no one will make you afraid. Leviticus 26:6*

CONTACT: Lama Bureau of H. H. the Dalai Lama, 10-A Ring Road Lajpat Nagar IV, New Delhi-110024, India

Eldrick "Tiger" Woods
Pro Golfer

Archive Photo

POINT OF IMPACT: According to *Sporting News,* few—if any—athletes in America currently have more influence than Tiger Woods, rated the number-one golfer in the world at present. Since he took the sports world by storm when he won the Masters in 1997—at age 21 the youngest winner ever—Woods has brought almost $700 million into the golf industry. Behind Tiger's image, Nike's golf apparel and footwear sales jumped 100 percent in 1997. Television ratings double in tournaments he plays in, and he has become a role model for young golfers everywhere, including America's inner cities. His Tiger Woods Foundation has contributed more than $2 million to family and inner-city youth programs, and Woods personally leads golf clinics for kids across the country. In addition, Woods—who is an ethnic mix of Chinese, Thai, African-American, and white—has helped redefine America's conversation about race. On Capitol Hill, the Tiger Woods Bill was proposed to give multiracial citizens their own "multi-ethnic category" in government classifications. "He's a real inspiration for the kids," says one involved with minorities in sports. "He's a pioneer."

He's one of the best role models in sports.

QUOTABLE: "My father has always instilled in me that there are only two things in life that you ought to do. You gotta care and you gotta share."

BEHIND THE SCENES: Woods was six months old when he began imitating his dad's golf swing. By age three, he shot 48 for nine holes, and by five, he was featured in *Golf Digest.* His father is a retired lieutenant colonel in the U.S. Army, and his mother is a native of Thailand. He was nicknamed "Tiger" after a Vietnamese friend and fellow Green Beret who saved his dad's life in Vietnam. Woods, single, lives in Orlando.

PRAYER STARTERS:

- Woods has said: "A role model is someone who embraces the responsibility of influencing others positively." Give thanks for his attitude, and pray that his influence will encourage and empower many today, especially the young.
- Ask that Woods will encounter Christians who can influence his spiritual journey.
- Pray for his protection from the many pressures of success at such a young age.

The man with two tunics should share with him who has none. Luke 3:11

CONTACT: Internat'l Management, 420 West 45th Street FL 3, New York, NY 10036

Paul A. Rader

President, Salvation Army

Griffith Photography, Torrance, CA

POINT OF IMPACT: General Paul Rader commands an army of officers, employees, and volunteers. And his "army" is usually easy to find—just go to ghettoes, flood-ravaged villages, shanty towns, and other desperate corners of the world. Rader, a New York native now based in London, is the Salvation Army's first U.S.-born leader. Founded in 1865 by William Booth in Great Britain, the ministry of the Salvation Army is organized in military-like rankings; its members are now at work in 103 countries. Dedicated to serving those in need, the Salvation Army offers tangible help such as food, clothing, and financial assistance. But their fundamental commitment is to faithfully preach the gospel. In 1998 Rader sent out the urgent call for one million senior soldiers to march into the new millennium (a 20 percent increase in their adult force).

He leads an army for God.

QUOTABLE: "Salvation begins with conversion to Christ, but it does not end there. The transformation of an individual leads to a transformation of relationships, of families, of communities, of nations."

BEHIND THE SCENES: Rader, 66, is the son of Salvation Army parents. During his undergraduate years, he met and married his wife, Kay, a Methodist minister's daughter who was training to be a teacher. After they were commissioned as officers, they chose missionary service and served in Seoul, South Korea, for 22 years. The Raders' two children are grown and have returned to Korea as missionaries.

PRAYER STARTERS:

- Give thanks for 135 years of faithful service by Salvationists around the world. Pray that future leaders will carry on Rader's legacy of service.
- Pray for God's continued blessing and guidance for General Rader and his family.
- Join with General Rader in his prayer request: "As we enter the twenty-first century, pray that God will grant to the Salvation Army a purifying and empowering baptism of His Spirit that will clear our vision, cleanse our hearts, and pour His love through us anew for the salvation of the lost and healing of the nations."

Now is the time of God's favor, now is the day of salvation. 2 Corinthians 6:2

CONTACT: Salvation Army, U.S. National Headquarters, P.O. Box 269, Alexandria, VA 22313; www.sarmy.org

Marilyn Manson
Rock Singer

Courtesy of Steve Gloemboski

POINT OF IMPACT: Marilyn Manson (born Brian Warner) is the lead singer in his "death rock" band by the same name. An avowed member of the Church of Satan, Manson's live concerts feature a wide range of acts for shock value, including caged or crucified girls, skinned goats' heads, nudity, and arson. At one concert he tossed a Bible to the crowd—but only after ceremonially ripping out some pages. His death-mask black-and-white makeup and his mismatched eyes (one blue, one brown, thanks to a contact lens) have become his trademark. Thirty-year-old Manson's influence can be seen in the hundreds of young fans who attend school wearing dark, Mansonlike clothing and makeup. "In this position I've put myself in," Manson admits, "I have the responsibility of influencing the minds of teenagers." His fans have propelled the band to platinum sales status and numerous MTV awards.

His death-rock lures angry youth.

QUOTABLE: "I think Jesus was the first sex symbol, rock star, magician, hippie, drug dealer—whatever he was. I don't think he was any different from someone like me. Some idiot hundreds of years from now may have a Marilyn Manson T-shirt, and a bunch of people are gonna pray to it, and they're gonna make little Marilyn Manson necklaces that everybody wears."

BEHIND THE SCENES: Often opposed by Christians when he comes to town, he says, "I've grown bored with me against the Christians, this whole battle that they've created. . . . If they want to ban me, they can. I like to do things of the moment and not be afraid of the repercussions." Manson is single; he lives in Florida.

PRAYER STARTERS:

- Pray that God will rescue Marilyn Manson from his spiritual prison of darkness.
- Pray the same for his band members: Twiggy Ramirez, Madonna Wayne Gacy, and Ginger Fish. Ask God to surround them with Christians who can be an example of, and an encouragement toward, true freedom in art and life (John 8:32).
- Pray for spiritual protection and deliverance for the music fans who embrace Manson's message of violence, paganism, and decadence.

> *For [God] has rescued us from the dominion of darkness and brought us into the kingdom of the Son he loves, in whom we have redemption, the forgiveness of sins. Colossians 1:13-14*

CONTACT: www.interscoperecords.com

John Grisham

Bestselling Author

POINT OF IMPACT: Books weren't John Grisham's first love: baseball was. But when his IQ outmatched his batting average, he turned to accounting and then eventually criminal law. But a pesky habit kept him from solely focusing on his new career: writing. In the mid-eighties Grisham woke up early to churn chapters, and *A Time to Kill* resulted. *The Firm* followed, and its sale to both Paramount and Doubleday led to Grisham's decision to write for a living. Books and films streamed forth, every one a bestseller and six of them movie material. "It's no exaggeration to say that thousands of media folk, from publishing and printing executives to bookstore owners, film producers, directors and actors and beyond, profit from, and to some extent depend upon, the annual Grisham blockbuster," says *Publishers Weekly*. His most recent release is *The Testament*.

He writes blockbusters about ethical dilemmas.

QUOTABLE: "I have never been tempted to resort to gratuitous sex, profanity, or violence. I couldn't write a book that I would be embarrassed for my kids to read a few years from now. Plus, my mother would kill me."

BEHIND THE SCENES: Grisham, who grew up in a small, close-knit Baptist family, devotes just six months a year to his writing—the other six he spends coaching his son's Little League team (he's built six ball fields near his home in Albemarle County, Virginia). Grisham, 45, and his wife, Renee, have two kids, Ty and Shea.

PRAYER STARTERS:

- Give thanks for John Grisham's commitments to social justice and personal ethics, and for the biblical values he brings to his writing.
- Pray that Grisham's work will have a positive impact on lawyers and our legal system.
- Ask for God's blessings on Grisham's marriage and family.

> *Do not exploit the poor because they are poor and do not crush the needy in court, for the LORD will take up their case.* Proverbs 22:22-23

CONTACT: Doubleday, 666 5th Avenue, New York, NY 10103

Craig Venter
Pioneer Gene Mapper

POINT OF IMPACT: *Time* magazine describes Dr. Craig Venter as "driven, impatient, demanding." But if you suffer from a genetic disease, this is one "mad" scientist you'll be rooting for. Widely expected to be nominated for a Nobel Prize, Venter, 54, has decoded more genes, and faster, than anyone in the world. In 1998 he shocked scientists with his assertion that his privately funded lab [now Celera Genomics Corporation] would decode the entire human DNA, or "genome," faster and for millions of dollars less than the Human Genome Project (a $3 billion government venture). A person's genome contains all the instructions (some 60,000 or so genes) needed to operate the human organism. Deciphering this "script" would yield information about human physiology and disease, as well as the potential to correct the faulty DNA that cause genetic disease. But it also could enable scientists to create an artificial life form, which raises concern—especially if such information ends up being owned by a private company.

He's leading the biggest race in science.

QUOTABLE: "I have concerns about negative uses. I don't want to do anything that could have negative consequences unless the positive outweighs them."

BEHIND THE SCENES: In high school, Venter was a chronic discipline problem who refused to take tests. But during the Vietnam war, his work in an emergency room impressed a senior officer, who urged Venter to go on to college. He did, and earned a Ph.D. in six years. His wife, Dr. Clare Fraser, a noted molecular biologist, works with him. They live outside Washington, DC.

PRAYER STARTERS:

- Pray for wisdom and success for Dr. Venter, as well as for all those involved in this high-impact area of research.
- Pray for ethicists, lawyers, researchers, and government agencies wrestling with the implications of properly handling the new genetic information becoming available.
- Ask God to bless Dr. Venter and his wife with evidence of His leading and care.

> *[God] reveals deep and hidden things; he knows what lies in darkness.*
> *Daniel 2:22*

CONTACT: Institute for Genomic Research, 9712 Medical Center Drive, Rockville, MD 20850

Bud Selig

Commissioner of Baseball

Courtesy of Major League Baseball

POINT OF IMPACT: Allan H. "Bud" Selig, for 33 years the owner of the Milwaukee Brewers, became baseball's ninth commissioner in July 1998. Before then, Selig had served as an interim, part-time commissioner after the forced resignation of Fay Vincent in 1992. He's probably best remembered as the guy at the helm during the 232-day players' strike that ended in the cancellation of the 1994 World Series. On a more positive note, this bespectacled, dark-haired man increased fan interest by doubling the number of teams that can make the playoffs. He also boosted game attendance and created new regional rivalries by introducing interleague play. One observer said that Selig accomplished "more for the game in his five or six years of temporary leadership than has been done in the history of baseball."

He's the top boss of baseball.

QUOTABLE: Speaking about Selig's appointment as baseball's commissioner, a colleague says, "Who has more interest than he has in this game being successful? He's put his whole life into it."

BEHIND THE SCENES: Selig was a car dealer who bought the Seattle Pilots baseball team in 1970 and brought them to Milwaukee as the Brewers. "They love him here," said one Brewers official. "They see him as the man who brought baseball back to Milwaukee." Selig resigned as president of the franchise to become commissioner. Selig's daughter, Wendy Selig-Prieb, took over as president and chief executive officer of the Brewers.

PRAYER STARTERS:

- Ask God to bless Bud Selig's work and family life.
- Give thanks for the wholesome enjoyment that baseball brings to fans and players.
- Ask for wisdom and discernment for Selig as he steers pro baseball into the future.
- Pray for the integrity and influence of outspoken Christian ball players. Pray that their witness will touch and encourage Selig.

The noble man makes noble plans, and by noble deeds he stands. Isaiah 32:8

CONTACT: Bud Selig, c/o 350 Park Ave., New York, NY 10022

Archive Photo

James Cameron
Movie Producer

POINT OF IMPACT: Producer James Cameron is best known for his film *Titanic,* the most expensive movie ever made ($200 million) and the most successful (it earned more than *Star Wars* or *E.T.* and won 11 Oscars). A notorious perfectionist, Cameron first gained attention as the writer and director of the highly successful *Terminator* movies and such hits as *True Lies* and *Aliens*. *Titanic,* however, represents the high-water mark of his career. And as a result of *Titanic's* success, it's being speculated that Hollywood will be open to more high-cost, high-risk ventures in the future. His next project is rumored to be either a Spiderman movie, for which he's already written a screenplay (copyright quibbles have stalled the project), or a sci-fi film called *Avatar*, which he plans to cast with nonhuman, digitally generated actors.

He made the highest-grossing film in history.

QUOTABLE: "The more decisions you've made before you ever get to the set, the better. But you have to stay open to the moments of discovery. You have to keep your heart open to the magic."

BEHIND THE SCENES: Cameron, a Canadian by birth, was one of five children. As a boy, he played endlessly with his father's video camera. He also organized his playmates in such adventurous endeavors as building a miniature diving vessel to send mice to the bottom of the Niagara River. Now 46, he's divorced from his fourth wife, actress Linda Hamilton, the mother of his daughter, seven-year-old Josephine.

PRAYER STARTERS:

- Pray that influential directors like James Cameron will use their creativity and impact wisely as they make movies that shape our imaginations.
- Ask God to bless Cameron's relationship with his daughter despite the family break-up; pray for healing and peace.
- Pray that Cameron will be drawn to God, and that in times of trouble he would seek and find hope in the Lord.

> *The engulfing waters threatened me, the deep surrounded me. . . . But you brought my life up from the pit, O* Lord *my God. Jonah 2:5-6*

CONTACT: Gregg Brilliant, 5555 Melrose Avenue, MOB Building #3211, Hollywood, CA 90038

Pope John Paul II

Primate of the Roman Catholic Church

POINT OF IMPACT: By nearly every estimate, Pope John Paul II is the single most influential person on earth. His every word or decision has direct impact on the estimated 1 billion Roman Catholics worldwide (one of every two Christians). Even compared to his predecessors, his papacy has been remarkable—as a world traveler, political activist, human rights spokesperson and evangelist, he has set new expectations for his office. He was the first non-Italian chosen as Pope in 456 years and the youngest in this century. At 61, he was seriously wounded in an assassination attempt, and he has been plagued with illness, including Parkinson's disease. Yet he is tireless in his efforts for the church and is the most-traveled pope in the 2,000-year history of the church. He speaks eight languages. John Paul II has reinforced such conservative traditions as men only in the priesthood, celibacy for priests, the importance of family life, protection for the unborn, and the ultimate authority of the church. He has called for health care for all and praises the dignity of human work.

He's the single most influential person on earth.

QUOTABLE: "In essentials, unity, in doubtful matters, liberty; in all things charity."

BEHIND THE SCENES: He was born Karol Joseph Wojtyla in 1920 in Poland. While still in childhood, he believed God was calling him to the priesthood. More than any other recent pope, he's been a man of arts and letters. As a young man in Poland he was a poet, playwright, and actor. His books include *Crossing the Threshhold of Hope.*

PRAYER STARTERS:

- Give thanks for John Paul II's example of integrity, courage, compassion, and love for Jesus Christ. Pray that God will keep him in health, strength, and peace.
- Pray for the continuing global impact of John Paul's concerns for families, health, spiritual renewal, and human dignity.
- Pray for the unity of all believers today.

> *Now to him who is able to do immeasurably more than all we ask or imagine, according to his power that is at work within us, to him be glory in the church.*
> *Ephesians 3:20-21*

CONTACT IN THE UNITED STATES: His Holiness John Paul II, Catholic Information Network, 9269 Mission Gorge Road #124, Santee, CA 92071

Courtesy of Franklin Covey Co.

Stephen Covey
Author, Speaker

POINT OF IMPACT: *Time* calls Stephen Covey the world's number-one author on personal and professional development. His 1989 book, *The 7 Habits of Highly Effective People,* has sold more than 10 million copies and been translated into 28 languages. In a *Chief Executive* magazine survey, *7 Habits* tied as the most influential business book of the twentieth century. In the mid-nineties, Covey wrote *The 7 Habits of Highly Effective Families.* The essence of Covey's message is that groups of people—families, corporations, schools, armies, governments—can achieve their maximum potential through nothing less than moral transformation. To do well, he says, you must do good, and to do good you must first be good. His seminars, taught in businesses, schools, prisons, governments, and churches worldwide, reach almost half a million people each year.

His books are highly effective.

QUOTABLE: "Conscience is a divine gift given to all of God's children. It is their native sense of right and wrong. It is a moral sense. The more they educate it by studying the great literature, which I think comes from God, the more their conscience becomes the source of their guidance, security, wisdom, and power."

BEHIND THE SCENES: A committed member of the Church of Jesus Christ of Latter-day Saints, Covey earned a doctorate at Brigham Young University, where he later taught. He also spent five years as a Mormon missionary in England and Ireland. Now in his sixties, Covey, a resident of Provo, Utah, is married and has nine children.

PRAYER STARTERS:

- Give thanks for the impact of Covey's principles of character-based leadership.
- Ask for good health for the Coveys and their extended family. Pray that they will come to "know the truth" in new ways (John 8:32).
- Pray that Covey's readers will act on the truths of his message and renew their consciences in the Bible.

> *He has showed you, O man, what is good. And what does the* Lord *require of you? To act justly and to love mercy and to walk humbly with your God.*
> Micah 6:8

CONTACT: Franklin Covey Co., 2200 West Parkway Blvd., Salt Lake City, UT 84119

Charles Colson

President, Prison Fellowship Ministries

Courtesy of Prison Fellowship Ministries

POINT OF IMPACT: Chuck Colson accepted Christ as his Savior shortly before he served time in prison for a Watergate-related offense (he was Special Counsel to President Richard Nixon). After his release, he founded Prison Fellowship in 1976 with proceeds from his best-selling autobiography, *Born Again.* His mission is to "exhort, equip, and assist the church in its ministry to prisoners, ex-prisoners, and victims and their families, and to promote biblical standards of justice in the criminal justice system." He also launched the Angel Tree Foundation (which meets the needs of at-risk children), hosts a radio program called *Breakpoint,* and writes a column for *Christianity Today.* In 1993 Colson won the Templeton Prize for Religion, worth more than $1 million.

He takes the gospel to jails.

QUOTABLE: "We should always pray with as much earnestness as those who expect everything from God; we should always act with as much energy as those who expect everything from themselves."

BEHIND THE SCENES: Among evangelicals, Colson is probably more responsible than anyone after Billy Graham for trying to promote unity in the church. He says, "The body of Christ, in all its diversity, is created with Baptist feet, charismatic hands, and Catholic ears—all with their eyes on Jesus." Some criticize, while others laud, his views. Colson, a trained lawyer, lives in Reston, Virginia, with his wife, Patty.

PRAYER STARTERS:

- Give thanks for Chuck Colson's life—for his highly publicized salvation, his example of servanthood, his rigorous intellect, and his quest for unity.
- Ask God to give care and comfort to Colson, his wife, and his family today.
- Pray for Prison Fellowship—for wisdom and influence, and for their financial and staff needs. Pray for those in prisons around the world—often in danger and despair—and for the needs of their families.

> *Remember those in prison as if you were their fellow prisoners, and those who are mistreated as if you yourselves were suffering. Hebrews 13:3*

CONTACT: Prison Fellowship, P.O. Box 17500, Washington, DC 20041-0500; (703) 478-0100

Elizabeth Dole

GOP Candidate, Former President of Red Cross

Archive Photo

POINT OF IMPACT: Elizabeth Dole's career of public service has included work for five U.S. presidents. She is the former Secretary of both Transportation and Labor, and past president of the American Red Cross, a post she resigned in January 1999 to consider making a bid for the presidency. In a magazine poll at the time, Dole was first choice by a wide margin as the woman believed most qualified to become the first woman president. The Gallup Poll has named her one of The World's Ten Most Admired Women. Given her national prominence, popularity among Republicans, and appeal to women, many strategists say Mrs. Dole will remain in the top tier of Republican presidential contenders unless she chooses otherwise.

She could become the first female president.

QUOTABLE: "On average, Americans give less than 2 percent of their income to charitable causes. Now if we're able to take the overall amount that goes to worthy causes and just get it up one percentage point, that would be 62 billion new dollars to help churches and humanitarian groups. I know it is something that can be done."

BEHIND THE SCENES: Dole, raised in a strong Christian family in Salisbury, North Carolina, admits that after moving to Washington, D.C., career and political concerns crowded out spiritual growth for a time. All that's changed today, she says. Now in her early sixties, Dole attends Washington's National Presbyterian Church, where she meets with a group of women for prayer and fellowship. Her husband, Bob, a former senator from Kansas, was himself a two-time presidential contender.

PRAYER STARTERS:

- Give thanks for Elizabeth Dole's leadership in relief work, and for her continuing legacy of integrity and competence in public service.
- Pray for God's blessings on Mrs. Dole's work, her marriage, her family, and her future. Ask for wisdom as the Doles chart their very public life.
- Pray for increased giving and genuine compassion for those in need—"Freely you have received, freely give" (Matthew 10:8).

> *Defend the cause of the weak and fatherless; maintain the rights of the poor and oppressed. Rescue the weak and needy. Psalm 82:3-4*

CONTACT: elizabethdole@nandomail.com

Laura Schlessinger
Radio Host, Author

AP/Wide World Photos

POINT OF IMPACT: As host of the fastest-growing syndicated radio program in history, Dr. Laura Schlessinger speaks to an average of 18 million listeners weekly. Some 60,000 people a day clamor to be one of the 20 or so callers who actually get on the show. A licensed marriage and family counselor in her early fifties, "Dr. Laura" earned her Ph.D. in physiology. Among her books is *The Ten Commandments: The Significance of God's Laws in Everyday Life*. A convert to Judaism late in life, she strongly defends stay-at-home moms, rails against feminism and abortion, and argues against sex education in public schools. "I want to reintroduce morals, ethics and conscience into everyday life," she says. "I have a value system. I'm blunt about it." Some critics claim she is too blunt, but fans welcome her "tough love" approach as an alternative to the self-indulgent approach of many contemporary therapists. A resident of Southern California, she's been awarded the industry's prestigious Marconi Award.

She's blunt about right and wrong.

QUOTABLE: "Sex should be saved for marriage. If we make sex meaningless and living together meaningless, then we make marriage meaningless."

BEHIND THE SCENES: The Dr. Laura Schlessinger Foundation funds charities that discourage abortion and teen sexuality, promote adoption, prevent the abuse and neglect of children, and provide support to stay-at-home parents. Dr. Schlessinger posts the Ten Commandments on her web page. Her newest book, *Everyday Evil*, focuses on "everyday" evils like gossiping, pettiness, vengefulness, and humiliations.

PRAYER STARTERS:

- Give thanks for the presentation of godly, moral principles through Schlessinger's radio programs; for her influence with persons who may never attend church or synagogue.
- Pray that she will seek all the wisdom and grace God has planned for her; pray for His blessing on her life, her work, and her family.
- Pray for a generational awakening to the truths of God's moral code and the promise of new life in Him.

> *Your statutes are wonderful; therefore I obey them. The unfolding of your words gives light; it gives understanding to the simple. Psalm 119:129-130*

CONTACT: www.drlaura.com

Peter Xu Yongze

Leader, Born Again Movement

Courtesy of Born Again Movement

POINT OF IMPACT: Peter Xu Yongze is currently serving a three-year jail sentence for leading a "banned religious cult, disrupting public order, and spreading religious heresy." It began 31 years ago as Yongze contemplated Christianity's future in China. He foresaw only oppression. As he climbed a mountain that day he prayed, "Dear Lord, please revive Your church!" Ever since, he's been spearheading that revival. His ministry, called the Born Again Movement, has reportedly grown to 3 million members (spin-off movements account for another 20 million). Because of his visibility, he's been a target of the communist government, who jailed him. China's constitution enshrines freedom of belief, but there is little corresponding freedom of worship. The Christian underground reports that beatings and electric-shock torture are common in prisons. More than 200 religious leaders of all faiths have signed a letter asking President Clinton to intervene for Xu and all religious prisoners in China.

He's jailed in China for Christian activities.

QUOTABLE: Jonathan Chao, President of China Ministries International, says of the pastors associated with Yongze's movement: "They believe jail is their seminary. Jail is like a battery that charges the believer and movement."

BEHIND THE SCENES: Xu Yongze's wife, Qing Jing, is also imprisoned. In prison, Xu Yongze's labor may include making Christmas ornaments for export. The number of Chinese believers is unknown but may approach 70–80 million in the house church movement alone.

PRAYER STARTERS:

- Thank God for Yongze's faith, and pray that many more will come to know Christ.
- Support him and Quing Jing with your prayers today. Ask for God's intervention and for their release; pray for his family's safety and welfare.
- Pray for a change in Chinese government's opposition to Christianity, and for the peace and comfort of Christ to surround Chinese believers.
- Pray that Chinese leaders will strive to end human rights abuses in their nation. Ask for prosperity and peace among China's 1.3 billion people.

> *Rejoice and be glad, because great is your reward in heaven, for in the same way they persecuted the prophets who were before you. Matthew 5:12*

CONTACT: Compass Direct News Service, compassdr@compuserve.com

Adam Werbach

President, The Sierra Club

Copyright Debra McClinton

POINT OF IMPACT: When Adam Werbach was elected to lead the San-Francisco-based environmental group in 1996, he was, at 23, the youngest president in the group's 108-year history. But he's not the least likely. At eight, he circulated a petition at school to get U.S. Secretary of the Interior (and mining supporter) James Watt removed from office. In high school he refused to dissect frogs and formed an animal rights group in protest. And he founded and directed the Sierra Club's national student program. Small surprise, then, that after earning a degree at Brown University, he found himself heading the 600,000-member grassroots organization. He wants to spread the Club's gospel—to "explore, enjoy, and protect the wild places of the earth"—via the internet and MTV. Some applaud Werbach's nineties sensibility; others question the wisdom of making glitz an ingredient in conservation. He was named one of the most powerful people in their twenties by *Swing* magazine.

Can a twenty-something save the planet?

QUOTABLE: "Protecting every last wild place in America is not a radical idea; it's relatively simple. To make sure drinking water is safe for every child in America is not a radical idea; it's pretty basic. And I can get those ideas across on MTV."

BEHIND THE SCENES: Werbach lives out of a hotel room in San Francisco. He's part of a music group called the Brown Derbies, and he's working on a Sierra Club CD tentatively titled *Rock the Planet* and his first book, *Act First, Apologize Later.*

PRAYER STARTERS:

- Pray for Adam Werbach's success in using the conservation work of the Sierra Club in ways that are truly beneficial for our society.
- Pray that Werbach and his colleagues will encounter the Lord of Creation in a personal way.
- Ask God to bless Werbach, his friends, and his family with wisdom, vision, and well-being.

> *May you be blessed by the LORD, the Maker of heaven and earth. The highest heavens belong to the LORD, but the earth he has given to man.*
> *Psalm 115:15-16*

CONTACT: The Sierra Club, 85 Second St., Second Floor, San Francisco, CA 94105-3441; e-mail: adam.werbach@sierraclub.org

David Brickner

Executive Director, Jews for Jesus

Photo compliments of Jews for Jesus

POINT OF IMPACT: Jews for Jesus began as a slogan in the seventies, but today it's an international organization whose purpose is to proclaim that Jesus is the Messiah of Israel and the Savior of the world. Calling themselves Messianic Jews, they worship Yeshua (the Hebrew name for Jesus) while retaining their Jewish cultural heritage. David Brickner took over as executive director from founder Moishe Rosen in 1996. "David is a creative, incisive thinker and a keen strategist," said Rosen at the time. Brickner has brought new vigor to an organization that's already one of the most confrontational of the estimated 150 Christian groups working among Jews. For example, a recent ad in New York bus shelters that read "Be More Jewish. Believe in Jesus" created an uproar. "We exist to make the Messiahship of Jesus an unavoidable issue to our Jewish people," says Brickner.

He boldly declares Jesus to the Jews.

QUOTABLE: On being a fifth-generation Jewish Christian: "I thought all Jews believed in Jesus until I went to elementary school. Then I quickly found out it was otherwise!"

BEHIND THE SCENES: A graduate of Moody Bible Institute and Fuller School of World Missions, Brickner is an ordained Baptist minister. He and his wife, Patti, have two children, Isaac and Ilana.

PRAYER STARTERS:

- Give thanks for the courage of Jewish Christians to carry out the Great Commission. Brickner has said, "The hardest thing about being the executive director is not knowing what you don't know." Pray that he will ask for and follow wise counsel today.

- Ask God to fill his family with His grace, and surround them with safety.

- Pray for a Jew you know; many are estranged even from an Old Testament faith.

> *The first thing Andrew did was to find his brother Simon and tell him, "We have found the Messiah" (that is, the Christ). John 1:41*

CONTACT: Jews for Jesus, 60 Haight Street, San Francisco, CA 94102; e-mail: jfj@jews-for-jesus.org

Barbara Bowman

President and Cofounder, Erikson Institute for Advanced Study in Child Development

Copyright Kathy Richland Photography

POINT OF IMPACT: For nearly half a century, Barbara Bowman has been teaching the world's teachers how to best teach the world's youngest children. President of the renowned Erikson Institute in Chicago, she's known internationally as one of the strongest, wisest voices in the realm of early childhood education. Over the years, she's spoken her mind on just about every childhood issue—from phonics to day care to kids and computers. "She is the most courageous voice," says a peer. "She's willing to speak boldly and audaciously." And for the most part, she's been heard. Today society recognizes what Ms. Bowman has long asserted—that what happens in the first five years of life frames the whole of a child's intellectual life.

She's an expert on a child's first five years of life.

QUOTABLE: "If we're raising children to grow up in a world where computer skills are a minimum daily requirement, all children need access to a keyboard. But computers can't supplant creativity. The child has the vision. He or she tells the computer what to do, and that's a very important lesson to learn. The machine is an active agent of their imaginations."

BEHIND THE SCENES: Bowman, now 70, is married to pathologist James Bowman. In the late fifties, the two lived for six years in Iran, where their daughter Valerie was born and where they helped start a 250-bed hospital, a medical school, and a nursing school in the ancient city of Shiraz.

PRAYER STARTERS:

- It is understood today that 90 percent of our capacity to learn is acquired by age 5. Give thanks for the new insights into child development championed by Barbara Bowman, and for the benefits to parenting and education.
- Pray for continued advances that will enhance the well-being of children in the midst of rapid technological and cultural changes.
- Ask God to favor the Bowmans today with health, honor, and fulfillment.
- Pray for a preschooler you know today.

> *Let the little children come to me, and do not hinder them, for the kingdom of God belongs to such as these. Mark 10:14*

CONTACT: Erikson Institute, 420 North Wabash Avenue, Chicago, IL 60611

117

AP/Wide World Photos

Kate Michelman

President, National Abortion and Reproductive Rights Action League (NARAL)

POINT OF IMPACT: As president of NARAL for the past decade, Kate Michelman's passionate support of a woman's right to choose abortion has helped NARAL grow into a major political force of 750,000 women. Frequently involved in public wrangles with pro-life forces, Michelman has been called by *Vanity Fair* "one of the most vocal abortion-rights activists in the country." A powerful lobbyist, she has testified on Capitol Hill against a proposed ban on late-term abortions, and in 1996 she addressed the Democratic National Convention.

She heads the nation's largest pro-choice group.

QUOTABLE: "I think there is an unusually high degree of focus on fetal life in this country. And that is not to say that there isn't value to fetal life, but there's been a preoccupation with it. . . . I had an abortion after having three children. I didn't need a picture to show me, or to enlighten me that I was terminating, you know, fetal life."

BEHIND THE SCENES: Michelman was raised a Catholic and didn't believe in abortion until her husband fell in love with another woman and left her with three children under age six—and a baby on the way. She had no job, no money, and no car. "For me it was a difficult choice," she says of her decision to have an abortion. "But as I look back, I know it was the right choice—and the moral choice." Michelman is remarried and has three grown daughters.

PRAYER STARTERS:

- Ask God to reveal His enduring mercies to Kate Michelman; pray for her well-being and that of her family.

- Pray for compassion for women facing unwanted pregnancies. Pray for the groups and individuals who are trying to meet the needs of these mothers.

- More than 40 percent of American women will have had at least one abortion by age 45. Pray today for their emotional and physical healing.

- Pray that God will impress on Michelman His truths about the value of life in the womb.

> *You knit me together in my mother's womb. I praise you because I am fearfully and wonderfully made. Psalm 139:13-14*

CONTACT: www.NARAL.com

Garrison Keillor

Radio Humorist, Bestselling Author

Photo credit: Carmen Quesada

POINT OF IMPACT: Since 1968, Garrison Keillor has been the writer and host of the legendary weekly radio series *A Prairie Home Companion,* produced by Minnesota Public Radio. Each week, more than 2.5 million people across the country tune in to the show, set in the imaginary Minnesota town of Lake Wobegon, which pokes fun at everything from religious piety to political correctness. Coming through all Keillor's satire on modern life is a small-town boy who grew up in a Christian home. He deftly taps into the angst of the boomer generation—leaving behind small-town roots and longing for more traditional values. Among his bestselling books are *The Book of Guys* and *Wobegon Boy.* *Atlantic Monthly* calls him "a national icon."

His radio show is down home.

QUOTABLE: "To know and to serve God, of course, is why we're here, a clear truth that, like the nose on your face, is . . . easily discernible but can make you dizzy if you try to focus on it hard. But a little faith will see you through. What else will do except faith in such a cynical, corrupt time? When the country goes temporarily to the dogs, cats must learn to be circumspect, walk on fences, sleep in trees, and have faith that all this woofing is not the last word."—from Keillor's book, *We Are Still Married*

BEHIND THE SCENES: Growing up, Keillor says, "We were not allowed to go to movies because they glorified worldliness. People drank in movies. They drank like fish. They smoked cigarettes. They danced. And we did not do those things," he says. But radio was acceptable—"I don't think people smoked as much on radio." Keillor, 56, is married to Jenny Lind Nilsson and they have two children.

PRAYER STARTERS:

- Give thanks for the gift of laughter, and for the life-affirming delight that Garrison Keillor brings to millions each week.
- Pray that Keillor's many references to God will encourage his listeners—especially those put off by other kinds of Christian media—to seek God.
- Ask God to bless Keillor and his extended family today.

All the days of the oppressed are wretched, but the cheerful heart has a continual feast. Proverbs 15:15

CONTACT: Minnesota Public Radio, 45 East Seventh Street, Saint Paul, MN 55101; e-mail: phc@mpr.org

Archive Photo

Jim Carrey
Actor, Comedian

POINT OF IMPACT: Jim Carrey, 38, was the most-talked-about film comic of the nineties. It all began in 1994 with an unheralded movie called *Ace Ventura: Pet Detective* that grossed $72 million. Carrey's physical style of slapstick followed in the tradition of Dick Van Dyke. By the end of the year, two other movies starring Carrey, *The Mask* and *Dumb and Dumber,* both easily exceeded the $100 million mark. Then in 1995, Sony paid Carrey $20 million—at the time the largest straight sum ever paid any actor for one movie—to secure his services for *The Cable Guy.* The rubber-faced comic took a break from broad comedy in 1998 to make the drama *The Truman Show,* and his performance generated an Oscar nomination. Carrey's recent movies include *The Incredible Mr. Limpet, The Secret Life of Walter Mitty,* and *Man in the Moon.* Carrey is especially popular with youth, but his brand of humor often contains crass sexual antics and bathroom jokes that some parents find objectionable.

His slapstick is redefining funny.

QUOTABLE: "One thing I hope I'll never be is drunk with my own power. And anybody who says I am will never work in this town again."

BEHIND THE SCENES: Carrey's seventh-grade teacher induced good behavior from him by allowing him to do 15-minute stand-up comic routines for the class. Carrey, who has no high-school diploma, left school in the ninth grade after his family fell on hard times that forced him to work long hours at a factory. Today he frequently contributes to Comic Relief, a charity that aids the homeless. He's divorced from his second wife, actress Lauren Holly, and has one daughter, Jane, from his first marriage. He lives in Brentwood, California.

PRAYER STARTERS:

- Ask God to bless Carrey and his family today; pray for positive, caring friends who can be the voice and touch of Jesus Christ to them today.
- Pray that Carrey would apply his amazing comic gifts to uplifting material.
- Pray that parents will set positive limits for their children and help them to understand the objectionable nature of certain humor.

The words of the godly are like sterling silver. Proverbs 10:20 NLT

CONTACT: United Talent Agency, 9560 Wilshire Blvd., Suite 500, Beverly Hills, CA 90212

Carly Fiorina

Group President, Global Service: Lucent Technologies

Courtesy of Lucent Technologies

POINT OF IMPACT: As president of Lucent's core division, Fiorina oversees the sales of big-ticket networking systems and software for telephone, internet, and wireless-service operators in 43 countries around the globe. "In short," says *Forbes* magazine, "she's at the center of the ongoing technology revolution that's changing how we live and work. . . . [She's] a star in nothing less than the hottest, most important industry in American business: telecommunications." In 1998, *Fortune* listed Fiorina as America's most powerful woman in business. Today Fiorina's division has sales of $19 billion a year, and Wall Street "adores her." Though Fiorina is often described as affable, stylish, and elegant, her boss, Rich McGinn, describes her simply as "wickedly smart." Record-high growth in revenues and profits have prompted hundreds of financial and industry analysts to visit Lucent's headquarters to look into its corporate operations.

She's the most powerful woman in business.

QUOTABLE: "Anytime you have a fiercely competitive, change-oriented growth business where results count and merit matters, women will rise to the top."

BEHIND THE SCENES: Fiorina's husband, Frank, has been consistently supportive of her career. When schedules became too hectic, he retired at 48 from his job as vice president at AT&T. Today he takes care of their three Yorkshire terriers and travels for business with his wife around the world. They enjoy spending time on their 55-foot yacht. The Fiorinas have two grown children.

PRAYER STARTERS:

- Ask for God's continued blessings on Carly Fiorina—her children, her husband, Frank, and their marriage—and through her the many with whom she has contact.
- Pray that Fiorina will be an influence for responsible business development worldwide.
- Pray that Fiorina and others in high-tech fields would seek the Lord of the future at every step—"This is what the Lord says, he who made the earth . . . 'Call to me and I will answer you and tell you great and unsearchable things you do not know' " (Jeremiah 33:2-3).

Commit to the LORD whatever you do, and your plans will succeed.
Proverbs 16:3

CONTACT: www.lucent.com

Garth Brooks
Country Singer

Archive Photo

POINT OF IMPACT: What's his magic? Garth Brooks, 37, the winner of four Country Music Entertainer of the Year awards, is a kindhearted, pudgy, balding country singer who has catapulted country music out of its blue-collar background into the ultrahip nineties. His story is one of drive, persistence, and success—with a lot of smarts. Brooks holds a degree in advertising and marketing and brings that commercial savvy to the stage. He incorporates rock-and-roll techniques into his performances: elaborate light shows, explosions, and even a harness so he can swing out above the crowd. And the fans love it— Brooks' concerts sell out in minutes and he is now the biggest-selling solo recording artist in U.S. history. *People* magazine writes, "The broad crossover appeal of Brooks' first three albums allowed him to sell more records with more velocity than any other artist in country music history."

He took country music from hick to hip.

QUOTABLE: "I think we've overshot paradise with a lot of things in life. We need to get the flag back out on the porch and God to the supper table."

BEHIND THE SCENES: Brooks is generous with his time, talents, and money for charity work—such as lobbying in Washington, DC for funding for arts and art education, performing benefit concerts for low-income families, and donating proceeds of his sales to Ronald McDonald House Charities. He and his wife have three daughters; they live in Goodlettesville, Tennessee.

PRAYER STARTERS:

- Ask God to bless Garth Brooks' personal life and family and pray for their spiritual well-being.
- Pray that God will expand Brooks' positive impact on individuals and organizations, especially those serving the needs of the less fortunate.
- Pray for more positive role models and uplifting lyrics in country music.

> *Blessed are all who fear the LORD, who walk in his ways. You will eat the fruit of your labor; blessings and prosperity will be yours. Psalm 128:1-2*

CONTACT: William Morris Agency, 151 El Camino Real Drive, Beverly Hills, CA 90212

Bartholomew I

Ecumenical Patriarchate:
Leader of Orthodox Christians

Courtesy of the Ecumenical Patriarchate

POINT OF IMPACT: Bartholomew, born Demetrios Archontonis in 1940, is believed by Orthodox Christians to be a direct successor of the apostle Andrew. He is the spiritual leader of Greek, Russian, Armenian, American, Abyssinian, and other Orthodox Christians, numbering around 300 million worldwide. He has become known as a voice for improved relationships between his church and the Jewish, Roman Catholics, Lutherans, Baptists, and Muslims. He travels extensively to that end and to promote preservation of the environment. Dubbed the "Green Patriarch," he has shared his views with leaders such as President Clinton and Prince Philip, and has launched seminars and discussions on the roles of morality and spirituality in reaching harmony between nature and man. When he assumed the role of Ecumenical Patriarch in 1991, he called for Orthodox unity, spiritual revival, Christian reconciliation, interfaith tolerance, and protection of the world's limited resources.

He's been dubbed the "Green Patriarch."

QUOTABLE: "There is a great hunger for spirituality; there is a thirst for transcendent meaning . . . and there has never been a greater need for spiritual leaders to engage themselves in the affairs of the world."

BEHIND THE SCENES: Bartholomew rose from humble beginnings; his father was a barber and coffee-shop owner in Turkey. He's well equipped to encourage relationships among different peoples; he speaks seven languages fluently.

PRAYER STARTERS:

- Give thanks for Patriarch Bartholomew's vision for spiritual revival in his church, and for his work for Christian unity and environmental concerns. Pray for wisdom and spiritual power for him as he pursues these priorities in a church that is steeped in traditionalism.

- Pray for Orthodox priests and lay workers around the world, that the new life of Christ would encourage and empower them today.

- Ask that God will bless Bartholomew and his family with grace and peace.

I have made him a witness to the peoples, a leader and commander of the peoples. Isaiah 55:4

CONTACT: Rum Patrikhanesi, 34220 Fener, Halic Istanbul, Turkey

123

Lloyd J. Ogilvie

Chaplain of the Senate

POINT OF IMPACT: He's the man who gets in the first word of the day in the Senate—and it's a word of prayer. Four years ago, Lloyd Ogilvie succeeded Richard Halverson in the high-profile post as Senate chaplain. Ogilvie's duties include providing spiritual care and counsel for the Senators, their families, and their staffs (a "congregation" of more than six thousand), and leading Bible studies, discussion sessions, and prayer meetings. Many first became familiar with Ogilvie's booming voice during the Clinton impeachment hearings. "He has an incredible preaching voice, like he was born to preach the Gospel," says Dr. Barry Hankins of the Dawson Institute of Church-State Studies. "He has incredible presence and great dignity in the pulpit." At 69, he's frequently named among the world's most admired preachers. Ogilvie prays for the Senators in groups of twenty each day as part of his morning devotional time.

He's the on-site pastor to the U.S. Senate.

QUOTABLE: "I see my role as Chaplain to be an intercessor, trusted prayer partner, and faithful counselor to the Senators as they seek to know God and discover His will in the monumental responsibilities entrusted to them."

BEHIND THE SCENES: For 23 years, Dr. Ogilvie was pastor of the Hollywood Presbyterian Church in Los Angeles. In that role, he led many in the film community to faith in Christ and exerted a significant spiritual impact in the city. The author of 44 books, Ogilvie and his wife, Mary Jane, have three children and four grandchildren.

PRAYER STARTERS:

- Give thanks for the tradition (since 1789) of the Chaplain's role in the Senate. Pray that Senators would genuinely seek God's wisdom for their decisions and His truth for their daily lives.

- Pray that Dr. Ogilvie's impact in Congress would bring honor to Christ and help to spread the Gospel in large and small ways.

- Ask God to bless the Ogilvies with health, strength, peace of heart, and joy.

By setting for the truth plainly we commend ourselves to every man's conscience in the sight of God. 2 Corinthians 4:2

CONTACT: Rotunda of the Senate Russell Building, Room 325-B, Washington, DC

National Teachers' Day

*"A teacher affects eternity; he can never
tell where his influence stops."*

HENRY ADAMS

- **Give thanks** for the tremendous contributions of teachers, coaches and mentors.
- **Pray for teachers and child-care workers in your community—** by name if possible. Pray for their patience, compassion, fulfillment and success.
- **Pray for the U.S. Secretary of Education, Richard Riley**: He says, "When I read a story to my grandchildren or call them up to congratulate them on their report card, I know why I get up in the morning and go to work. Our children and grandchildren represent who we are and what America will become." Ask God to give Riley strength and biblically based counsel. **Contact:** 400 Maryland Ave. S.W., Washington, DC 20202
- **Pray for Bob Chase, president of the National Education Association,** which represents more than 2.4 million teachers. Pray that Chase will help teachers improve their classroom success and be a strong advocate for teaching both life virtues and academic excellence. **Contact:** www.nea.org
- **Pray for the Boys & Girls Clubs of America:** Spokesman Gen. Colin Powell asks, "Wouldn't you invest in a company if it were growing so fast it opened four locations a week?" More than 2,800,000 boys and girls worldwide participate at Club activity centers. Give thanks for dedicated, integrous volunteers; pray for more. **Contact:** www.boysandgirlsclub.org
- **Pray for the Girl Scouts and Boy Scouts:** The world's largest voluntary youth movement, Scouting boasts 25 million members. Programs stress character-building, leadership, citizenship, and personal fitness. Pray for the success of scoutmasters around the world. **Contact:** www.bsa.scouting.org; www.gsusa.org

*Hold on to instruction, do not let it go; guard it well, for it is your life.
Proverbs 4:13*

Mark McGwire
Baseball Player

Courtesy of St. Louis Cardinals

POINT OF IMPACT: Sex, lies, and Monica dominated headlines during the summer of 1998—but Mark McGwire helped us set our sights beyond them. For one magnetic baseball season, he proved there are still heroes in the world. Yes, McGwire hit more home runs—70—in a single season than anyone in history, breaking Roger Maris' 26-year-old record of 61. But in addition to raw power, McGwire showed uncommon grace and respect for opponents, publicly hugged and adored his son after hitting home runs, cried on national television over sexually abused children, and then committed $1 million a year to help them. After the season, columnists and commentators credited McGwire with helping to save the game of baseball, carrying a country's tawdry burdens on his broad shoulders, and giving kids—finally—a genuine hero. "The quantity and sheer power of Mark's home runs have put him in a class of his own, but his moving example of selflessness and loyalty have made him equally unique," said the *Sporting News,* naming McGwire its 1998 Sportsman of the Year.

He brought the apple pie back to baseball.

QUOTABLE: "I know we're role models. And you may have a favorite baseball player, but how can that person be your hero? You don't even know him. That really bothers me. Your hero should be your father, or your mother, or an aunt, or an uncle. Look to your family, to people around you."

BEHIND THE SCENES: Among his charity projects is his Mark McGwire Foundation for Children. McGwire, 37, is divorced and lives in Orange County, California, near his teenage son, Matthew.

PRAYER STARTERS:

- Give thanks for Mark McGwire's positive example.
- Pray that McGwire will send a strong message to aspiring athletes about striving for personal and professional excellence.
- Pray that McGwire's relationships, especially with his son, will prosper. Ask God to draw the McGwire family closer to Himself.

> *Do nothing out of selfish ambition or vain conceit, but in humility consider others better than yourselves. Philippians 2:3*

CONTACT: Busch Stadium, 250 Stadium Plaza, St. Louis, MO 63102

Bill Bright

Founder and President,
Campus Crusade for Christ

POINT OF IMPACT: Over the past 40 years, Bill Bright has helped to take the gospel to more than 1 billion people. His organization, Campus Crusade for Christ, is now comprised of 13,000 full-time staff and more than 100,000 trained volunteers in 161 countries. Its ministries include outreaches to inner cities, numerous professions, and entire governments. Bright's organization was instrumental in producing *The Jesus Film,* which has now been translated into 455 languages and viewed by 1.2 billion people. Bright, 79, has written 50 books. When he was awarded the 1996 Templeton Award for religious service, Bright used the $1 million prize to spread the gospel around the world and to promote fasting and prayer for spiritual revival.

He's helped take the gospel to a billion people.

QUOTABLE: "I believe that people are hungry for God. Nobody who really understands the truth would say no to God if he understood how much God loves him, and how great is His forgiveness."—an *NPR interview*

BEHIND THE SCENES: During a 40-day fast in 1998, Bright prayed for worldwide spiritual revival. Now he's asking that 2 million believers join him on similar fasts. His goal is to get the gospel to 6 billion people in 2000, with at least 1 billion receiving Christ and 1 million churches planted. Bright and his wife, Vonette, residents of Orlando, Florida, have two sons, Zachary and Brad.

PRAYER STARTERS:

- Give thanks for Bright's 50 years of commitment to telling others about Jesus Christ. Praise God for the impact of Campus Crusade.
- Ask for the continued impact of *The Jesus Film,* especially in areas and cultures where the gospel isn't otherwise available.
- Ask God to bless Bill and Vonette with health, peace, and the joy of His presence. Ask for protection and blessing for their extended family.
- Today is National Day of Prayer. Pray for courage, unity, and effectiveness for worldwide prayer and renewal ministries.

> *Go and make disciples of all nations, baptizing them in the name of the Father and of the Son and of the Holy Spirit. Matthew 28:19*

CONTACT: Campus Crusade for Christ, 100 Sunport Ln., Orlando, FL 32809-7875

Edgar Bronfman, Jr.
CEO, Seagram Co. Ltd., Universal Studios

Archive Photo

POINT OF IMPACT: One entertainment executive compared him to a piñata: "Hit him and money comes out." Edgar Bronfman, Jr., chief executive and president of Seagram Co., Ltd., not only heads one of the world's largest distillers but also one of the world's largest, most influential entertainment businesses: Universal Studios. Universal is a leader in the film industry, runs theme parks, and dabbles in television. In 1998 Universal purchased music heavyweight PolyGram, whose well-known record labels—including Motown, Geffen, A&M, and Mercury—account for 25 percent of all music sold around the world. Now the world's most powerful music mogul, Bronfman must find it a comfortable fit—his first love has always been music (he's a professional lyricist himself under the name Sam Roman).

He's the world's most powerful music mogul.

QUOTABLE: On Hollywood: "It's a dumb town."

BEHIND THE SCENES: As a boy of 11 or 12, Bronfman was flown alone on a company jet across New England to look at boarding schools while his father was busy running Seagram. "Are you here with your father?" one headmaster asked as they walked across the campus. "No," young Edgar replied, "I'm here with my pilot." Now in his mid-forties, he's so publicity-shy that he once tried to buy every copy of every photograph of himself in existence so he couldn't be on the cover of *Business Week*. He's married to Clarissa Alcock and has four children; he lives in New York and Los Angeles.

PRAYER STARTERS:

- Pray that Edgar Bronfman, Jr. would use his enormous influence to become a leading force for personal and social renewal in the new century.
- Pray that Bronfman and other executives in Seagram and Universal Studios would follow biblical values in their business decisions today.
- Ask the Lord to bless the Bronfmans with spiritual, emotional, and physical well-being.

> *He who gets wisdom loves his own soul; he who cherishes understanding prospers. Proverbs 19:8*

CONTACT: Seagrams, 1430 Peel St., Montreal, Quebec H3A 1S9, Canada

Sarah Ferguson

Duchess of York, Author,
Weight Watchers' Spokesperson

Archive Photo

POINT OF IMPACT: Sarah Ferguson, nicknamed "Fergie" by the media, is one of the best-known British royals, but her claim to fame wasn't always positive. After her 1986 marriage to Prince Andrew, she was tormented by the press for being outspoken, undignified, and overweight. She eventually divorced her husband and was for a time estranged from members of the royal family. And yet, Ferguson has proven that she has what it takes to overcome her own image. The 40-year-old found answers to her eating disorder and lost weight with Weight Watchers. The now svelte redhead says she used her diet and self-improvement program to work out her anger against the media and others. Now she regularly travels as a Weight Watchers' spokesperson, and is committed to promoting awareness about obesity. "Obesity kills and we have to talk about it," she says. Recently she was honored by the *Journal of Women's Health* for her "challenge, compassion and commitment" to women's health issues, and she continues her work in charities for children.

She's a royal crusader.

QUOTABLE: "I was never cut out for the job of being royal."

BEHIND THE SCENES: Ferguson, now engaged again, has two daughters, Beatrice and Eugenie. Ferguson resides at Sunninghill Park, an estate owned by the Queen outside of London, with her children and former spouse, although in separate living quarters.

PRAYER STARTERS:

- Pray that Sarah Ferguson's example of determination to triumph over her personal difficulties will inspire others.
- Ask for blessings upon Sarah Ferguson as she encourages women on issues such as obesity and breast cancer.
- Pray for Sarah and her family in their private lives, that they will "seek first the kingdom of God and His righteousness" (Matthew 6:33).

I am the bread of life. He who comes to me will never go hungry, and he who believes in me will never be thirsty. John 6:35

CONTACT: Weight Watchers International, www.weightwatchers.com

Michael Medved
Film Critic, Author

Courtesy of Listen America

POINT OF IMPACT: Michael Medved, 51, is one of the nation's most vocal critics of the film and television industry. As host of a syndicated radio talk show and a frequent guest host for the Rush Limbaugh radio program, he wages war on "the enemies of traditional family values." Medved continues to assert, as he has for years, that one of the most important steps parents can take is to reduce the amount of television their kids watch. He reviewed films for years on PBS's *Sneak Previews* and currently does so for the *New York Post*. His latest book, coauthored with his wife, Diane, is *Saving Childhood: Protecting Our Children from the National Assault on Innocence* (HarperCollins, 1998). Among advocates for positive family values in the media, Medved often gets listened to in New York and Los Angeles while critics from the Christian right get tuned out.

He preaches less TV for kids.

QUOTABLE: "And what is the TV saying to the child? It is hardly saying to the child: 'Rejoice in the world around you. Celebrate in this world that God has made for you.' The TV is saying to the child: 'Take everything for granted. Feel impatient. Feel wanting. Feel desirous. Feel restless.'"

BEHIND THE SCENES: The Medveds, who live in Mercer Island, Washington, are observant Jews. They eat only kosher foods and rest on the Sabbath (which includes refraining from driving, cooking, talking on the phone, or using any electrical devices). They watch no TV whatsoever, and the children—Sarah, Shayna, and Danny—watch only six hours of parent-approved videos each week. Medved's wife, Diane, is host of an internet show, a clinical psychologist, and author of several books (including one on the family cowritten with Dan Quayle).

PRAYER STARTERS:

- The average family with children keeps the TV on 60 hours a week, and children spend more time in front of the tube than in school or at play. Pray that parents will have the wisdom and fortitude to limit TV viewing.
- Pray that children will be protected today from all TV-related harm.
- Ask God to bless the Medved home with grace, peace, and joy. Pray that he and his wife will experience great success in their mission.

> *There is a way that seems right to a man, but in the end it leads to death.*
> Proverbs 14:12

CONTACT: HarperCollins, 10 East 53rd Street, New York, NY 10022

George W. Bush
Governor of Texas
GOP Candidate

POINT OF IMPACT: Called "George W." or "Junior" so as not to confuse him with his father, Governor George W. Bush of Texas is the eldest son of former President George Bush. He's touted by some as the savior of the Republican Party as it looks at the next century. Bush, 54, has earned a reputation as a "compassionate conservative" who reaches out to minorities and promotes a message of family values, sexual abstinence before marriage, and the need to "usher in the responsibility era." Bush is seen as a unifying figure: instead of seeking confrontation with Democrats, he has sought consensus; instead of shocking the troops with hard-edged rhetoric, he has encouraged Republicans to soften their language. Even Democratic consultant Mark McKinnon described him as "someone who really tries to understand the human side and human consequences of politics." Yet on hot-button social issues such as abortion, same-sex marriages, and school prayer, Bush is in sync with conservatives.

He's a compassionate conservative.

QUOTABLE: "You cannot lead unless you unite people. People don't want to follow someone who's divisive. People will not follow someone who lumps people into groups. I judge individuals based upon their hearts and souls."

BEHIND THE SCENES: As a college student, Bush earned a reputation as a hard-drinking party boy and had numerous scrapes with the law. He abruptly gave up alcohol the day after his fortieth birthday and is now "a loyal husband of 21 years and a dedicated dad." Friends say he reads the Bible through every year or two. He's an active member of the Methodist church. He and his wife, Laura, have twin teenage daughters, Jenna and Barbara. They live in Austin.

PRAYER STARTERS:

- Pray that in the post-Clinton era, George W. Bush can be a force for reconciliation and bipartisanship in both state and national arenas.
- Give thanks for the record of public service in the Bush family.
- Ask God to bless George and Laura and their girls today with His favor and a keen awareness of His presence.

I will lead them beside streams of water on a level path. Jeremiah 31:9

CONTACT: Office of the Governor, P.O. Box 12428, Austin, TX 78711-2428

Gabriel García Márquez
Nobel Prize-Winning Author

Courtesy of Pantheon

POINT OF IMPACT: Thought by many to be one of the world's greatest living authors, Colombian writer Gabriel García Márquez pioneered the writing style called Magical Realism, which blends the reality of political oppression and injustice with the magic of strong beliefs in the divine and supernatural. His masterpiece, *100 Years of Solitude,* has sold 20 million copies in 18 languages. Over the years, his highly political and leftist books—he is a good friend of Fidel Castro—have incited revolutionary passion throughout Latin America. Yet Márquez, 71, continues to funnel some of his money into political and social causes. He was awarded the Nobel Prize for Literature in 1982. He lives in Mexico City with his second wife, Mercedes.

His novels blend reality and magic.

QUOTABLE: "Spelling should be pensioned off. . . . It terrorizes human beings from birth."

BEHIND THE SCENES: In 1965, Márquez put his wife in charge of the family, and retired to his room where he wrote every day for 18 months. His wife sold the car and pawned almost every household appliance so she could feed the family and keep him supplied with a constant river of paper and cigarettes. His friends called his smoke-filled room "the Cave of the Mafia," and after awhile the whole community began helping out, as if they collectively understood that he was creating a magnum opus. Credit was extended, appliances loaned, debts forgiven. The result was *100 Years of Solitude*—a novel that's one of the century's greatest.

PRAYER STARTERS:

- Pray that Gabriel García Márquez would experience a powerful encounter with Jesus Christ that would bring him new and eternal inspiration.
- Ask God to give Márquez health and peace during his later years.
- Pray for the poor and oppressed in Central and South America today, that those in positions of influence over them would work for justice.

Whatever you do, work at it with all your heart, as working for the Lord, not for men. Colossians 3:23

CONTACT: Rizzoli International Publications, 1000 3rd Ave., New York, NY 10022

Ben Carson

Surgeon

Courtesy of Cosby Bureau

POINT OF IMPACT: Ben Carson was once an angry, self-destructive street fighter. Today he's an inspiring and life-saving surgeon and Director of Pediatric Neurosurgery at the world-renowned Johns Hopkins Medical Institution. Carson's 1987 surgery to separate twins joined at the head catapulted the doctor to celebrity status. His autobiography, *Gifted Hands,* chronicles the road from a broken home, poverty, and poor grades to his life today. His second book, *Think Big,* elaborates on his philosophy for success in life. Carson frequently speaks at medical-school commencements, high-school classes, and elementary-school assemblies in an effort to inspire young people to achieve greatness.

He operates on hearts—and inspires minds.

QUOTABLE: "We cannot wait for someone to do something for us. We have to do it for ourselves."

BEHIND THE SCENES: As a teenager, Carson had a "pathological temper." In one fit of rage, he almost killed a friend with a camping knife. Afterward he locked himself in the bathroom and cried out to God for help. Since then he's become a Seventh-Day Adventist, a husband, and a father, and he says he no longer loses his temper. Today he performs as many as ten operations a week, praying before each one. He and his wife, Candy, have three sons. They live in Maryland.

PRAYER STARTERS:

- Give thanks for the children's lives saved under Dr. Carson's care; for the pioneering surgical work of Dr. Carson and his coworkers.
- Give thanks for Carson's outspoken faith, and for his zeal to inspire others to excellence, especially the young and disadvantaged.
- Pray for continued success and medical advancements at Johns Hopkins and other medical centers that specialize in the needs of children.
- Ask for health, rest, and blessing for Carson's marriage and family.

You make me glad by your deeds, O LORD; *I sing for joy at the works of your hands. Psalm 92:4*

CONTACT: Johns Hopkins Children's Center, 600 North Wolfe St., Baltimore, MD 21287

133

Alanis Morissette
Pop Singer

POINT OF IMPACT: When Madonna was asked what she thought of Alanis Morissette, she replied, "She reminds me of me." Morissette, 25, has the fan base of a cult figure with the sales base of a megastar. Her lyrics have been called "at best, painfully honest and, at worst, incredibly nasty." But the Canadian singer didn't always have the hard edge that now defines her. In Canada, she was a young teen pop/dance sensation, singing the national anthem "O Canada" at high-profile events. When she moved from Canada to Los Angeles, her songs evolved with a fury. Jarringly angry, serious, and intelligent, Morissette's new style has resulted in great success and recognition. She has the distinction of having the best-selling U.S. debut album of all time by a female solo artist.

She may be the next Madonna.

QUOTABLE: "People have always said I was an old soul. They said I was always a little more intense and introspective than everyone was used to seeing girls be, so they didn't know where to categorize me. I want to walk through life instead of being dragged through it."

BEHIND THE SCENES: Morissette was "discovered" in a children's music revue at the 1987 Springtime Tulip Festival in her hometown. At 13 she recorded her first album, *Alanis,* which proved to be a big hit in Canada and won her a JUNO Award (Canada's version of the Grammys) as the most promising new female vocalist. She is single and lives in Los Angeles.

PRAYER STARTERS:

- Morissette plays "God" in Kevin Smith's controversial film *Dogma.* Pray that Morissette will experience a genuine encounter with God's saving love.
- Many young women respond enthusiastically to Morissette's angry lyrics. Pray that her music will help fans move past disillusionment to healing.
- Ask that Alanis will hear God's Spirit inviting her to new life and new purposes in Him.

> *I pray also that the eyes of your heart may be enlightened in order that you may know the hope to which he has called you. Ephesians 1:18*

CONTACT: Creative Artists Agency, 9830 Wilshire Blvd., Beverly Hills, CA 90212

Süleyman Demirel
President of Turkey

UN/DPI Photo by E. Schneider

POINT OF IMPACT: For Turkish president Süleyman Demirel, civil unrest has made governing his country a constant challenge. One of his greatest domestic hurdles is balancing secular traditions with the Islamic political influence. Known for his respect for Islamic traditions, antisocialist orientation, and pro-West sympathies, he nonetheless has described the Turkish state as a "democratic, secular and social state." He wants to reduce Turkey's inflation, which in 1998 was running at an annual rate of 62 percent, and to cut the huge domestic debt. As president, he's survived an assassination attempt allegedly motivated by his signing of a treaty with Israel.

He walks a political tightrope.

QUOTABLE: Following a year in America: "My own personal experience in life led me to understand the full importance of social mobility, providing full opportunities to all citizens regardless of birth, origin, and creed, and thus ensuring a full development of individual talents and initiatives."

BEHIND THE SCENES: Demirel, 75, the oldest of four children, was born to a farm family in Asia Minor. He takes pride in describing himself as a "peasant boy" and in his image as a "man of the people." He is the first prime minister to speak in a peasant's dialect. He speaks English and French fluently. He and his wife of 50 years have no children.

PRAYER STARTERS:

- Pray that President Demirel and his cabinet will exercise wisdom and vision as they lead Turkey through a time of economic difficulty and religious strife. Pray for peace with Greece, and for justice and provision for displaced Iraqis and Kurds who look to Turkey for help.
- Pray for the physical and spiritual well-being of Demirel and his wife.
- Turkey is predominantly Muslim. Pray for the church there—both Orthodox and evangelical—and for the spread of the gospel.

> *Seek the LORD while he may be found; call on him while he is near.*
> Isaiah 55:6

CONTACT: Office of the President, Cumhurbas-Kanligi Kosku, Cankaya, Ankara, B, Turkey.

Nancy Brinker

Cancer Activist

Courtesy of Komen Foundation

POINT OF IMPACT: After Susan Komen died of breast cancer at age 36, leaving behind her husband and two young children, her sister, Nancy Brinker, established The Susan G. Komen Breast Cancer Foundation. That was in 1982. Two years later, Nancy herself was diagnosed with breast cancer. Having learned from Susan's experience, she took charge of her own health—and survived her cancer. Today, the Komen Foundation sponsors "Race for the Cure" events across the country and is the nation's largest private funder of research dedicated solely to advancing breast cancer research, education, screening, and treatment. Brinker has served under three U.S. presidents on the National Cancer Advisory Board and is the author of a book, *The Race Is Run One Step At a Time.*

She runs a race against breast cancer.

QUOTABLE: "When I went home to visit her [Susan] for the last time, she said, 'I want you to help me do something for other women and their families so they don't have to go through what we have. I want you to help cure this disease.'"

BEHIND THE SCENES: Armed with only a few hundred dollars and a shoe box of friends' names, she began her campaign by visiting a lingerie company. "I thought a bra company was a natural," she says. But she was wrong. "The president said, 'We sell beauty and glamour; we don't sell disease,'" and asked Brinker to leave. Today, many fashion industries embrace breast cancer awareness. Brinker lives in Dallas with husband, Norman, and son, Eric.

PRAYER STARTERS:

- Breast cancer will strike one woman in eight, killing one in three. Give thanks for Nancy Brinker's dedication to breast cancer prevention and research. Pray for success in her continuing efforts.

- Pray that many will participate in this year's "Race for the Cure" fundraising event. Also pray for a woman you know who is fighting breast cancer, or building a new life in its aftermath.

- Ask God to bless Brinker with courage, peace, and reassurance of His love.

He sent forth his word and healed them; he rescued them from the grave.
Psalm 107:20

CONTACT: 5000 LBJ Freeway, Ste. 370, Dallas, TX 75244; www.breastcancerinfo.com

Bertha Holt

Adoption Activist

POINT OF IMPACT: Bertha Holt, along with her husband, Harry, who died in 1964, founded Holt International Children's Services, which has placed more than 60,000 orphans from around the world into U.S. homes since 1956 and pioneered the way for countless others. "Though Harry held the reins, he constantly affirmed that it was the Lord's work," says Holt. Known as "Grandma Holt," she has received many honors, including Mother of the Year and Woman of the Year. At 95 years old, she continues to work and travel extensively.

Photo by: John Aeby

She pioneered international adoptions.

QUOTABLE: "Holt's adoption work was started by the Lord Himself. . . . God knew there would be a war in Korea and that Amer-Asian children would be left helpless and homeless. . . . The Lord chose an old farmer without a Ph.D. to come to their rescue. He didn't press buttons to bring up his name; He knew it from the beginning. He prepared him with a mixture of stubborn persistence, solid faith in God, [and] a caring responsibility to children."

BEHIND THE SCENES: Bertha set a world record for her age group (90-94) in the 400-meter race at Eugene Oregon's Hayward Classic Masters Track and Field Championships. She completed the race in just under 4 minutes. She continues to write hundreds of letters by hand to her "family" around the world, which includes her six children by birth and many adopted children.

PRAYER STARTERS:

- Thank God that in Bertha Holt's brave determination to mother orphans around the world, we hear His voice. Pray for her continuing health. Ask God for peace and harmony among those in her organization.
- Pray for orphans everywhere, that they might find a home.
- Celebrate Mother's Day by asking God to bless the institution of mothers around the world, granting them strength, wisdom, and stamina.

> *Can a mother forget the baby at her breast and have no compassion on the child she has borne? Though she may forget, I will not forget you!*
> *Isaiah 49:15*

CONTACT: P.O. Box 2880, 1195 City View, Eugene, OR 97402

Eddie Vedder

Rock Singer

Archive Photo

POINT OF IMPACT: Eddie Vedder and Pearl Jam pioneered and then outlived the genre of grunge. Now they are determined to prove their music still matters. "Having survived the end of one era, these fellas have no intention of either burning out or fading away," says *Entertainment Weekly*. This eclectic quintet—proud of its antiestablishment image—is "the flagship band for disaffected youth," says one magazine. Vedder's trademark themes of alienation, the glory of youth, and mortality are resonant throughout his lyrics. In the mid-nineties, the group became explosively popular, winning an American Music Award and three Grammy nominations. *Entertainment Weekly* says, "Pearl Jam is now a classic-rock act."

His music resonates with disaffected youth.

QUOTABLE: "Man is the end-all thing on earth. Man comes out of the muck, three million years later he's still standing. Now he's controlling everything and killing it. . . . So what are we doin' here?"

BEHIND THE SCENES: The band performs many benefit concerts, donating money to their favorite charities. They played in an abortion rights benefit, and have performed on behalf of AIDS, public schools, disabled kids, youth recreation, and most recently, an anti-death penalty "Dead Man" concert.

PRAYER STARTERS:

- Vedder is described as having that "I'm-a-superstar, feel-my-pain persona." Pray that God's Spirit will bring him healing and hope, and draw Vedder and his bandmates to Himself. Pray for their safety.

- Give thanks for the band's social sensitivites. Pray that their desire to make a difference will be channeled in positive directions.

- Pray for a teenager you know today who may be struggling with depression, alienation, or a lack of purpose in his or her life.

    You, O LORD, keep my lamp burning; my God turns my darkness into light.
    Psalm 18:28

CONTACT: www.sonymusic.com; e-mail: tenclub1@aol.com (fan club)

Geoffrey Bible

CEO, Phillip Morris Companies

AP/Wide World Photos

POINT OF IMPACT: Australian Geoffrey Bible is chairman and CEO of the Phillip Morris Companies, the largest cigarette seller worldwide, producing 2 billion cigarettes a day. Public health officials estimate that as many as 450,000 Americans die every year from smoking-related sickness, yet for years the industry has disputed medical evidence and waged war against health advocates. In 1998, Geoffrey Bible sought peace. The chief Marlboro man, along with the $50 billion-a-year U.S. tobacco industry, agreed to pay $206 billion to settle a mountain of state lawsuits that will help pay health-care costs for sick smokers. About half of this stunning sum will be paid by Phillip Morris alone. Phillip Morris is also the biggest consumer-products company on the planet. It owns Kraft Foods, America's number-two food business, and Miller Brewing, the number-three beer producer.

He's the man behind the Marlboro man.

QUOTABLE: Bible once said, "What do you think smokers would do if they didn't smoke? You get some pleasure from it, and you also get some other beneficial things, such as stress relief. Nobody knows what you'd turn to if you didn't smoke. Maybe you'd beat your wife. Maybe you'd drive cars fast. Who knows what . . . you'd do."

BEHIND THE SCENES: Bible started out as an accountant who worked for the United Nations in Switzerland. Now in his early sixties, he's an unapologetic pack-a-day smoker (he smokes Marlboros). He started smoking at age 14.

PRAYER STARTERS:

- Bible has said, "Next to my wife and family, the stock (of Phillip Morris) is the most important thing in my life." Ask God to bless Bible's marriage and family today, and to grant him wisdom at home and in his corporate leadership.
- Pray for healing and comfort for those with smoking-related illnesses.
- Pray for the thousands of smokers who want to quit; pray for creativity and impact for the health groups who are trying to discourage the habit.

> *Long life to you! Good health to you and your household! And good health to all that is yours! 1 Samuel 25:6*

CONTACT: Phillip Morris, 120 Park Ave., New York, NY 10017

Photo by Rick Reinhard, Washington, DC

Al Gore
Vice President of the United States

POINT OF IMPACT: As congressman, senator and then vice president, Al Gore made his mark as a champion of the environment. He's been quoted as saying that "protection and preservation of the earth's environment is one of the most important issues facing this generation." He's also a recognized leader in developing the National Information Infrastructure (he coined the term "information superhighway"). He led "Reinvent Government" initiatives that resulted in reforming and cutting the size of government by 351,000 employees to create the smallest federal government, on a percentage basis, since the thirties. Despite his reputation as an uninspiring public speaker, he's viewed as the front-runner for the Democratic nominee for the 2000 presidential election.

He's passionate about the environment.

QUOTABLE: On internet safeguards for families—"Blocking your own child's access to objectionable internet content is not censoring; it's parenting. And it is essential."

BEHIND THE SCENES: Gore, 52, grew up in a newspaper family with a high profile in Tennessee politics. His family attends a Missionary Baptist church when they're home in Carthage, Tennessee. His wife, Tipper, has been active in the drive to protect children from objectionable music lyrics. The Gores have four children.

PRAYER STARTERS:

- Give thanks for Al Gore's forward-looking service to the nation. Ask God to bless and protect the Gore family.

- Gore openly supported reformers during a regional summit in Malaysia in 1998, ruffling many Asian powers. Pray that Gore will continue to seek God's guidance on important issues, taking courageous stands where necessary.

- Pray that Gore's influence will help restore integrity to the White House.

Obey me, and I will be your God and you will be my people. Walk in all the ways I command you, that it may go well with you. Jeremiah 7:23

CONTACT: The White House, 1600 Pennsylvania Ave. N.W., Washington, DC 20500; e-mail: vicepresident@whitehouse.gov

Deepak Chopra
Endocrinologist, Health Teacher, Author

Archive Photo

POINT OF IMPACT: Dr. Deepak Chopra has been called today's most influential and esteemed spokesperson for the $30 billion-a-year business of alternative/New Age medicine. The son of a prominent cardiologist in India, Chopra moved to the United States and completed residencies in internal medicine and endocrinology. He later turned to Ayurveda, the ancient Hindu science of healing. This system's guiding principle is that the mind exerts the deepest influence on the body. A balance of correct diet, exercise, meditation, and learning to live in present time, Chopra believes, can help a person live whole and well for at least 120 years. In 1993 he became executive director of the Sharp Institute for Human Potential and Mind Body Medicine, and the chief consultant to the Center for Mind Body Medicine. Chopra speaks all over the world and is frequently featured on U.S. public television. He is the author of 11 books including the mega-seller *Ageless Body, Timeless Mind.*

He believes you can live to be 120.

QUOTABLE: "To realize 'I am love' is not reserved only for those who marry. It is a universal realization, cherished in every spiritual tradition. Or to put it most simply, all relationships are ultimately a relationship with God."

BEHIND THE SCENES: Chopra is fascinated by the English King Arthur legend. Arthur and the wizard Merlin, Chopra says, are aspects of personality we all have within us. The Christian Research Journal labels as "nonsense" his teachings that disease and death are ultimately only manifestations of an imperfect awareness.

PRAYER STARTERS:

- Pray that Deepak Chopra will look to the Bible for the truth about eternal life, and that he will encounter articulate Christian health practitioners.
- Pray that the Holy Spirit would draw this generation of seekers to God by awakening a hunger for healing and an awareness of sin.
- Ask God to bless Chopra and his family with health of body, mind, and spirit.

> *For you who revere my name, the sun of righteousness will rise with healing in its wings. Malachi 4:2*

CONTACT: The Chopra Center for Well Being, 7630 Fay Avenue, La Jolla, CA 92037; e-mail: info@chopra.com

UN/DPI photo by E. Schneider

Yasser Arafat

*Leader of the Palestinian
Liberation Organization*

POINT OF IMPACT: Yasser Arafat was only a teenager when Israel was becoming a nation in the 1940s. In 1956 Arafat founded Al Fatah, an underground terrorist organization. After losing the 1967 War, Arabs made Arafat the leader of the Palestinian Liberation Organization (PLO). Arafat eventually turned from terrorism to diplomacy. In 1988 he told the United Nations that the PLO would recognize Israel as a sovereign state. And in 1993 the unthinkable happened: peace talks in Norway led to the Oslo Peace Accords between Arafat and Israeli Prime Minister Yitzak Rabin. The agreement granted limited Palestinian self-rule and earned Arafat, Rabin, and Israeli foreign minister Shimon Peres the 1994 Nobel Peace Prize. Yet peace remains elusive. For his peacemaking efforts, Rabin was assassinated. And for now, the wily man in the black-and-white turban remains critical toward any lasting settlement.

His PLO is Israel's greatest enemy.

QUOTABLE: "We shall continue to act against the settlement onslaught to save holy Jerusalem from the Judaizing monster Israel and the despised settlements."

BEHIND THE SCENES: Arafat, 71, has Parkinson's disease and suffers from memory loss and fainting spells. His wife, Suha Tawil, is 35 years his junior. Though raised a Palestinian Christian, she converted to Islam for the marriage. Arafat and his wife take care of dozens of orphans from Palestinian refugee camps, and have adopted several. They have one daughter, Zahwa, and live in Gaza City.

PRAYER STARTERS:

- Ask God to heal Yasser Arafat in body, mind, and soul.
- Pray for the peace of Jerusalem and the security of the Israelis. Pray for justice, safety, and provision for the Palestinian people, among the Middle East's poorest.
- Give thanks for progress toward peace in Israel and the occupied territories. Pray for a stronger consensus on all sides, and for Arafat's role in this process.
- Pray for Christians—of both Jewish and Palestinian heritage—that they will be ambassadors for peace and draw others to the Savior by their example.

> *Pray for the peace of Jerusalem: "May those who love you be secure. May there be peace within your walls and security within your citadels." Psalm 122:6-7*

CONTACT: U.S. Consulate PLO Office, 818-18 St. N.W. 620, Washington, DC 20006

Arlene Klasky and Gabor Csupo

Creators of Rugrats

AP/Wide World Photos

POINT OF IMPACT: If a baby could talk and he came upon a toilet for the first time in his life, what would he say? This idea sparked the imaginations of animators Arlene Klasky and Gabor Csupo, who, with partner Paul Germain, brought the Rugrats to life. Now the number-one rated kids' television program, *Rugrats* attracts more than 23 million viewers every week and has so far garnered three Emmy awards. Now the Rugrats are considered the most recognized animated characters in the marketplace and are more popular with kids than Bugs Bunny and Mickey Mouse. The animated stars of the half-hour program—which contains two 15-minute cartoons—became movie stars with the 1998 major motion picture release, *The Rugrats Movie.* Many credit the Klasky–Csupo studio with breathing new, eccentric life into the animation world.

Their animated babies are big-time stars.

QUOTABLE: "This is a show where parents are comfortable sitting with their children and they don't have to be bored. It's not a silly, one-gag oriented cartoon. [It is] more like storytelling. And once you learn the characters . . . you want to find out what else is going to happen to them."—Gabor Csupo

BEHIND THE SCENES: Csupo (pronounced "CHOO-poh") left communist-ruled Hungary for Sweden, where he met Klasky, an American graphic designer. They married and in 1981, formed Klasky Csupo, Inc. Their company has grown to a studio of 260 employees. In addition to *Rugrats,* they've created *Ahhh! Real Monsters, Duckman,* and *The Wild Thornberries.* Now divorced, Klasky and Csupo remain creative partners. They have two children and live in New York.

PRAYER STARTERS:

- Pray that the entertainment industry will increasingly endeavor to produce cartoons for kids that are creative, entertaining, and edifying.
- Ask God to encourage and bless Klasky and Csupo, and pray that they would know and delight in an intimate relationship with their Creator.
- Pray that Klasky and Csupo's relationship remains amicable and that they, together, make their roles as parents a top priority.

Surely then you will find delight in the Almighty and will lift up your face to God. Job 22:26

CONTACT: c/o Nickelodeon, 1515 Broadway, 37th Floor, New York, NY 10036

Reinhard Bonnke

Evangelist, Founder, Christ for All Nations

Courtesy of Christ for All Nations

POINT OF IMPACT: Reinhard Bonnke was a "preacher's kid" in Germany who gave his life to Christ at age nine, and says he heard a call to Africa before he was a teenager. He began by preaching in a tent that accommodated 800. But it proved too small. In 1984, he commissioned the construction of a tent capable of seating 34,000 people. Once again, attendance soon exceeded capacity. Today, he hosts "Fire Conferences" in many countries to train leaders for evangelism. During the nineties, he conducted nearly 100 major crusades and ministered to more than 17 million people. Around 3.6 million accepted Christ and joined local churches. He and his wife reside in Frankfurt, Germany.

He takes the Great Commission to heart.

QUOTABLE: "I see something like a big harvest net rolling across America, scooping up every lost soul in its path, bringing them into the kingdom of God. America is the greatest missionary-sending nation on earth. For many years, she has been casting her bread upon the water. Now, some is coming back to her in a mighty harvest for God."

BEHIND THE SCENES: A simple mail campaign can win people to Christ, Bonnke says, referring to a British woman's testimony. "She said her husband never wanted to accept Jesus. After he died, she grieved because he didn't know Christ. But a few months later, she found our evangelism booklet, and in the back, her husband had filled out the card for salvation. He never mailed it to us, but we're sure a much higher authority recognized her husband's action."

PRAYER STARTERS:

- Thank God for Bonnke's dedication to the gospel. Pray for his stamina and effectiveness; ask for blessing and protection for his wife and family.
- Pray for those who hear Bonnke's message, that God will soften their hearts to the promise of salvation and that they will choose to respond.
- Pray for the church in Africa—growing and beleaguered in many ways but now sending missionaries around the world.

Pray also for me, that whenever I open my mouth, words may be given me so that I will fearlessly make known the mystery of the gospel. Ephesians 6:19

CONTACT: Christ for All Nations, P.O. Box 277440, Sacramento, CA 95827

144

Gary L. Bauer
Political Activist

Courtesy of Family Research Council

POINT OF IMPACT: At just over five feet tall, Gary Bauer is a diminutive but highly visible conservative activist who has made family values his calling card on Capitol Hill. In 1999 he declared himself a candidate for the presidency. His goal: to create "a society that's stable, where marriage means something, where the virtue deficit is being dealt with, where kids are being taught reliable standards of right and wrong." He is chairman of the Campaign for Working Families and was recruited by James Dobson of Focus on the Family to run their Family Research Council. In ten years, he's built the now-independent operation from four employees and a $200,000 budget into today's $14-million, 100-employee enterprise with a base of nearly 500,000 donors. Bauer's books include *Children at Risk: The Battle for the Hearts and Minds of Our Kids,* a book he coauthored with Dobson.

His calling card is family values.

QUOTABLE: "The best way to be victorious is to be right and to have the courage to believe you're right."

BEHIND THE SCENES: Gary Bauer, 53, grew up in Newport, Kentucky, called "Sin City" during the fifties. While still in high school, he was a civic activist, working to get corrupt forces thrown out. "People were doing whatever they wanted if it felt good and they thought they could get a quick buck. And you could see the obvious downsides in all that in the broken families, in spousal abuse, in violence in the schools—all those things that I think we've learned in the years since can affect a republic if you begin to overthrow virtue." Bauer lives in Virginia with his wife, Carol, and their three children—Elyse, Sara and Zachary.

PRAYER STARTERS:

- Give thanks for the influence of Gary Bauer and those who work alongside him in defense of America's foundational values during these times of change and confusion.
- Pray that the media will give Bauer's strong family message a fair hearing.
- Pray for safety, health, and peace for Bauer and his family.

I will make your faithfulness known through all generations. Psalm 89:1

CONTACT: 801 G Street N.W., Washington, DC 20001

Courtesy of Yahoo!

Jerry Yang

Cofounder, CEO, Yahoo!

POINT OF IMPACT: Few people have become richer or more famous from the internet than Jerry Yang, the cofounder of Yahoo! Inc. Since starting Yahoo! with David Filo while both were in grad school at Stanford, Yang has become the world's best-known internet geek and the face of the hugely popular doorway to the internet. The company has distinguished itself from its competitors by being pop-culture cool. And as director, chief spokesperson, and visionary for the company, Yang deserves much of the credit. Today Yahoo! contains organized data on tens of thousands of computers linked to the web, helping users navigate quickly through vast amounts of information. It has branched out with guides for France, Germany, and Japan. In just over three years, Yang's grasp of "cool" has made him a billionaire—though his nickname around the office is Grumpy.

He's a world-famous internet geek.

QUOTABLE: "We'd never done any of these things before. We didn't know the right protocols. . . . And the whole money thing, it's still weird. . . . I lived on $19,000 a year as a grad student and I could live on $19,000 today. It's nice to know that your family is provided for, but the money isn't that important."

BEHIND THE SCENES: Born Yang Chih-Yuan in 1968 in Taiwan, Yang moved with his family to San Jose when he was ten. As a doctoral student at Stanford, his office was in a junk-strewn trailer on campus. That's where he hatched plans for Yahoo! with Filo. Since then they've donated $2 million to Stanford. Yang's wife, Akiko, a marketing consultant, is a Costa Rican of Japanese descent.

PRAYER STARTERS:

- Give thanks that it remains possible in America for even the youngest or poorest entrepreneurs to succeed in pursuing their dreams.
- Pray for wisdom, creativity, and vision for Yang and others who are pioneering web access and usability.
- Ask God to bless Jerry and Akiko Yang today with spiritual *access* and *usability*—"I am the way and the truth and the life" (John 14:6).

> *He who pursues righteousness and love finds life, prosperity and honor.*
> Proverbs 21:21

CONTACT: Yahoo!, 635 Vaqueros Ave., Sunnyvale, CA 94086; jerry@yahoo.com

Frank Peretti
Bestselling Author

Courtesy of Thomas Nelson Publ.

POINT OF IMPACT: Christian fiction has emerged as one of the most powerful forces in publishing, and no one is more responsible than the king of the theological thriller, Frank Peretti. According to *Time* magazine, "Peretti gave birth to the genre—and the current surge in Christian fiction, in general." Since the release of *This Present Darkness* in the mid-eighties, his novels about spiritual warfare and demonic influences in contemporary culture—abortion, the media, New Age, and public education—have sold almost 10 million copies, putting Peretti among the 20 top-selling general fiction writers in the country. Besides *This Present Darkness*, his novels include *Piercing the Darkness, The Oath, Prophet,* and *The Visitation.* His work is frequently compared with that of Stephen King—with a theological spin. Even some Hollywood producers are converts: a group that includes producer Howard Kazanjian (*Raiders of the Lost Ark*) recently bought film rights to the *Darkness* stories.

He's called "Stephen King with a theological spin."

QUOTABLE: "Many Christians have succumbed to the world's shallowness and no longer build their strength on spiritual depth. Instead of Bible study we have spiritual warfare video games, instead of worship we have staged musical extravaganzas."

BEHIND THE SCENES: After high school he became a banjo player in a bluegrass band called the Kimberlys, which toured the country playing engagements in local taverns. He quit when he realized that "God had better things for me to do." The former Assembly of God pastor and his wife live in Coeur d'Alene, Idaho.

PRAYER STARTERS:

- Praise God for how Peretti's works have helped believers become more alert to the spiritual dimension of daily life.
- Ask for God's continued blessing on Peretti's writing ministry, and for safety and happiness in his home and marriage.
- Pray for those struggling against the powers of darkness, that God will deliver them.

> *This is no afternoon athletic contest that we'll walk away from and forget about in a couple of hours. This is for keeps, a life-or-death fight to the finish against the Devil and all his angels (Ephesians 6:11-12, THE MESSAGE)*

CONTACT: Ambassador Speakers Bureau, P.O. Box 50358, Nashville, TN 37205

147

Courtesy of Marc Klaas

Mark Klaas with Polly in 1991

Marc Klaas
Founder and President,
Marc Klaas Foundation for Children

POINT OF IMPACT: Marc Klaas has lived every parent's nightmare. In 1993 his daughter, Polly, was kidnapped at knifepoint from her bedroom in Petaluma, California. A massive search—compared by the FBI to that conducted in the case of the Lindbergh baby kidnapping—ended two months later with the discovery of the 12-year-old's body near an abandoned sawmill. Her killer, an ex-convict with a history of kidnapping women, was caught and convicted. Since his daughter's death, Marc Klaas has devoted his life to protecting children. In 1994 he formed the Marc Klaas Foundation for Children (now the Klaas Kids Foundation), which has spurred a series of reforms in the criminal justice system, including changes in how authorities handle missing children cases and the enactment of tough new laws for dealing with repeat offenders, especially those who prey on children. According to Officer Mike Meese, who handled Polly's case, "The FBI now has a much closer involvement with local law enforcement and even developed a protocol for handling cases based on this kidnapping."

His daughter's murder prompted change.

QUOTABLE: "The happiest day of my life was when Polly was born, and the worst was when they told me she was dead."

BEHIND THE SCENES: Prior to Polly's abduction, Klaas was a manager of a Hertz car rental franchise. He and Polly's mother, Eve Nichols, have been divorced since Polly was two years old. His current wife, Violet, works at a real estate agency. They live in Sausalito, California.

PRAYER STARTERS:

- There are 12 attempted stranger abductions of a child daily (at least one of these children will never be heard from again); one child is murdered every four hours. Pray for the safety of our kids, and for better laws to protect them.
- The Klaas Kids Foundation is funded by donations. Pray for major sponsors to partner financially with the Foundation.
- Ask God to bless Klaas with peace and healing, and his marriage with love.

Rescue me, O LORD, from evil men; protect me from men of violence. Psalm 140:1

CONTACT: KlaasKids Foundation, P.O. Box 925, Sausalito, CA 94966; e-mail: klaas@crl.com, www.klaaskids.org

Denzel Washington

Actor

Archive Photo

POINT OF IMPACT: Asked to name his priorities, Denzel Washington replies, "God, family, work, football." Achieving great success in three of the four has made him unique in Hollywood and a powerful role model. He earned an Oscar for his work in *Glory,* starred in other big-grossing films like *The Pelican Brief, Crimson Tide, Philadelphia,* and *Malcolm X,* and now earns $12 million per movie. Director Kenneth Branagh says, "[Denzel] has intellectual weight, spiritual gravity, and a powerful sexual and romantic presence." He's been happily married to Pauletta Pearson, an actress and cabaret singer, for 18 years. They have four children—John David, Katia, Malcolm, and Olivia. "When we had that first child, acting became making a living. The child was life. It's an absolute miracle that happens." And tying the whole package together: "I think every event in my life has been touched by God," he says simply. They attend an evangelical church in Los Angeles.

This star knows what matters.

QUOTABLE: "I want [my children] to realize that you don't have to stab anybody in the back. You don't have to scratch anybody's eyes out. Just be honest, work hard and have faith. That will take them further in life than anything."

BEHIND THE SCENES: Five years ago, Denzel, 46, and Pauletta renewed their vows on a vacation to South Africa; Archbishop Desmond Tutu officiated. The couple is very active in charitable causes, among them the Boys & Girls Clubs of America, the Nelson Mandela Children's Fund, and an AIDS clinic.

PRAYER STARTERS:

- Give thanks for Washington's strong professional and spiritual example. Ask God to bless his career and charitable work with success.
- Pray for Denzel and Pauletta's marriage—ask for spiritual and moral protection for them in their high-profile, high-pressure circumstances.
- Ask for safety for their children today, and a growing love for Jesus.

As God's chosen people, holy and dearly loved, clothe yourselves with compassion, kindness, humility, gentleness and patience. Colossians 3:12

CONTACT: ICM, 8942 Wilshire Blvd., Beverly Hills, CA 90211

Courtesy of Major League Soccer

Ronaldo Luiz Nazario da Lima

Soccer Player

POINT OF IMPACT: Ronaldo Luiz Nazario da Lima is, in every sense, the biggest name in soccer, and perhaps in the entire world of sports. Only Michael Jordan could claim to have greater name recognition outside the United States, and he's retired. In 1996-97, soccer's world federation named da Lima World Player of the Year, which *Sports Illustrated* described as "a title with few rivals in the international arena." At only 24 he hammers in goals the way Mark McGwire hits homers, is the highest-paid player in soccer history, and is often compared with the legendary Pele. Ronaldo merchandise is sold on every continent, and fans swoon over him as they would an international rock star. When da Lima appeared in cyberspace in 1998 to promote a Rome-based United Nations food bank, the server took 6 million hits in 30 minutes, then crashed. Da Lima is also involved in many social causes in his native Brazil, including programs that get poor kids out of the slums and into soccer camps.

His legs are insured for $26 million.

QUOTABLE: How he feels after scoring: "That particular moment is difficult to describe. Because you are out of this world. You can't hear anyone. You don't see anyone. You are blind, you are deaf, you just want to run and scream."

BEHIND THE SCENES: Da Lima grew up in a slum outside Rio de Janeiro—the family house had no doors or windowpanes. When he signed his first pro contract at 16, he used some of the money to reupholster the family's tattered furniture. Today, his legs are insured for $26 million. He is engaged to Suzanne Werner and lives in Milan, Italy.

PRAYER STARTERS:

- About the source of his talent, Ronaldo says, "Mainly, it is God." Pray that through word and deed he would use his talent to bring glory to God.
- Pray that da Lima's example inspires impoverished children worldwide.
- Ask for da Lima's safety and health. Pray that those who love the Lord would be a source of encouragement and wisdom in da Lima's life today.

If anyone serves, he should do it with the strength God provides. 1 Peter 4:11

CONTACT: www.ronaldinho.com

Bill Hybels

Senior Pastor,
Willow Creek Community Church

Courtesy of Willow Creek Community Church

POINT OF IMPACT: Under Hybels' innovative direction, Willow Creek Community Church, located outside Chicago, has become the second largest church in America. He emphasizes a "seeker sensitive" approach to worship that has had a major influence on churches in the United States and the world. The proof: about 16,000 people attend the 4,500-seat auditorium. Willow Creek stands out from mainline churches in several ways: attendees are encouraged not to give financially until they're sold on the church; they're matched, via informal tests and counselors, to one of the church's 90 ministries; and both men and women are encouraged to participate in leadership roles. Hybels developed his church model from a survey of the unchurched he took 15 years ago. He became convinced that what people wanted was a "positive, Bible-centered church that appealed to their desire for anonymity, gave them plenty of time to make a decision for Christ, and provided excellence in programming, creativity, and contemporary worship."

His "seeker sensitive" church is a model around the world.

QUOTABLE: Part of his message to President Clinton, with whom he has met regularly since the president's inauguration: "Know in the depth of your being that you are loved by God, and not incidentally by many, many of us."

BEHIND THE SCENES: Among his bestselling books are *Rediscovering Church* (coauthored with his wife, Lynne), *Too Busy Not to Pray*, and *Becoming a Contagious Christian* (with Mark Mittelberg). He also serves on the board of World Vision. He and his wife have two children, Shauna and Todd.

PRAYER STARTERS:

- Give thanks for the fresh ideas and energy that Bill Hybels has brought to church ministries, and for the many who have been influenced for the gospel by Willow Creek Community Church.
- Pray that Hybels and his pastoral team would be sensitive to the leading of God and pursue without compromise their mission to the unchurched.
- Ask God to surround the Hybels family with safety and peace; pray that Bill and Lynne's marriage will bring joy and fulfillment to them both.

The Son of Man came to seek and to save what was lost. Luke 19:10

CONTACT: 67 E. Algonquin Rd., South Barrington, IL 60010-6143

General Henry H. Shelton
Chairman of the Joint Chiefs of Staff

POINT OF IMPACT: Before the crisis in Yugoslavia, most Americans didn't recognize his name. But as Chairman of the Joint Chiefs of Staff, Henry Shelton is the president's principal military advisor and America's "general of generals." Prior to his appointment, Shelton led the U.S. Special Operations Command and boasts a stellar 35-year military career. He's the third Army general in a row to head the Joint Chiefs, and the first general ever plucked from the Special Forces Command for the military's top post. An imposing North Carolinian, Shelton frames his top priorities for the military: "Are we ready? Are we taking care of our people and their families? And are we preparing adequately for the future?"

He's the President's principal military adviser.

QUOTABLE: From a recent Memorial Day address: "Since 1869, the nation has consecrated this holiday to the memory of Americans who have died in war. Since then, many more American men and women have nobly fought and died, proving that our ideals and way of life will continue to be challenged and will be won anew only at extreme cost."

BEHIND THE SCENES: Four-star General Shelton, 57, earned degrees from North Carolina State University and Auburn University. He did two tours in Vietnam, headed a joint task force in Haiti, and spent seven months as part of Operations Desert Shield and Desert Storm. He and his wife Carolyn have three sons.

PRAYER STARTERS:

- Give thanks for peace in North America. Pray for peace in the world.
- Pray that Shelton—along with the president, the Secretary of Defense, the National Security Adviser, and other key military and civilian advisers—will humbly seek divine guidance in their decisions today.
- Ask the Lord to bless General Shelton and his family with peace, joy, and a growing awareness of His purposes for their lives.

> *You give me your shield of victory, and your right hand sustains me; you stoop down to make me great. Psalm 18:35*

CONTACT: 9999 Joint Staff, The Pentagon, Washington, DC 20318

Jewel

Singer, Songwriter

Archive Photo

POINT OF IMPACT: It wasn't long ago that Jewel Kilcher, 26, was living in her VW van and washing her hair in Kmart bathrooms. Since winning the 1995 American Music Award for Best New Artist, though, she's also become a bestselling poet (*Night Without Armor*) and an actress (*Ride with the Devil*). *Time* magazine, which featured the singer on its cover, exclaimed that Jewel has "the improbable match of slender youth and that voice—an astonishingly versatile instrument ranging from soul-shattering yodels to the most eloquent of whispers to arch Cole Porter-ish recitatives." After her parents divorced, she lived with her father and brothers in a rustic cabin in Alaska. She learned to perform by trailing her father to bars and Eskimo villages. After high school, she sang in coffee houses, living out of her van. Her first album, *Pieces of You*, sold 10 million; her second, *Spirit*, was released in 1998.

Her voice astonishes critics.

QUOTABLE: "People look at me in magazines and feel like I'm a phenomenon, as if what I've accomplished is beyond their ability. I tell them to knock it off. If you respect what I've done, then do something yourself."

BEHIND THE SCENES: A turning point occurred in Jewel's life when at age 14 she was "adopted" by an Ottawa Indian tribe. Through her participation in a ceremony called a "talking circle," she realized the power and gift of the spoken word and determined that she would do more than write—she would sing. Jewel's first love is horses—in her teens she had one named Clearwater.

PRAYER STARTERS:

- Give thanks for the wonder of music—and especially today for how music speaks so powerfully for the hopes and dreams of the young.
- Pray that Jewel's artistry in music and poetry will draw her audience into an encounter with truth and a desire to know God.
- Ask God to bless Jewel with safety, meaningful relationships, success, and a growing sense of His presence and purposes in her life.

Worship the LORD with gladness; come before him with joyful songs.
Psalm 100:2

CONTACT: e-mail: JewelJK@aol.com

153

Copyright © Kathleen King.

Paul Allen

Chairman, Vulcan Ventures

POINT OF IMPACT: Paul Allen is cofounder of Microsoft (where he engineered such breakthrough products as MS-DOS and Word) with Bill Gates, and is currently chairman of Vulcan Ventures, where he pursues his vision of a "wired world" that links entertainment with technology through a variety of independent companies. Allen's current passion is interactive TV. He recently bought two cable companies, combining them into the nation's number-seven cable system, with 2.4 million subscribers. *Time* magazine and *Vanity Fair* have named him among the most powerful people in the telecommunications industry; *Entertainment Weekly* calls Allen one of the most powerful men in Hollywood, where he has invested in DreamWorks and his own studio. Now in his late forties, Allen owns the Portland Trailblazers and Seattle Seahawks and is worth $25 billion.

He envisions a "wired world."

QUOTABLE: On what it's like to be a billionaire: "It's . . . a lot . . . of . . . money. . . . Hopefully, you find some way to put that in charitable hands, to do something good for society as a whole."

BEHIND THE SCENES: He left Microsoft in 1983 after a battle with Hodgkin's disease, which led him to reevaluate his priorities and devote himself to causes he truly believes in. Through his six foundations, he's donated more than $100 million to various causes. A bachelor, Allen has homes in Mercer Island, Washington; Beverly Hills, California; Manhattan; France; and aboard a 199-foot yacht.

PRAYER STARTERS:

- Give thanks for Paul Allen's record of philanthropy and compassion.
- Pray that Allen and others working on the leading edge of interactive media will pursue their objectives with integrity and with forethought for positive applications.
- Ask God to give Paul Allen longevity and fulfillment, and a richness of spirit to match his personal wealth.

> *Remember the LORD your God, for it is he who gives you the ability to produce wealth. Deuteronomy 8:18*

CONTACT: Vulcan Northwest, Inc., 110 110th Ave. N.E., Suite 550, Bellevue, WA 98004-5840

Michael Crichton
Bestselling Author, Film Director

Archive Photo

POINT OF IMPACT: Few writers have had more success in today's popular culture than Michael Crichton, who is called "father of the techno-thriller." He has written 24 novels, ten of them bestsellers, including *Sphere, Jurassic Park,* and *The Lost World.* Eight of his books have been turned into movies (he directed six of them himself), including *Jurassic Park.* Crichton, a 1969 Harvard med-school graduate, is also creator of the Emmy Award-winning television program *ER.* While his work encompasses intricate scientific knowledge, it also influences the way viewers and readers perceive and grapple with major social issues, including sexual harassment, genetic manipulation, dangers of technology, international economics, and corruption of media.

He's the father of the techno-thriller.

QUOTABLE: "Quitting medicine to become a writer struck most people like quitting the Supreme Court to become a bail bondsman."

BEHIND THE SCENES: Crichton made it through medical school despite almost passing out each time he had to draw blood. Every year of medical school he tried to quit, but family and friends persuaded him to continue. Crichton paid his way through med school by writing thrillers under pseudonyms. Even during school, he wrote about 10,000 words a day. Crichton is 58 and lives in California with his wife, Ann Martin, and a daughter.

PRAYER STARTERS:

- Ask for Michael Crichton and his family to encounter God's pursuing love and surpassing peace.
- Give thanks for Crichton's creative gifts. Pray that he will successfully pursue projects that educate and uplift viewers and readers.
- Crichton is an atheist with a longstanding interest in the paranormal. Pray that he will come to read the Bible and be changed by its truths—"Man does not live by bread alone, but on every word that comes from the mouth of God" (Matthew 4:4).

> *We fix our eyes not on what is seen, but on what is unseen. For what is seen is temporary, but what is unseen is eternal. 2 Corinthians 4:18*

CONTACT: 433 N. Camden Dr. #500, Beverly Hills, CA 90210

Jesse Helms
Senator, North Carolina

POINT OF IMPACT: For more than 25 years, archconservative icon Senator Jesse Helms has butted heads with the most powerful people in Washington and hasn't budged an inch. His anticommunist, antiabortion, antigay rights stands are legendary—as is his support for segregation, the tobacco industry, nuclear armament, and elimination of U.S. international aid. Helms' often-successful efforts to delay, in some cases halt presidential nominations or to sabotage legislation, have earned him the nickname "Senator No." In his fifth term, at age 79, he's more powerful than ever as the imperious chairman of the Senate's foreign relations committee. Using his position, he's pushed U.S. foreign policy firmly to the right. While the *Weekly Standard* in Washington calls Helms "the most important conservative of the last 25 years," the *New York Times* calls him "a mean-spirited, loose-lipped legislator" who has become a "global liability for the nation."

He butts heads with liberals.

QUOTABLE: "The Lord did not make me impossible of error. All I've had to offer you is the total dedication in serving you as best I know how. And I've always leveled with you knowing that everyone will not agree with me."

BEHIND THE SCENES: According to the *Los Angeles Times*, Helms learned his authoritarian ways from his six-foot five-inch father, the local fire and police chief. He is married to Dorothy Jane Coble and has three children: Jane, Nancy, and Charles.

PRAYER STARTERS:

- Pray that Senator Helms' influence in Washington will be for good, combining integrity and respect for tradition with compassion and insight.
- Pray that Congressional leaders will exercise wisdom in resolving vexing issues in a rapidly changing world—e.g., military spending, immigration, foreign aid, and foreign relations.
- Ask God to bless the Helmses today with health, safety, and contentment.

As we have opportunity, let us do good to all people. Galatians 6:10

CONTACT: 403 Dirksen Senate Office Building, Washington, DC 20510-3301

Bill Nye

Host of Bill Nye, The Science Guy

Courtesy of KCTS-TV, Seattle

POINT OF IMPACT: He's done for science what no book could do. As host of Disney's six-time Emmy Award-winning television show *Bill Nye, The Science Guy*, Bill Nye combines his love of science with his own blend of hip comedy, MTV-type graphics, and zany camera moves to make science more fun and accessible. Beloved by adults and kids alike, an estimated 4.4 million viewers catch the show seven days a week on PBS and many commercial stations. Igniting interest in science among youth is a big deal in an age when many fear that scientific advances are outstripping the number of students in the next generation who are interested in science or capable of keeping up. *Family PC* magazine says, "The Science Guy should have an Honorary Degree in Imagineering." At the invitation of President Bill Clinton, Nye visited Washington, DC to talk about science education at the White House Conference on Children's Television.

He makes science a blast.

QUOTABLE: "I want people to get more excited about science, so in the future, we'll have more scientists. If we don't have a scientifically literate society, this is a formula for disaster."

BEHIND THE SCENES: Bill Nye's career began when friends pressured him into entering a Steve Martin look-alike contest. After winning, he began performing as a stand-up comic. "It occurred to me to do some of the science demonstrations at the comedy shows," he told *USA Today*. ". . . and that's when the thing was born." The Seattle-based scientist rides his bicycle to work and has tutored inner-city preteens and teens as part of the I Have a Dream program.

PRAYER STARTERS:

- Pray for Bill Nye's spiritual well-being and for continued success in his professional endeavors.
- "My modest little goal is to change the world," says Nye. Pray that science education will engage both the imaginations and the spirits of students.
- Pray for your child's science teacher today—for encouragement, imagination, and a new awareness of God's creative power.

> *The heavens declare the glory of God; the skies proclaim the work of his hands. Psalm 19:1*

CONTACT: KCTS TV, 401 Mercer St., Seattle, WA 98109; e-mail: billnye@nyelabs.com

Rich Stearns

President, World Vision

Courtesy of World Vision

POINT OF IMPACT: A trip to Haiti in the eighties changed Rich Stearns' life. He visited a community where World Vision was building a well. "It was something very simple," he explains. "It struck me how little they probably needed to make their lives better." Today he's president of World Vision, the largest privately funded Christian relief and development organization in the world. It raises more than $350 million a year to provide food, education, health care, economic assistance, and the gospel to more than 60 million people in almost 100 countries, and runs one of the world's largest child-sponsorship programs. According to the *Seattle Times,* World Vision's size and impact make Stearns a key figure in helping the poor worldwide.

He helps the poor around the globe.

QUOTABLE: On his previous job as president and CEO of Lenox: "I'm doing something that has a tangible effect on people's lives. At Lenox, we made fine dishes. Our china is in the White House. But they are just dishes."

BEHIND THE SCENES: At his previous job, Stearns had an eight-foot-long desk, a view of quiet ponds, a company-owned, sky-blue Jaguar, and a marbled office bathroom. At World Vision, he has a windowless cubicle and uses the employee restroom. And for those perks, he took an 80-percent pay cut. Stearns, 51, is married to Reneé and they have five children: Sarah, Andrew, Hannah, Peter, and Grace. They live near Seattle.

PRAYER STARTERS:

- Give thanks for the mercy, provision, and evangelism that World Vision delivers in needy corners of the globe. Ask for more supporting partners.

- Pray that Rich Stearns will listen to the "still, small voice" of God's leading today, and that he'll benefit from a unified and proactive management team. Pray, too, for World Vision aid workers worldwide, that God's power will keep them safe and flow through them for the good of others.

- Ask the Lord to surround the Stearns family with His grace and peace.

I was hungry and you gave me something to eat. Matthew 25:35

CONTACT: P.O. Box 9716, Federal Way, WA 98063; e-mail: mpublow@worldvision.org

Jeff Gordon
Stock-Car Racer

Archive Photo

POINT OF IMPACT: Stock-car racing is the fastest growing spectator sport in the United States, and one big reason is the man everyone calls "the Michael Jordan of the racing world": Jeff Gordon. In a sport where few participants start winning before the age of 30, Gordon is already rewriting the record books at 29. But winning races is only part of Gordon's mystique. He's young, he's married to a former Miss Winston Cup, he's been named on *People* magazine's list of America's Most Beautiful People, and he's won almost $30 million in prize money since 1993. He also prefers milk to champagne after winning, he never swears, he donates time and money to several cancer and children's charities, and he's an outspoken Christian. Says Charles Barkley, "He's never in trouble, he's very religious, and he's always kicking butt. What more would you want in an athlete?"

Thousands idolize this godly speedster.

QUOTABLE: "If I win, it allows me to be on a platform to glorify God, and if I finish dead last, it allows me to thank Him for even having the opportunity to race."

BEHIND THE SCENES: While growing up in Charlotte, North Carolina, Jeff was beating drivers 17 and older when he was only nine. He won three sprint-car track championships before he was old enough to get a driver's license. Today, he spends every night before a race attending a Bible study with his wife, Brooke. Before the race starts, she selects a passage of Scripture, types it up, and tapes it to his steering wheel. "They're always different," Gordon says. "It reminds me that I'm able to overcome anything." The Gordons live in Highland Beach, Florida.

PRAYER STARTERS:

- Give thanks for the example of faith and excellence that Jeff Gordon brings to racing.
- Pray that his example would influence many for good, especially those "wanna-be racers" who may tend to mix driving and drinking.
- Pray for Gordon's safety, and for God's best for his marriage and future.

> When the righteous triumph, there is great elation; but when the wicked rise to power, men go into hiding. Proverbs 28:12

CONTACT: Hendrick Motorsports, P.O. Box 9, Harrisburg, NC 28075

Donna Shalala

Secretary of Health and Human Services

AP/Wide World Photos

POINT OF IMPACT: In Washington political circles, Donna Shalala's forceful style has earned her the nickname "Boom Boom." Appointed Secretary of the Department of Health and Human Services by President Clinton in 1993, she runs the nation's largest federal agency with aggressive focus and no-nonsense pragmatism. She's made important gains in the area of health-care reform and was instrumental in bringing Clinton's health-care reform bill to a vote in Congress. Her style has been called "competitive" and "razor sharp" by *Harper's Bazaar,* yet even her critics respect her sincerity. Although she has sometimes been branded a liberal, the 58-year-old is from a culturally conservative background. Shalala continues to work for better funding for Head Start programs, AIDS research, and drug education.

She's got your health in mind.

QUOTABLE: "I am a feminist committed to a wide range of progressive issues who's been a member of the establishment for a long time. I'm one of the few outsiders on the inside."

BEHIND THE SCENES: Of Lebanese-American descent, Shalala was born in Cleveland, Ohio to working-class parents. In announcing her appointment, then-President-elect Clinton noted her "astonishing leadership abilities"—and her love of mountain climbing. "My parents taught me to never give up," says Shalala, "whether scaling a peak or forging a career, and I think that's a good lesson for everyone."

PRAYER STARTERS:

- Thank God for Donna Shalala's work to improve health care and social services in America.
- Pray for wisdom, vision, and integrity at all levels of the federal human services network. Pray that Shalala would seek God's will today.
- Ask the Lord to protect Shalala and her family, and draw them to Himself.

> *"I will restore you to health and heal your wounds," declares the* LORD.
> *Jeremiah 30:17*

CONTACT: Secretary of Health and Human Services, 440D Hubert Humphrey Building, 200 Independence Ave. S.W., Washington, DC 20201

Leonardo DiCaprio

Actor

Archive Photo

POINT OF IMPACT: Leonardo DiCaprio first received critical raves in *This Boy's Life* with Robert DeNiro. Next, as Johnny Depp's retarded younger brother in *What's Eating Gilbert Grape* he was, at age 19, nominated for an Academy Award. Then he starred in what became the biggest-grossing picture of all time, *Titanic*. The movie quickly propelled DiCaprio to stardom, spawning "DiCaprio fever" reminiscent of Beatle Mania. Tearful, screaming fans mauled the actor in public, and thousands more gobbled up photos and articles about him (fittingly, his next movie was Woody Allen's *Celebrity*). No one's talking Oscar these days, and speculation abounds: Is DiCaprio only Hollywood's flavor of the month, or on his way to Tom Cruise-like success? For his starring role in *The Beach* he received no less than $20 million.

Is he more than a teen heartthrob?

QUOTABLE: "School, I never truly got the knack of. I could never focus on things I didn't want to learn. I used to, like, take half of the [kids in] school and do break-dancing skits with my friend in front of them at lunchtime."

BEHIND THE SCENES: DiCaprio got his name when his pregnant mother was visiting a museum in Florence. While admiring a Leonardo da Vinci painting, she felt the baby kick. The rest is marquee history. DiCaprio's father approves scripts and his mother manages his finances.

PRAYER STARTERS:

- Do you know a teenager who's enamored of DiCaprio or another film heart-throb? Pray that she or he will let the Lord shape and protect their dreams and ideals, and use their passions to draw them toward His best.
- Pray that DiCaprio will use his influence responsibly, choosing to be a standout for good life choices regardless of the pull of others.
- Ask the Lord to bless him—professionally, personally, and spiritually.

> *He who gets wisdom loves his own soul; he who cherishes understanding prospers. Proverbs 19:8*

CONTACT: 955 South Carrillo Drive, Suite 300, Los Angeles, CA 90048

Ralph Reed
Political Consultant

POINT OF IMPACT: Ralph Reed is best known as the founder of the Christian Coalition, a 1.9-million-member political force with clout at every level of the Republican Party. Recently, Reed left the Christian Coalition to start Century Strategies, a political consulting firm whose goal is to help elect 100 religious-right, "pro-family, pro-faith, pro-free enterprise" candidates to Congress over the next decade. At one point Reed was informally advising no fewer than seven men with aspirations for the presidency. At only 39, Reed's clout in Washington is astounding. He's able to propel candidates into the spotlight and connect them with networks of activists and contributors. *USA Today* says, "Reed offers politicians not only smart strategic analysis but also contacts with the Christian right throughout the nation. To many Republicans, the package is irresistible."

He hopes to make Congress pro-family.

QUOTABLE: "Be who you are. Say who you are. Don't apologize or be defensive about holding moral values. And more than likely you will win."

BEHIND THE SCENES: Reed says the turning point in his life and career came when he was in college and drinking heavily. After observing a drunk congressman in a restaurant, he changed his ways. "I just thought, if I'm going to represent the values that I'm fighting for in my public life, I want to make sure that in my private life I exemplify those same values." Reed's private life includes wife Joanne and four children. They live in Atlanta, Georgia.

PRAYER STARTERS:

- After Reed quit drinking, he experienced a spiritual awakening. "When God got ahold of him," his mother says, "it was just like somebody turned a switch." Pray that he will guard his integrity and listen for God's leading.
- Ask for blessing, safety, and peace for the Reed family.
- Pray that conservative politicians would increasingly combine compassion, humility, and personal virtue with their public positions on right and wrong.

Be wise in the way you act toward outsiders; make the most of every opportunity. Let your conversation be always full of grace. Colossians 4:5-6

CONTACT: c/o 277 Mallory Station Rd., Franklin, TN 37064; e-mail: online@premierespeakers.com.

Jocelyn Bell Burnell

Astrophysicist

POINT OF IMPACT: In 1967 Jocelyn Bell Burnell was a graduate student at Cambridge University when she came upon unusually regular radio waves. She jokingly labeled them "LGMs" for "Little Green Men." She had discovered the first pulsar—superdense, rotating neutron stars that beam flashes of radiation as they spin, somewhat like a lighthouse. To find it, she'd analyzed by hand 400 feet of paper chart that represented four days of complete coverage of the sky. Her supervisor Tony Hewish received the Nobel Prize in Physics for this discovery, triggering a public uproar, as many thought the award should be shared with Bell Burnell. Nonetheless, her professional contributions have resulted in many awards over the last 30 years and have significantly influenced the study of astrophysics. Now head of the physics department at Open University in England, Bell Burnell is one of only two female full professors in Britain. She describes herself as "a role model, a spokeswoman, a representative, and a promoter of women in science."

She's a promoter of women in science.

QUOTABLE: "I've been very lucky and it's been very good fun."

BEHIND THE SCENES: Born in Belfast, Northern Ireland, Burnell, 57, is a gentle woman with a lyrical Irish-Scottish brogue. "I started by failing," she quips. At age 11 she took an examination which was part of Britain's stringent requirements for pursuing higher education—and failed. It spurred her family to send her to a boarding school in England, where she met up with an inspiring physics teacher. She married in 1968 and has one son.

PRAYER STARTERS:

- Thank God for the impact Bell Burnell has on discoveries in astronomy, and for her influence on students as she shares her love of the heavens.
- She says her research has convinced her of the existence of God. Pray that she will have a far-reaching impact among her nonbelieving peers.
- Pray that she will enjoy good health and family blessings.

> You alone are the LORD. You made the heavens . . . and all their starry host. . . . You give life to everything, and the multitudes of heaven worship you. Nehemiah 9:6

CONTACT: e-mail: S.J.B.Burnell@open.ac.uk

Archive Photo

Billy Corgan
Singer, Smashing Pumpkins

POINT OF IMPACT: Despite their name, the Smashing Pumpkins have nothing to do with Halloween. They are Billy Corgan, James Iha, and D'Arcy Wretzky—one of the most successful and influential alternative rock bands of recent years. Yet perhaps their greater legacy is as philanthropists. They spent a large portion of 1998 on a 15-city charity tour that made $2.8 million. They donated 100 percent of the ticket sales to various nonprofit groups—mostly for children—which put the band at a loss for covering the tour's expenses. Pretty impressive, considering they're part of a world littered with drug casualties and bands decimated by ego and excess. Their latest album, *Adore,* nominated for a Grammy, contains less of the usual pessimism and anger the Pumpkins are famous for—the music is more hopeful. On the other hand, the band is revered for their unpredictability. "If they were more consistent, they'd doubtless be a less interesting band," says Virgin Records.

His band gives back a lot.

QUOTABLE: "Talk is cheap. The [charity] money is very important, on a literal level. But the rippling effect of the symbolism and trying to influence other people around us is hopefully going to be an even longer-lasting legacy of what we are trying to do."—Billy Corgan

BEHIND THE SCENES: The Smashing Pumpkins have always tried to keep their ticket prices low because they know what it is like to work at a record store or coffee shop and not have money for concert tickets. Corgan is separated from his wife; D'Arcy and Iha are single. They all reside in Chicago.

PRAYER STARTERS:

- Give thanks for the charitable commitments of Billy Corgan and his band.
- Pray for a deep spiritual awakening in Corgan and his bandmates, that their influence on music fans would be redemptive in every way.
- Ask God to keep the Pumpkins safe in a risk-filled world, whole in body and spirit, and always listening for His voice.

He put a new song in my mouth, a hymn of praise to our God. Psalm 40:3

CONTACT: Smashing Pumpkins Fan Club, P.O. Box 578010, Chicago, IL 60657

Carlos Annacondia

Evangelist

Photo by Pastor Charlie Sweet, Utica, NY

POINT OF IMPACT: Already a successful Argentinian businessman, super-evangelist Carlos Annacondia came to Christ in 1979 during a crusade. Today, his vision is to evangelize Argentina and the rest of South and Central America. He's world-renowned for miracles, healings, and deliverance, and an estimated 2 million people have received salvation through his ministry in recent years. C. Peter Wagner and others consider his ministry one of the driving forces behind the Argentine Revival, which has swept Latin America and has been sustained for more than 15 years. He is considered a father of the revival that has also touched Pensacola and Toronto. Annacondia secures a broad base of support from pastors and other Christian leaders in the target areas for his revivals. He's had no formal theological training.

He's a force for spiritual revival.

QUOTABLE: "The crucial factor is this: In any city where I do a crusade, if the pastors are in 10 percent unity, there's 10 percent power at my meetings. If the pastors are in 80 percent unity, there's 80 percent power. The degree of unity among the pastors in a city determines the degree of power in which I can minister."

BEHIND THE SCENES: Though soft-spoken, Annacondia is best-known for his passionate tirades against demonic power. When he ministers in Argentina, sometimes people involved in occult practices scream or writhe on the ground until trained deliverance ministers order the demonic spirits to leave. His popular book *Listen to Me, Satan!* was released by Creation House. He and his wife, Maria Lujan Revagliatti, have nine children and live in Buenos Aires.

PRAYER STARTERS:

- Thank God for the ministry of Carlos Annacondia and other evangelists like him who are spreading the gospel and bringing renewal to the church.
- Pray for revival on every continent, and that God's name may be glorified.
- Ask God to bless and protect Annacondia and his family from spiritual and physical harm. Ask God to to surround Annacondia with mature leaders.

> *He commanded us to preach to the people and to testify that he is the one whom God appointed as judge of the living and the dead. Acts 10:42*

CONTACT: c/o Ed Silvoso, Harvest Evangelism, 6155 Alamaden Expressway, Suite 400, San Jose, CA 95120

Archive Photo

Sonia Gandhi
Leader, Congress Party, India

POINT OF IMPACT: In recent years, it's been increasingly hard to put a single face on the seeming chaos of Indian democracy. Governments rise and fall within months of each other in this nation of nearly 1 billion. But one name still speaks of India's greatest hopes and fears—Sonia Gandhi. She is the wife of one assassinated Gandhi (Rajiv) and the daughter-in-law of another (Indira), both prime ministers. Yet Sonia Gandhi is Italian by birth and, at 54, has never run for office or held a government post. In 1998 she emerged as the leader of the Congress Party, India's largest, though in mid-1999, in the midst of running for prime minister, she offered to step down as a candidate. Whatever develops, Gandhi is likely to remain a dominant player in India's future. A Roman Catholic, she has become an Indian citizen and speaks Hindi.

Just her name speaks of India's greatest hopes and fears.

QUOTABLE: "Though born in a foreign land, I chose India as my country. I am a daughter of India, and I will remain so till my last breath."

BEHIND THE SCENES: Gandhi is almost aggressively shy and treats the press like a contagion. She has two children and lives in New Delhi.

PRAYER STARTERS:

- India faces daunting economic problems with a historic mix of resignation and resourcefulness. Pray for wise leaders to be elected into office to guide the country into prosperous and secure future.
- Pray for the protection of Sonia Gandhi—as with the Kennedy family in the United States, the Gandhi clan carries a tragic legacy of political assassinations. Pray that Sonia will seek and obey God's purposes for her public and private life.
- Ask for the Lord to bless Gandhi and her family, and draw them to Himself.

> *The LORD will protect him and preserve his life; he will bless him in the land and not surrender him to the desire of his foes. Psalm 41:2*

CONTACT: shalu@indiancongress.org

Ruth Westheimer
Therapist

Archive Photo

POINT OF IMPACT: Dr. Ruth Westheimer is a world-renowned psychosexual therapist and America's most famous dispenser of sexual advice. She appears on numerous radio and TV programs, including Lifetime's *The Dr. Ruth Show* and King Features Entertainment's *Ask Dr. Ruth*. She's authored 15 books and pioneers what she refers to as "sexual literacy"—a credo that emphasizes fulfillment and taking responsibility, but declines to address sexuality in terms of moral values. She's passionate about preventing unintended pregnancies and sexually transmitted diseases. It was her experience working for Planned Parenthood, she says, that led her to study human sexuality. Widowed and the mother of two, she is presently an adjunct professor at New York University. She travels often to speak, and has twice been named College Lecturer of the Year.

She offers advice on sex to millions.

QUOTABLE: On her most popular book: "I didn't want to do *Sex for Dummies*. I said, 'I don't write for dummies. I write for intelligent people.' Then I looked at other books in the Dummies series and . . . saw they were very interesting. Maybe I could prevent an unintended pregnancy or somebody from getting AIDS."

BEHIND THE SCENES: Born in Germany, she was ten years old when her parents sent her to a Jewish orphanage in Switzerland to avoid the Nazi rampage. At 16, Westheimer went to Palestine, where she fought as a member of the Haganah for an independent Jewish state. "I am really very pleased every time when I go to Israel to say, 'Look, I was part of that effort of creating a country for Jews.'"

PRAYER STARTERS:

- Thank God for blessing us with the wonders and joy of sexuality.
- Ask God to bless Dr. Ruth today, and to make His love known to her in a profound way, gently guiding her toward truth.
- Pray for all those seeking Dr. Ruth's advice—that they would make sexual choices that are truly best for them and in line with God's will for their lives.
- Pray for people everywhere who are confused or hurting about their sexuality.

You are not your own; you were bought at a price. Therefore honor God with your body. 1 Corinthians 6:19-20

CONTACT: www.drruth.com

Hugh Ross

Physicist

Courtesy of Hugh Ross

POINT OF IMPACT: Hugh Ross was not raised as a Christian. However, his logical bent eventually caused him to study the Scriptures out of curiosity, and he came to the rational conclusion that the Bible is true. Today, Ross is still amazed at how many people believe in God without checking the evidence. His life focus has been to bridge the perceived gap between science and faith; he believes the two should be allies, not enemies. Ross earned his Ph.D. in astronomy from the University of Toronto and researched galaxies and quasars at the California Institute of Technology. He is the founder of Reasons to Believe, a worldwide ministry whose mission is to affirm the scientific accuracy of the Bible. He believes his work is a faith-building discovery: "Every discovery about the cosmos adds more evidence to the already weighty case for a transcendent, personal Creator."

He bridges the gap between science and faith.

QUOTABLE: "As a physicist, I have never seen a fundamental particle called a neutrino. But I have faith in its existence and act accordingly because of certain well-established facts. As a Christian, I have never seen God. But I have faith in His existence and act accordingly because of well-established facts."

BEHIND THE SCENES: He's an ordained minister on staff at the Sierra Madre Congregational Church. Ross and his wife, Kathy, have two sons, Joel and David. They live in Pasadena, California.

PRAYER STARTERS:

- Praise God for Christian scientists like Hugh Ross, who are using their gifts and expertise to lead others to a greater faith and understanding of God's glory.
- Pray that Christians will not allow themselves to be contentiously divided over differing theories of how God created the universe.
- Ask God to bless Dr. Ross and his family with safety, honor, and contentment.

> *The heavens declare the glory of God; the skies proclaim the work of his hands. Day after day they pour forth speech; night after night they display knowledge. Psalm 19:1-2*

CONTACT: Reasons to Believe, P.O. Box 5978, Pasadena, CA 91117

Alice Walker

Pulitzer Prize-Winning Author

Archive Photo

POINT OF IMPACT: Feminist icon and social activist Alice Walker is best known for her Pulitzer Prize-winning novel (and popular movie) *The Color Purple*, which was recently named one of the most important books of the past 100 years. Walker has written more than 20 novels and books of poetry and essays since the early seventies, exploring such topics as the experience of American black women, domestic violence, sexual liberation, lesbianism, racial equality, female genital mutilation, and paganism. Her books include *By the Light of My Father's Smile, The Temple of My Familiar,* and *In Search of Our Mothers' Gardens,* which have earned her acclaim as the world's leading black feminist writer. At the same time, 56-year-old Walker's controversially explicit prose has made her one of the most frequently banned authors in U.S. schools and libraries.

She's a leading black feminist writer.

QUOTABLE: "No one could wish for a more advantageous heritage than that bequeathed to the black writer in the South: a compassion for the earth, a trust in humanity beyond our knowledge of evil, and an abiding love of justice. We inherit a great responsibility . . . for we must give voice to centuries not only of silent bitterness and hate but also of neighborly kindness and sustaining love."

BEHIND THE SCENES: At age eight, Walker was playing with her brothers when she was accidently blinded in her right eye by a BB gun pellet. "I no longer felt like the little girl I was," she remembers. "I felt old, and—because I felt I was unpleasant to look at—filled with shame. I retreated into solitude, and read stories and began to write poems." She has a daughter and lives in Mendocino, California.

PRAYER STARTERS:

- Give thanks for Walker's literary legacy and impact for social justice.
- Pray that her personal views will be powerfully influenced by biblical truths.
- Pray that God's grace and healing will touch Alice Walker today. Ask Him to bless her with well-being in body, mind, and spirit.

> *The LORD watches over the alien and sustains the fatherless and the widow, but he frustrates the ways of the wicked. Psalm 146:9*

CONTACT: Random House, 201 E. 50th St., New York, NY 10022-7703

Archive Photo

Juan Antonio Samaranch
President, International Olympic Committee (IOC)

POINT OF IMPACT: As president of the IOC since 1980, Juan Antonio Samaranch of Spain is widely considered "the most powerful sports figure in the world," according to the *New York Times*. As such, he has provoked controversy about everything from his role in Franco's fascist regime to his decisions as IOC president: allowing professional athletes to compete in the games; encouraging lucrative partnerships by letting commercial sponsors link their names with the Olympics; granting top Olympic awards to former communist dictators. Samaranch, whose slight build belies his boundless energy, is also instrumental in the fight against drugs in sports. In early '99, the IOC became embroiled in allegations of bribery associated with the placement of the 2002 winter games in Salt Lake City.

His job links the world through sports.

QUOTABLE: "I have the opportunity to meet very important people, heads of state, prime ministers, important business people, and I am always asking about the future of sports and the Olympic movement. I can assure you that always the answers are the same: that sports and the Olympic movement part of sports will be even much more important in our society in the years to come."

BEHIND THE SCENES: Samaranch is the first Hispanic to head the IOC. At 78, he travels more than 100,000 miles each year and works 15 hours a day. He's married and has two grown children. In addition to his native Spanish, he speaks French and English fluently and has a good working knowledge of German and Russian.

PRAYER STARTERS:

- Give thanks for the inspiration of the Olympic Games to challenge thousands of young athletes to aim high.
- Pray for a commitment to the highest ethical standards in all IOC dealings.
- Ask for safety, health, and rest for Samaranch, especially during his travels. Pray for his marriage and family.
- Pray for wisdom and tact for Samaranch. International ties formed because of the Olympics often help pave the way for smoother diplomatic relations.

Your strength will equal your days. Deuteronomy 33:25

CONTACT: IOC, Chateau de Vidy, CH-1007, Lausanne, Switzerland

Jan Karon
Bestselling Author

Courtesy of Penguin

POINT OF IMPACT: Jan Karon's five novels about an Episcopal priest in the fictional small town of Mitford—*At Home in Mitford, A Light in the Window, These High, Green Hills, Out to Canaan,* and *A New Song*—have created "Mitford mania." In 1996, 1997, and 1998, the American Booksellers Association voted her *Mitford* series their favorite books to recommend to customers. Her book *Out to Canaan* reached number five on the *New York Times* bestseller list, leading to numerous "copy-cat" series. Now there's talk in Hollywood about putting Mitford on the big screen, and Hallmark is developing a line of greeting cards based on the series. "Jan Karon," writes *Christianity Today*, "has shown that the world still pines for the consolation of a Christian world-view." Says Karon: "Where else can people find their value system represented? Can you find it in *Vogue* magazine, on *Roseanne,* watching Geraldo? No. But when people go to Mitford, they go home. It's familiar, and it is consoling. And that's what I want to give my readers."

Her books take readers home.

QUOTABLE: "I think there are thousands upon thousands of readers out there looking for a clean read. You can be looking for a casserole recipe in a magazine and all you can find is how to have a better orgasm."

BEHIND THE SCENES: Janice Meredith Karon didn't start writing novels until she was 51. "I stepped out on faith to follow my lifelong dream of being an author. I made real sacrifices and took big risks. But living, it seems to me, is largely about risk." At 62, she lives in Blowing Rock, North Carolina (which her fans visit by the bus load) near her grown daughter, Candace, and her mother.

PRAYER STARTERS:

- Give thanks for Jan Karon's gifts of humane insight and spiritual encouragement to her many readers.
- Praise God for her convincing evocations of interesting, everyday Christians.
- Ask the Lord to bless her personal life with health, joy, and creativity, and her professional life with continued success.

> *Hope does not disappoint us, because God has poured out his love into our hearts by the Holy Spirit, whom he has given us. Romans 5:5*

CONTACT: Penguin USA, 375 Hudson St., New York, NY 10014

Mark Bryan

Author, Crusader

POINT OF IMPACT: As author of *The Prodigal Father* and director of the Boston's Father Project counseling center, Mark Bryan has spent nearly a decade helping thousands of estranged fathers reunite with their kids. A one-time absentee father himself, he knows what he's talking about. *"Prodigal Father* is the book I wish I had read when I was hurting and longing to see my son." The how-to book that encourages dads to reconnect with their kids has been so successful that Oprah Winfrey invited Bryan to speak on her talk show as a "change your life" expert. Bryan has also written *Codes of Love*. As a result of his crusade on behalf of estranged fathers (many of whom he personally counsels), thousands of men have reconciled with children they never knew or whom they abandoned.

He helps "prodigal fathers."

QUOTABLE: On the term "deadbeat dads": "It's shaming and doesn't help solve the problem. It's more true that they are brokenhearted dads. Shame is one of the reasons that fathers become disengaged. If we keep shaming them, we're never going to get them back with their kids."

BEHIND THE SCENES: Bryan became a father when he was 17. He married his girlfriend, but their marriage lasted only three years. When his ex-wife remarried, Bryan dropped out of his son's life and didn't reenter it again until 14 years later. Now he and Scott, 29, enjoy a close relationship. Bryan lives in Massachusetts.

PRAYER STARTERS:

- Give thanks for Mark Bryan's example of reconciliation, and for fathers who are active in their children's lives. Pray for a dad you know who may be facing obstacles in this area.

- Father's Day can be painful for the some 22 million children in the United States who are growing up in homes in which the biological father is absent; half of these see their dads once a year or less. Ask God to comfort them today, and pray that absentee dads will reconnect with their kids. Pray for comfort and strong male role models for children who grow up without fathers.

- Pray that God will continue to bless Mark Bryan's impact on fathers and his own relationship with his son, Scott.

In you the fatherless find compassion. Hosea 14:3

CONTACT: Father Project, 1 Waterhouse St., Cambridge, MA 02138-3615
mark@fatherproject.com

Paul Harvey
Radio Journalist and Commentator

ABC News

POINT OF IMPACT: *"Hello, Americans."* Paul Harvey has been called "the most recognized and trusted voice in the nation." As host of the coast-to-coast *News and Comment* and *The Rest of the Story* radio programs, Harvey shares his optimistic and usually conservative point of view with more than 20 million Americans each week. Harvey is especially influential with older listeners. One internet critic says, "Who still takes Paul Harvey seriously? I called my mom and asked her, and she said that older people still trust him and view him in almost reverential terms as a bastion of truth and integrity." Paul Harvey News is the largest one-man network in America, syndicating his distinctive newscasts to more than 1,200 radio stations, 400 Armed Forces Network stations worldwide, and 300 newspapers. In 1997 Harvey received the Marconi Award, the industry's highest honor.

He's the voice America trusts.

QUOTABLE: "Each morning, I get up like a prospector going panning for gold. I can't wait to get on to the teletypes and telephones and the copier and find out what foolish and heroic things 200 million people have been doing all night for me to talk about."

BEHIND THE SCENES: Harvey literally grew up in radio newsrooms and began making his own radio sets while still a boy. In high school he hung out at the local radio station until they gave him a job. Now in his eighties, Harvey still reportedly rises for work at 4:00 A.M., and he plans to be the voice America trusts well into the next century. He and his wife, Lynne, live in Chicago. They have one son, Paul, Jr.

PRAYER STARTERS:

- Give thanks for Paul Harvey's legacy of upbeat news, traditional values, and common sense that has encouraged millions.
- Ask God to bless the Harvey family today with health and happiness.
- Pray for an elderly person you know today who may derive an important sense of connectedness with the outside world through the commentaries of Paul Harvey.

> *Apply your heart to instruction and your ears to words of knowledge.*
> Proverbs 23:12

CONTACT: 333 N. Michigan Ave., Suite 1600, Chicago, IL 60601

Bill Bradley

Senator, New Jersey

Courtesy of Bill Bradley for President

POINT OF IMPACT: When Bill Bradley announced his retirement from the Senate in 1996, he said, "Politics is broken." But many think he's the guy who can go back in and fix it. In December 1998 Bradley became the first candidate to announce that he was running for president in 2000. Bradley said he wants to "help unleash the enormous potential of the American people" and deal with "an agenda of obligations," including persistent poverty among children and the absence of health insurance for millions. As a senator from 1978 to 1996, Bradley earned a reputation as a brilliant legislator and shaper of public opinion, speaking out against racism, the dwindling sense of community in America, and the tobacco industry, while advocating tax reform and strengthening families. *Wall Street Journal* columnist Al Hunt calls Bradley "the most admirable senator of this era."

Can he fix politics?

QUOTABLE: "Helping parents help their children must be a national priority. Children need a caring adult in their lives, and America needs a next generation that appreciates a meaning in life that is deeper than just the acquisition of material goods."

BEHIND THE SCENES: Bradley, 57, is a former Rhodes scholar at Oxford and Olympic gold medalist. During his ten-year career with the New York Knicks, he was a member of two NBA championship teams. His book, *Life on the Run,* has become a classic in sports literature. He and his wife, Ernestine, have one daughter.

PRAYER STARTERS:

- Give thanks for Bill Bradley's legacy of civility and conviction. Ask that his influence will continue to shape the American political process for good.

- Ask for God's wisdom and blessing for the Bradleys as they consider their options for future public service.

- Pray that God will raise up leaders who are not just successful politicians but also moral and visionary caretakers of the public trust.

> *He who loves a pure heart and whose speech is gracious will have the king for his friend. Proverbs 22:11*

CONTACT: Bill Bradley for President, 395 Pleasant Valley Way, West Orange, NJ 07052

Wesley Stafford

President, Compassion International

POINT OF IMPACT: When he was growing up in Africa's Ivory Coast, Wesley Stafford often heard tribal drums at night signalling the names of his friends who had died—most from preventable causes like measles, smallpox, and diarrhea. He pledged to make a difference. Today he oversees a global ministry that cares for more than 260,000 needy children in 22 countries. "He's a quality leader with a genuine passion for serving children and their Creator," says a colleague. Prior to joining Compassion, Stafford coordinated more than 50 projects for six international relief and development agencies in Haiti. "It doesn't matter whether a person is a major donor, an acquaintance in an airport, or a needy child," Stafford asserts. "The truth is, in God's economy there are no disposable people."

He's on a mission to care for needy kids.

QUOTABLE: "There's no greater privilege on earth than to rescue children from the clutches of hopelessness and poverty and place them lovingly on the lap of Jesus."

BEHIND THE SCENES: This former missionary kid is fluent in several languages and has earned three undergraduate degrees and a doctorate in education from Michigan State University. But at 49, he says his education all boils down to "people development." An avid outdoorsman, he lives outside Colorado Springs, Colorado, with his wife, Donna, and their two daughters, Jenny and Katie.

PRAYER STARTERS:

- Give thanks for Compassion's work with children around the world. Pray for sponsors and supporters and for Compassion's staff.
- Pray that Dr. Stafford will seek and follow God's wisdom.
- Pray that Compassion's children will grow up to know spiritual, economic, social and physical well-being.
- Ask God to protect Stafford and surround his marriage and family with His care.

> *Jesus called the children to him and said, "Let the little children come to me, and do not hinder them, for the kingdom of God belongs to such as these."*
> *Luke 18:16*

CONTACT: 3955 Cragwood Dr., Colorado Springs, CO 80997; e-mail: ciinfo@us.ci.org; (719) 594-9900

Archive Photo

Jiang Zemin
President of China

POINT OF IMPACT: Jiang Zemin, 74, is the unchallenged head of the world's most populous nation (1.3 billion), and he faces the formidable task of reversing the country's 200 years of cultural and economic decline. To do this President Zemin is trying to modernize China's outmoded political system without undermining Communist power. He has pledged to maintain China's open-door economic strategy, but he has little enthusiasm for democratic reforms. He continues to jail dissidents despite U.S. backlash. But Zemin has redirected his country's foreign policy, especially in the recent annexation of Hong Kong, improved relations with neighboring Taiwan, and a visit to Washington in early '99. Beijing is also cooperating with the U.S. to defuse North Korea's nuclear threats as well as making efforts to contain the Asian financial crisis. "He's very shrewd," says Lin Chong-pin, vice-chairman of Taiwan's Mainland Affair Council.

He's the unchallenged leader of 1.3 billion people.

QUOTABLE: At a speech in December 1998 to party members, President Zemin declared that China's present political order "must not be shaken, weakened, or discarded at anytime." He specifically rejected copying Western-style political reforms. Shortly after these remarks, the founders of the China Democracy Party received tough prison sentences.

BEHIND THE SCENES: Jiang Zemin was once a candy factory manager and an electrical engineer. He and his wife, Wang Yeping, have two grown sons; they live in Beijing.

PRAYER STARTERS:

- Despite opposition and persecution, the number of Christians has increased significantly in China recently. Pray for their protection and encouragement.
- Ask God to soften President Zemin's heart, that his materialist assumptions will crumble, that he will see his—and his people's—acute need of God.
- Thank God that many Christians are able to enter China as teachers, businesspersons, or medical workers. Pray they'll find appropriate opportunities to share their faith.
- Ask God to bless Jiang Zemin and his family with goodness and mercy.

> *Rise up, O God, judge the earth, for all the nations are your inheritance.*
> *Psalm 82:8*

CONTACT: Embassy, People's Republic of China, 2300 Connecticut Ave. NW, Washington, DC 20008.

Jay Leno

Host, The Tonight Show with Jay Leno

Archive Photo

POINT OF IMPACT: Jay Leno's "everyman" personality and famous lantern chin (astronaut Curtis Brown told Leno he could spot it from orbit when they passed by California) have made him famous all over the world. Nearly 6 million viewers tune in every weeknight to watch Leno, who used to be a regular stand-in host for Johnny Carson. Since he took over *The Tonight Show* in 1992, Leno has created his own style of humor, talk, and entertainment. But how well he's succeeded the legendary Carson is hotly debated. The *New York Post* gushes, "Everybody said late-night TV would never be the same without Johnny, and they were right. Late-night TV isn't the same—it's much better." But a reviewer for the *New York Daily News* accuses 49-year-old Leno of buying into the dumbing down of America syndrome, and says he's "spent the last six years turning the former jewel of late-night television into an unwatchable cesspool of jokes for drunken frat boys."

You can almost see his chin from outer space.

QUOTABLE: On his wife, Mavis: "We were, and are, opposites. . . . Which I love. . . . She has deep focus, and I fly off in 20 directions at once. . . . She loves European travel; I don't want to go anywhere people won't understand my jokes."

BEHIND THE SCENES: His fifth-grade report card read, "If Jay spent as much time studying as he does trying to be a comedian, he'd be a big star." Today he and Mavis have one of the longer, and reportedly stronger, Hollywood unions—he wrote about it glowingly in his autobiography, *Leading with My Chin.* Recently, Mavis has been tireless in campaigning on behalf of oppressed women in Afghanistan.

PRAYER STARTERS:

- Pray for the blessings of shared commitment, friendship, and harmony for Jay and Mavis Leno today.
- Pray that Leno would use his gifts of humor for kindness and encouragement.
- Leno has said, "I don't consider myself to have much of a spiritual side." Pray that the Holy Spirit would open his heart to God's great love.

A cheerful heart is good medicine. Proverbs 17:22

CONTACT: 3000 W. Alameda Ave., Burbank, CA 91523

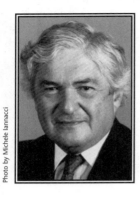

Photo by Michele Iannacci

James Wolfensohn
President, World Bank

POINT OF IMPACT: When James Wolfensohn became president of the World Bank in 1995, his foremost concern was to aid impoverished countries such as Mexico. His goals were lofty and difficult: to manage the flow of $20 billion in loans into developing nations while keeping 178 member states and financial markets satisfied. But economic collapses in Asia, Mexico and Brazil have thrust Wolfensohn into the spotlight and tested his resolve. But this "loan officer to the nations" has proven a match for any crisis so far. In fact, his human touch in working to correct ruling-class corruption by actually visiting slums and his attention to environmental causes are changing the way the World Bank does business. He's known in Washington and New York art circles as the "Renaissance man in pinstripe" for his keen interest in the arts. He also has a reputation for enjoying a "good Australian beer" in the company of working-class people.

He's loan officer to the world.

QUOTABLE: "There is a human dimension to the financial crisis—and social responses are as important as financial responses if we want global stability."

BEHIND THE SCENES: Wolfensohn, 67, is an amateur cello player and was a member of the 1956 Australian fencing team. He became a naturalized U.S. citizen in 1980. His wife, Elaine, is an education specialist; they have three children—Sara, Naomi, and Adam—and live outside Washington, DC.

PRAYER STARTERS:

- A large part of Wolfensohn's role is trying to control corrupt use of World Bank funds by those in power. Pray that he'll have wisdom, creativity and endurance in his work with troubled economies.
- Give thanks for Wolfensohn's empathetic, relational approach.
- Ask that God will bless Wolfensohn and his family with a clear sense of His presence and favor; pray for a humble, seeking response.

> *He who gives to the poor will lack nothing, but he who closes his eyes to them receives many curses. Proverbs 28:27*

CONTACT: The World Bank, 1818 H Street N.W., Washington, DC 20433

Paige Patterson

President, Southern Baptist Convention and Southeastern Baptist Theological Seminary

POINT OF IMPACT: The Southern Baptists—largest denomination in the United States, with 40,000 churches and more than 15 million members—elected "fundamentalist" Paige Patterson president in 1998. Also president of Southeastern Baptist Theological Seminary, he's generally regarded as one of the architects of the conservative resurgence in the SBC. He's perhaps most known for his opposition to women having leadership positions in the church and his emphasis on wives submitting to husbands. Yet his focus is much broader: Patterson wants to see one million people saved in the year 2000. "My ultimate goal is to have a denomination with a heart for evangelism and missions," he says.

He leads America's largest denomination.

QUOTABLE: "That's the only thing that wakes me up in the middle of the night and troubles me: Am I doing enough to get the gospel to all people?"

BEHIND THE SCENES: Dr. Patterson, 57, inherited his love for literal interpretation of the Bible from his father, Reverend T.A. Patterson. Paige grew up a "feisty conservative" ready to debate anyone on modern biblical scholarship. He feels his calling was set from birth. Patterson's mother longed for a son but couldn't conceive after her last daughter was born nine years earlier. Still, she prayed—for a Southern Baptist minister—and Paige was born. He's married to Dorothy; they have two adult children and one grandchild.

PRAYER STARTERS:

- Thank God for Paige Patterson's commitment to the reliability of Scripture. Pray for a growing hunger for God's Word in our culture.
- Pray that Dr. Patterson's leadership of the Southern Baptists would be marked by integrity, wisdom, and peacemaking. Pray for spiritual renewal and effective ministry for a Baptist church in your community.
- Ask God to grant the Pattersons health, peace, and family blessings.

> *We preach Christ crucified . . . the power of God and the wisdom of God.*
> *1 Corinthians 1:23-24*

CONTACT: Southeastern Baptist Theological Seminary, 222 N. Wingate Street, Wake Forest, NC 27588

Photo by Rick Reinhard, Washington, DC

Hillary Rodham Clinton
First Lady of the United States

POINT OF IMPACT: Hillary Rodham Clinton has distinguished herself as a formidable and controversial power in national politics. She's frequently cited as the most influential First Lady since Eleanor Roosevelt. She's drawn public attention to the need for adequate health care, education, jobs, and credit, and the plight of the world's underprivileged. Her 1996 book *It Takes a Village* was a call for communities to care for their children. She's traveled internationally on solo trips more than any other First Lady. Yet she may be most remembered for the stoic grace she displayed when her husband's marital infidelities came to light. She's widely expected to remain a political contender in some capacity after the Clinton administration leaves office.

She's the most influential First Lady since Eleanor Roosevelt.

QUOTABLE: "As long as discrimination and inequities remain so commonplace around the world—as long as girls and women are valued less, fed less, fed last, overworked, underpaid, not schooled and subjected to violence in and out of their homes—the potential of the human family to create a peaceful, prosperous world will not be realized."

BEHIND THE SCENES: A lifelong Methodist, Mrs. Clinton is open and diligent about her Christian faith. In the days following her husband's confession to an extramarital affair, *Time* magazine reported that she had to come to grips with the fact that she could not "not forgive him and still call herself a Christian." The First Lady is 53, and loves art, especially sculpture.

PRAYER STARTERS:

- She's said she most wants to be remembered for her work for women and children around the world. Give thanks for her efforts in this arena. Pray for her continuing effectiveness as an ambassador and catalyst for change.

- Pray for restoration, strength, and love in the Clintons' marriage.

- Pray for Chelsea Clinton today—that she'll thrive in her studies, friendships, and activities despite external pressures.

> *The LORD is my strength and my shield; my heart trusts in him, and I am helped. Psalm 28:7*

CONTACT: The White House, 1600 Pennsylvania Ave. N.W., Washington, DC 20500; first.lady@whitehouse.gov

Raymond V. Gilmartin

CEO, Merck & Co.

Courtesy of Merck & Co.

POINT OF IMPACT: On Ray Gilmartin's second day on the job as Merck's new CEO, someone handed him his speech. It was a 50-year-old script, originally delivered by a previous CEO, that read, "We try never to forget that medicine is for the people. It is not for profits. The profits follow, and if we have remembered that, they have never failed to appear." Gilmartin still delivers the speech—with "almost irritating regularity" according to the *Financial Times*. And the profits continue to roll in. Merck is the number-one drugmaker in the United States and tied for first in the world, with yearly revenues of $30 billion. It exerts enormous influence on health care worldwide. As one Nobel Prize researcher noted, "Without Merck, most, if not all, antibiotics that we isolated would have remained bibliographic curiosities." Some of Merck's success stories include treatments for AIDS (Crixivan), hypertension (Vasotec, Prinivil), osteoporosis (Fosamax), and male baldness (Propecia).

He's CEO of America's largest drugmaker.

QUOTABLE: "The reason Merck has continued to be at the leading edge of science is because our core values attract excellent people and generate tremendous support from the physicians and patients we serve."

BEHIND THE SCENES: Gilmartin, 58, is a Washington, DC native who studied electrical engineering, then earned an MBA from Harvard. He's received numerous awards. He's married with three children and lives in New Jersey.

PRAYER STARTERS:

- Merck developed and distributes free a preventative drug for river blindness (a common tropical disease). Sixty million cases have been treated to date. Give thanks for this significant charitable work.

- Gilmartin has said that a Merck priority is to find suitable AIDS treatments for those infected in developing countries (about 90 percent of all cases). Pray for breakthroughs that will be affordable and practical; pray for wisdom for Gilmartin and his team of executives and researchers.

- Ask for God's tender mercies to be evident in the Gilmartin family.

> *Praise the LORD, O my soul, and forget not all his benefits—who forgives all your sins and heals all your diseases. Psalm 103:2-3*

CONTACT: 1 Merck Drive, Whitehouse Station, NJ 08889; www.merck.com

Joan M. Garry

Executive Director, Gay and Lesbian Alliance
Against Defamation (GLAAD)

AP/Wide World Photos

POINT OF IMPACT: Joan M. Garry describes GLAAD as a "media advocacy organization promoting fair, accurate and inclusive representation of gay men and lesbians in all forms of media." Executive director since 1997, Garry has 16 years' experience in the entertainment industry—she helped launch MTV and spent seven years with Showtime. Celebrities such as gay activist Chastity Bono (daughter of Cher and the late Sonny Bono), who served as executive director of GLAAD previously, have joined Garry in talking with studio executives about gay stereotypes in films. Garry and GLAAD support and defend same-sex marriages and gay couples having children.

She fights discrimination against gays.

QUOTABLE: "Our work is rooted in one simple assumption: that how we view the world is shaped largely by media images—the films we see, the newspapers and magazines we read."

BEHIND THE SCENES: While Garry is known as an entertainment executive with media savvy and programming expertise, she is also very involved with her home life in Montclair, New Jersey. She defends her family—a same-sex partner of 18 years and three children—by challenging anyone to "sit down with our daughter and explain to her that her moms are diseased."

PRAYER STARTERS:

- Pray for homosexual men and women around the world, that they would be protected from those who resort to unlawful tactics in their stand against homsexuality.
- Pray that the Christians Garry encounters would communicate Christ's love, truth, power, and mercy instead of condemnation and rejection only.
- Pray for peace, safety, and a keen awareness in her family of God's love.
- Pray for sexual purity and healing in America, and for compassion and clear understanding in our differences. Pray that God's eternal truths would bring freedom from ignorance and sin (John 8:32).

We love because he first loved us. 1 John 4:19

CONTACT: klein@glaad.org

Abigail Van Buren

Advice Columnist

POINT OF IMPACT: "Dear Abby" has been a household name for decades, and the woman behind the title, Abigail Van Buren, remains the most widely syndicated columnist in the world (a claim at times made for both her and her sister, Ann Landers). At an age when most people have long retired (82), Abby continues to work eight to ten hours and reviews hundreds of letters on an average workday. She's been married for more than 60 years and has written six bestselling books. In spite of a full workload, she still finds time to champion equal rights for women, the mentally ill, and the physically disabled. She's founding director of the National Foundation of AIDS Research as well as an advocate for the humane treatment of animals.

Her columns reflect—and shape—our culture.

QUOTABLE: "Fear less; hope more. Eat less; chew more. Talk less; say more. Hate less; love more. . . . [And] never underestimate the power of forgiveness."

BEHIND THE SCENES: She and her twin sister, Ann Landers, grew up in Sioux City, Iowa, as Pauline Esther Friedman and Esther Pauline Friedman. Abby was the first sister to launch an advice column. She's been known to make personal calls to people who sound suicidal in their letters. "Once I called a woman's doctor for her," says Abby. "I told the nurse, 'This is Dear Abby. I heard from a patient of yours, and she sounds desperate. She said she can't get an appointment for two weeks—please see her as soon as possible.' The doctor saw her that day." Abby and her husband, Morton Phillips, live in Beverly Hills and are the parents of two children: Jeanne and Edward.

PRAYER STARTERS:

- Give thanks for the countless number of people Abigail Van Buren has helped during her four decades of writing.
- Pray for her health today; pray for grace and favor in her marriage, and a keen and growing awareness of God's presence and purposes for her.
- Ask for impact for good through her advice column and her work with charities. Pray that she'll give sound advice that doesn't contradict the Bible.

Plans fail for lack of counsel, but with many advisers they succeed.
Proverbs 15:22

CONTACT: Dear Abby, P.O. Box 69440, Los Angeles, CA 90069

Archive Photo

Tom Brokaw

Anchor and Editor, NBC Nightly News

POINT OF IMPACT: The anchor of weekday *NBC Nightly News* since 1983, Tom Brokaw, almost 60, began his journalism career in Omaha and Atlanta before joining NBC News in 1966. He was the White House correspondent for NBC News during Watergate, and from 1976 to 1981 he anchored *Today* on NBC. His career has been a series of firsts: he conducted the first American one-on-one interview with Mikhail Gorbachev, and he was the only U.S. anchor on the scene the night the Berlin Wall fell. He was the first to report on human-rights abuses in Tibet and to conduct an interview with the Dalai Lama. And in 1995 Brokaw was the first network evening news anchor to report from the site of the Oklahoma City bombing; in 1996, from the scene of the TWA Flight 800 tragedy. After 15 years of interviews, research, and writing, Brokaw recently published a bestselling book, *The Greatest Generation.*

He brings the news home.

QUOTABLE: "In the spring of 1984, I went to the northwest of France, to Normandy, to prepare a documentary on the fortieth anniversary of D-Day. . . . Ten years later, I returned to Normandy and by then I had come to understand what this generation of Americans meant to history. It is, I believe, the greatest generation any society has ever produced."

BEHIND THE SCENES: Brokaw has received every major broadcast award, including a Peabody, Emmys, and a National Headliner Award from the National Conference of Christians and Jews for advancing the understanding of religion, race, and ethnicity. He and his wife, Meredith, have three daughters and residences in Manhattan and Montana.

PRAYER STARTERS:

- Pray that Tom Brokaw will be guided by divine insights and biblical principles today in all of his news decisions.
- Pray that the American news media will value objective reporting and significance over sensationalism.
- Pray for blessing, safety, and spiritual well-being for Brokaw and his family.

> *How beautiful on the mountains are . . . those who bring good news.*
> Isaiah 52:7

CONTACT: NBC News, 30 Rockefeller Plaza, New York, NY 10112

Jean Chretien

Prime Minister of Canada

UN/DPI Photo by G. Kinch

POINT OF IMPACT: The day before he turned 65, he took his first snowboarding lesson. But Canadians need a person with just such nerve as they face stubborn problems like disunity, unemployment, and government reform. Jean Chretien, head of Canada's Liberal Party, has already had to undertake some very conservative business while in office—send Canadian troops into U.N. war zones and scale back government social programs, for example. But the native Quebecois has remained popular, and successful—so far—in keeping Canada's fractious provinces and political parties all going in the same direction. As one observer remarks, "[Chretien] is likely the best finger-in-the-wind politician in the business. It is not so much his knowing what is right as it is his unerring judgment of what he can get away with, or what Canadians will put up with."

He has the nerve Canada needs.

QUOTABLE: A relative comparing Chretien and Clinton—"These are two men who have struggled hard to get to the top; nobody gave them their jobs. Because they are not from wealthy families, they have an understanding and sympathy for the little guy in common."

BEHIND THE SCENES: Chretien is seen as a driven, complicated, private person unawed by the trappings of power. Joseph Jacques Jean Chretien, 66, was born the eighteenth of 19 children—only nine of the Chretien children survived infancy. Chretien and his wife, Aline Chaine, have three grown children.

PRAYER STARTERS:

- Pray for unity, peace, and prosperity for all Canadians. Pray for a spiritual awakening, especially among those who are indifferent to Christianity.

- Pray that Chretien will lead by wisdom, morality, and personal example; pray that he will help to articulate Canada's future in the new millenium.

- Ask God to draw the Chretiens to Himself, and keep them safe in His care.

Through the blessing of the upright, a city is exalted. Proverbs 11:11

CONTACT: RM 311-S, Centre Block, House of Commons, Ottawa, Ontario K1AOA6, e-mail: comments@ottawa.com

Courtesy of Promise Keepers

Bill McCartney

Founder and CEO, Promise Keepers (PK)

POINT OF IMPACT: Many people believe that former University of Colorado football coach Bill McCartney has done a better job of motivating Christian men toward good living than any layman in the twentieth century. As president of Promise Keepers since its inception in 1990, McCartney has pulled together three million men for stadium events and several times that in small accountability groups. PK's goal is "to encourage men to live godly lives and to keep seven basic promises of commitment to God, their families, and fellow man." PK has also been the target of vehement opposition from groups like the ACLU and the National Organization for Women. McCartney frequently receives hate mail, and former Representative Pat Schroeder (D-Colo.) once called him "a self-appointed Ayatollah." Responds McCartney: "We're calling men to do what the Bible says: lay down your lives for your wives; come alongside them and serve them like Christ serves the church."

He motivates men toward good living.

QUOTABLE: "The heroes are not the guys scoring the most touchdowns. It's the guys who wash the dishes, change the diapers, take out the garbage."

BEHIND THE SCENES: In 1997, Promise Keepers underwent a financial and organizational restructuring. The group's goals remain the same; however, McCartney now refuses to charge admission for stadium events. This has put PK under considerable financial strain. McCartney and his wife, Lyndi, live in Denver; they have four adult children. His latest book is *Sold Out*.

PRAYER STARTERS:

- Give thanks for Bill McCartney's example of transparency. Ask God to bless Bill and Lyndi with harmony and fulfillment in their marriage.

- Praise God for the influence of Promise Keepers. Pray for this year's stadium events, and for men's groups meeting around the world.

- Pray for some Christian husbands—"heroes in the making"—whom you know and appreciate.

> *Live as free men, but do not use your freedom as a cover-up for evil; live as servants of God. Show proper respect to everyone. Love the brotherhood, fear God, honor the king. 1 Peter 2:16-17*

CONTACT: www.promisekeepers.org

Elton John

Pop Singer, Songwriter

Archive Photo

POINT OF IMPACT: Elton John, 53, is one of pop music's most influential and flamboyant personas. Since his arrival on the music scene in 1970, he's sold more than 200 million records. One key to his success was his creative partnership with lyricist Bernie Taupin. Together they scored 23 top-40 hits—including "Your Song," "Goodbye Yellow Brick Road," and "Rocket Man." He has been on the cover of *Time* magazine and has played concerts to crowds of more than 100,000 people. In 1992 he formed the Elton John AIDS Foundation, which funds patient care and prevention programs. In 1994 his soundtrack work on Disney's *The Lion King* won him both a Grammy and an Oscar. And his 1997 tribute to Princess Diana, "Goodbye, England's Rose," became the biggest-selling single of all time. Says one music critic, "Not only is he an enormous talent with worldwide recognition and appeal, but he's built a reputation as someone with great concern for humanitarian issues."

He's a music icon—and a humanitarian.

QUOTABLE: "I'm a compulsive/impulsive person. I can't have one drink and I can't have one drug and I can't ever have one pair of glasses or one car. That's my makeup."

BEHIND THE SCENES: He learned to play the piano at four and entered the Royal Academy of Music at 11. His father forbade rock-and-roll in the house. His mother, however, sneaked in Little Richard and Jerry Lee Lewis records. In 1990 he confirmed he's gay; he lives in England with his partner, David Furnish.

PRAYER STARTERS:

- Give thanks for Elton John's contributions to humanitarian causes.
- Pray for God to bless him in tangible ways that draw him to Himself. Ask for credible Christians in the industry to befriend him.
- Pray for strength for those who work with AIDS patients. Pray for healing and comfort for AIDS sufferers, especially in Africa and Asia.

> *For your name's sake, O LORD, preserve my life; in your righteousness, bring me out of trouble. Psalm 143:11*

CONTACT: Elton John AIDS Foundation, 9744 Wilshire Blvd., Suite 301, Beverly Hills, CA 90212

Archive Photo

Harrison Ford
Actor

POINT OF IMPACT: Harrison Ford's rise to fame began 30 years ago when he accepted a small part in *American Graffiti*—even though it paid half of what he was earning as a carpenter. Today Ford is acknowledged as the most successful actor in the history of motion pictures. His roles in the *Star Wars* trilogy and *Indiana Jones* films are only a part of the story; Ford has appeared in six of the 30 highest-grossing films of all time and 19 of his movies have grossed more than $2 billion. The 57-year-old actor is almost universally admired for the roles he's taken through the years—men with consummate integrity who will fight for truth, regardless of the consequences. (He played the United States president in *Air Force One.*) He's been named Star of the Century by the National Association of Theatre Owners. As one movie executive said, "You know with a Harrison Ford movie, turnstiles will be ringing and tickets will be sold."

He's Hollywood's favorite good guy.

QUOTABLE: On acting: "I'm an assistant storyteller. It's like being a waiter or a gas-station attendant, but I'm waiting on six million people a week, if I'm lucky."

BEHIND THE SCENES: Harrison, who grew up in Illinois, doesn't cite any religious or political affiliations, but along with his screenwriter wife, Melissa Mathison, he has been active in promoting the Tibetan Freedom movement. He has four children and lives in New York and Wyoming. Ford is an accomplished pilot certified to fly a variety of aircraft and helicopters.

PRAYER STARTERS:

- Pray that Harrison Ford will use his influence in the movie industry for good; pray that he will humbly seek God's wisdom in his choices.
- Pray that film writers and producers would invest in the power of heroic figures to win audiences and influence society for good.
- Ask God to bless the Ford family and bring them to a fuller knowledge of Himself.

May integrity and uprightness protect me, because my hope is in you.
Psalm 25:21

CONTACT: McQueeney, 10279 Century Woods Dr., Los Angeles, CA 90067

Janet Reno
Attorney General of the United States

Photo by Rick Reinhard, Washington, DC

POINT OF IMPACT: As Attorney General, Janet Reno is both the nation's top law enforcement officer and the first woman to hold the position. Nominated by Bill Clinton and sworn in during March 1993, Reno was again appointed by Clinton in 1997. During her time in office, she has often become involved in highly controversial issues. The Waco crisis ended badly; her decision to appoint Ken Starr to investigate Whitewater and then Lewinsky gained her many enemies, as did her failure to appoint an independent counsel to investigate alleged Democratic fundraising violations. One of the most recognizable political figures of our times, Reno is seen by many as an icon of female power and tenacity. She is also one of the most parodied people in the country. This may be because, as one writer put it, "Reno doesn't appear to care what anybody thinks. The sort of approval that comes from wearing the right clothes, having the right haircut, putting people at ease by schmoozing and joking seems irrelevant to her."

She's the country's top cop.

QUOTABLE: On her advocacy for diversity: "We must always honor this country as a nation of immigrants."

BEHIND THE SCENES: Reno, 62, who once described herself as an "awkward old maid," is frequently visited in Washington by family. She enjoys hiking and canoeing, reading poetry, and listening to music ranging from opera to country-and-western.

PRAYER STARTERS:

- Give thanks for the rule of law in America and for those who support it.
- Pray for wisdom for Janet Reno today in all her decisions—that God would grant her sensitivity to the needs of the weak, the needy, and the oppressed.
- Ask God to bless her with strength, personal peace, and a receptivity to His love.

> *Do not pervert justice; do not show partiality to the poor or favoritism to the great, but judge your neighbor fairly. Leviticus 19:15*

CONTACT: Dept. of Justice, Constitution Ave. & 10th St. N.W., Washington, DC 20530

Burnett Photography, Rialto, CA

Larry Poland

Founder, Chairman,
CEO of Mastermedia International

POINT OF IMPACT: Dr. Larry Poland is changing hearts in Hollywood. As leader of Mastermedia International, Poland keeps Christians informed of the spiritual dynamics inside media while ministering to professionals in film and television. Poland says that while Hollywood often lives up to its reputation as being spiritually and morally bankrupt, many professionals there maintain effective Christian witnesses. More than 1,700 media personnel receive assistance from Mastermedia. Dr. Poland is former director of the Agape Movement, an international volunteer service organization under Campus Crusade for Christ International. He's traveled to 77 countries and authored five books, including *The Last Temptation of Hollywood*. He currently hosts a radio feature, *The Mediator,* which airs daily on more than 900 radio stations.

He's changing hearts in Hollywood.

QUOTABLE: Poland says he once prayed, "God, give me a job so great that if You don't undertake, I'll never be able to do it." The next day he was offered a college presidency.

BEHIND THE SCENES: Poland, 59, is a native of Ohio and a graduate of Wheaton College (Illinois) with a degree in sociology. Dr. Poland also earned advanced degrees from Purdue University and Grace Theological Seminary. He and his wife, Donna Lynn, have six children—Christian, Desiree, Cherish, Destiny, Chalet, and Valor. They live in Redlands, California.

PRAYER STARTERS:

- Thank God for Larry Poland's acceptance and influence in the film industry. Ask that his relationships in Hollywood will flourish spiritually.
- Ask God to favor the Poland family with His generous provisions and a sweet sense of His presence today.
- Pray that God will raise up more godly, successful filmmakers and actors.
- Pray for these who also have strategic ministries in Hollywood: Father Elwood Kaiser, the Reverend Tim Storey, the Reverend Bob Rieth of Media Fellowship International, and Ted Baehr of the Christian Film and Television Commission.

> *By setting forth the truth plainly we commend ourselves to every man's conscience in the sight of God. 2 Corinthians 4:2*

CONTACT: 330 North Sixth St., Ste. 110, Redlands, CA 92374-3312; www.mastermedia.com

Denton A. Cooley, M.D.

President, Texas Heart Institute

Archive Photo

POINT OF IMPACT: As one writer puts it, "the life of Denton Cooley has centered around hearts—hearts that beat too fast, hearts that don't beat fast enough, and hearts that stop." A world-renowned heart surgeon, Cooley's career is marked by a series of amazing medical firsts. He perfected the first heart-lung machine; performed the first open-heart surgery in the southern United States; introduced "bloodless" heart surgery; performed the first successful heart transplant in the United States; and implanted the first totally artificial heart in a human. More recently, this spare, tall Texan performed what was scheduled to be the first open heart surgery live on the internet (another doctor team beat him to the punch by a few days). As president of Houston's Texas Heart Institute, Cooley remains at the forefront of the study and treatment of diseases of the heart. A Stanford medical professor who studied with Cooley says simply, "Dr. Cooley has taken the mystery out of open-heart surgery." To date, he and his team have performed more than 90,000 open-heart surgeries.

He took the mystery out of open-heart surgery.

QUOTABLE: "The heart has been considered the seat of the soul, the source of courage. But I look upon the heart only as a pump—a servant of the brain. Once the brain is gone, the heart becomes unemployed. Then (via transplant) we can find it other employment."

BEHIND THE SCENES: Dr. Cooley, 79, grew up in Houston, graduating from the University of Texas at Austin and Johns Hopkins University School of Medicine. He and his wife Louise are active supporters of UT—a foundation there which bears his name supports two professorships and a varsity basketball scholarship.

PRAYER STARTERS:

- Thank God for giving doctors like Denton Cooley the knowledge, skill, and motivation to save lives. Pray for more advances in cardiac surgery.
- Pray for success today for Dr. Cooley and the entire medical team at the Texas Heart Institute. Ask that they will seek God's wisdom.
- Ask that God's peace and grace will surround the Cooley family.

> *May the favor of the LORD our God rest upon us; establish the work of our hands for us—yes, establish the work of our hands. Psalm 90:17*

CONTACT: Texas Heart Institute, P.O. Box 20345, MC 3-117, Houston, TX 77225

King Abdullah
Ruler of Jordan

Archive Photo

POINT OF IMPACT: Until he was named Crown Prince days before the death of his father, King Hussein, Jordan's King Abdullah headed the Jordanian army's elite special forces, garnering him the loyalty and support of the armed forces. U.S. officials privately call him "a chip off the old block" in terms of his dynamic personality and intelligence. "He clearly understands his mission," said President Clinton. One issue facing Abdullah is his country's faltering economy. Another issue is Israeli-Palestinian peace negotiations. Sitting between Israel and Iraq, and between Syria and Saudi Arabia, Jordan is at the core of the Palestinian question. All matters decided about the final status of an independent Palestinian state—from borders to refugees, Jerusalem, and water supply—will affect Jordan. "Jordan is too small and too weak to be immune from trouble on its borders," a diplomat told the *New York Times.* "And so just like his father, [King Abdullah] is going to have to choose when to stand firm and when to make accommodations."

His small country sits in a hot spot.

QUOTABLE: "I and all of my brothers and sisters have absorbed my father's teachings. We know what we are supposed to do, and I intend to do it."

BEHIND THE SCENES: King Abdullah, 37, is the eldest son of King Hussein and British-born Princess Muna, whom he later divorced. Abdullah has three full siblings and eight half-siblings. Abdullah was British- and American-educated from the age of four, making English his first language, a fact that disgruntles some of his strict Muslim countrymen. His wife is a Palestinian.

PRAYER STARTERS:

- Pray for wisdom and discernment for King Abdullah as he leads his country through a difficult transition and intractable political issues.
- Give thanks for Jordan's commitment to peace. Pray that Jordan and Israel will deal honorably and patiently with each other.
- Ask God to protect and bless King Abdullah and his family.

> *The LORD will be king over the whole earth. On that day there will be one LORD, and his name the only name. Zechariah 14:9*

CONTACT: Embassy of the Hashemite Kingdom of Jordan, 3504 International Drive N.W., Washington, DC 20008; e-mail: Jordaninfo@aol.com

Philip Yancey
Author

POINT OF IMPACT: Probably no nonfiction writer is reaching educated baby boomer readers with the Christian message better than Philip Yancey. Since 1978 he's won eight Gold Medallion Awards—the pinnacle achievement for Christian books—by scratching where contemporary Christians are itching. His 12 books have sold more than 5 million copies, including such bestsellers as *The Jesus I Never Knew, Disappointment with God,* and *What's So Amazing About Grace?* Lewis Smedes of Fuller Theological Seminary called Yancey's *The Jesus I Never Knew* "the best book about Jesus I have ever read, probably the best book about Jesus in the whole century." And Billy Graham says, "There is no writer in the evangelical world that I admire and appreciate more." Yancey started as a writer for *Campus Life.* Along with Chuck Colson, Yancey has been a back-page columnist for *Christianity Today* for many years.

He helps readers grasp God's grace.

QUOTABLE: "It seems to me Christians are too busy trying to stuff up the cracks and correct those imperfections. It's all right to try to fix our defects, but if it keeps us away from grace, it's not good. Light only gets in through the cracks."

BEHIND THE SCENES: Yancey grew up in the South, attending a fundamentalist church he calls "a mutant strain of Christianity." Its members measured spirituality by works, Yancey recalls, and judged each other on issues such as wearing makeup, reading the Sunday paper, and mixed swimming. "They used all the words from the Bible, but they meant the opposite of what they said," he recalls. "They said 'God is love,' but they meant 'God is hate.' They said they lived under grace, but it seemed a lot like law to me." Yancey, 51, lives with his wife, Beth, in Colorado.

PRAYER STARTERS:

- Give thanks for the intelligence and impact of Yancey's published works.
- Ask for a growing understanding among believers about the wonders of grace, the reality of Jesus Christ, and the trustworthiness of God.
- Pray for Yancey and his wife today—for their marriage and their work together. Pray for the success of Yancey's current projects.

> *For it is by grace you have been saved, through faith—and this not from yourselves, it is the gift of God—not by works, so that no one can boast.*
> *Ephesians 2:8-9*

CONTACT: c/o Zondervan Publishing House, 5300 Patterson S.E., Grand Rapids, MI 49530

Courtesy of Xerox Corp.

Paul Allaire

CEO, Xerox Corporation

POINT OF IMPACT: As top man at Xerox, Paul Allaire is consistently named among America's most respected CEOs. Under the guidance of this mild-mannered and unpretentious man, Xerox—the world's copier and document processing giant—is leading the way in combining business and social values. Even Wall Street skeptics are saying Xerox is the business model for the future. For example, in 1994 Xerox won the Business Enterprise Award for showing "consistent corporate leadership and social vision in the face of unprecedented change, and a sense of idealism in the face of daunting social and economic problems." Xerox has also initiated pioneering programs in job training, minority contracting, and community volunteering and paid social-service sabbaticals for employees. An eight-year environmental protection initiative—Xerox calls it, "developing green machines"—now actually saves the corporation $200 million annually. Allaire is also committed to promoting diversity; Xerox recently invested $100 million in South Africa to prepare black workers for management positions.

His company is a business model for the future.

QUOTABLE: "Our failure to develop our human resources not only harms individuals, it holds back the nation as a whole. America must have world-class education and training programs if we are to compete successfully in the twenty-first century. Competitiveness depends on lifelong learning."

BEHIND THE SCENES: Paul Allaire, 59, and his wife, Kathleen, have two grown children, Brian and Christiana. They live in New Canaan, Connecticut.

PRAYER STARTERS:

- Give thanks for the humanitarian influence of the Xerox Corporation around the world.
- Ask that Paul Allaire will seek God's wisdom in all his decisions; pray for the health and well-being of his family.
- When you use or pass by a copier today, pray that Christian decision-makers at Xerox and other major corporations will "copy" Christ's example.

Be imitators of God, therefore, as dearly loved children and live a life of love, just as Christ loved us and gave himself up for us. Ephesians 5:1-2

CONTACT: Headquarters, 800 Long Ridge Road, Stamford, CT 06904; www.xerox.com

Jerry Springer
Host, The Jerry Springer Show

AP/Wide World Photos

POINT OF IMPACT: Jerry Springer is host of the nation's number-one rated daytime series—a daily talk show seen in more than 190 U.S. markets and 40-plus foreign countries. *The Jerry Springer Show* became the first talk show to knock Oprah Winfrey's out of first place. The show's highly sensational content (often guests are involved in various forms of sexual betrayal, and enraged guests physically attack one another regularly) has been credited with taking TV tastelessness to an all-time low. Robert W. Peters, president of Morality in Media, lays some of the blame on sponsors as well: "Jerry Springer would not be able to bring vicious fighting, in-your-face cursing and a parade of sexual abominations, including bestiality, into the living rooms of America without local TV stations airing it and mainstream companies sponsoring it." Springer's video collection of shows has become the bestselling video nationally and internationally. Springer has also written *Ringmaster*, and starred in a feature film based on his show.

He's taken TV schlock to an all-time low.

QUOTABLE: "I don't know if I can be shocked by anything. We've seen it all. It's not the subjects that amaze me—it's the fact that people are willing to share their secrets."

BEHIND THE SCENES: In 1998, a New York-based chocolate company offered to send free sweets to the first 1,000 people who swore off Springer's show and agreed to have their household trash delivered to the show's producers. Springer was born in London in 1944 as his Jewish family fled from the Holocaust. At age five, he emigrated to New York City with his family. He has been an award-winning news anchor and a former mayor of Cincinnati. In recent years, he has served as vice president of the Muscular Dystrophy Association, and he frequently cohosts Jerry Lewis' annual Labor Day telethon. He has one grown daughter.

PRAYER STARTERS:

- Pray that those who make influential choices in regard to the types of shows aired on television would opt for morally decent and uplifting programs.
- Ask for the health and well-being of Jerry and his family.
- Ask God to bring Christian influences into the lives of Jerry Springer and his family.
- Pray for a new cultural consensus against unregulated trash on TV.

> *Create in me a pure heart, O God, and renew a steadfast spirit within me.*
> *Psalm 51:10*

CONTACT: Jerry Springer Show, 454 N. Columbus Drive, Chicago, IL 60611

Sam Moore
CEO, Thomas Nelson Publishers

Courtesy of Thomas Nelson Publ.

POINT OF IMPACT: Sam started out in 1949 as a Lebanese immigrant with $600 and his father's advice to "work hard, be honest, and don't be afraid to take risks." Today Sam Moore leads the largest Christian business conglomerate in the world and directs the creation and distribution of more Bibles, Christian books, and other products than any other individual. Combined with its Word imprint, Thomas Nelson publishes such major Christian authors as Max Lucado and Charles Stanley. Nelson also has interests in television, music, home shopping, and radio. As part of Moore's vision for Nelson's future, the company is creating media alliances with enterprises like CompuServe, QVC, and Tele-Communications, Inc. The company is contemplating venturing into filmmaking, recently optioning Frank Peretti's novel *This Present Darkness.*

He's the top man in Christian publishing.

QUOTABLE: "I believe so strongly in the work that we are doing. I want people to look at me as a businessman and at Thomas Nelson as a company that represents Christianity in the marketplace through integrity, honesty and honorable character in all of our business dealings."

BEHIND THE SCENES: As a youth growing up in Lebanon, Moore attended an evangelical school where he heard the basics of the Christian faith. Early one morning he discovered the body of a murdered friend under an olive tree. Shaken, he placed his faith in Christ with the help of a Christian neighbor. Now 70, he lives in Nashville with his wife, Peggy. They have three grown children and three grandchildren.

PRAYER STARTERS:

- Pray that Sam Moore and his coworkers will uphold high standards for content, marketing strategies, and quality.
- Ask the Lord to bless Sam and Peggy Moore with strength and joy (they've been married 42 years).
- Give thanks for the visionary leadership of Moore in Christian publishing, for the impact of Nelson books and Bibles around the world, and for the company's high profile in many non-traditional outlets.

> *I want you to be able always to recognize the highest and the best, and to live sincere and blameless lives until the day of Christ. Ephesians 1:9-10,* PHILLIPS

CONTACT: Thomas Nelson, 501 Nelson Place, Nashville, TN 37214-3600

Gloria Feldt
President, Planned Parenthood

AP/Wide World Photos

POINT OF IMPACT: As president of the Phoenix Planned Parenthood affiliate, she increased fundraising income by more than 2,000 percent and battled tenaciously with groups such as Catholics United for Life. Today Gloria Feldt runs both the Planned Parenthood Federation of America (PPFA), the nation's oldest and largest reproductive health-care organization, and its political arm, the Planned Parenthood Action Fund. PPFA's 137 affiliates operate 900 health centers nationwide. Since assuming the national leadership post in 1996, Feldt has overseen a dramatic revitalization of PPFA. Her goals are to increase services that prevent unintended pregnancy, to improve the quality of reproductive health care, and to ensure access to safe, legal abortion. Feldt reports that abortion services represent only about 2 percent of the organization's energies.

She battles tenaciously for reproductive rights.

QUOTABLE: Feldt told *Mother Jones* magazine: "It's absolutely incumbent on us to put our agenda forward and let our adversaries justify why they don't support it. Let them run the risk of looking like unreasonable Neanderthals."

BEHIND THE SCENES: Feldt married her college-age boyfriend at age 15 and had three children by the time she was 20. Later, while attending community college, she became interested in politics and women's issues. Feldt, 58, is married to Alex Barbanell; they have six grown children and nine grandchildren.

PRAYER STARTERS:

- Pray for God's blessing upon Gloria Feldt, her family, and upon every Planned Parenthood worker. Ask God to give them a growing awareness of the sacredness of human life in the womb.

- In 1997, 1.4 million abortions were performed in the United States. Pray for a decline in unwanted pregnancies and in the practice of abortions worldwide.

- Ask for God's forgiveness for misapplied medical interventions; ask for moral renewal for our nation and for grace and healing for those in need.

> *This is what the LORD says—your Redeemer, who formed you in the womb: "I am the LORD, who has made all things. . . ." Isaiah 44:24*

CONTACT: e-mail: communications@ppfa.org

Jacques Chirac

President of France

UN/DPI Photo by G. Kinch

POINT OF IMPACT: French President Jacques Chirac believes that his country—as the world's fourth largest economy, a permanent member of the United Nations Security Council, and a contributor of United Nations peacekeeping operations—has the right to exert influence on world affairs. Along with Germany, France plays a key role in the emerging united Europe. France has long been the dominant cultural and economic power in West Africa. And recently Chirac has attempted to increase France's influence in the Middle East by being a peacemaker. He's been characterized as a man who "knows how to take a beating, recover and bounce back." He's been a major player in French politics since the late sixties, and has served as prime minister twice while simultaneously serving as mayor of Paris. After he was made president in 1995, he caused an international uproar by testing nuclear weapons in the Pacific.

He wants to increase France's influence.

QUOTABLE: On the "euro," the new monetary unit for the European Union: "One cannot hope for world financial stability while at the same time accepting unstable exchange rates. We must aim for more stable relations between currencies. This is a daunting task."

BEHIND THE SCENES: Chirac, 67, is the child of a banker and his wife. He speaks of a "deep affection" for his mother and says he was "a spoiled child, very very spoiled." He and his wife, Bernadette, have two daughters.

PRAYER STARTERS:

- Chirac, a practicing Catholic, often says that his religion is important to him. Pray that he'll protect and nourish his faith amidst the pressures of public service, and that he will seek God's guidance in his decisions.
- Pray for Chirac's role as middleman and peacemaker, especially in the Middle East, Algeria and West Africa, and through the United Nations.
- Pray for safety and family blessings for the Chiracs today.

> *The God of Jacob . . . will judge between many peoples and will settle disputes for strong nations far and wide. Joel 4:2-3*

CONTACT: Palais de l'Elysée, 55-57 rue du Faubourg Saint-Honoré, 75008 Paris, France

August Busch III

President, Anheuser-Busch

POINT OF IMPACT: In his high-school yearbook, a photograph of Busch holding a mug of Budweiser beer is accompanied by the caption: "Most likely to succeed." And succeed he did. In 1975 August Busch III, impatient and worried about the future, wrested Budweiser from his father's company in a bitter proxy fight. Today he's president and CEO of Anheuser-Busch Companies, one of the largest brewers in the world. With about 45 percent of the market, the company is the largest beer maker in the United States. The company also sells beer in China, Japan, Mexico, several South American countries, and throughout Europe. Busch III is the man responsible for turning Budweiser into a marketing machine. Its "critter" ads, headed by frogs, then lizards Frank and Louie, have been among the most popular ads in America—even among children. That has made alcohol-awareness groups hopping mad. Busch III, 62, is also responsible for backing the Lou Rawls Parade of Stars telethon, which has raised more than $132 million in cash.

His company is the largest beer maker in the United States.

QUOTABLE: "Make sure your standards are high, and if someone doesn't meet those standards, take them out. I don't care whether it's family or not."

BEHIND THE SCENES: Within hours after August Busch III was born, his father ordered the doctor to put five drops of Budweiser from an eyedropper into the baby boy's mouth. It's now a family tradition whenever a male is born. Busch and his wife, Virginia Lee, live in St. Peters, Missouri, and have two sons and two daughters.

PRAYER STARTERS:

- Pray that August Busch III will lead the brewing industry in helping to curb underage drinking and promoting safe driving.
- Pray for spiritual renewal among the Busch clan today. Ask God to bless the marriage and family of August and Virginia Lee Busch.
- Gives thanks for Busch's charitable giving.

Jesus answered, "Everyone who drinks this water will be thirsty again, but whoever drinks the water I give him will never thirst." John 4:13-14

CONTACT: Anheuser-Busch Inc., 1 Busch Place, Saint Louis, MO 63118

Calvin Butts

Pastor, African-American Activist

POINT OF IMPACT: He leads one of the biggest Baptist churches in New York and possibly America. But Reverend Calvin Butts of Harlem's Abyssinian Baptist Church doesn't stop with preaching: through the Abyssinian Development Corporation, Butts and his church have completed housing construction and renovation projects for the homeless, seniors, and moderate-income buyers. The corporation has acquired two historic landmarks in Central Harlem for preservation and has been instrumental in establishing the Thurgood Marshall Academy for Learning and Social Change, a public inter-mediate school and high school. Butts is also Chairman of the Harlem Foundation for Arts and Culture, and has taught urban affairs and black church history at New York colleges. He led a group that painted over liquor and cigarette ads displayed on inner-city buildings. An inspiration around the country, he has been listed twice as a New York power broker and has been recognized as a living treasure by the New York City Chamber of Commerce and Industry.

He's Harlem's "living treasure."

QUOTABLE: "There would be no America without the African river flowing through it."

BEHIND THE SCENES: Actively preaching against rap music, Butts recently announced that he will pile up CDs, music videos, and cassettes produced by rap artists and run over them with a truck. He has launched a campaign against use of anti-women words in rap lyrics, begging for a return from derogatory language to "brothers" and "sisters."

PRAYER STARTERS:

- Thank God for Calvin Butts' work in Harlem. Ask God to bless every person ministering through his church. Pray for their protection.

- Pray for the next generation of African-American Christian leaders whom God is calling.

- Ask God to provide for the needs of the Butts family, leading them in green pastures, giving them rest, and restoring their souls (Psalm 23:1-3).

> *Defend the cause of the weak and fatherless; maintain the rights of the poor and oppressed. Psalm 82:3*

CONTACT: Abyssinian Baptist Church, 132 W. 138th Street, New York, NY 10039

Bud Paxson

CEO, Paxson Communication,
Creator of PAX TV

Courtesy of Paxson Communications Corp.

POINT OF IMPACT: Lowell "Bud" Paxson is trying to change TV—or at least one channel on your dial. The program lineup on his new network, PAX TV, takes a stand for the American family—and against vulgar language, violence, and explicit sex. Wall Street still isn't sure what Paxson is up to. But there doesn't seem to be an inch of doubt in this 6-foot, 6-inch TV legend who made a fortune in infomercials and the Home Shopping Network, which he cofounded in 1982. In 1998, Paxson, a born-again Christian, launched the nation's seventh television network, which broadcasts on 95 stations, 78 of which Paxson owns. He says PAX TV is not a Christian network, but features programming "with a touch of spirituality." Says Paxson, "I think that *Touched by an Angel* does more for the kingdom of God than all of the televangelists combined."

His network offers family-safe fare.

QUOTABLE: "I can't tell what God would want to watch [on television]. But I want to try to prevent anything going on there that I think He wouldn't want to watch."

BEHIND THE SCENES: Paxson, 63, says the spiritual turning point in his life came when his second wife left him for another man on Christmas Day in 1986. He realized he was partly to blame: he'd spent about 260 days a year on the road. Devastated and alone in a hotel room on New Year's Eve, he picked up a Gideon Bible and found instructions inside on how to receive Christ, which he did. A divorced father of five, Paxson lives down the street from his friend Donald Trump in Palm Beach, Florida.

PRAYER STARTERS:

- Pray for the success of the PAX TV network and other efforts to infuse television with wholesome programming: for high-quality, entertaining shows; for strong advertising support; and for sincere community interest.

- Pray that people would recognize their need for God and respond in other positive ways through PAX TV programming.

- Ask God to bless Bud Paxson and his family today with creativity, stamina, and peace.

I will set before my eyes no vile thing. Psalm 101:3

CONTACT: www.pax.net/contact_new.htm

Courtesy of Ian Wilmut

Ian Wilmut
Embryologist

POINT OF IMPACT: Dr. Ian Wilmut of Scotland, 55, rocked the scientific world as well as the public in 1997 when he announced the creation of a sheep named "Dolly," the first mammal to be cloned from adult cells. "This is huge," exclaimed Princeton University biology professor Dr. Lee Silver. "It basically means there are no limits." Dolly's birth set off a global debate on the ethics and direction of cloning research. Some scientists are exhilarated by the potential for creating; others worry about the Dr. Frankenstein effect: *Can the dead be cloned?* (No, says Wilmut.) *Could human cloning turn out some kind of monster?* (Yes, says Wilmut.) Wilmut prefers to focus on the beneficial results. "I think the technology can be used in other ways for all sorts of treatments." He insists the primary purpose of cloning is to advance drug therapies and tissue transplantation.

He's the scientist who cloned a sheep.

QUOTABLE: On cloning humans: "We [at the Roslin Institute] would find it ethically unacceptable to think of doing that. Any kind of manipulation with human embryos should be prohibited."

BEHIND THE SCENES: He concedes there's "a remote possibility there could have been a mix-up" with Dolly. It took 400 tries to create her. "Cloning is a very inefficient procedure," he admits. In April 1998, despite concerns that clones might be sterile, Dolly had a little lamb, conceived the old fashioned way.

PRAYER STARTERS:

- Give thanks for scientific discoveries that promise medical breakthroughs.
- Pray that the thrust of cloning research worldwide will be toward responsible and ethically desirable ends.
- Pray that Ian Wilmut will be drawn closer to his Creator in his work; ask for spiritual and physical blessings in his family.

> *The secret things belong to the LORD our God, but the things revealed belong to us and to our children forever, that we may follow all the words of his law.* Deuteronomy 29:29

CONTACT: Roslin Institute, Roslin, Midliothian EH259PS, United Kingdom; e-mail: ian.wilmut@bbsrc.ac.uk

Evander Holyfield
Boxing Heavyweight Champion

Courtesy of Thomas Nelson Publ.

POINT OF IMPACT: Evander Holyfield is the only other boxer besides Muhammad Ali to win the heavyweight boxing title three times. His pay-per-view boxing matches gross millions of dollars and are seen worldwide. And his fights are always a spectacle. For example, in Holyfield's 1998 bout with "bad boy" Mike Tyson, Tyson bit off a piece of Holyfield's ear before being disqualified. But Holyfield has also gained attention with his "nice guy" attitude and amazing work ethic. His recent book is titled *Holyfield: The Humble Warrior.* In post-fight interviews Holyfield regularly credits Jesus with his victories. But his much disputed draw in a '99 bout with Lennox Lewis left a cloud over Holyfield and his sport.

In a brutal sport, he fights the good fight.

QUOTABLE: On boxing: "I don't know why I stayed. I just assumed I would quit before I got to, say, 18. . . . I knew there came a time when you could get hurt, your nose would be bloody, your eye cut. I'd quit before that happened."

BEHIND THE SCENES: Holyfield, 37, grew up fatherless in Alabama. He has five children and has admitted to fathering two children out of wedlock. In 1991 a heart condition forced Holyfield into early retirement, but an apparent healing by televangelist Benny Hinn during a crusade brought him back to boxing. Holyfield lives in Houston and Atlanta. In April of 1999, he and his third wife, Dr. Janice Itson, an internist, filed for divorce.

PRAYER STARTERS:

- Pray that Evander Holyfield lives out his Christian commitment with integrity in the tumultuous world of boxing; pray that by both word and example he influences many boxing fans.
- Pray for health and safety for Holyfield as he continues to compete.
- Ask that Holyfield's family will respond to God's purpose for their lives and enjoy His best today.

> *I can do everything through him who gives me strength. Philippians 4:13 (the verse Holyfield has posted on his website)*

CONTACT: www. evanderholyfield.com

Dick Armey

U.S. Congressman, House Majority Leader

Photo by Rick Reinhard, Washington, DC

POINT OF IMPACT: As House Majority Leader, Representative Dick Armey (R.,Texas) has the second most powerful position in the U.S. House of Representatives. "As second-in-command, Armey has assumed far more power than past majority leaders, making critical decisions about which bills come up and when," says *Time* magazine. Armey, 60, is an outspoken advocate for families, moral values, free markets, and flat taxes. He opposes national health care, defense cuts, abortion rights, and the National Endowment for the Arts. Armey says that Republicans controlling the House have a responsibility to set a course for the nation that is in keeping with the Founding Fathers' principles. That includes an acknowledgment of the importance of God in influencing those principles. "We are the most unique experiment in faith-based democracy in the history of the world," he says.

He leads the House in conservative style.

QUOTABLE: On facing the wrath of fellow Republicans following their loss of several seats in November 1998: "Every day I pray for humility, and all of a sudden I've got 222 people helping me with it."

BEHIND THE SCENES: In 1996 Armey experienced a conversion to faith in Christ. "I finally got over being stubborn and prideful and accepted Christ as my Savior. It's been a remarkable change in my life." When they're not in Washington, he and his wife, Susan Byrd, live in Irving, Texas. They have five grown children.

PRAYER STARTERS:

- Ask that Representative Armey will be granted God's wisdom in his leadership role in Congress.
- Pray that God's grace and peace will bless the Armey home today.
- Pray for those who take strong stands in Congress on behalf of family values, including alternatives to abortion—that they will be examples of courage, integrity, and effectiveness.

The fear of the LORD is the beginning of wisdom. Proverbs 1:7

CONTACT: 301 Cannon House Office Building, Washington, DC 20515-4326; 9901 East Valley Ranch Parkway, Suite 3050, Irving, TX 75063

Marianne Williamson

Lecturer, Author

Archive Photo

POINT OF IMPACT: Marianne Williamson has been called the "guru of the moment in Hollywood." Delivering New Age lectures to packed houses at rented churches in Hollywood and New York, the 47-year-old daughter of a wealthy Texas attorney has a knack for "blending spirituality with show-biz," according to *Time* magazine. Inspired by the book *A Course in Miracles* by the late Jewish psychologist Ruth Schucman, Williamson weaves together Christian exhortations, meditative slogans, and psychotherapeutic advice. One of her slogans, "Align your mind with God and watch miracles happen," inspired talk show diva Oprah Winfrey to invite Williamson to her show. While many celebrities aren't real followers, they have volunteered and contributed to Williamson's charitable organizations, which provide meals and home help for those with life-threatening diseases. Some call her the "Mother Teresa of the nineties" while others criticize her message and tactics.

She's a New Age guru with flair.

QUOTABLE: On her course: "It teaches us to relinquish a thought system based on fear and acceptance instead of a thought system based on love."

BEHIND THE SCENES: Williamson is a single mom who lives in a modest two-room apartment in West Hollywood with her young daughter, India. Williamson admits to a "dramatic personality" but insists her motivation is purely to help others.

PRAYER STARTERS:

- Pray that Marianne Williamson will continue to serve people in need through her charitable organizations.
- Pray that her teachings will increase the hunger of her listeners to investigate the whole message of the Bible and the claims of Christ.
- Pray for Williamson's safety and for her success as a mother.

> *You are the God who performs miracles; you display your power among the peoples. With your mighty arm you redeemed your people. Psalm 77:14-15*

CONTACT: www.marianne.com

Pete Sampras

World Tennis Champion

Courtesy of ATP Tour

POINT OF IMPACT: Ranked as the number-one pro tennis player for six straight years and winner of 11 Grand Slam victories, Pete Sampras, 29, is one of the world's most admired athletes. "Pete Sampras is the greatest tennis player of all time. And he's so young, he'll still be in the game for another 6 or 7 years," says tennis pro Greg Cinko. Sampras is best known for his ace serves, earning him the nickname "Pistol Pete." Sampras is always a gentleman in a game that has sorely longed for worthy role models (remember Jimmy Connors, Ilie Nastase, and John McEnroe?). In 1996 Sampras' coach, former tennis pro Tim Gullikson, died of a brain tumor at age 44. Sampras has since created a charity entitled Aces for Charity, to which he donates $100 per ace to cancer foundations.

He's an ace role model.

QUOTABLE: "A nice guy playing good tennis. That's how I'd like to be remembered."

BEHIND THE SCENES: Sampras never attended formal tennis schools. He picked up a racquet in his parent's basement at age seven and began hitting the ball against the wall. By age 11, with lessons, he was considered a prodigy. Sampras' parents, Greek immigrants, seldom watch him play tennis because they get too nervous. Sampras is unmarried and lives in Tampa, Florida.

PRAYER STARTERS:

- Give thanks that Pete Sampras is a positive role model both on and off the court. Pray that he will remain consistent in his reputation and influence, especially with teenagers and children who are hungry for a sports hero.
- Pray for God's blessing upon Sampras' charity work and his personal life.
- Ask God to reveal Himself to Sampras today—through other people, circumstances, the Bible, or the leading of the Holy Spirit.

> *A good name is more desirable than great riches; to be esteemed is better than silver or gold. Proverbs 22:1*

CONTACT: IMG, 1 Erieview Plaza, Suite 1300, Cleveland, OH 44114

Pat Robertson

Founder—Christian Broadcasting Network,
Christian Coalition, Regent University

Photo by Rick Reinhard, Washington, DC

POINT OF IMPACT: M.G. "Pat" Robertson is the internationally recognized religious broadcaster who founded The Christian Broadcasting Network (CBN). Every day 1.5 million viewers in 90 different countries tune in for CBN's flagship program, *The 700 Club*. He is the founder of Regent University, Operation Blessing (an international relief and development effort), the American Center for Law and Justice, and International Family Entertainment (a TV production and distribution company). Robertson wields influence in the political arena as the founder of the Christian Coalition and as a past candidate for the presidency. One liberal critic says the Christian Coalition is "singularly responsible for the right turn that the national Republican Party has taken in the past 20 years." *The End of the Age* is his most recent book.

His *700 Club* reaches 90 countries.

QUOTABLE: "When you pray for your enemies, asking God to meet their needs and manifest Himself to them, you are overcoming evil with good. You are now on the side of your enemy; you have a spiritual stake in his well-being. If God answers your prayer, which you want Him to do, the person prayed for will be blessed, and you will learn about redemption, the ultimate form of forgiveness."

BEHIND THE SCENES: Robertson, 70, and his wife, Dede, have four children and 13 grandchildren. They live in Virginia Beach, Virginia, the same state where Pat was born. Before starting his TV ministry, Robertson fought in Korea and earned degrees from Yale Law School and New York Theological Seminary.

PRAYER STARTERS:

- Give thanks for Pat Robertson's pioneering work in media, humanitarian relief, and politics. Pray that he will use his influence wisely.
- Pray for all who produce *The 700 Club* and its guests—that they will create a positive influence for Christ in homes and in the media worldwide.
- Ask God to bless the Robertson family with the joy of the Lord today.

> *"Not by might nor by power, but by my Spirit," says the LORD Almighty.*
> *Zechariah 4:6*

CONTACT: Christian Broadcasting Network, 977 Centerville Turnpike, Virginia Beach, VA 23463

Scott Sassa
President, NBC Entertainment

Courtesy of NBC Entertainment

POINT OF IMPACT: Scott Sassa thrives on challenges. Good thing, because he's been charged with no less than saving TV's most popular and prosperous network, which has lost audiences and profits since *Seinfeld* departed. But Sassa has qualities that impress the brass: former boss Ted Turner calls him "brilliant," and says another former boss, Barry Diller, head of Fox, "He's savvy. He's got very good instincts. Firing Scott was one of my supreme mistakes." This likability is very much on Sassa's side. According to TBS President Bill Burke, "Scott is different from your typical 'suit.' He goes out of his way to learn people's names. He sends thank-you notes for doing a good job." Sassa made headlines in 1998 when he announced plans to make NBC programming less sexy, more "mom-and-pop," racially varied, and set in non-New York locations. "In some cases," he said, "we could use a few more words between 'Hello' and 'Would you sleep with me?' "

He's a TV exec who suggests less sex.

QUOTABLE: "If you're in the right place and do bad work, you get more attention than if you're in the wrong place and do good work. The karma at the hot place is powerful."

BEHIND THE SCENES: Sassa, 39, grew up in Los Angeles, a third-generation Japanese-American. Not surprisingly, this eternal optimist was a cheerleader in his college years. And he spreads his sense of fun to his work environment: Sassa took his Turner staff bowling and drag racing. He is usually seen wearing jeans and a T-shirt.

PRAYER STARTERS:

- Pray for Scott Sassa's success in bringing more family-friendly, morally uplifting programming to NBC.
- Pray that the Lord will bring competent and respected Christian friends into his life, both personally and professionally.
- Ask God to bless him with good ideas, personal fulfillment, and health.

> *Your hands made me and formed me; give me understanding to learn your commands. Psalm 119:73*

CONTACT: NBC, 30 Rockefeller Plaza, New York, NY 10112

Daniel S. Goldin
Administrator, NASA

Archive Photo

POINT OF IMPACT: After 40 years of breaking space and technology barriers, NASA's reputation had slipped. "They make space as boring as possible," once grumbled then House Speaker Newt Gingrich. And as expensive. Many areas of research and exploration are being turned over to the commercial space industry. But since becoming NASA Administrator in 1992, Daniel Saul Goldin has tackled NASA's shaky financial situation and put the space agency back in orbit. Goldin is best known for his "faster, cheaper, better" slogan, and for the budget discipline he's provided in an agency long known for excess. He's championed the Discovery Program, which launches smaller, more frequent missions in cooperation with businesses and universities. Under his leadership, the orbiting space station (operated jointly with Russia) was redesigned to make it more affordable. By 2010, Goldin wants to launch PlanetFinder, a probe in orbit around Jupiter that will gather data on Earth-like planets in other star systems.

He has his eye on Mars.

QUOTABLE: "I want to get astronauts to Mars," says Goldin. "And I don't want to wait 30 years. We're not moving fast enough."

BEHIND THE SCENES: Daniel Goldin, 60, was born in New York City. He studied mechanical engineering at City College, then began his career working as a research scientist at NASA's Lewis Research Center. For 25 years he was associated with the TRW Space and Technology Group in California. Goldin and his wife, Judith, have two adult daughters.

PRAYER STARTERS:

- Pray for ongoing successs for NASA's many projects. Pray for safety, creative insight, and helpful scientific advancements.
- Thank God for Daniel Goldin's achievements in making NASA more efficient and productive.
- Ask for Goldin and his family to be keenly aware of their loving, personal Creator; pray for joy and health for them all.

> *By wisdom the LORD laid the earth's foundations, by understanding he set the heavens in place. Proverbs 3:19*

CONTACT: NASA Headquarters, Washington, DC 20546; www.nasa.gov

Bill Cosby

Actor, Comedian, Bestselling Author

Archive Photo

POINT OF IMPACT: Bill Cosby, 63, is the famous, familiar face behind the *Fat Albert* cartoon, the enormously successful eighties sitcom *The Cosby Show*, several bestselling books and highly praised comedy albums, the TV shows *Cosby* and *Kids Say the Darndest Things*, and has enjoyed success in almost every medium, winning Grammys and Emmys alike. "Just seeing Bill Cosby's face makes me feel better about life," explains one fan. Many aren't aware that although Cosby dropped out of high school to join the Navy, he later earned a doctorate in education and has a strong commitment to schooling, which he supports with millions in personal charity. He and his wife, Camille, who also has a doctorate in education, have donated hundreds of thousands of dollars to cancer research, athletics, and earthquake victims.

His life and humor inspire millions.

QUOTABLE: "I wasn't always black. There was this freckle, and it got bigger and bigger."

BEHIND THE SCENES: In January 1997 Cosby's son, Ennis, a 27-year-old doctoral student, was murdered in a Los Angeles burglary gone wrong. At the same time, a young woman named Autumn Jackson attempted to extort $40 million from Cosby, alleging she was his illegitimate daughter. Cosby stood firm over the next several months as Ennis' killer was tracked down and imprisoned and Jackson was sentenced to jail and fines. Through it all, he is still at work—making people laugh. "Somebody's got to give [people] relief," he said. The Cosbys have four daughters— Erika, Erinn, Ensa, and Evin—and live in Massachusetts.

PRAYER STARTERS:

- Pray for continued emotional healing for Bill and Camille Cosby and their family. Ask God to bless the family with peace.
- Give thanks for the high-quality entertainment that Bill Cosby has brought to American audiences for decades.
- Pray that up-and-coming comedians would choose wholesome, insightful humor over the cheap and degrading.

Those who sow in tears will reap with songs of joy. Psalm 126:5

CONTACT: William Morris Agency, 151 El Camino Drive, Beverly Hills, CA 90212

George Strait
Singer, Country Music

Archive Photo

POINT OF IMPACT: One day, George Strait placed a sign on a university bulletin board that read, "Singer looking for a band." Soon he teamed up with the Ace-in-the-Hole Band, which, with few exceptions, has been with him ever since. Strait has been called a "new traditionalist" who reintroduced classic country sounds to the genre and "caused a retro-revolution that has been influencing younger artists ever since." To date, Strait has more number-one hits than any other solo country performer—32 in all. Each of his 19 albums has gone either gold or platinum.

He reintroduced classic sounds to country.

QUOTABLE: Despite his popularity, 48-year-old Strait cherishes his privacy. After filming his movie *Pure Country* in 1992, Strait was approached by a studio publicist who introduced herself by saying, "Hi, I'll be doing press for your new movie." Strait reportedly smiled, extended his hand, and said, "Hi, I'm George Strait, and I won't be doing press for my new movie."

BEHIND THE SCENES: Strait earned a degree in agricultural education from Southwest Texas State University. When he's not singing, he enjoys rodeo riding (he's a regular on the professional roping circuit). He is married to his high-school sweetheart, Norma. They live in Texas with their son, George, Jr. (a daughter, Jennifer, died in a 1996 car accident).

PRAYER STARTERS:

- Pray for Strait's safety and health when he's on the road.
- Ask God to bless Strait's marriage and his relationship with his son. Ask for continued emotional healing.
- Pray for the positive impact of Christian recording artists; for more wholesome entertainment in the country music industry.

> *Be on your guard; stand firm in the faith; be men of courage; be strong. Do everything in love. 1 Corinthians 16:13-14*

CONTACT: MCA Records, Inc., 60 Music Square East, Nashville, TN 37203-4325

CBS 1996 Dan Epstein

Mike Wallace
TV Journalist, CBS' 60 Minutes

POINT OF IMPACT: An old *60 Minutes* ad hanging on his office wall reads, "The four most dreaded words in the English language: 'Mike Wallace is here.'" And at 82 years of age, Mike Wallace is, remarkably, still here. For 30 years, Wallace and his peers on CBS' newsmagazine, *60 Minutes,* have been doing the world the favor of exposing deadbeats, crooks, and scammers, as well as making more than a few politicians, presidents, and corporate CEOs squirm. The longest-running and most successful news program in history, the show is viewed weekly by 20 million people and has racked up a record 20 seasons in Nielsen's top ten. A spin-off, *60 Minutes II,* began airing in early 1999. Wallace, still known for his brusque, hard-nosed manner and straight-to-the-jugular questions, has signed a new multimillion-dollar contract.

He makes politicians, presidents, and CEOs squirm.

QUOTABLE: "I love the urgency of what we do. I like the battles that take place, the jousting. There are a lot of newsmagazines out there now, but people still recognize ours as the most responsible and most serious."

BEHIND THE SCENES: Recently, Wallace raised awareness of depression among men by talking about his own struggles in the HBO documentary *Dead Blue: Surviving Depression.* Wallace lives in New York City. He's married to his fourth wife, Mary; he has two children and seven grandchildren.

PRAYER STARTERS:

- Give thanks for the generally positive impact of the free press and for the tradition of investigative journalism that *60 Minutes* represents.
- Pray for emotional and physical health for Mike Wallace today and for God's best for his extended family.
- Depression strikes about 17 million American adults each year. Pray for someone you know who may be affected; ask God to show you how you could bring encouragement.

> *Humble yourselves, therefore, under God's mighty hand, that he may lift you up in due time. 1 Peter 5:6*

CONTACT: *60 Minutes,* CBS, 524 W. 5th, New York City, NY 10019

William F. Schulz

Executive Director,
Amnesty International USA

AP/Wide World Photos

POINT OF IMPACT: Fifty years after the U.N. adopted a Universal Declaration of Human Rights—designed to guarantee due process and to protect citizens from government violence—one-third of the world's countries are killing their own citizens without charge or fair trial. These "crimes against humanity" make up Dr. William Schulz's caseload every day. Since 1994, he's been director of the American chapter of Amnesty International, a Nobel Prize-winning human rights organization. The group provides a global media platform for those who are persecuted for religious beliefs or who are fighting for freedom peacefully. Amnesty International increasingly tries to persuade governments that a good human rights record is good for business. Schulz's opinions and inside information are a catalyst for political decisions in the United States and abroad. He's a frequent guest on *60 Minutes*, CNN, and BBC, among other media.

He monitors crimes against humanity.

QUOTABLE: "In Indonesia, a 9-year-old boy who stole a bicycle was burned on his feet with cigarettes, beaten, and forced to torture his mother. These are the crimes that Amnesty International is working to stop."

BEHIND THE SCENES: Dr. Schulz and his wife, Beth Graham, are both Unitarian Universalist ministers. He's also served on the boards of People for the American Way, Planned Parenthood Federation, and Americans United for the Separation of Church and State. He lives on Long Island, New York, and has two grown children from a previous marriage.

PRAYER STARTERS:

- Pray that good will come from Amnesty International efforts worldwide. Pray that government-sponsored injustice and violence would be curbed.
- Pray that William Schulz will seek God's wisdom each day and be strengthened by His power.
- Ask God to bless Schulz and his wife and family with safety and with a fresh encounter with the truths of the Bible.

> *Deliver me, O my God, from the hand of the wicked, from the grasp of evil and cruel men. Psalm 71:4*

CONTACT: Amnesty International, 322 8th Ave., New York, NY 10001

213

Courtesy of Tim LaHaye

Tim LaHaye
Bestselling Author

POINT OF IMPACT: As the millennium draws to a close, many authors of both fiction and nonfiction are focused on the end of the world. A leader in these end-times reflections is Tim LaHaye, the widely known prophecy expert and the bestselling author of *Spirit-Controlled Temperament* (more than 1 million copies sold). With co-writer Jerry Jenkins, LaHaye has also produced the phenomenally successful *Left Behind* fiction series, including *Left Behind, Tribulation Force, Nicolae, Soul Harvest,* and *Apollyon.* Together they have sold more than 5 million copies and reportedly prompted thousands of conversions. LaHaye has written 40 other books, with more than 12 million copies in print. As president and founder of Family Life Seminars, he's conducted more than 900 seminars in the United States and Canada. He also produces the *Capitol Report,* a newsletter on current events that affirms traditional values and religious liberty.

He readies his readers for the end-times.

QUOTABLE: "I have dedicated the rest of my life to teaching and preaching Bible prophecy and heralding the soon coming of Christ. Nothing inspires Christians to holiness, evangelism, and missions like good Bible teaching on prophecy."

BEHIND THE SCENES: For 25 years he pastored a church in San Diego that expanded to three locations. Jenkins, his co-writer on the *Left Behind* series, has more than 100 books to his credit, including a biography with Nolan Ryan. LaHaye's wife, Beverly, is the founder of the 600,000-member public policy group, Concerned Women of America. The LaHayes have four grown children. They live in Southern California.

PRAYER STARTERS:

- Give thanks for Tim LaHaye's faithfulness over many years as a minister of the gospel, and in recent years, for the influence of his end-times novels.
- Ask God to bless Tim and Beverly LaHaye with health, strength, and joy.
- Pray that believers will live "without spot or blame until the appearing of our Lord Jesus Christ" (1 Timothy 6:14-15). Pray that alarmists and opportunists in the church would be quickly discredited.

Be patient and stand firm, because the Lord's coming is near. James 5:8

CONTACT: Family Life Seminars, 370 L'Enfant Promenade S.W., Suite 801, Washington, DC 20024; also, www.leftbehind.com

Amartya Sen
Economist, 1998 Nobel Laureate

AP/Wide World Photos

POINT OF IMPACT: Amartya Sen, a native of India, has to do something about suffering when he sees it. Sen was just 10 when the Bengal famine killed 5 million people in his homeland (now Bangladesh). Remembering the dying begging for "a few drops of rice starch," he grew up to spend his energies searching for the causes of such disasters, as well as educational and gender-related abuses. He's researched famines and found ways to predict and quell them. He's created means to more accurately measure poverty so that programs to treat it are more effective. His latest book, *Hunger and Public Action*, which he co-wrote with Jean Dreze, has been described by economists as "the most important work of the decade on hunger and famine." He teaches at Trinity College (Cambridge University), is the first Asian to be appointed the head of a college in England, and the first Indian to win the Nobel Prize in Economics.

His life is devoted to ending hunger.

QUOTABLE: "All people must have the same possibilities of choice, even if they don't have the same means."

BEHIND THE SCENES: Born in 1933, Sen earned his Ph.D. in economics in England, then taught at Harvard before becoming a Master at Trinity College. Sen drives a reliable Ford Taurus. He's married to his third wife, Emma Rothschild, a philosophy professor at Cambridge. Sen is the father of four children: Antara, Nandana, Indrani, and Kabir. Many parents in India are reportedly naming their sons after him.

PRAYER STARTERS:

- Give thanks for the progress Amartya Sen has brought to our understanding of famine in underdeveloped countries.
- Pray for advances in famine response by nations and relief agencies, and for better farming techniques in famine-plagued regions.
- Pray that Amartya Sen would know God's love for him personally; ask that God's grace and peace would surround him.

> *Do not reap to the very edges of your field or gather the gleanings of your harvest. . . . Leave them for the poor and the alien. Leviticus 19:9-10*

CONTACT: Trinity College, Cambridge, CB2 1TQ, United Kingdom

Roseanne Barr
Comedian, Actress, TV Talk-Show Host

Archive Photo

POINT OF IMPACT: Roseanne Barr is among that small number of stars recognizable by their first name alone. She began her career as a stand-up comic, but fame came with her groundbreaking, top-rated TV sit-com *Roseanne.* The show depicted her as the loud, straightforward mother of a blue-collar family and dealt with sexuality, drugs, and family issues in a way that many people found hilarious—and some found offensive. The show was on the forefront of an aggressive media wave (including *The Simpsons,* Howard Stern, and Jerry Springer) that, as one writer put it, "leaves few assumptions about taste or privacy unassaulted." After the controversial series ended, she got her own TV talk show, which debuted to mixed reviews. Roseanne once said of her TV series audience, "I want them to feel healed. I want them to feel happy. I want them to feel like, at least, there's a real woman-mother on TV."

She changed notions about "family" television.

QUOTABLE: "I am the person who is most qualified to host a talk show: I have five kids from three different men, I come from a trailer court as a Jew passing as a Mormon in Salt Lake City, my sister and brother are both gay, I am a woman with multiple personalities, and I've been reunited with my eldest daughter whom I gave up for adoption and was found years later by the *National Enquirer.*" [All true.]

BEHIND THE SCENES: Famous for going to war with people on and off the set, Roseanne, 48, seems to have turned a corner. "I don't want to sound like Pat Robertson, but I have seen that the old straight and narrow may be the way to go. I don't want to be fighting everybody anymore." Roseanne, a single mother, has one child, Buck, still at home; her other children are Brandi, Jessica, Jennifer, and Jake.

PRAYER STARTERS:

- Pray for the viewers of Roseanne's shows, especially those who feel unnoticed or undervalued. Ask God to reveal His tender care to them today.
- Pray that Roseanne will use her talents to encourage and uplift her viewers.
- Ask God to bless Roseanne and her family with emotional fulfillment and spiritual direction and refreshment.

> *If it is possible, as far as it depends on you, live at peace with everyone.*
> Romans 12:18

CONTACT: The Lee Solters Company, 8383 Wilshire Blvd., Suite 850, Beverly Hills, CA 90211

216

George F. Will

Political Commentator, Author

Courtesy of Washington Post

POINT OF IMPACT: George Will, a highly respected and award-winning conservative political columnist, summed up Clinton's recent repentance this way: "Clinton's current confessional theme . . . is: 'I am ashamed of what I did to conceal behavior I was ashamed of, so now I have nothing to be ashamed of.'" Will's *Washington Post* column, which appears in 450 newspapers nationally, won him the Pulitzer Prize in 1977; his *Newsweek* column earned him the 1978 National Headliners Award; and a 1985 *Washington Journalist Review* readers' poll named Will "best writer, any subject." He's a regular on ABC's *This Week*, where he analyzes the state of the nation with other Washington-watchers. Will has also published a number of books, including *The Pursuit of Happiness and Other Sobering Thoughts* and *Statecraft as Soulcraft*. Says Frank Price, "[Will's] trademark wit, wry observations, and elegant prose make him America's premier conservative writer and political commentator."

He's the country's premier conservative sage.

QUOTABLE: "Heroes make vivid the values by which we try to live."

BEHIND THE SCENES: George F. Will was born in 1941 in Champaign, Illinois. He's a devoted baseball fan—specifically the Baltimore Orioles—and has written extensively on it in books like *Men at Work: The Craft of Baseball* and most recently *Bunts: Curt Flood, Camden Yards, Pete Rose, and Other Reflections on Baseball*. Will and his wife, Mari, have four children: Jonathan, Geoffrey, Victoria, and David.

PRAYER STARTERS:

- Pray that George Will and other analysts will be blessed by God with perspective, clarity, compassion, and a passion for truth.

- Give thanks for George Will's ability to articulate and defend traditional, Judeo-Christian values in a way that gives them impact with readers across the religious and political spectrums.

- Ask the Lord to bless Will and his family with grace, peace, and plenty.

Hold on to faith and a good conscience. 1 Timothy 1:19

CONTACT: Washington Post Writers Group, 1150 15th St., N.W., Washington, DC 20071-9200

Carol M. Browner

*Administrator, Environmental
Protection Agency (EPA)*

POINT OF IMPACT: As head of the EPA, Carol Browner is trying to "reinvent" environmental protection to achieve the best public health and environmental protection for the least cost. "The science demands we take action," she argues in her typically forthright manner, which has earned her the title "The Queen of Clean Air." The *New York Times* calls her "a new type of environmentalist" who views economic development and environmental protection as complementary goals. When Browner proposed a set of strict, new clean-air rules in the mid-nineties, she was lambasted from every direction—even some within the EPA thought she should be fired. But when Clinton approved her recommendations in July 1997, it was clear her tenacity had paid off. Key issues in the coming decade are disposing of nuclear waste, water quality, and damage to the upper atmosphere.

She's "The Queen of Clean Air."

QUOTABLE: "Imagine turning on your tap and not knowing whether the water is safe enough for your children to brush their teeth. Or watching raw sewage being dumped into the lake in which your family loves to swim and fish. This administration . . . must provide the leadership necessary to guarantee public health and natural resource protection for all Americans."

BEHIND THE SCENES: Browner, who worked as legislative director for Vice President Al Gore during his stint in the Senate, reportedly did much of the research for Gore's bestselling book *Earth in the Balance.* She's married, with one child.

PRAYER STARTERS:

- Pray that Carol Browner will find success in her efforts to protect children from environmental risk.
- Pray that Browner will have wisdom to know how to reconcile many competing interests.
- Ask for God's presence and favor to be made plain to Carol Browner and her family.

God saw all that he had made and it was very good. Genesis 1:31

CONTACT: United States EPA, 401 M Street S.W., Washington, DC 20460; e-mail: browner.carol@EPAmail.epa.gov

John Updike
Author

Archive Photo

POINT OF IMPACT: Over the past 40 years, author John Updike has been accused of spawning the sexual liberalism of the sixties, reviled for encouraging the self-indulgence of the seventies, celebrated for his spiritual insights in the eighties, and universally acclaimed as America's master of the English language. His career has spanned 50 books, including *Rabbit Is Rich* and *Rabbit at Rest,* which both won Pulitzer Prizes. His novels typically include graphic sex, death, middle-class angst, the grace of God, and the struggle for faith in the midst of hedonistic popular culture. In short, Updike is considered the most prolific and shrewd observer and chronicler of modern times. Critic William H. Pritchard once wrote of Updike, "He is putting together a body of work which in substantial intelligent creation will eventually be seen as second to none in our time."

His stories chronicle the struggles of modern living.

QUOTABLE: "I have an incorrigible religious streak from my God-fearing father. I believe humankind is a religious as well as sexual animal. My conservative feeling is that it's natural to affiliate with the religious institutions that exist. We all want to link up with something bigger."

BEHIND THE SCENES: Updike, 67, lives in Beverly Farms, Massachusetts. He has suffered from a lifelong speech impediment. He was raised in a conservative Christian home and regularly attends an Episcopal church near Boston. He credits Karl Barth and Søren Kierkegaard with shaping his spiritual views. He's married and the father of four children.

PRAYER STARTERS:

- Give thanks for John Updike's literary achievements, and for his capacity to see and communicate that God is intrinsic to modern life.
- Pray that he will walk—and write—in truth. Ask for the well-being of his wife and family.
- Pray that Updike's readers will embrace the grace and claims of Jesus Christ.

If you utter worthy, not worthless, words, you will be my spokesman.
Jeremiah 15:19

CONTACT: Alfred A. Knopf, Inc., Random House, 201 E. 50th St., New York, NY 10022-7703; www.aaknopf.com

Archive Photo

Betsy King
Golfer

POINT OF IMPACT: No one in the history of professional women's golf has made more money than Betsy King, a three-time LPGA Player of the Year, winner of more than 30 tournaments, and member of the LPGA Hall of Fame—the most exclusive Hall in sports, with only 14 members. Yet despite all her professional success, King has always considered what she does off the links more important. She's active in the LPGA Christian Fellowship, she builds houses for Habitat for Humanity, in 1993 and 1994 she traveled to Romania to work with orphans, and she's a frequent guest at Christian youth camps. As *Sports Illustrated* said, "King is the least trivial of golf champions. Other winners buy cars and clothes; King comforts Romanian orphans. Other stars complain about paying taxes; King pounds nails for Habitat for Humanity. Other Hall of Famers talk of their exploits; King makes listeners squirm with her religious fervor and antiabortion views."

She's the least trivial of golf champions.

QUOTABLE: "I think the mental part of golf is overplayed. Visualizing success is fine, but I can beat any 18 handicapper in the world, I don't care what the person's attitude is. He can picture hitting it 250 yards all he wants, but if he doesn't have the swing to do it, he can't do it."

BEHIND THE SCENES: In 1987 she won the Samaritan Award, which acknowledges humanitarian and charitable efforts by a player. King, 45, is single and lives in Scottsdale, Arizona.

PRAYER STARTERS:

- Give thanks for the consistent and inspiring example of Betsy King on and off the greens.
- Pray for her continuing impact in the fast-growing game of golf and among its fans (women are taking up the sport at a faster rate than men).
- Ask for God's favor and loving presence to surround her like a shield (Psalm 5:12).

Each of you should look not only to your own interests, but to the interests of others. Philippians 2:4

CONTACT: LPGA, 100 International Golf Drive, Daytona Beach, FL 32124-1092

Bishop Charles E. Blake

*Pastor, West Angeles
Church of God in Christ*

Courtesy of Charles E. Blake

POINT OF IMPACT: Converted at age 16 and preaching by 17, Charles Blake started his own church several years later with 50 members. Under his dynamic leadership, the congregation at the West Angeles Church of God in Christ has grown to 17,000 members—the largest of its denomination in the world. Blake encourages more than soul saving. What makes his church unique is its strong emphasis on community involvement—an example for, and challenge to, other urban churches. The West Angeles Church offers some 80 ministries, including the Community Development Corporation, a counseling center, and prison and skid row ministries. The church has become popular with celebrities of faith (Denzel Washington attends).

His church is a model of social concern.

QUOTABLE: "If we want to promote positive change, we cannot rely solely on our politicians to institute change on our behalf. Only by becoming involved in our churches and civic organizations can we prepare a more hopeful future for our children."

BEHIND THE SCENES: Blake, 60, inherited his passion for ministry from his father, the late Bishop J.A. Blake, who was also a pastor. He is married to Mae Lawrence Blake, who is President of West Angeles Women Affairs, and is the father of Kimberly Roxanne, Charles Edward II, and Lawrence Champion. He has two grandsons, Joseph and Jared.

PRAYER STARTERS:

- Give thanks for the positive impact of Bishop Charles Blake among African-American believers and in Southern California.
- Pray that God will bless Bishop Blake's ministry and the far-reaching impact of his church. Pray for the success of Christian ministries in greater Los Angeles, especially among large minority and immigrant populations.
- Ask God to favor the Blake family with health, plenty, and peace.

> *He calls his own sheep by name and leads them out. After he has gathered his own flock, he walks ahead of them, and they follow him because they recognize his voice. John 10:3-4 NLT*

CONTACT: West Angeles Church of God in Christ, 3045 Crenshaw Blvd., Los Angeles, CA 90016-4264

Archive Photo

Peter Jennings

Anchor and Senior Editor,
ABC's World News Tonight

POINT OF IMPACT: Peter Jennings reports on and interprets world events for millions of news viewers every evening. Among his fellow network anchormen, he's the master at conveying personable confidence. Unlike some anchors, Jennings has a reputation for being highly involved in what is aired. Nicholas Regush, an ABC producer, notes, "If Peter feels a story is inappropriate or unfair, there is no chance it gets on air." He's covered many of the pivotal events that have shaped the last half of the century. He was there for the raising and falling of the Berlin wall, the civil rights movement, and the struggle for equality in Southern Africa. He reported the repression of communism in the Soviet Union, and then its demise. He has a particular interest in children and has done several live news specials for children on subjects ranging from growing up in the age of AIDS to the effects of prejudice.

He gets the final say on news.

QUOTABLE: "I am not an intellectual. I have a good quality by TV standards, which is to reduce complicated ideas to literal or literate packages which people can understand."

BEHIND THE SCENES: Jennings' accomplishments make it hard to believe that he never finished high school. Despite working in U.S. media for many years, Jennings has retained his Canadian citizenship. At 62, he stays fit through canoeing, skiing, sailing, and tennis. Married to ABC producer Katherine Freed, he has two grown children by a previous marriage.

PRAYER STARTERS:

- Pray for God's provisions and peace for the Jennings family, and that they would recognize His hand in the world around them.
- Ask for discretion and moral courage for news professionals today.
- Pray today for news reporters the world over, that as they gather and communicate news, they would also be exposed to the good news of faith and love (1 Thessalonians 3:6).

> *Many are the plans in a man's heart, but it is the LORD's purpose that prevails.*
> *Proverbs 19:21*

CONTACT: ABC, 47 West 66th Street, New York, NY 10023

Mary Robinson
High Commissioner for Human Rights,
United Nations

UN/DPI Photo by Evan Schneider

POINT OF IMPACT: Mary Robinson's job every day is to go up against some of the globe's most brutal dictators and disheartening problems: genocide in Rwanda, child prostitution in Thailand, female genital mutilation in the sub-Sahara, hushed-up political murders in Algeria. She's described as strong-minded ("a stubborn girl is our Mary," says one Irish politician). In fact Koffi Annan, the United Nations' Secretary General, is counting on her to radically restructure how the Geneva-based commission does business—often, it's been slow to act and ineffective. If she succeeds, she'll have accomplished internationally what she did in Ireland, where, as the nation's first president (1990–97) she took a largely ceremonial position and used it to galvanize the Irish public to deal with major change. Her achievements in that position have been called "one of the wonders of contemporary politics."

She's a chief defender of the world's oppressed.

QUOTABLE: "People I admire have two qualities: a kind of simplicity, and generosity of spirit. It seems to me that the more impressive people are in what they have done, the simpler they tend to be in how they talk to you, or in what they say or write."

BEHIND THE SCENES: Robinson, 56, grew up in a convent school. After graduate study at Harvard, she married Nicholas Robinson, a lawyer by training but a cartoonist and author by profession. Since he was Protestant, their wedding shocked her Catholic family, who boycotted it. But after the birth of their children—Tessa, William, and Aubrey—family relations warmed.

PRAYER STARTERS:

- Give thanks for the dedication and competence of public servants like Mary Robinson.
- Pray for teamwork and willingness to change in the U.N.'s human rights efforts; pray that Mary Robinson will be empowered by God for her task.
- Remember the weak, abused, and dispossessed in your prayers today.
- Ask the Lord to keep Robinson and her family safe and blessed in His care.

Speak up for . . . all who are destitute. Proverbs 31:8

CONTACT: Palais des Nations, 8-14 avenue de la Paix, CH 1211 Geneva 10, Switzerland

Don Imus
Radio Talk-Show Host

POINT OF IMPACT: John Donald Imus, Jr. was one of radio's first bad boys. Today his *Imus in the Morning* reaches an audience of 10 million each day. He's been listed by *Time* magazine as one of America's 25 Most Influential People, and in a *Newsweek* cover article he was described "as powerful as, if not more powerful than, a network anchor." He's still brash, angry, and irreverent, but recently he's moved away from general commentary into politics. Critics say that he's now loved by some who used to hate him, and his star-studded guest list remains a hot ticket. In his recent biography, *Don Imus: Mouthing Off*, he chronicles his battle with drugs and alcohol. Imus is the only three-time recipient of the prestigious Marconi Award.

He's one of radio's original bad boys.

QUOTABLE: "Mort Saul made the original observation that people who talk most about family values are all on their second and third wives. And I would point out they all have families you could rope off and charge admission to view."

BEHIND THE SCENES: Imus, 60, is a high-school dropout who grew up in Southern California. His bestselling novel, *God's Other Son,* tells the story of a lecherous evangelist. He and his second wife, the former Deidre Coleman, are the parents of Fredric Wyatt Imus and live in New York. Imus has four daughters from his first marriage.

PRAYER STARTERS:

- Don Imus has raised millions for the Tomorrow's Children Fund and the CJ foundation for SIDS. Give thanks for his concern for children's health.
- Pray that Imus' widespread influence would be used with discernment—that it would be constructive and helpful.
- Ask God to bless the marriage and children of Don and Deidre Imus; pray that God's love expressed in people, circumstances, and the Bible would draw each family member to Him.

> *May the words of my mouth and meditation of my heart be pleasing in your sight, O LORD, my Rock and my Redeemer. Psalm 19:14*

CONTACT: www.MSNBC.com

Anne Lamott
Author

Photo credit: Mallory Geitheim

POINT OF IMPACT: There was a time, says ground-breaking author Anne Lamott, when "I really would have rather died than to have my wonderful brilliant left-wing non-believer friends know that I had begun to love Jesus." But these days she lets the whole world know. Her latest bestseller, *Traveling Mercies*, is a personal chronicle of her spiritual journey. But don't look for it in Christian bookstores. Her approach is sometimes irreverent, bracingly honest, and funny. Lamott, 46, has the ear of the "wired" generation through her monthly essays for the online magazine *Salon*. *Time* magazine calls her column "the best thing on the internet." She's the author of five novels as well as two nonfiction books. In a day when evangelicals are often cut off from mainstream readers, Lamott's impact is noteworthy.

She invites the "wired" generation on a spiritual journey.

QUOTABLE: "I never felt like I had much choice with Jesus; He was relentless. I didn't experience Him so much as the hound of heaven, as the old description has it, but as the alley cat of heaven, who seemed to believe that if it just keeps showing up, meowing outside your door, you'd eventually open up. . . ."

BEHIND THE SCENES: Lamott was an alcoholic for much of her adult life. But in 1986 she quit drinking and began attending church. She was attempting to get her life back in order when in 1988, she became pregnant. "These people [in the congregation] whipped into action . . . to show up with everything we needed. They walked right into my house. They walked right into my heart." Lamott lives with her son outside San Francisco.

PRAYER STARTERS:

- Give thanks for the writing gifts of Lamott and for her boldness to proclaim Christ. Ask God to help her flourish in her faith.
- Pray for a growing number of Christian writers who can reach pagan and "post-Christian" readers, especially those who resist traditional church.
- Ask God to bless her and her son with good health in both body and soul.

> *Here I am! I stand at the door and knock. If anyone hears my voice and opens the door, I will come in and eat with him, and him with me. Revelation 3:20*

CONTACT: Steven Barclay Agency, 321 Pleasant Street, Petaluma, CA 94952

Abdurrahman Wahid

Chairman, Nahdlatul Ulama Indonesia

Courtesy of World Vision

POINT OF IMPACT: Frequently called "one of the world's most powerful Muslim leaders," Abdurrahman Wahid was once snubbed by President Suharto, Indonesia's former strongman. Now Wahid, better known in his own country as Gus Dur, is violence-torn Indonesia's best hope for bridging the traditional divide between secular and Islamic politics. He is supported by all 30 million followers of the Nahdlatul Ulama Islamic organization. The government of Indonesia has tolerated the group in part because of Wahid's stature and public reputation. Wahid recently set up a discussion group to examine democratic reforms. More than simply a political or religious leader, he manages to have a foothold and exercise power in both camps. He has worked well with minorities in Indonesia, including Christians. Personal health problems, including a stroke and failing eyesight, haven't limited his effectiveness.

He bridges deep divides in Indonesia.

QUOTABLE: "Muslims must not be tricked into action, which seems to be a religious affair, because there are political interests behind it."

BEHIND THE SCENES: Wahid, 60, loves classical music. Recovering from a stroke in January 1998, he listened to Beethoven for hours. Wahid is married and the father of four children.

PRAYER STARTERS:

- Pray for peace in Indonesia, a country of 225 million in the throes of wrenching political and economic change. Pray for Christians there, who often suffer opposition and discrimination.
- Pray that Wahid's influence (Indonesia is 90 percent Muslim) will be for good—helping to fight corruption, and bringing stability and vision.
- Ask God to bring Wahid healing and vigor, and protect him and his family from danger.

> *May the nations be glad and sing for joy, for you rule the peoples justly and guide the nations of the earth. Psalm 67:4*

CONTACT: Pengurus Besar Nahdlatul Ulama, Jl Kramat Raya 164, Jakarta, Indonesia

LeAnn Rimes

Singer, Actress

AP/Wide World Photos

POINT OF IMPACT: LeAnn Rimes burst onto the country music scene in 1996 with her debut single "Blue." Just 13 at the time, the singer won immediate acclaim for her mature voice and style. Awards showered: the Academy of Country Music's Single of the Year, Song of the Year, and Top New Female Vocalist, and Grammys for Best Female Country Vocal Performance and Best New Artist. In Rimes' brief but amazing career, she has released three multiplatinum albums, starred in an ABC holiday movie, and crossed over into pop music realms with her hit single, "How Do I Live?" The *Houston Chronicle* writes that her "sound seems to come from the past, like some lost Patsy Cline radio broadcast that's been hidden away for 35–40 years. Yet the voice is fresh and young and remarkably full." Rimes, now 18, is the only country singer ever to have an album (*You Light Up My Life: Inspirational Songs*) debut at number one on the pop, country, and contemporary Christian charts all at once.

She simultaneously tops pop, country, and Christian charts.

QUOTABLE: "I don't let it all go to my head. It could all disappear overnight. So I remind myself of that and how hard I've worked to get here."

BEHIND THE SCENES: Rimes began singing at 18 months, and she won her first song and dance competition at age five. The pretty blond was discovered when songwriter Bill Mack heard the nine-year-old sing the national anthem at a sporting event; he thought her voice would be perfect for "Blue," a song he'd written for Patsy Cline. Rimes lives in Garland, Texas.

PRAYER STARTERS:

- Rimes is considering pursuing speech therapy in college. Pray that she will seek God's guidance in the significant decisions about her future.
- Pray that Rimes' wholesome influence among country music fans will encourage many to make good life choices and examine the claims of Christ.
- Ask that God will favor LeAnn Rimes with lasting Christian friendships, maturity as she faces career pressures, and success.

Remember your Creator in the days of your youth. Ecclesiastes 12:1

CONTACT: www.curb.com/Artists/mail.html; e-mail: larfans@leann.com

Don't drift from humble works. Every work of love is a work of peace, no matter how small it is.

There is so much hatred and hurt! We will not overcome this with fighting, or with bombs; not with things that hurt, but with things that will bring love, joy, and peace.

I believe Saint Vincent de Paul used to tell the young aspirants, "Remember, the poor are our masters: love and obey them."

If we go to the poor with that longing to give God to them, to bring the joy of Jesus which is our strength, I think the world will soon be full of peace and full of love.

—MOTHER TERESA
in *My Life for the Poor*

James Dobson
Founder, President, Focus on the Family

POINT OF IMPACT: Seen by some as the Christian version of Dr. Spock and by others as an overbearing conservative, Dr. James Dobson has for 20 years been the preeminent physician and counselor to Christian families. Even among non-Christians, his views on child-rearing, education, and politics have often ended up framing the national agenda. Focus on the Family, his 23-year-old nonprofit organization, produces his international radio program heard daily in America on more than 2,900 radio stations as well as in 17 other countries. Focus also distributes nearly a dozen magazines read by more than 2.3 million monthly, and offers counseling and referrals to 1,500 therapists. His best-selling books include *The New Dare to Discipline* (a copy of which is in the White House library) and *Love Must Be Tough*. Presidents Carter, Reagan, and Bush have all consulted him on family issues.

His family focus sets national agendas.

QUOTABLE: "[Our] first love has not changed, nor will it ever. We still try to help moms and dads raise healthy, productive children who are committed to the gospel of Jesus Christ. There is no higher calling than that."

BEHIND THE SCENES: James Dobson, 63, grew up in Kansas, where his father was a Nazarene pastor. Dobson was Associate Clinical Professor of Pediatrics at the University of Southern California for 14 years before he founded Focus on the Family. His wife, Shirley, is chairperson of the National Day of Prayer and is a widely sought speaker on family and women's issues. The Dobsons have two grown children and live in Colorado.

PRAYER STARTERS:

- Give thanks for James Dobson's strong voice for parents, kids, and the range of Christian family concerns.
- Pray that Focus on the Family will impact for good America's ongoing conversation about family, education, sexuality, and morality.
- Ask God to bless James and Shirley Dobson with health and strength. Pray for continued healing for Dr. Dobson, who has suffered from health setbacks.

As for me and my household, we will serve the LORD. Joshua 24:15

CONTACT: 8605 Explorer Drive, Colorado Springs, CO 80920; www.family.org

Geraldine Laybourne

Chairman, CEO, Oxygen Media

Archive Photo

POINT OF IMPACT: Geraldine Laybourne, 53, heads Oxygen Media, a new cable channel for women and children. Laybourne and her husband, Kit, have teamed up with prime-time powerhouse Carsey-Werner-Mandabach Productions as well as Oprah's Harpo Entertainment Group to launch the channel. It debuts in January 2000. Laybourne is former president of Disney/ABC Cable Networks. Before that, she ran Nickelodeon, molding it into one of cable's leading channels. "I'm passionate about women," she told CNN. ". . . They have been underserved and they've been underrepresented. Our goal is to . . . be squarely on their side." Oxygen Media will practice what she calls "telefusion" by having companion sites on AOL that will help drive traffic to the channel and vice versa. In 1996 she was named one of the 25 most influential people in America by *Time*.

Her new TV channel is run by women for women.

QUOTABLE: On being ranked by *Fortune* magazine as one of America's most powerful female executives: "You're ranking the women? That's a nonfemale thing to do. Ranking is the opposite of what women are all about. Women are best at creating win–win environments, collaborating, working to make a contribution rather than working to be No. 1."

BEHIND THE SCENES: Laybourne says her inspiration comes from her family. She lives in Manhattan, where she and husband, Kit (a TV producer and author), are the parents of Emmy and Sam.

PRAYER STARTERS:

- Laybourne has said, "Media, whether it's television, or magazines, or whatever, comes with a set of stereotyped views about what women want, what kids want, that I just don't subscribe to." Pray that she succeeds in defining a more truthful and uplifting kind of TV programming.
- Ask God to surround her with positive influences who can help her succeed.
- Pray that the Laybourne family would experience a deep awareness of God's nearness, realness, and love.

Make every effort to do what leads to peace and to mutual edification.
Romans 14:19

CONTACT: www.oxygen.com

Richard Gere

Actor, Activist

Archive Photo

POINT OF IMPACT: It's hard to know in which arena Richard Gere, a devout Buddhist, has the most influence—through his movies, his politics, or his religion. On-screen, his first hit was *An Officer and a Gentleman* in 1982, but it was his role in *Pretty Woman* (1990) that finally secured his star status. Recent hits are *Primal Fear* and *Red Corner.* Offscreen he uses his high visibility to promote various ecological and political causes. In recent years, he's become the most prominent spokesman—outside of his friend and spiritual guide, the Dalai Lama—for the movement to free Tibet from Chinese occupation. To advance his causes, he founded the Tibet House in New York and the Gere Foundation. Meanwhile, recent projects including *Runaway Bride* with Julia Roberts promise to keep him, and his causes, in the spotlight.

He's a star advocate for the Tibetan cause.

QUOTABLE: "There was a lot of glassing over when I first started talking about Tibet. But now, when I walk into a room, that's what people are really interested in. . . . The Dalai Lama has elevated the whole issue to very high symbolism. Saving Tibet is saving the best part of ourselves."

BEHIND THE SCENES: Gere, 51, once said of his girlfriend, Carey Lowell, "She's very committed to Buddhism, which makes life a lot easier. If you're on a path, it's almost impossible if your partner is not on the same path." Gere is divorced from supermodel Cindy Crawford.

PRAYER STARTERS:

- Thank God for Richard Gere's compassion for, and work on behalf of, the Tibetans; pray that many others would support his work.
- Pray for Tibet's people, for their freedom from oppression, corruption, and violence. Pray that God will make Himself known there.
- Pray that Gere would be positively influenced by Christian individuals in media work and that his spiritual hunger would draw him to God.
- Ask God to bless Gere today with peace, wisdom, and health.

> *Salvation is found in no one else, for there is no other name under heaven given to men by which we must be saved. Acts 4:12*

CONTACT: ICM, 8942 Wilshire Blvd., Beverly Hills, CA 90211

Philip F. Anschutz

CEO, Anschutz Corporation

POINT OF IMPACT: One of America's richest men (worth $8.8 billion), Philip Anschutz built his fortune the old-fashioned way—through oil and railroads. But these days his corporation is trying to dominate the telecommunications industry through Qwest Communications International. Qwest is laying thousands of miles of fiber-optic cables along Anschutz's railroad lines. The network plans to serve 92 cities, representing 65 percent of all the long-distance and internet traffic in the United States. Information, entertainment, and shopping will travel over Anschutz's fiber channels. Anschutz has contributed hundreds of thousands of dollars to Republicans, which gives him significant political clout. He and his wife recently donated $900,000 to Princeton University. In 1998, *Forbes* listed him as one of the three smartest entrepreneurs in the world (along with Bill Gates and Prince al Saud).

His company wants to dominate telecommunications.

QUOTABLE: On career setbacks—"It's important to have your back to the wall. It teaches you how to think outside the box."

BEHIND THE SCENES: Philip Anschutz, a regular churchgoer, doesn't buy new cars because he's convinced they're a waste of money. These days, he drives a five-year-old Lexus. Anschutz, 61, gets up at 4:30 each morning to train for his next marathon; he's already run 15, many with his two grown daughters, Sarah and Elizabeth. He and his wife, Nancy, live in Denver.

PRAYER STARTERS:

- Ask that Philip Anschutz seeks God's wisdom in his decisions about business strategy, investments, and philanthropy.
- Pray that influential, capable, and forward-thinking Christians will be positioned in the telecommunications industry in the new millennium.
- Ask for physical and spiritual blessings for Anschutz and his family today, and that they'll be aware of Christ's loving presence.

> *Dishonest money dwindles away, but he who gathers money little by little makes it grow. Proverbs 13:11*

CONTACT: 555 17th Street, Suite 1000, Denver, CO 80202; www.qwest.net

Yo-Yo Ma

cellist

AP/Wide World Photos

POINT OF IMPACT: Violinist Isaac Stern says of Yo-Yo Ma, "He is probably the most perfect instrumentalist I have ever seen." The Chinese-born Ma is the master cellist for his generation and the inspiration for countless music students. Yet what he does best is *play*—he's collaborated with archictects, designers, ice dancers, choreographers, film makers, fiddle players, even African Bushmen to find new musical expressions. "There's no pure music," Ma likes to say, "everything is crossover." A prodigy since he was four, Ma has released 50 albums, won 12 Grammys, and poured his formidable energies into a hectic schedule of performing and teaching. His friend, pianist Emanual Ax, says of Ma: "Yo-Yo is in a way the right man at the right time. I think we need people like him if music is to remain a truly vital force."

In classical music, he's the "right man at the right time."

QUOTABLE: "To be a really good performer, you have to make sure that your ego is not the center but at the service of something else. To go one on one with Beethoven, you have to figure out who the guy is, what he's doing, and how that's encoded in the music. And then . . . you have to realize that you are not Beethoven."

BEHIND THE SCENES: Ma's father, Hiao-Tsiun Ma, taught music at Nanjing University in China before the family moved to New York in 1962. At five, Ma was assigned Bach's monumental Cello Suites (all six of them) to memorize. As a Harvard student, Ma skipped classes to perform around the world. Now 44, he lives in Boston with his wife, Jill Hornor, and their two teenagers.

PRAYER STARTERS:

- Give thanks for Yo-Yo Ma's extraordinary giftedness and enthusiasm for teaching young students ("Beautiful things need nurturing," he says).
- Pray for a serious music student you know, that he or she would discover the joy of serving God and others with their lives and abilities.
- Pray for Ma's safety in travel, and for strong and fufilling relationships at home. Pray for his continued positive influence in art and music.

> *Praise the Lord . . . Praise him for his acts of power; praise him for his surpassing greatness . . . Praise him with the strings and flute." Psalm 150:1-2,4*

CONTACT: BSO, 301 Massachusetts Ave., Boston, MA 02115; www.cello.org

Archive Photo

Thomas Middelhoff
CEO, Bertelsmann AG

POINT OF IMPACT: In 1998 Thomas Middelhoff had scarcely settled into the driver's seat of Bertelsmann AG, the world's third-largest media company, when he engineered two major publishing coups. First, he acquired Random House (whose luminaries include John Grisham, John Updike, and Maya Angelou), making his German company the largest English-language trade-book publisher in the world. Second, he negotiated a partnership with Barnes & Noble, bringing the 160-year-old company into the modern age of electronic commerce. At 46, he's the youngest CEO in the world's giant media groups. Insiders say he's blessed with new-media savvy, and most of all, an exceptional ability to lead. Says one media executive, "Thomas knows just where he wants to go and exactly how he wants to get there." The Bertelsmann company—known in publishing circles simply as "the Germans"—also owns such familiar enterprises as BMG Music Clubs and Bantam Books.

His German company is rewriting the book on American publishing.

QUOTABLE: "The groundwork we are laying today will help tomorrow's generation learn more."

BEHIND THE SCENES: Middelhoff lives in a country house outside Munich with his wife and five children. They have four dogs, two horses, chickens, pigs, and ducks in the pond out back. Middelhoff spends about one week a month in New York. Leaving home late in the afternoon, he can take a private plane to Paris, hop on the Concorde, and arrive in Manhattan in time for dinner.

PRAYER STARTERS:

- Ask for wisdom for Middlehoff and the directors of the Bertelsmann group as they make decisions that impact millions.
- Pray for his safety as he travels, and for provision for his family when he is away. Ask for spiritual blessings on his marriage.
- Twenty percent of American adults are considered functionally illiterate. Pray that they have the opportunity and the desire to learn to read.

Of making many books there is no end. Ecclesiastes 12:12

CONTACT: Verlagsgruppe Bertelsmann GmbH, 81673 Munchen, Neumarkterstr. 18, Germany

Sammy Sosa

Baseball Player, Chicago Cubs

Stephen Green Photography

POINT OF IMPACT: Over the summer and fall of 1998, Mark McGwire and Sammy Sosa captured the world's imagination as they raced to break Roger Maris' 26-year-old record of 61 home runs in a season. Both of them did. McGwire finally set the new record at 70. But in Sosa's native Dominican Republic and much of Central America, Sosa is "The Man." He hit an incredible 66 home runs, and led the Chicago Cubs to the playoffs. Back home, kids call him "Sammy Claus" for his gifts of computers to schoolchildren and donations to the homeless. Since Hurricane George devastated the island in 1998, the Sammy Sosa Foundation has provided millions of dollars of relief. President Clinton honored Sosa at the White House in January 1999. "Sports records are made, and sooner or later, they are broken," he said. "But making other people's lives better—and showing our children the true meaning of brotherhood—that's something that lasts forever."

In Latin America, he's a hero second to none.

QUOTABLE: "At one time I told myself that Sammy Sosa belonged to Sammy Sosa. But now I belong to my people."

BEHIND THE SCENES: Sosa's father died when Sammy was seven. He grew up in a one-room apartment with five siblings, his mother, and stepfather, and helped support the family as a shoe-shine boy. But every spare moment he played baseball—with a glove made from a milk carton, a ball made from rags, and a bat made from a tree branch. Today at 32, Sosa has homes in Chicago and Santo Domingo. He and his wife, Sonia, have four children.

PRAYER STARTERS:

- Give thanks for the inspiration and physical support that Sammy Sosa has brought to disaster-stricken Central America.
- Pray that, despite the pressures of fame, Sosa's continuing legacy in baseball will be that of a standout humanitarian and family man.
- Ask God to bless the Sosa's marriage and family today with His peace and protection, and a keen sense of His purposes.

Be devoted to one another in brotherly love. Romans 12:10

CONTACT: Chicago Cubs, Wrigley Field, 1060 W. Addison St., Chicago, Illinois, 60613-4397.

Harry Langdon Photography

Jack Hayford
Pastor, Evangelical Leader

POINT OF IMPACT: Jack Hayford, senior pastor of the 10,000-member Church on the Way (Van Nuys, California), is the driving force in the West-Coast based Foursquare denomination, one of the world's fastest-growing churches. Tall and energetic, Hayford has been called the "dean of reconciliation" among evangelical, charismatic and pentecostal groups. Several years ago, he and Lloyd Ogilvie (now Senate Chaplain) cofounded the "Pastors Love L.A." prayer meetings to support civic leaders and promote racial harmony. Says Ogilvie, "Hayford has the fire and dynamism of a charismatic, yet he understands the relevance of social responsibility." Located in the heart of L.A.'s film industry, Hayford's church ministers to a dynamic ethnic and cultural mix. In 1998, Hayford opened The King's Seminary, the first on the West Coast in the charismatic tradition.

His megachurch reaches out to love L.A.

QUOTABLE: "Fewer and fewer people are brought up in a family atmosphere which cultivates a sense of worth. More and more people tend to feel like cosmic accidents. There is nothing like the truth of God's Word to settle this issue: Every person is a case of 'planned parenthood'—God planned you!"

BEHIND THE SCENES: Hayford, 65, has written more than 20 books and composed over 400 songs, including the popular chorus "Majesty." These days he spends less time preaching and more time mentoring young pastors. "Pastors sense in him what they are longing to be," says Ogilvie. Hayford and his wife, Anna, have four children and 11 grandchildren.

PRAYER STARTERS:

- Pray that Jack Hayford's church will continue to impact the Los Angeles community, leading many to Christ and strengthening the faith of believers.
- Pray that God will use Pastor Hayford for His purposes in his mentoring role with pastors and lay workers.
- Ask God to bless the Hayfords with health, harmony and a renewed sense of His love for each of them.

We have not received the spirit of the world but the Spirit who is from God,
that we may understand what God has freely given us. 1 Corinthians 2:12

CONTACT: 14300 Sherman Way, Van Nuys, CA 91405; www.tcotw.org

Phillip E. Johnson
Law Professor, UC Berkeley

Courtesy of Phil Johnson

POINT OF IMPACT: This grandfatherly lawyer is "stirring up the pea patch in respectable scientific circles by insisting that neo-Darwinism is naturalistic philosophy and not science," says Access Research Network. Claiming that logic is on his side, Phillip Johnson uses his well-honed debating skills to provide arguments on the absence of evolution's clear physical proof. His books, *Darwin on Trial* and *Defeating Darwinism by Opening Minds*, are regarded as some of the most influential books in the century: "Unquestionably the best critique of Darwin I have ever read," says scientist and author Michael Denton. Johnson, a Christian, is careful to discuss the origins of life question not as a believer but as a disinterested skeptic. He believes the real adversary is a dogma that insists life arose solely by chance and denies contrary evidence a hearing: "Neo-Darwinism survives only by the selective use of evidence, and because materialist philosophy has no alternative. They [evolutionists] rely heavily on ridicule and on appeals to their own authority to defend their position. I'm not proposing another theory; I'm explaining why I'm not convinced by theirs."

He leads the argument against Darwin's theories.

QUOTABLE: "When the truth is that we don't know, it's best to say so."

BEHIND THE SCENES: He's on the faculty at the University of California in Berkeley and has taught law for more than 30 years. Critics complain that he's not a scientist and is unqualified to analyze scientific theories. His method, however, is to analyze the logic of arguments and identify the assumptions that lie behind them. "Logic is logic wherever it is utilized," he says.

PRAYER STARTERS:

- Praise God for giving Phillip Johnson a credible and influential platform to seek and debate the issues of origin and human development.

- Ask God to open the minds and imaginations of readers of Johnson's treatises, where he challenges the concept of God as a "blind watchmaker."

- Ask God to bless Johnson and his family with health and happiness.

The discerning heart seeks knowledge, but the mouth of a fool feeds on folly. Proverbs 15:14

CONTACT: e-mail: philjohn@uclink4.berkeley.edu

Rush Limbaugh
Radio Personality

Archive Photo

POINT OF IMPACT: Rush Limbaugh is one of America's most popular radio talk-show hosts and an outspoken political commentator. As the self-appointed loudmouth for the blue-collar traditionalist, "Rush" has become a synonym for down-home, conservative, wisecracking horse sense. He follows in the tradition of political humorists like Mark Twain and Will Rogers. *The Rush Limbaugh Show* has often been ranked the nation's number-one radio talk show, reaching more than 20 million listeners every week. Limbaugh is also the author of two bestsellers, *The Way Things Ought to Be* and *See, I Told You So*. Limbaugh hosts his own syndicated television show, which appears on 222 television stations nationwide.

He's a blue-collar political funny man.

QUOTABLE: "The way to improve our schools is not more money, but the reintroduction of moral and spiritual values, as well as the four 'R's': reading, 'riting, 'rithmatic, and Rush."

BEHIND THE SCENES: Limbaugh, 49, was born and raised in Cape Girardeau, Missouri, where he began his radio career at the age of 16. He attributes his firm political beliefs and wit to a "stern, conservative lawyer father" and a "talkative, wisecracking mother" (He insists his mother is the funniest person he's ever known). He lives in New York City with his third wife.

PRAYER STARTERS:

- Give thanks for Limbaugh's commitment to pro-life issues and abstinence.
- Pray that Limbaugh will seek and follow God's wisdom; pray for protection and spiritual enrichment for Limbaugh and his family.
- Ask that Limbaugh would influence the lives of his listeners in a positive and God-honoring way.

> *Let your conversation be always full of grace, seasoned with salt, so that you may know how to answer everyone. Colossians 4:6*

CONTACT: The Rush Limbaugh Show, 515 W. 57th St., New York, NY 10019

Harville Hendrix

Psychologist, Pastoral Counselor

Helen Hunt

Author, Women's Advocate

Photo by Michael Ian

POINT OF IMPACT: Described as "one of the leading therapeutic voices of the 1990s," for 35 years, Dr. Harville Hendrix and his wife, Helen Hunt, have been teaching that the challenges of parenting and marriage are less like problems than opportunities for healing and growth. In bestsellers like *Giving the Love that Heals: A Guide for Parents,* Hendrix and Hunt teach that spouses and parents can learn to relate "intentionally," thus breaking "the legacy of wounding" that can get passed from generation to generation. "I know of no better guide for couples who genuinely desire a maturing relationship," says M. Scott Peck. More than 1,400 clinicians present hundreds of seminars annually worldwide. Dr. Hendrix's multiple appearances on Oprah Winfrey's show have won him the "most socially redemptive" daily talk show award.

Together they help to heal relationships.

QUOTABLE: "Every time we have a conversation with another person or an interaction with another person we are either healing ourselves or wounding ourselves further."—Harville Hendrix

BEHIND THE SCENES: Hendrix, 65, was educated at Mercer University, the Theological Seminary of New York, and the University of Chicago Divinity School. Helen Hunt, 51, has earned three degrees from Southern Methodist University. They have raised six children and live in New Jersey.

PRAYER STARTERS

- Thank God for the hope and help Harville and Helen have brought to thousands of couples. Pray for their continuing influence and success.
- Helen Hunt has been a voice in feminist theology, and a force in several women's organizations. Pray for compassion, insight, and fidelity as Christian women wrestle with issues of identity and purpose.
- Ask God to favor Hendrix and Hunt with peace, health, and happiness.

Love one another deeply, from the heart. 1 Peter 1:22

CONTACT 335 North Knowles Ave., Winter Park, FL 32789; www.imagotherapy.com

Courtesy of William Morris Agency

Sam Haskell
West Coast President,
The William Morris Agency (WMA)

POINT OF IMPACT: Haskell's greatest talent (he's a talent agent, after all) may be to shatter the Hollywood stereotype of the teflon, spritually bankrupt powerbroker. As one writer observed, "Though he swims in Hollywood's riptides, Haskell is more guppy than shark." He oversees 65 other agents, but personally handles 40 clients, including Kathie Lee Gifford, Bill Cosby, and George Clooney—and he does it with legendary kindness and integrity. Says one network executive, "Haskell mesmerizes you with that down-home charm. We get all soft and mushy and the next thing you know our hands and feet are tied and we're just squirming. We've been hog-tied by Sam more than once. The amazing thing is we come back for more." Recent Haskell/WMA projects include *Mad About You, Suddenly Susan,* and *Everybody Loves Raymond.*

He swims with the sharks in Hollywood.

QUOTABLE: On people asking about his success: "People want me to talk about a deal for Kathie Lee or Bill Cosby or some show I sold that made ga-billions of dollars. But my greatest success is that I'm exactly the same person today as I was when I arrived here 19 years ago."

BEHIND THE SCENES: Haskell has been married to his college sweetheart, Mary Donnelly Haskell, a former Miss Mississippi, for 16 years. He eats breakfast with his kids, Sam IV and Mary Lane, every morning and reserves weekends for family. In 1991, in his mother's memory, he set up the Mary Kirkpatrick Haskell Scholarship Foundation, which helps underprivileged youth in Mississippi go to college.

PRAYER STARTERS:

- Give thanks for the charitable contributions Haskell makes to youth in need.
- Ask God to bless Haskell's career, and pray that he'll continue to be an inspiring example of integrity and caring to many in Hollywood.
- Ask God to bless his family with unity, health, and spiritual wholeness.

The man of integrity walks securely. Proverbs 10:9

CONTACT: WMA, 151 El Camino Drive, Beverly Hills, CA 90212

William C. Steere, Jr.
CEO, Pfizer, Inc.

Courtesy of Pfizer, Inc.

POINT OF IMPACT: William Steere's drug company, Pfizer, Inc., is a leading maker of consumer health products and prescription medicines. And while it rates behind industry giant Merck, Pfizer owns the dream product of the decade, Viagra. Sales for the impotence treatment are expected to top $2 billion by 2001. And what Steere and his team are realizing is that Viagra's sudden success is just a hint of things to come. Says one pharmaceutical analyst, "The aging baby boomer population wants to remain young and is very willing to use drugs that counteract some of the ravages of aging." Steere points to future products that will minimize problems like weight loss, baldness, wrinkling, and memory or hair loss. Since Steere took over, Pfizer has risen from number 13 to number four in worldwide prescription drug sales.

He runs the company that owns Viagra.

QUOTABLE: "Viagra crystallized some things I'd been thinking about. It struck me that a quality-of-life drug for aging would be a real winner. Look at the volume in cosmetics, which are nostrums that don't really do anything."

BEHIND THE SCENES: Steere, 64, graduated from Stanford with a degree in biology. He got started in the drug business as a salesman for Pfizer in 1959. Ever since, "it's been a one-wife, one-company life," he likes to say.

PRAYER STARTERS:

- Give thanks that modern pharmaceuticals relieve so much suffering and enhance health.
- Pray that William Steere and others in the drug industry would proceed responsibly, creatively, and successfully in their quest.
- Ask that Steere will seek God's wisdom and favor in his professional and private life; pray for physical and spiritual health for his whole family.

> *He asked you for life, and you gave it to him—length of days, for ever and ever. Psalm 21:4*

CONTACT: 235 E. 42nd St., Floor 28, New York, NY 10017-5755; www.pfizer.com

Archive Photo

Patricia Ireland

*Feminist; President, National Organization
for Women (NOW)*

POINT OF IMPACT: As the head of NOW since 1991, Patricia Ireland draws from her experience as an attorney and activist to keep NOW in the news. Since it was formed three decades ago, NOW has grown into the largest, most visible feminist organization in the country and boasts 300,000 members. Under Ireland's leadership, NOW has become more active in promoting abortion rights as well as gay and lesbian rights. Out of concern over growing threats to abortion rights, she developed the project Stand Up for Women, which trains activists for major lobbying and litigation efforts as well as on-site clinic defense. A NOW goal is to elect 2,000 new feminists to office by the year 2000. She's written a book chronicling her beliefs, called *What Women Want.*

She heads the most visible feminist organization.

QUOTABLE: "While we do express a healthy, legitimate anger over women who are battered or raped, we're also a lighthearted group because we act instead of letting rage eat at us."

BEHIND THE SCENES: Ireland learned the satisfaction of fighting back while a flight attendant for Pan Am in 1968. "I was underpaid and undervalued in an industry that actually seemed to invite sexual harassment with ads such as 'We really move our tails for you' or 'I'm Cheryl; fly me,'" she says. Just as maddening was the company's refusal to pay for her husband's oral surgery—though it routinely paid claims for the spouses of male employees. She teamed with NOW, which helped get the airline to cough up the cash and kill its biased policy. Before accepting her post at NOW, she worked pro bono on many discrimination cases. She lives in Washington, DC.

PRAYER STARTERS:

- Pray for hurting women in the United States and around the world who need health services and protection from violence and discrimination.
- Ask the Lord to make His presence and love very real to Patricia Ireland.
- Pray for a growing influence of biblical principles and values among the members of NOW.

> *I will walk about in freedom, for I have sought out your precepts.*
> *Psalm 119:45*

CONTACT: www.now.org

Josh McDowell

Author, Speaker

POINT OF IMPACT: Youth minister and writer Josh McDowell is best known for his books *Evidence That Demands a Verdict* and *More Than a Carpenter,* which have reached millions with compelling arguments about the historical and intellectual evidence supporting Christianity. Over the past 30 years, as a traveling representative for Campus Crusade for Christ, he's written more than 50 books and visited 700 college campuses, bringing the gospel to youth in 84 countries. His new campaign, *Right from Wrong,* educates parents and youth about the moral decline in society. He also has a weekly radio program, *The Josh McDowell Ministry.* He says the secret to his success is simple: "You have to get older, but you don't have to grow up." He routinely hangs out at the mall to spend time with students; his standard apparel, whether at home or on stage, is a polo shirt and jogging pants.

He campaigns for the difference between right and wrong.

QUOTABLE: "When everything is leveled out, when we accept everything in culture, we lose the ability to discern right from wrong. We don't have morality anymore, just different opinions: 'You can choose what's right or wrong, but don't impose your values on me.'"

BEHIND THE SCENES: After he accepted Christ while in college, McDowell noticed changes in his life. The biggest was in his relationship with his alcoholic father. McDowell's hatred for him had turned into love. He and his wife, Dottie, live in Dallas with two of their four children.

PRAYER STARTERS:

- Give thanks for the millions of high school and college kids who've been helped to make good life choices and to consider the reality of Christ through the ministry of Josh McDowell. Pray for his continued impact.
- McDowell, 60, has a grueling travel schedule, here and abroad. Pray for his strength and good health.
- Ask God to bless the McDowell family with quality time together.

> *What I received I passed on to you as of first importance: that Christ died for our sins according to the Scriptures, that he was buried, that he was raised on the third day. 1 Corinthians 15:3-4*

CONTACT: P.O. Box 1000, Dallas TX 75221; www.josh.org

Bob Dylan
Singer, Songwriter

Archive Photo

POINT OF IMPACT: Hailed as the most influential pop musician of his generation, Bob Dylan's influence on music and lifestyles has spanned 40 years. Born Robert Zimmerman, he took the name and experimental language of Welsh poet Dylan Thomas as his stage identity and the folk style of Depression-era legend Woody Guthrie as his sound. Soon after he moved to New York in the early sixties, he began extending the boundaries of traditional music—first to protest songs like "Blowing in the Wind" and "A Hard Rain's Gonna Fall." But it was his personal songwriting that transformed every genre of pop music. Even the Beatles' shift toward introspective lyrics in the mid-sixties is attributed to Dylan. Bruce Springsteen says of Dylan, "He invented a new way a pop singer could sound, broke through the limitations of what a recording artist could achieve and changed the face of rock-and-roll forever." His influence is still evident in rap (angry, spoken rhymes) and grunge (dark lyrics, rough voiced, and unorthodox chording). His 1997 album *Time Out of Mind* (his fiftieth) garnered three Grammy awards.

He's changed the sound and substance of rock-and-roll.

QUOTABLE: "Just because you like my stuff doesn't mean I owe you anything."

BEHIND THE SCENES: In 1978 Dylan shocked the music world when he converted to Christianity. "I truly had a born-again experience, if you want to call it that." His first album following his conversion, *Slow Train Coming,* earned him his first Grammy award. Now Dylan, 59, calls the period his "Christian phase" and says he subscribes to no organized religion. He's a divorced father of four. Son Jakob leads his own hit band, The Wallflowers.

PRAYER STARTERS:

- Pray that Dylan's lyrics will inspire the young to not only seek the honest truth, but to live by it as well.
- Pray that he'll be renewed in his conviction that Jesus is indeed his Savior.
- Pray that Dylan will find peace and refreshment in his personal life. Ask for God's felt presence and blessings in his family.

> *Why are you downcast, O my soul? Why so disturbed within me? Put your hope in God, for I will yet praise him, my Savior and my God. Psalm 42:5-6*

CONTACT: Creative Artists Agency, 9830 Wilshire Blvd., Beverly Hills, CA 90212

Donald Laub

Founder, International Chair, Interplast

Jim Warych Photography, Campbell, CA

POINT OF IMPACT: Thirty years ago, Donald Laub—then Chief of Reconstructive and Plastic Surgery at Stanford University Medical Center—learned about Antonio, a 14-year-old Mexican boy with a cleft lip and palate. When he found there were few if any surgeons available near Antonio's home in Mexico who could help, he decided to bring Antonio to Stanford and perform the needed surgery himself. Laub then learned of many other Mexican children who needed surgery. He enlisted support and arranged to send a team of physicians and nurses to Mexico to perform surgeries on-site in a "charity hospital." Thus the idea for Interplast was born. Since then, it has grown into an international organization that provides 3,000 free surgeries annually to children all around the world. Interplast volunteers generally treat children born with life-debilitating deformities or who have suffered crippling injuries, such as severe burns.

He treats poor children with deformities for free.

QUOTABLE: On receiving a $1 million donation from Ronald McDonald House in 1998, the single largest gift Interplast has ever received: "I've been waiting 30 years for a gift like this."

BEHIND THE SCENES: Interplast depends solely on private donations to fund their trips overseas; it has no affiliations and accepts no financial support from any government. Ninety-four percent of Interplast's revenues are spent to directly support medical services. All care is free, all medical teams volunteer their time, and almost all equipment and supplies are donated.

PRAYER STARTERS:

- Thank God for Donald Laub's compassionate work. Pray for children suffering from injuries and deformities, and for medical personnel who are trying to help. Pray for the continued impact of Interplast.
- Ask God to bless Laub and his family with His love and grace.
- Ask for the gift of mercy, and an opportunity to express it today.

Show mercy and compassion to one another. Zechariah 7:9

CONTACT: Interplast, 255 Route 108, Somersworth, NH 03878; e-mail: e-news@interplast.org

Boris Berezovsky

Russian Businessman, Politician

UN/DPI photo by Evan Schneider

POINT OF IMPACT: Boris Berezovsky, billionaire tycoon and one of Russia's most influential men, is the "man behind the Man"—the advisor and financier to Russian president Boris Yeltsin. Called the "Kremlin kingmaker," Berezovsky helped Yeltsin defeat the Communists and Nationalists in the 1996 election. Later, in ill health, Yeltsin appointed him the Deputy Chief of his National Security Council. As such, Berezovsky helped negotiate peace in the rebel province of Chechnya. He also helped to restore the flow of oil through the strongly nationalist territory. Yet he's often described as a "dark force" because he seems to exist outside the law. One Kremlin official said he is at the heart of a "demented, warped irresponsible capitalism."

This tycoon is Russia's "kingmaker."

QUOTABLE: He made his first millions from car sales, but now his empire stretches from oil to media. "Poke a stick into a Russian company at random and you'll find Berezovsky at the end of it," said one Muscovite journalist.

BEHIND THE SCENES: He once boasted that he and six colleagues controlled half the Russian economy. In Russia, where city streets are rife with crime and wealthy men send their families abroad for safety, Berezovsky has a personal security force of more than 100 people. At 53, the small, inscrutable, dark-haired man is often described as "dapper." His private life is cloaked in secrecy—some say he's been married three times and has six children.

PRAYER STARTERS:

- Pray that Boris Berezovsky and his colleagues will use their influence for Russia's good, and that they'll turn away or be restrained from corruption.
- Pray for political and economic stability and democratic reform for Russia. Pray for those who suffer from food shortages, crime, unemployment, and currency devaluations. Pray for Christians there.
- Ask for God's blessing on Berezovsky; pray for a genuine spiritual awakening in his whole family.

> *He who fears the LORD has a secure fortress, and for his children it will be a refuge. Proverbs 14:26*

CONTACT: LOGOVAZ, Gorokhovski per.3, 103064 Moscow, Russia

Tom Hanks

Actor, Director, Screenwriter

Archive Photo

POINT OF IMPACT: Tom Hanks has turned his nice-guy screen persona into one of the most amazing careers in Hollywood. *Entertainment Weekly* says "In a town where actors are often treated like cattle, he's a sacred cow, adored by studio heads, directors, writers, filmgoers, everyone alike." Proving himself adept at both comedy and drama, he won back-to-back Best Actor Oscars for his starring roles in *Philadelphia* and *Forrest Gump*. With *That Thing You Do* and his HBO series *From Earth to Moon* (winner of three Emmys), Hanks, 42, added screenwriting and directing to his résumé. His Oscar-nominated performance in *Saving Private Ryan* further cemented his reputation as adaptable. However, he invariably plays characters who represent what is admirable and good—a sensitive crusader, a brave astronaut, a war hero.

He's Hollywood's most adaptable—and likeable—actor.

QUOTABLE: "Going into anything, I have an innate kind of hopefulness that we're gonna do something cool. I think that is what can set me apart. . . . I am a hopeful person—both first thing in the morning and last thing at night."

BEHIND THE SCENES: Hanks was five when his parents split up. He stayed with his father, a cook who moved a lot, but he considers the San Francisco Bay area home. At 43, he has two kids from his first marriage and two with his second wife, actress Rita Wilson.

PRAYER STARTERS:

- About making his movie *That Thing You Do*: "It's easy to write swear words in order to communicate something. It's harder to write regular words." Give thanks for Tom Hanks' efforts to bring civility to cinema.

- In high school, he made a decision for Christ. Pray that the Lord would continue to draw Hanks to Himself, working through him in surprising and powerful ways to influence popular culture.

- Ask the Lord to bless Hanks' marriage and family with His best.

> *The boundary lines have fallen for me in pleasant places; surely I have a delightful inheritance. Psalm 16:6*

CONTACT: PMK, 955 S. Carillo Dr., Suite 200, Los Angeles, CA 90048

Thilo Bode

Executive Director, Greenpeace

Courtesy of Greenpeace

POINT OF IMPACT: One of the world's best-known environmental groups, Greenpeace burst on the scene in the seventies with TV images of bludgeoned baby seals and daredevils in inflatable boats climbing aboard nuclear subs. After a period of declining influence, Thilo Bode, the group's new chief eco-warrior, has cleaned up Greenpeace's hippie image. "We've got to go beyond boarding whaling ships," says Bode. Today Greenpeace boasts 3.1 million dues-paying members, a $140 million budget, 1,000 full-time staff members, 43 offices worldwide and a fleet of oceangoing vessels. "Our strategy is based on winning," declares an Australian Greenpeace activist. "Whatever works, whatever it takes." The hit list of current concerns includes nuclear testing and aging nuclear plants, global warming, ancient forests, and marine life.

He leads the world's most confrontational environmentalists.

QUOTABLE: "Glaciers are melting. Forests are retreating. We are changing the seasons. We are running out of fish in the sea. We are poisoning our children with persistent organic pollutants and accumulating waste. And as carbon emissions increase, we find ourselves running out of sky . . ."

BEHIND THE SCENES: Thilo Bode, 52, grew up Roman Catholic in Bavaria, Germany. An economist by training, Bode's mild manner hides a tough managerial style and fierce commitment—three years ago he spent 36 hours in a Beijing jail for unfurling an antinuclear banner in Tiananmen Square.

PRAYER STARTERS

- "The ecological fate of mankind will be decided in Asia," says Bode. Pray for progress in environmental awareness and protections in Asia.
- Bode notes world progress in air and water quality and waste disposal. Give thanks for this better stewardship of God's creation. Pray for clarity, consensus, and action on the world's key environmental challenges.
- Ask God to bless Thilo Bode with wisdom, health, and spiritual understanding.

> *Speak to the earth, and it will teach you. . . . Which of all these does not know that the hand of the LORD has done this? Job 12:8-9*

CONTACT: 1436 U Street N.W., Washington, DC 20009; www.greenpeaceusa.org

Jerry Lewis

Comedian, Humanitarian

Courtesy of Jerry Lewis

POINT OF IMPACT: Jerry Lewis turned one of the century's most successful careers in comedy into one of its most effective crusades for compassion. In fact, for his annually televised war against muscular dystrophy, Lewis is probably the world's best-known charity spokesperson. The Muscular Dystrophy Association calls him "the most effective fund-raiser in television history." In the past 30 years, his Labor Day telethons have raised more than $800 million. A nominee for the Nobel Peace Prize, Jerry Lewis is described by one college president as a "shining example for the people everywhere that one person can have an impact on society and change the world." Lewis made his entertainment debut in 1931 at age five, singing, "Brother, Can You Spare a Dime?" at a hotel in New York. But the key to his career was a comedy partnership with Dean Martin that began in 1946. Their crazy antics and improvised banter made them world-famous and rich.

He's the most effective charity fund-raiser in TV history.

QUOTABLE: Lewis jokes: "People hate me because I am a multifaceted, talented, wealthy, internationally famous genius."

BEHIND THE SCENES: Born Joseph Levitch, Jerry Lewis, 74, has five sons from a 36-year marriage to Patti Lewis, plus seven grandchildren and one great granddaughter. Lewis married SanDee "Sam" Pitnick in 1983; their daughter, Danielle, eight, is the "light of their lives and the air of their lungs."

PRAYER STARTERS:

- Give thanks for the benefits to both giver and receiver in Jerry Lewis' long career in charity appeals to benefit muscular dystrophy. Pray for his continued success, and for great progress in the fight against muscular dystrophy.
- Ask for God's provision and saving love to be apparent to Lewis and his family.
- Pray for someone you know suffering from a chronic illness or handicap.

> *Whatever you did for one of the least of these brothers of mine, you did for me. Matthew 25:40*

CONTACT: Muscular Dystrophy Assn., 3300 E. Sunrise Dr., Tuscon, AZ 85718

Paul and Jan Crouch

Broadcasters, Trinity Broadcasting Network (TBN)

Courtesy of TBN

POINT OF IMPACT: Trinity Broadcasting Network is the world's largest Christian media empire, a nerve center for more than 700 broadcast, cable, and satellite affiliates. As network founders and cohosts of its lead program, *Praise the Lord,* Paul and Jan Crouch are the most powerful figures in televangelism—the Christian equivalent of media moguls Rupert Murdoch or Ted Turner. In fact, for millions of TV watchers, the Crouches *are* evangelical Christianity. Along with other TBN preachers like Kenneth Copeland and Benny Hinn, the Crouches evoke strong reactions from fellow believers—ranging from enthusiasm to outrage. In 1998 TBN opened a new headquarters in a lavish, white-marble, 65,650-square-foot complex. The Crouches defend their opulence by contending that Christ was a wealthy merchant. Viewers are told if they give money, God will reward them with health and wealth.

They run the world's largest religious media empire.

QUOTABLE: "I would rather be charged by men for trying to secure too many stations than to be charged by God for trying to secure too few."—Paul Crouch

BEHIND THE SCENES: Paul Crouch, 64, is the son of Assemblies of God missionaries; he graduated from Central Bible College, Springfield, Missouri. Along with Jim and Tammy Faye Bakker, Paul founded the original TBN station in Santa Ana, California, in 1973.

PRAYER STARTERS:

- Pray that Paul and Jan Crouch will use TBN's enormous influence to advance the kingdom of God and minister to people's deepest needs.
- Ask God to favor the Crouches with health, wisdom, and peace.
- The 2,500 TV and radio preachers in the United States collectively take in more than $3 billion each year from supporters. Pray for accountability and integrity in every context where Christ's name is used to solicit funds.

> *Wealth is worthless in the day of wrath, but righteousness delivers from death.*
> *Proverbs 11:4*

CONTACT: Trinity Broadcasting Network, P.O. Box A, Santa Ana, CA 92711

Shirley Ann Jackson
Former Chief,
Nuclear Regulatory Commission (NRC)

POINT OF IMPACT: Over the past 25 years, the Nuclear Regulatory Commission has frequently been criticized for ignoring the dangers posed by the nation's nuclear power plants. Then Shirley Jackson took over. In 1996 she publicly acknowledged the truth of many allegations and shut down three questionable plants for sweeping repairs. She set about to completely reorganize the NRC. Since Jackson's shaking of the moribund organization, the NRC has displayed new regulatory teeth, earning renewed public trust. "Jackson is the toughest chairman we've seen," says Bill Magavern, director of Critical Mass Energy Project at Ralph Nader's Public Citizen watchdog group. In 1999, Jackson left the commission but continues to influence the next generation of scientists as president of Rensselaer Polytechnic Institute (RPI). She is the first African-American woman to lead one of the nation's top technological universities.

She's shaping the next generation of nuclear scientists.

QUOTABLE: "Leadership must begin with setting an example—an example of hard work, creative thinking, and commitment to ideals and mission."

BEHIND THE SCENES: In 1973, Shirley Jackson became the first African-American female to receive a doctorate from Massachusetts Institute of Technology—in any subject. She was inducted into The National Women's Hall of Fame in 1998 for her contributions as a distinguished scientist and advocate for education, science, and public policy. Jackson and her husband have one son.

PRAYER STARTERS:

- Thank God for Shirley Jackson's example of bold and creative leadership in the important field of nuclear power.
- Pray that Jackson will shape and inspire young African-Americans in her new position as president of RPI.
- Ask God to bless her family and marriage, and draw them to Himself.
- Pray that the risk of nuclear terrorism would diminish worldwide.

We have different gifts, according to the grace given us. . . . If it is leadership, let him govern diligently. Romans 12:6,8

CONTACT: Rm. 6049, Jonsson Engineering Center, RPI, Troy, NY 12180-3590

Michael W. Smith

Recording Artist

AP/Wide World Photos

POINT OF IMPACT: If Amy Grant is the leading lady of Christian pop, then Michael W. Smith is the leading man. In fact, he got his start by playing keyboard and opening for Grant's "Age to Age" tour in 1982. Eighteen years later, he's sold over 7 million records and performed for millions around the world, including two presidents, Pope John Paul II, and Billy Graham. His awards include two Grammys and six Dove awards. For *People* readers, he's just another pretty face (recently voted one of America's most beautiful). But what really sets "Smitty" apart is his passion to encourage young believers to take a stand for Christ. Just look at his album titles—"Change Your World" and "Live the Life"—and his youth devotionals—"Old Enough to Know" and "Time to Be Bold."

He's a gifted musician with a heart for young believers.

QUOTABLE: "Music is not my ministry. My ministry is driving my kids to school in the morning, reading books to them while they sit on my lap by the fireplace, listening to their prayers at bedtime, and taking their mother on dates. Entertainment is what I do for a living; 'family' is what I am."

BEHIND THE SCENES: Smith, 42, grew up in Kenova, West Virginia. Though his early aspirations were focused on baseball, others noticed he had a gift for songwriting. Smith's outreach program for youth in the Nashville area is named "Rockettown" after one of his best-known hits. He and his wife, Deborah, have five children.

PRAYER STARTERS:

- Give thanks for Smith's clear message to young Christians to put their faith to work in the world. Pray that many would respond.
- Pray that Smith will be strengthened with wisdom and singleness of purpose today in his musical and professional choices.
- Ask God to bless the Smith family with safety, joy, and peace.

> *Fight the good fight of faith. Take hold of the eternal life to which you were called when you made your good confession in the presence of many witnesses.*
> *1 Timothy 6:12*

CONTACT: 1501 LBJ Freeway, Suite 650, Dallas, TX 75324; www.michaelwsmith.com

Julia Roberts

Actress

Archive Photo

POINT OF IMPACT: Whether she performs in a theater smash or a box-office bomb, Julia Roberts comes up smiling. Maybe it's because her losses have added up to an important gain: she's figured out that audiences like her best (and almost solely) in romantic comedies like *Pretty Woman*. Even with her uneven success, Roberts commands attention and big bucks. Recently she signed to play in *The Runaway Bride,* a romantic comedy with Richard Gere, for $17 million. It was her pivotal role in *Mystic Pizza* that put her on the movie map; roles in *Steel Magnolias* (for which she was nominated for an Oscar) and *Pretty Woman* solidified her status as America's favorite. Besides wielding enormous influence in which movies get made, "Julia is everybody's sister and best friend," says one writer. "She stands for hope, for something good in American life and womanhood that we all aspire to."

Her megawatt smile draws moviegoers.

QUOTABLE: "What's nice about my dating life is that I don't have to leave my house. All I have to do is read the paper: I'm marrying Richard Gere, dating Daniel Day-Lewis, parading around with John F. Kennedy, Jr., and even Robert DeNiro was in there for a day."

BEHIND THE SCENES: At 33, Roberts' personal life has been stormy. She's endured a broken engagement with actor Kiefer Sutherland and a brief but amicable marriage to singer Lyle Lovett before hooking up with Benjamin Bratt. The actress has contributed to UNICEF and other charitable organizations and made goodwill trips to Haiti and India. She has homes in New York, Hollywood, and Taos, New Mexico.

PRAYER STARTERS:

- Pray that Julia Roberts will exercise wisdom in her professional and personal life.
- Pray that she will use her considerable influence in the film industry for good.
- Ask the Lord to draw her to Himself in clear and meaningful ways, and bless her with health and peace.

Banish anxiety from your heart and cast off the troubles of your body.
Ecclesiastes 11:10

CONTACT: ICM, 8942 Wilshire Blvd., Beverly Hills, CA 90211

Courtesy of Paxson Communications Corp.

Jeff Sagansky

President, CEO, Pax TV

POINT OF IMPACT: Jeff Sagansky, 47, has spent more than 20 years in influential positions in the television industry. Some of his previous credits include *Cosby* at NBC and *Touched by an Angel, Dr. Quinn, Medicine Woman,* and *Christy* on CBS. "It is no secret that Jeff Sagansky is one of the most successful programming and network brand developers in television history," says one network leader. Now, as CEO of the new PAX TV network, which launched in the fall of 1998, Sagansky is trying to bring back family TV. The nation's seventh broadcast television network promises programming that emphasizes the values of family, community, and faith. "I want to offer positive role models and strong messages and optimism," says Sagansky.

He's applying his programming genius to family television.

QUOTABLE: "We have this radical idea that there's an audience out there for programs that you can watch with a child, a parent or any member of your family and not be embarrassed or just plain angry about the language, attitude or visual content."

BEHIND THE SCENES: Sagansky, who is Jewish, has personal reasons to care about spiritual and family values on television. "Really, this is the kind of programming I've always succeeded with in my career," he says, "and these are programs that I personally like to watch, particularly now that I have two girls, 4 and 9."

PRAYER STARTERS:

- Give thanks for Sagansky's determination to produce good family programming that reflects positive values in entertainment.
- Ask God to bless his efforts with success and with many new viewers tuning in to the network.
- Pray for God's blessing on Jeff Sagansky and his family. Pray that Sagansky would experience personally the full depth of God's love and redemption.

> *Commit your way to the LORD; trust in him and he will do this: He will make your righteousness shine like the dawn, the justice of your cause like the noonday sun. Psalm 37:5-6*

CONTACT: Pax TV, 601 Clearwater Park Road, West Palm Beach, FL 33401

254

Gloria Steinem

Author, Feminist Crusader

Archive Photo

POINT OF IMPACT: Gloria Steinem has been America's most visible and enduring feminist, coming up with generation-defining statements like, "Women won't be equal outside the home until men are equal partners inside the home." Always striking and articulate, she founded *Ms.,* the landmark feminist magazine. In 1998, when dwindling subscriptions forced *Ms.* to shut down, Steinem put together a group of investors and re-launched. "*Ms.* is necessary now more than ever," she declares. "Other women's magazines are like mail-order catalogs. Their editorial pages are so taken up with how to put your blush on and recipes and completely uncritical fashion photos that complement the ads, they should be given away." Steinem has written four books and works tirelessly for feminist causes, including the Women's Political Caucus.

She's the famous face of the feminist movement.

QUOTABLE: "When the right wing tells me I'm wrong, I always know I'm right."

BEHIND THE SCENES: Steinem, 66, grew up poor in Toledo, Ohio. After graduating from Smith College, Steinem became a journalist; one assignment involved going undercover as a Playboy bunny for *Show* magazine. She has never married, but has reportedly maintained a long relationship with Blair Chotzinoff, a writer for *The Boulder Planet.*

PRAYER STARTERS:

- Bella Abzug once said of Steinem, "She's crystallized the emotions and yearnings of our entire gender." Pray that women's desires for significance and fulfillment would be realized in positive ways and lead them to God.

- Pray that secular and biblical factions in the women's movement will reach a greater understanding and mutual respect, and that the values of personal morality, marriage, and family will be affirmed.

- Pray that Steinem will know the depths of God's love for her; pray for her health and strength.

Above all else, guard your heart, for it is the wellspring of life. Proverbs 4:23

CONTACT: 20 Exchange Place, 22nd Fl., New York, NY 10005; e-mail: Ms@echonyc.com

Stephen J. Gould

Biologist, Professor, Author

POINT OF IMPACT: Stephen J. Gould, America's best-known advocate for evolution, is Professor of Geology and Zoology at Harvard University, where he has taught since 1967. Preferring to call himself an evolutionary biologist, Gould is an internationally celebrated paleontologist and prolific author. In his recent book, *Rocks of Ages: Science and Religion in the Fullness of Life,* he argues that religion and science shouldn't mix in moral decisions but must coexist for humankind to experience a full life. Gould, 59, is considered by many the grandmaster of contemporary science writers. He wields his influence beyond the classroom as a member of the Council on Ideas, a panelist for the Modern Library's list of the 100 best nonfiction books, and keynote speaker for a semi-annual symposium of the world's 100 most renowned dinosaur experts.

He's the grandmaster of science writers.

QUOTABLE: "Humans are not the end result of predictable evolutionary progress, but rather a fortuitous cosmic afterthought, a tiny little twig on the enormously arborescent bush of life, which if replanted from seed, would almost surely not grow this twig again."

BEHIND THE SCENES: When Gould was a kid, he was nicknamed "fossil face" because of his passion for fossil digging. He is a lifelong baseball fanatic and Red Sox fan who frequently uses baseball as an analogy to explain and explore evolutionary issues.

PRAYER STARTERS:

- Pray that the Holy Spirit would lead Stephen Gould into all truth (John 16:13). Pray for new understandings both of the potential and the limitations of human reason.
- Ask for spiritual and physical blessings for Gould and his family.
- Pray for a spiritual awakening in the scientific community—for a growing awareness of God as both Creator and Redeemer.

Does the rain have a father? Who fathers the drops of dew? Job 38:28

CONTACT: c/o Harvard University, MCZ 151, 26 Oxford St., Cambridge, MA 02138

Max Lucado

Bestselling Author

Courtesy of Word Publishing

POINT OF IMPACT: Inspirational writer Max Lucado has written more than 23 books that have sold more than 11 million copies. For his books *In the Grip of Grace* and *When God Whispers Your Name,* he became the first author to win Christian publishing's Gold Medallion Book of the Year Award twice. At one time, Lucado had three top-ten bestsellers simultaneously. In fact, a Max Lucado title has appeared on the Christian Booksellers hardcover bestseller list every month for the past seven years. Lucado, a pastor and former missionary to Mexico, excels at bringing Bible stories to life in vivid and deeply affecting prose. The *Washington Times* calls Lucado "an easy sell for Christian book junkies, but he also is beloved by big lugs of guys who tell him, 'Y'know, I never read, but I read your books.'" Lucado's 60-second radio program, *UpWords*, airs on 800 Christian stations.

His bestsellers bring the Bible to life.

QUOTABLE: "So many Christians underestimate God's grace and create neurotic souls who live in doubt of God's love. We must understand that there is nothing we can do to increase or diminish God's love!"

BEHIND THE SCENES: Lucado was raised in a Christian family, but as a student at Abilene Christian College, he was a hard-drinking party boy. One night as he was sitting in his truck, he thought, *There's got to be something more to life than this.* Then he called upon the mercies of God and recommitted his life to Christ. The experience of God's mercy continues to be a hallmark of Lucado's books. He is the pastor of Oak Hills Church of Christ in San Antonio, Texas. He and his wife, Denalyn, have three daughters.

PRAYER STARTERS:

- Give thanks for the widespread influence of Max Lucado's writing, especially for his ability to reach those who don't usually buy Christian books.
- Pray that many would discover Christ's mercy and seek to follow Him.
- Ask God to bless the Lucado family with health, provision, and safety.

Because of the LORD's great love we are not consumed. Lamentations 3:22-23

CONTACT: 8308 Fredericksburg Road, San Antonio, TX 78229

Scott Adams
Cartoonist, Dilbert

Photo by Eric Millette

POINT OF IMPACT: When *Time* magazine named Scott Adams, creator of the comic strip *Dilbert*, one of 1997's most influential people, it wasn't merely because of the laughs he generates in work cubicles worldwide. While business gurus like Tom Peters help managers find new ways to succeed, Adams uses humor and scathing satire to help employees. That might explain why 300 million readers in 51 countries make Adams a part of the day. "Walk around any big, hierarchical corporation on a Monday morning, and you'll see pockets of people chuckling and nodding as they pass around a small strip of newspaper," says Chicago consultant Rich McLaughlin. "Dilbert, the corporate warrior/survivor, is the voice of the people." In fact, it's been said that the true health of any large organization can now be gauged by the number of *Dilbert* cartoons tacked on its cubicle walls—along with *Dilbert* mugs, calendars, books, and novelties.

He helps corporate America laugh at itself.

QUOTABLE: "I have a grudge against idiots. Unfortunately the world is full of them, and a disproportionate number are promoted to management."

BEHIND THE SCENES: Before Adams, 43, created his comic strip, he held a variety of "humiliating and low-paying jobs," including bank teller (he was robbed twice at gunpoint). Adams entertained himself during boring meetings by drawing insulting cartoons of his coworkers and bosses. Eventually a bespectacled character named Dilbert emerged from the doodles. In 1988 United Features Syndicate plucked *Dilbert* out of thousands of submissions and offered Adams a contract. He has a longtime relationship with Pam Okasaki; he lives in Dublin, California.

PRAYER STARTERS:

- Give thanks for the comic relief that Scott Adams' wit gives to millions of working people.
- Pray that Adams' insights would help harmony, mutual respect, and common sense to prevail in the world's fast-changing business environment.
- Pray that Adams and his partner Pam Okasaki would seek the Lord and His goodness.

> *From [Christ] the whole body, joined and held together by every supporting ligament, grows and builds itself up in love, as each part does its work.*
> *Ephesians 4:16*

CONTACT: e-mail: scottadams@aol.com

Slobodan Milosevic
President of Yugoslavia

Archive Photo

POINT OF IMPACT: For more than ten years, Slobodan Milosevic has been the deciding factor in Europe's most volatile hot spot—the republics of the former nation of Yugoslavia. Called by some "the butcher of the Balkans" and "the man who brought you the Bosnian war," Milosevic was president of Serbia from 1990–97 and has been president of Yugoslavia since 1997. But his aim has not changed: to build a greater Serbia from the ruins of the former Yugoslavia. His policies are rooted in race and violence. He has been directly linked to war crimes (300,000 civilians in Bosnia alone), especially against the Muslim minority. His term for such atrocities is "ethnic cleansing." Recently, Milosevic again refused to stop ethnic killing, this time in the province of Kosovo, which resulted in NATO air strikes and a mass exodus of fearful minorities.

He's often compared to Hitler.

QUOTABLE: "No one outside this country can decide on changes in it. Only its own citizens can."

BEHIND THE SCENES: Milosevic, 59, encountered tragedy early, reports *The Toronto Star.* When he was a young boy, Milosevic's favorite uncle killed himself. Then his father, an Orthodox priest, committed suicide. A decade later, his mother hanged herself in the family living room. One U.S. envoy says Milosevic can be charming in private but has no fixed principles: "He's not a democrat, a communist, a nationalist or even a Greater Serbian—he's pro-Milosevic." He and his wife, Mira Markovic, a professor of Marxism, have two children.

PRAYER STARTERS:

- Pray that Slobodan Milosevic will encounter the Prince of Peace and turn away from hate and violence. Pray that he will be restrained from doing any more harm.
- Pray for those who have been harmed by the Bosnian war; pray for families whose loved ones have been raped, forced to flee, or killed.
- Pray for safety for medical, relief, and peace-keeping personnel.
- Pray for peace among the rival religious and ethnic groups in the region.
- Pray that God's mercies rest on and are apparent to Milosevic's family today, especially to his children.

Let us fall into the hands of the LORD, for his mercy is great. 2 Samuel 24:14

CONTACT: Yugoslavian Embassy, 2410 California St. N.W., Washington, DC 20008

Joan Ganz Cooney

Founder, Children's Television Workshop;
Creator of Sesame Street

POINT OF IMPACT: Could Big Bird change the world? Joan Cooney thought so. Starting in 1969, the 8-foot, 2-inch yellow bird and his colorful puppet playmates forever linked the words "educational" and "television." Cooney, a one-time teacher, won the support of the Carnegie Corporation to launch a "brightly colored vehicle for teaching inner-city kids their ABC's and numbers, as well as cooperation and tolerance." She wanted a counter to the pointless, product-hyping cartoons that left inner-city children ill-prepared for school. Today, Cooney's writing and the late Jim Henson's puppetry have become the gold standard of children's TV programming. Big Bird and his pals present the single most pervasive children's TV influence on the globe. Says one media expert, "The effect is so monumental it dwarfs everything else that's on television."

She created the gold standard of children's TV programming.

QUOTABLE: "There is a young and impressionable mind out there that is hungry for information. It has latched on to an electronic tube as its main source of nourishment."

BEHIND THE SCENES: Joan Ganz Cooney, 70, says her three-year-old granddaughter Chloe is her best market researcher. "I've actually learned an immense amount watching *Sesame Street* with her. I'll go in to the studio the next day and say, 'This doesn't work. This does.'" As you might expect, the "enemy" crops up in the darndest places—one Halloween, Chloe came by in a red Teletubby costume.

PRAYER STARTERS:

- Give thanks for the education, inspiration, and friendship that the imaginary world of "Sesame Street" has brought to millions of children.

- Pray that Joan Cooney and other programmers will pursue fresh ways to encourage learning and emotional health among preschoolers.

- Ask God to bless Cooney and her family with health, joy, and peace.

> *Train a child in the way he should go, and when he is old he will not turn from it. Proverbs 22:6*

CONTACT: CTW, One Lincoln Plaza, New York, NY 10023-7129

Gwyneth Paltrow
Actress

Archive Photo

POINT OF IMPACT: Just a few years ago, the media often identified Gwyneth Paltrow as "Blythe Danner's daughter" (her mother is a Tony Award-winning theatrical actress). Today, Gwyneth can get by on her first name alone. In an era when flash and trash sell, she mesmerizes both teen and adult women with her poise and porcelain-fine appearance (says *In Style* magazine, "Millions of women watch her every move"). But it's her acting that mesmerizes directors. "It's amazing to work with Gwyneth," says director Alfonso Cuaron. "You can give her *The Communist Manifesto* and tell her it's a romantic comedy, and she would read it as a romantic comedy. Anything that comes out of her mouth always comes with the right emotion." Recent movies include *Great Expectations, Sliding Doors,* and her Oscar-winning performance in *Shakespeare in Love*. Next stop: a thriller with Matt Damon, *The Talented Mr. Ripley.*

She's been compared to Grace Kelly and Audrey Hepburn.

QUOTABLE: "For my mom, the family always came first. I can't believe the movies my mother turned down. But she didn't want to leave us. She's not ambitious like that, and I'm not really either, as a result."

BEHIND THE SCENES: After her much-publicized romance with Brad Pitt, Paltrow, 27, determined to keep her private life—including her next relationship, with Ben Affleck—under tighter wraps. Paltrow has turned down roles that called for extensive nudity. "I don't want to embarrass my grandfather," she says. "It's not worth it to me."

PRAYER STARTERS:

- Pray that Paltrow's personal and professional choices would inspire women to reach for God's best in their lives, making difficult, unpopular choices where necessary.

- Paltrow says, "You get to a point where you're thinking, *What kind of life do I want?* One day I hope to have the power to determine my destiny." Pray that she will seek and follow God's loving guidance for her life.

- Ask God to protect her from harm; pray that she would be blessed with friends who are wholeheartedly following God.

Dear friends, do not imitate what is evil but what is good. 3 John 11

CONTACT: Creative Artists Agency, 9830 Wilshire Blvd., Beverly Hills, CA 90212

Randy Tate

Executive Director, Christian Coalition (CC)

Courtesy of Christian Coalition

POINT OF IMPACT: He's been called the "poster boy of the radical right," but not many boys carry his kind of clout. Randy Tate's two-million-member Christian Coalition advises candidates, defines national issues, and funds causes for the conservative faithful. One item high on the CC agenda is the elimination of the so-called marriage penalty that can mean higher taxes for couples when both work. The Christian Coalition, founded in 1989 by Pat Robertson, has been called the largest and most effective grassroots political movement of Christian activists in U.S. history. Before succeeding Ralph Reed as CC Director, Randy Tate served as a U.S. Representative from Washington state.

He leads the largest grassroots movement of Christian activists.

QUOTABLE: "Julie and I pray for the president. We should pray for all our elected officials, regardless of whether we agree with them on public policy issues. For people of faith, I don't think it's an option."

BEHIND THE SCENES: Tate, 34, is the third of five children who grew up in Puyallup, Washington. "My grandfather lived in a sod house and my grandmother wouldn't marry him until he built a stick house," recounts Tate. "I'm the son of a union worker who worked three jobs. Mine is not the lineage of the elites, but it's the story of America." Randy and his wife, Julie, have two children and live in Washington, DC.

PRAYER STARTERS:

- Pray that Randy Tate and the Christian Coalition would seek and exercise "the wisdom that comes from heaven" (James 3:17). Pray that their efforts will have a positive impact on the U.S. political process.

- Tate has said, "We are increasingly becoming what our founders fought against: a nation where a sizeable majority of individuals believe that the laws do not apply equally to all." Pray for trial attorneys, juries, and judges at work in the U.S. legal system today, that justice for all would prevail.

- Ask for safety, harmony, and fulfillment for the Tate family.

Blessed is the nation whose God is the Lord. Psalm 33:12

CONTACT: 1801-L Sara Drive, Chesapeake, VA 23320; www.cc.org

Jackie Chan

Actor

Archive Photo

POINT OF IMPACT: The box-office smash *Rush Hour* catapulted Hong Kong action star Jackie Chan into one of the few Asian actors who have made it big in Hollywood—after 15 years of trying. Chan is more than a veteran martial arts showman. His blend of wit, good looks and physical comedy make him the appealing Asian "everyman." Chan refuses to portray villains; his clean-living characters offer a role model to Asia's kids, in keeping with Asian social values. Chan's days of wild stunt work are probably numbered, but he prides himself on never using a stuntman. He's already had several close brushes with death. "I've broken bones from my skull to my toes, but broken legs and fingers don't matter. I hurt for a few weeks or months, but my films give people memories that they can keep for a hundred years."

He's Asia's onscreen role model for kids.

QUOTABLE: "If I did things Bruce Lee-style—punching and kicking—there would have been no way for me to succeed. Instead, I mixed action with comedy. I looked at Lee's films. When he kicks high, I kick low. I put more expression in my face. And I added humor."

BEHIND THE SCENES: Chan grew up in a dilapidated boarding school while his parents worked as servants for the American Embassy in Australia. Chan says his success has brought him so many sponsor endorsements that "I really don't have to buy anything." He supports a foundation that sends needy kids to school. Chan is married to actress Lin Fung-Chiao.

PRAYER STARTERS:

- Give thanks for the relatively wholesome message of Chan's characters. Pray that he will continue to use his influence for good.
- Pray for the generation coming of age in Asia—for the preservation of strong family values in rapidly changing societies, for the vigorous spread of Christianity, and for the strength of the church.
- Ask God to bless Chan and his family and reveal Himself to them.

Look to the LORD and his strength; seek his face always. 1 Chronicles 16:11

CONTACT: 145 Waterloo Road, Kowloon Tong, Hong Kong, S.A.R. China

dc Talk

Christian Music Group

Courtesy of Forefront Records

POINT OF IMPACT: dc Talk is a Grammy-winning band comprised of Toby McKeehan, Kevin Max, and Michael Tait, who believe that the Christian message and secular musical appeal can go together—and sell. Their rap/rock CD, *Jesus Freak*, scored a record for first-week sales for a Christian album with 85,000 sold. Though the group's musical style has evolved over the years, its bold, gospel-driven proclamations remain front and center. As Max notes, "dc Talk usually hits the message straight on, lights on, high beam heading straight for it." In 1998 the group's fifth CD, *Supernatural,* came out under the Virgin Records label, guaranteeing the group an even larger secular audience. Phil Fox, Virgin's Director of Product Management, says, "We saw them as wonderfully gifted songwriters and musicians. We don't want to dilute what they say. If it happens to have a heavy spiritual message, so be it." dc Talk recently launched a campaign to promote racial unity, ERACE (Eliminating Racism and Creating Equality).

They're Jesus freaks who win secular music fans.

QUOTABLE: "People often talk about being color-blind, but I don't want to be color-blind. I want to recognize all the colors and appreciate the beauty that they bring to society."—Toby McKeehan

BEHIND THE SCENES: The band members live in Nashville. McKeehan is married to Amanda; they are the parents of one. Max is married to Alayna, and Tait is single. They started their music career as students at Jerry Fallwell's Liberty University in Virginia.

PRAYER STARTERS:

- Give thanks for dc Talk's boldness and success in combining contemporary music appeal and the gospel.
- Pray that the band's move to a secular label leads to a significant impact with new audiences of non-Christian youth.
- Pray for God's blessing and protection for Toby McKeehan, Kevin Max, and Michael Tait and for their families.

We do not preach ourselves but Jesus Christ as Lord. 2 Corinthians 4:5

CONTACT: dc Talk, P.O. Box 1107, Brentwood, TN 37067

Michael P. Farris

*President and Founder, Home School Legal
Defense Association (HSLDA)*

Peter Cutts Photography, Washington, DC

POINT OF IMPACT: Twenty years ago home schooling was a hippie habit. Today it's championed by many
Christians, along with an increasing number of secular
families as the best means of providing quality, family-
based education. Michael Farris is undisputedly the
movement's leading advocate on the national level and
one of the leading pro-family activists on Capitol Hill.
Newsweek recently reported that 1.5 million children
are now being taught at home. Farris' HSLDA has a
staff of 60, including eight lawyers who lobby on Capitol Hill. The organization represents 12,600 families in California alone (Farris says he can generate 100 telephone calls to every congressional office within hours). A constitutional lawyer by
training, he's argued cases before the United States Supreme Court. His daily radio
show, *Home School Heartbeat,* airs on more than 800 outlets.

He's the top advocate for home schooling in Washington.

QUOTABLE: "Rampant problems . . . in our nation's schools are compelling parents to find alternatives. Home schooling allows parents to promote good academics, common-sense morality, and family unity."

BEHIND THE SCENES: Farris, 48, decided to educate his six-year-old daughter at
home when he realized that she cared more about the approval of friends than of
her own family. "Real life," he says, "does not consist of age-segregated herds." He
and his wife, Vickie, have ten children.

PRAYER STARTERS:

- Give thanks for Michael Farris' advocacy for high-quality moral and religious education. Pray for the HSLDA's continued positive impact.
- Pray for the millions of parents who are teaching their children at home
  today; pray that they'll teach with patience, imagination, and competence.
- Ask God for continued success for home-based education around the world;
  pray for health, harmony, and happiness in the Farris family.

  *My son, keep my words and store up my commands within you . . . and you
  will live. Proverbs 7:1-2*

CONTACT: P.O. Box 3000, Purcellville, VA 20134; www.hslda.org; (540) 338-5600

Wynton Marsalis

Jazz and Classical Musician,
Pulitzer Prize-Winning Composer

AP/Wide World Photos

POINT OF IMPACT: Few musicians move between jazz and classical music as effortlessly or as compellingly as trumpeter Wynton Marsalis. For young jazz fans, Marsalis exemplifies discipline, clean living, and virtuosity—and lures them into the riches of classical music. He tours widely and has recorded more than 30 jazz and classical albums, yet he still finds time to serve as artistic director for the "Jazz at Lincoln Center" program that he cofounded in 1987. In 1994 *Time* magazine named him among America's most promising leaders under the age of 40. Marsalis has won eight Grammys for jazz and classical recordings, and in 1997, he won the first Pulitzer Prize for Jazz for writing *Blood on the Fields*, a three-hour jazz oratorio about slavery.

He trumpets the wonders of both jazz and classical music.

QUOTABLE: On his home-video series, *Marsalis on Music:* "It is my hope that children who see these programs will find it easier to make music a part of their lives in a way that is meaningful and beautiful for them. We'd like to painlessly beckon our children into the magical world of music."

BEHIND THE SCENES: Marsalis' father, Ellis, is also a well-known jazz musician (as is his brother, Branford). Marsalis insists he didn't show early promise. "When I auditioned for my high school band," he recalls, "the band director was excited because my father was known to be a great musician. But when he heard me, he said, 'Are you sure you're Ellis' son?'" Marsalis, 29, has played in 30 countries and performed more than 120 concerts in each of the past 12 years.

PRAYER STARTERS:

- Give thanks for Marsalis' interest in children and his ability to relate to them, and ask God to bless his efforts.
- Pray that Marsalis encounters people in the music industry who will encourage him in his spiritual journey.
- Ask for health and protection for Wynton Marsalis while he travels.

Remember to extol His work, which men have praised in song. Job 36:24

CONTACT: Columbia Records, 1815 JFK Boulevard, Philadelphia, PA 19103

Dick Gephardt

U.S. Congressman, House Minority Leader

Photo by Rick Reinhard, Washington, DC

POINT OF IMPACT: Hailed by *USA Today* as "the perfect combination of a fiery populist and a quiet, backroom pragmatist," Dick Gephardt of Missouri is one of the Democrats' chief strategists and spokespersons on major issues. Early in his career, Gephardt was known as one of the party's conservative opponents of abortion. Since then he has become a powerful advocate of abortion and gay rights and earned a reputation as a populist who fights for working families. He is also the principal architect of the Democrats' Families First agenda. Once widely touted as a presidential candidate in 2000, Gephardt, 59, is poised to become Speaker of the House should the Democrats regain control. According to the *Wall Street Journal*, "Gephardt remains the buoy marking the Democratic channel."

He's the flagbearer for key concerns of Democrats.

QUOTABLE: "America at its core is an idea. And it is a failure of the idea of democracy and freedom and liberty if we continue to discriminate against our citizens for any reason."

BEHIND THE SCENES: After several Republicans went public in 1998 with their views that homosexuality is sinful, Gephardt volunteered to speak at the world's largest gay church, the 2,000-member Cathedral of Hope in Dallas. During Gephardt's hour-long question-and-answer session, he impressed his audience with his sincerity, says a cathedral spokesperson. Gephardt is married to Jayne Byrnes; their children are Matt, Chrissy, and Katie.

PRAYER STARTERS:

- Pray that the Democratic leadership will honor biblical truths and seek God's guidance as they shape their legislative agenda for the new century.
- Pray for Dick Gephardt in his influential position on the national stage; pray that he will lead by integrity, compassion, and wisdom.
- Ask God to bless the Gephardts with rest, health, and spiritual renewal.

Never tire of doing what is right. 2 Thessalonians 3:13

CONTACT: 1226 Longworth House Office Building, Washington, DC 20515; e-mail: gephardt@hr.house.gov

Courtesy of Koop Institute

C. Everett Koop

Health Services Reformer;
Former Surgeon General

POINT OF IMPACT: More than ten years after he left his job as U.S. Surgeon General, most Americans still recognize the uniformed, Lincolnesque figure of Dr. C. Everett Koop. But not many understand how much he's changed American health and medicine, and even fewer know that, at 83, the fearsome Dr. Koop is still at work. Through his C. Everett Koop Institute at Dartmouth College, he continues to tackle the big issues of health information and health reform. Koop recommends a public/private partnership, plus harnessing the power of the internet, to create a health care network. Koop also still champions one of his lifelong passions: getting kids to school physically and mentally ready to learn.

He's still working to change the way we stay well.

QUOTABLE: On health care reform: "As Congress and the country found out, there are no easy answers, only hard choices."

BEHIND THE SCENES: As Surgeon General during the eighties, Koop revolutionized government attitudes toward smoking and the tobacco industry, crusaded on nutrition and environmental issues, and helped define the nation's response to the AIDS epidemic. An evangelical Christian, Koop is married to the former Elizabeth Flanagan. They live in New Hampshire; they have three living children and seven grandchildren.

PRAYER STARTERS:

- Koop opposes both government-controlled health care and what he calls "private medicine run amuck." Pray for Koop and others who are working to shape America's health care system. Pray for doctors and nurses in your community.

- Give thanks for progress in key issues championed by Koop, including AIDS treatments and national attitudes toward tobacco use.

- Ask God to bless the Koops with health, safety, and personal fulfillment.

> *Jesus went throughout Galilee, teaching in their synagogues, preaching the good news of the kingdom, and healing every disease and sickness among the people. Matthew 4:23*

CONTACT: C. Everett Koop Institute, Dartmouth College, Hanover, NH 03755

268

Quincy Jones
Composer, Producer

Archive Photo

POINT OF IMPACT: Quincy Delight Jones, at one time a composer, arranger, trumpeter, and bandleader, won three of his 15 Grammy awards by producing one of the biggest-selling albums of all time, Michael Jackson's *Thriller.* In the sixties he broke ground by becoming one of the first black executives in a major recording firm, and then the first black composer accepted by Hollywood. Of Jones' accomplishments *Life* magazine says, "No one in the history of contemporary American music has cut so wide a path." Jones founded his own recording company, Qwest Records, in 1981. He masterminded the 1986 hit single, "We Are the World," which featured 30 stars and brought aid to famine victims in Ethiopia. Among other projects, 66-year-old Jones is currently developing an extensive history of black music. "Not only is almost no one else in the business so widely admired," says *U.S. News & World Report*, "but Jones still manages to bring new vigor and curiosity to each job—a rarity in a jaded industry."

No one in contemporary music has left a stronger mark.

QUOTABLE: On how he got started: "A blind man said to me, 'Listen to everything you can, and don't play the fool by putting ropes around yourself.' That was Ray Charles teaching me, a know-nothing 14-year-old squirt, how to write music."

BEHIND THE SCENES: A child prodigy who was performing professionally by age 15, Jones was one of nine children raised in Seattle by his stepmother and his father Quincy, Sr., a carpenter. Jones studied music in Paris and toured Europe extensively with his own big band in the fifties. He lives in New York and Los Angeles, and is the divorced father of five children.

PRAYER STARTERS:

- Ask God to draw Quincy Jones to Himself and bless him; pray for God's influence on his career as well as his relationships with his children.
- Give thanks for Jones' example of passion and excellence in music.
- Pray that Jones, as well as the rest of the recording industry, will strive to produce music that is both entertaining and responsible.

> *Worship the LORD with gladness; come before him with joyful songs.*
> *Psalm 100:2*

CONTACT: Warner Brothers Records, 3300 Warner Blvd., Burbank, CA 91505

Vaclav Havel
President of the Czech Republic

UN/DPI photo by Greg Kinch

POINT OF IMPACT: As a young man, Vaclav Havel was a playwright. Today he's the Czech Republic's leading man. But the road here wasn't easy. In 1977 he and hundreds of artists and intellectuals signed Charter 77, which protested the government's human rights violations. He was arrested and sentenced to four-and-a-half years of hard labor, during which time he nearly died from pneumonia and a lung infection. After becoming president of Czechoslovakia in 1989—just eight months after his last prison term—Havel said that the best way for the United States to help his country and the rest of eastern Europe was to help the Soviet Union find its way to democracy. In 1993 he was elected to a five-year term as president of the Czech Republic, after it and Slovakia had split into two nations. He remains an influential spokesman for human rights.

This former playwright is the Czech's leading man.

QUOTABLE: On communism's worst legacy to Czechoslovakia—"a spoiled moral environment: We have become morally ill because we are used to saying one thing and thinking another. We have learned not to believe in anything, not to care about each other."

BEHIND THE SCENES: Born to a wealthy Prague family, Havel has written poems and prose since childhood. In his twenties, he became a stagehand with Prague's ABC Theatre. His plays often mock the absurdity of power. Now he says, "Sometimes I feel like a character in one of my own plays." Havel, 63, is short with graying sandy hair. He lives with his second wife, Dagmar, in Prague.

PRAYER STARTERS:

- Pray for countries that are struggling with post-communist problems. Ask that Czech leaders will achieve Havel's vision of a "moral environment."
- Pray for God's goodness and mercies to be evident in Vaclav Havel's life.
- Havel, a secular humanist, says his worldview arose "from a Christian background, from a certain Christian experience of being." Pray that he will encounter Jesus Christ in a personally meaningful way.

I will restore them because I have compassion on them. Zechariah 10:6

CONTACT: Kancelßr prezidenta republicky, 119 08 Prague Hrad, Czech Republic

Reggie White
Football Player, Pastor

Courtesy of Green Bay Packers

POINT OF IMPACT: They call Reggie White, number 92 for the Green Bay Packers, the "Minister of Defense" for his ability to crush opposing linemen as he pursues a jumpy quarterback. At six feet, five inches and 290 pounds, he's the leading sacker in NFL history, and with his team, champion of the 1997 Super Bowl. Though he retired in 1999, White still makes waves for his uncompromising stance on issues of morality and faith. In March 1998, he stirred up controversy nationwide with his remarks to the Wisconsin Assembly when he called homosexuality a sin. A reporter remarked, "You can start a conversation with the NFL's all-time leader in sacks, but you usually wind up speaking with the ordained minister." A Green Bay colleague says, "If you were to look at one guy whose demeanor and whose mode of living is an example for all of us to follow, it's Reggie White."

He's still football's "Minister of Defense."

QUOTABLE: "Some people consider me a success because I'm a good football player and because I make a lot of money. But if my heart isn't right—if I'm not living in a way that pleases the Lord—then I'm a failure."

BEHIND THE SCENES: White is assistant pastor at the Inner City Community Church, Knoxville, Tennessee, and founder of Urban Hope, a charity that addresses inner-city problems. In 1993, after he signed on with Green Bay, Packers' Coach Mike Holmgren admitted he had left this message on the free agent's answering machine: "Reggie, this is God. Go to Green Bay." White and his wife, Sara, have two children. He's the author of *God's Play Book*.

PRAYER STARTERS:

- Give thanks for Reggie White's positive example to millions of young people and for his unswerving, outspoken devotion to God.
- Ask for White's continuing influence for good inside professional sports; ask for blessing and guidance for White in his role as pastor.
- Pray for spiritual oneness in White's marriage and for health, protection, and blessing for his family.

> *Whoever acknowledges me before men, I will also acknowledge him before my Father in heaven. Matthew 10:32*

CONTACT: Inner City Ministries, c/o Inner City Community Development Corp., 1503 Magnolia Ave., Knoxville, TN 37917; www.reggie-white.com

271

Courtesy of AP/Wide World Photos

Louis Gerstner

CEO, IBM Corporation

POINT OF IMPACT: For decades, his company's name has been synonymous with terms like blue chip, white collar, and the birth of the computer age. Today, IBM (often called "Big Blue") remains the world's top provider of computer hardware and number two in software. But Louis Gerstner isn't looking back. He's pushed "Big Blue" into the fastest-growing areas of the computer business: networking equipment and the internet. "If one billion people are going to do online banking, banks have to change the way they work," he says. Gerstner, a lifelong education promoter, established a program at IBM called Reinventing Education, to which the company has committed $35 million. Both *Time* and *Vanity Fair* magazines place Gerstner in the forefront of influential leaders in communications.

He's a blue-chip CEO with a heart for kids.

QUOTABLE: "A network is an important tool, but it won't replace brilliant teachers who can motivate a classroom of kids, parents who support their kids, and administrators with high standards. Technology is not a silver bullet."

BEHIND THE SCENES: Gerstner, 57, coauthored the 1994 book *Reinventing Education: Entrepreneurship in America's Public Schools*. He is vice chairman of the New American Schools Development Corporation and co-chairs Achieve, an organization created by U.S. governors and business leaders to set higher academic standards for public schools.

PRAYER POINTS:

- Notes Gerstner, "Technology is not the hard part. The hard part is what has to be done to take advantage of technology." Pray for Louis Gerstner and others like him at the leading edge of computer applications—for wisdom, social responsibility, and imagination.

- Pray for the success of all of Gerstner's endeavors to improve public education.

- Ask God to surround Gerstner and his family with protection, strong family ties, and peace.

> *Teach us to number our days aright, that we may gain a heart of wisdom.*
> Psalm 90:12

CONTACT: IBM, New Orchard Rd., Armonk, NY 10504

Diane Sawyer

Television Newscaster

Courtesy of ABC Photo

POINT OF IMPACT: She's been called the most wanted woman in broadcasting and "Sharon Stone on nice." Diane Sawyer, co-host of ABC's *Prime Time Live,* has won multiple Emmy awards for her investigative pieces (including reports on racism, televangelism, and mammograms) and high ratings with interviews of celebrities like Fergie, Michael Jackson, and Mark Fuhrman. Sawyer first came to Washington as a press aide for Richard Nixon, and after his resignation spent three years helping him write his memoirs. Later she became the first woman correspondent on CBS's *60 Minutes.* These days, she co-anchors three different weekly magazine shows, and her only competition among female celebrity anchors is Barbara Walters. Sawyer is considered the front runner to take over Dan Rather's anchor job on the *CBS Evening News* when he retires.

She's the most wanted woman in broadcast media.

QUOTABLE:. "You have to take risks, even career-altering, death-defying, triple-jumps-from-the-trapeze risks. If I'm going to play it too safe, what is the point of this job?"

BEHIND THE SCENES: Diane Sawyer, 54, was born in Glasgow, Kentucky; as a teenager, she won the national Junior Miss contest. She is a Wellesley graduate who's known for a quick sense of humor, a love of poetry, and a shy streak. She's married to film director Mike Nichols and lives in New York.

PRAYER STARTERS:

- Pray that Diane Sawyer would bring compassion and insight to her reporting, and listen carefully for God's leading.
- Pray for those who make significant daily news judgments that affect what we know, when we know, and often what we think. Pray that they would exercise the highest levels of integrity and civic responsibility.
- Ask the Lord to bless Sawyer's professional and personal life with His best.

You will know the truth, and the truth will set you free. John 8:31

CONTACT: 47 West 66th Street, New York, NY 10023

Reverend Leon Sullivan

International Civil Rights Activist,
Pastor, Businessman

Courtesy of Leon Sullivan

POINT OF IMPACT: Reverend Leon H. Sullivan, 77, changed the way corporations invest overseas. When he was a member of General·Motors' board of directors, he framed the Sullivan Principles that link foreign investment with a country's civil rights record. Now Pastor Emeritus of Zion Baptist Church in Philadelphia, the charismatic Dr. Sullivan has been a leading light in self-help and job training among the unemployed for more than 30 years. In 1964 Sullivan founded Opportunities Industrialization Centers of America, Inc. (OICA) to help untrained Americans learn job skills. Since its start OICA has helped more than 1.5 million people find meaningful work. Sullivan has also coordinated five African/African-American Summits, attended by world figures such as Nelson Mandela and Reverend Jesse Jackson. Recently, Sullivan has been helping Ethiopia through his International Foundation for Education and Self-Help.

He helps light the way for the unemployed.

QUOTABLE: At the Fourth African/African-American Summit: "We have come to follow an idea at the invitation of God, to attempt to deal with the problems of a continent that has been pushed to the side of the map in the interest of the rest of the world."

BEHIND THE SCENES: Leon Sullivan, who grew up in poverty in Philadelphia, is often described as being cut from the same mold as Martin Luther King, Jr.—a visionary, builder, and motivator. Sullivan lives in Phoenix, Arizona. He and his wife, Grace, have three grown children.

PRAYER STARTERS:

- Give thanks for the impact Leon Sullivan has had on job training and work attitudes among the disadvantaged and unemployed.

- Pray for ongoing wisdom and guidance for Dr. Sullivan. Pray that his problem-solving attitudes would continue to impact the world.

- Ask for health and spiritual abundance for Dr. Sullivan and his family.

> *He who works his land will have abundant food, but he who chases fantasies lacks judgment. Proverbs 12:11*

CONTACT: Opportunities Industrialization Centers International, 240 West Tulpehocken Street, Philadelphia, PA 19144; e-mail: oica@aol.com

Woody Allen
Writer, Director, Actor

Archive Photo

POINT OF IMPACT: Woody Allen began his comedic career writing one-liners for gossip columns at age 15, and during college he was a joke writer for Bob Hope. Today, his artistic reputation as a brilliant humorist and director allows him to assemble talented ensemble casts and exercise almost limitless creative freedom. Famous for his persona as a "cynical, upwardly mobile Jewish intellectual," Allen, now 65, has amassed a long list of distinguished films, including 1978's *Annie Hall.* That picture won him three Academy Awards, including Best Director and Best Screenplay, and he's garnered 13 more nominations since then. Allen is an enduring influence only partly because of his humor. In nearly every script, he wrestles with the big questions of meaning and purpose in life ("What if everything is an illusion and nothing exists? In that case, I definitely overpaid for my carpet").

His films capture the humor and angst of modern man.

QUOTABLE: "The movie industry has changed tremendously since I started making films but, for me personally, the way I make movies hasn't. I'm still interested in pretty much the same things: human relationships, and the unanswerable questions in life about aging, death, loneliness."

BEHIND THE SCENES: In 1992, Allen was swept up in a scandal about his affair with Soon-Yi Previn, the 21-year-old adopted daughter of his common-law wife, Mia Farrow. In 1997, the two wed in Venice. When he's not shooting a movie, he plays clarinet at Michael's Pub in Manhattan every Monday night. He has two sons, Satchel and Moses, and a daughter, Dylan Farrow.

PRAYER STARTERS:

- "The same anxieties that plagued me at 30 still plague me at 62. I've made no progress on the things that are important in life." On Allen's behalf, pray for a life-changing encounter with God's love and mercy.

- Give thanks for Allen's talents, so evident in the art and entertainment that he has brought audiences worldwide.

- Ask God to bless Woody Allen and his family with harmony and health.

> *No one can understand what goes on under the sun. Despite all his efforts to search it out, man cannot discover its meaning. Even if a wise man claims he knows, he cannot really comprehend it. Ecclesiastes 8:17*

CONTACT: Norma Lee Clark, 130 W. 57th St., New York City, NY 10019

Martha Williamson

Executive Producer, Touched by an Angel

CBS Photo

POINT OF IMPACT: Martha Williamson is best known as the producer of *Touched by an Angel.* Not an immediate hit, the TV series' popularity grew because a loyal audience created word-of-mouth buzz. And the program has done more than entertain people. Said House Majority Leader Dick Armey when he awarded Williamson the Freedom Works Award, "Countless letters have poured in to the show with stories of marriages that have been restored, debts that have been forgiven, and suicides that have been averted as a result of the uplifting messages of Martha's work." Williamson bases each show on three givens: that God exists, that He loves people, and that He wants to be part of their lives. It works. One writer says, "This faith is utter and abiding, expressed with a clarity so earnest, relevant and immutable that it demands respect whether you share it or not." The show has spawned numerous other sitcoms based on spirituality and religion.

She proved that God could "make it" on prime time.

QUOTABLE: "We don't get ministers, priests, and rabbis complaining about anything that's in this show. We do hear a lot of reports that they recommend our episodes to their congregations."

BEHIND THE SCENES: Williamson grew up in a Methodist family in Denver, where she sang in a church choir and taught Sunday school. For a time early in her career she lost her grip on her faith, but she recommitted herself in 1980. Today she attends a Baptist church in Los Angeles, where she lives with her husband.

PRAYER STARTERS:

- Give thanks for the broad appeal of Williamson's TV work, and for its positive impact both with viewers and with media creators.
- Pray that all shows depicting Christians and the reality of God in our lives will be helpful, accurate, and honoring to God. Pray that the shows would lead many to an encounter with Jesus Christ.
- Ask God to bless Williamson's creative endeavors and guard her health.

> *He will command his angels concerning you to guard you in all your ways.*
> *Psalm 91:11*

CONTACT: CBS, 51 W. 52nd St., New York, NY 10019

Jose Ramos-Horta and Bishop Carlos Belo

*Nobel Peace Prize Winners,
Human Rights Activists*

Copyright Nobel

POINT OF IMPACT: The plight of the tiny Asian island of East Timor caught the attention of the world because of two men—activist Jose Ramos-Horta (shown) and Bishop Carlos Belo. For 25 years, this island has been ruled by Indonesia, the world's largest Muslim nation, yet most of the 800,000 people on Timor are Roman Catholic. Indonesia has refused to give up control, despite international appeals, and its domination has meant thousands of deaths, along with imprisonment, disease, and famine. Ramos-Horta has agitated for independence for nearly all of that time, to no avail. Then in 1989, after learning that at least 100,000 Timorese had been killed by Indonesian forces, Bishop Belo wrote a letter to the United Nations asking for help. The East Timorese were "dying as a people and as a nation," he pleaded. For their efforts, despite overwhelming Indonesian opposition, the two were awarded the 1996 Nobel Peace Prize. Their example continues to influence powers in a region where individual rights are often little valued.

Their David-and-Goliath example inspires others.

QUOTABLE: "Empires have melted away. We are used to valiant talk by dictators. We are patient."—Jose Ramos-Horta

BEHIND THE SCENES: Ramos-Horta, 51, has been forced to flee the island many times for his activities. Four of his siblings have been killed by the Indonesian military. Currently, he lives in exile in Lisbon; his ex-wife, Ana Pessoa, lives in Mozambique with their son Loro. Carlos Belo, 55, is the first Roman Catholic bishop to receive a Nobel Prize. Belo and Ramos-Horta split the $1 million award and both funneled the money back into their cause.

PRAYER STARTERS:

- Give thanks for the inspiring example of Carlos Belo and Jose Ramos-Horta. Pray that democracy and justice will prevail in Southeast Asia.
- Recent developments in East Timor hold promise. Pray for resolution to the conflict, and for an end to human rights abuses.
- Pray for protection for both Ramos-Horta and Belo and for their families (both men have received death threats).

    *A ruler who oppresses the poor is like a driving rain that leaves no crops.
    Proverbs 28:3*

CONTACT: c/o University of New South Wales, Sydney 2052, Australia

Millard Fuller
Founder, Habitat for Humanity

Courtesy of Habitat for Humanity

POINT OF IMPACT: Once a millionaire, Fuller gave away his fortune out of a desire to emulate Jesus' service to the poor. In 1976 he founded Habitat for Humanity, an international Christian organization that helps low-income families build their own houses. Once the houses are completed, Habitat transfers ownership to the new owners at no profit and with interest-free loans. Volunteers help during construction, often using donated supplies. Fuller calls his approach "biblical economics." In just two decades, Habitat has become the largest nonprofit housing organization in the United States, with an annual budget of $78 million. It has built an estimated 55,000 houses worldwide. Key to their success has been Fuller's knack for mobilizing support across economic, religious, racial, and political lines, as well as his recruitment of high profile volunteers, including former president Jimmy Carter. When awarding Fuller the Medal of Freedom, President Clinton declared, "I don't think it's an exaggeration to say that Millard Fuller has literally revolutionized the concept of philanthropy."

He builds homes for low-income families.

QUOTABLE: "How can you say that you love your neighbor as much as you love yourself when you live in a big high-rise and your neighbor across town lives in a roach-infested tenement?"

BEHIND THE SCENES: Married 40 years to wife Linda, they live in a modest house in Americus, Georgia. In his early sixties, Fuller usually walks the nine blocks to work. Despite Georgia's sweltering heat, he doesn't use air-conditioning in his home, and has turned down raises, saying what he earns is enough.

PRAYER STARTERS:

- Give thanks for the life, generosity, and example of Millard Fuller. Pray for God's blessings on him and his family today.
- Pray for the work of Habitat for Humanity and its volunteers.
- Today remember those without shelter. Habitat reports that in the United States alone, 7.6 million live in deficient housing conditions.

> *You have been a refuge for the poor, a refuge for the needy in his distress, a shelter from the storm and a shade from the heat. Isaiah 25:4*

CONTACT: e-mail: public_info@habitat.org

Fred Rogers

TV Host and Creator of
Mister Rogers' Neighborhood

Courtesy of Family Communications, Inc.

POINT OF IMPACT: Fred McFeely Rogers is the host and writer of the longest-running children's program on public television. *Mister Rogers' Neighborhood,* which debuted in 1968, reaches 8 million households and child-care settings. College kids to aging baby boomers cite Rogers as a favorite childhood influence. His untiring message of caring, gentleness, and respect for children has often been at odds with commercial TV programming. In 1996, *TV Guide* named Fred Rogers one of the 50 greatest TV stars of all time. The tribute fittingly read: "*Mister Rogers' Neighborhood* makes us, young and old alike, feel safe, cared for and valued. Wherever Mister Rogers is, so is sanctuary."

It's a beautiful day in his neighborhood.

QUOTABLE: "Everybody longs to be loved. And the greatest thing we can do is let somebody know that they are loved and capable of loving."

BEHIND THE SCENES: Rogers still writes and produces several weeks of new programs each season. He continues to sing "Won't You Be My Neighbor?" at the start of each show and wear a trademark cardigan sweater. (The Smithsonian keeps one of Rogers' sweaters in its permanent collection.) Fred and his wife, Joanne, have two grown children and two grandchildren.

PRAYER STARTERS:

- Give thanks for Fred Rogers' 30 years of positive impact on young children.
- Rogers is an ordained Presbyterian minister who considers his viewing audience his congregation. Pray for his continued health and strength, and for the influence of his media company, Family Communications.
- Pray for parents who may be struggling today to express love and care to their children. Rogers has said, "Children get their earliest notions of God from their earliest caregivers. A good prayer for parents is: 'Jesus, help me grow right along with this little one, and help me to see how I have grown.'"

Unless you change and become like little children, you will never enter the kingdom of heaven. Therefore, whoever humbles himself like this child is the greatest in the kingdom of heaven. Matthew 18:3-4

CONTACT: Family Communications, 4802 5th Ave., Pittsburgh, PA 15213

Archive Photo

The Chemical Brothers: Tom Rowlands and Ed Simons
Music Group

POINT OF IMPACT: This eccentric British duo met in college and started deejaying at parties. They wanted a new, slightly different sound, so Simons and Rowlands seamlessly stitched together snippets of R&B, hip-hop, Latin beats, and random sound bites. Their wholly successful concoction cast a spell over English dance floors and within three short years, their sensation spread to the United States. The Brothers, both 30, are on the wings of a growing American "Electronica" push. *Entertainment Weekly* describes this new genre as "artificially flavored pop that relies heavily on synthesizers, samples, loops, and dance-beat—and less on guitars or vocals." They were nominated for a Best Instrumental Grammy in 1998 and cracked *Billboard* charts with "Setting Sun."

Their music chemistry captures listeners.

QUOTABLE: "The last ten years, the most exciting place to be is at the dance floor."
—Ed Simons

BEHIND THE SCENES: Some critics question whether the Chemical Brothers' frenetic sound is trying to replicate a drug experience. On the video of "Setting Sun" there is an impression of a girl "tripping" on drugs. "I think we both like music that confuses you and makes you feel like you're somewhere else, and you're being given new sounds and a good funky beat. It's all quite a psychedelic experience," replies Simons. "It's just about being together with other people. It's not necessarily about being on drugs or whatever."

PRAYER STARTERS:

- Simons insists, "In spite of our name, drugs mean nothing to us." Pray that they stand against the use of so-called designer drugs, which are common to dance clubs.
- Ask God to bless both the Chemical Brothers and their loved ones.
- Pray that Christian artists will influence the Chemical Brothers to seek a relationship with God.

    How can a young man keep his way pure? By living according to your word. Psalm 119:9

CONTACT: www.musicfanclubs.org/chemical

Steve Case

CEO, America Online (AOL)

Archive Photo

POINT OF IMPACT: Well over 47 million Americans were connected to the internet last year, more than half of them subscribers to America Online. In other words, AOL founder and CEO Steve Case has turned his interactive village into a bona fide mass medium, reaching more people than all the top newspapers in the country combined. AOL is the world's number-one producer of online services, with subscribers in Europe, Australia, Canada, Japan, and Hong Kong. Case's goal is to create a new medium that will someday be as ubiquitous as telephone or television—and eventually even more useful and indispensable to everyday life. But Case is about more than money; the company's AOL Foundation supports grassroots internet programs that help foster community, enhance teaching and learning, and improve lives.

Online, he reaches more people than the top newspapers combined.

QUOTABLE: "What you're witnessing is the birth of an NBC on the internet."

BEHIND THE SCENES: Case once marketed hair conditioner for Procter & Gamble and tested pizza toppings for Pizza Hut. But by 1998 *Time* and *Vanity Fair* had named Case, worth around $200 million, among the ten most influential people in the communications industry. That same year Case, now in his early forties, married Jean Villaneuva, AOL's former communications chief, in a ceremony performed by Case's friend, the Reverend Billy Graham (they met online). The ceremony was private—only their five children attended.

PRAYER STARTERS:

- Pray that Steve Case and his leadership team would have the imaginative ability to help take the internet to its full potential for good, and the integrity and moral commitment to help minimize its potential for harm.
- Ask the Lord to bless the Cases' marriage and their personal life with affection, commitment, and a strong sense of His presence and purposes for them.

There are different kinds of gifts, but the same Spirit. There are different kinds of service, but the same Lord. 1 Corinthians 12:4-5

CONTACT: 22000 AOL Way, Dulles, VA 20166; SteveCase@aol.com

Carol Bellamy

*Executive Director, United Nations
Children's Fund (UNICEF)*

Photo Credit: UNICEF/HQ93-1893

POINT OF IMPACT: Her Brooklyn gumshoe accent and hard edge can't hide the fact that Carol Bellamy has hungry kids on her mind—millions of them. A seasoned political activist, she had extensive contacts within the Democratic party that won her the Clinton administration's backing for her current post as executive director of UNICEF in 1995. Yet the seminal experience in her life was a two-year stint as a Peace Corps volunteer. She served as the director of the Peace Corps from 1993 to 1995. Now head of the only U.N. organization devoted to children, Bellamy oversees UNICEF's supplying of health care, education, and sanitation in many countries. She has been called one of the world's most powerful "can-rattlers"—it is her task to pry out of donor governments money that will determine what a day will bring for millions of children the world over.

She's a powerful "can-rattler" for the world's poor children.

QUOTABLE: "UNICEF's commitment has always been articulated in terms of child survival, but I think now that more children are surviving, we have to consider what kind of a world we are bringing these children into. That is a challenge for me. I can't think of anything else I'd rather be doing."

BEHIND THE SCENES: Brooklyn-born Carol Bellamy, 58, says, "I don't moan and groan; I just play the cards I'm dealt." She twice voted as a legislator against laws to require medical care for babies born alive after induced abortions. Bellamy lives in New York.

PRAYER STARTERS:

- Pray for new momentum for the initiative (begun by Jody Williams and Princess Diana) to ban land mines. America's failure to sign the Ottawa treaty banning land mines was a particular blow to Bellamy.
- Pray for Bellamy's leadership, and for UNICEF's work around the world today. In Bangladesh alone, 700 children die each day of malnutrition.
- Ask God to bless Bellamy with safety and peace, and a desire to seek Him.

> *And he took the children in his arms, put his hands on them and blessed them.*
> Mark 10:16

CONTACT: 333 East 38th Street, New York, NY 10016

Jerry Seinfeld
Comedian, Actor

Archive Photo

POINT OF IMPACT: "Now why does moisture ruin leather? Aren't cows outside a lot of the time? When it's raining, do cows go up to the farmhouse and say, 'Let us in! We're all wearing leather!'" Such funny, albeit pointless, observations turned Jerry Seinfeld's show "about nothing" into one of the most successful TV series in history. On *Seinfeld*, which first aired in 1990, he played himself—a single comic in New York coping with the trivialities of modern life. "Seinfeld manages to articulate the concerns of the unremarkable majority whose idea of a major contemporary issue is the difficulty of finding your car in a shopping-mall car park," explains one writer. Some criticized him for his Jewish jokes and the way he and his "desperately selfish and ludicrously childish friends" fell in and out of bed with a gaggle of partners. Seinfeld, 45, ended the show in 1998. Today he's watched almost as widely as ever in reruns.

His show about nothing strikes the world's funny bone.

QUOTABLE: "I knew I was going to be a comedian at a very young age. I remember one time I made a friend laugh so hard that he sprayed a mouthful of cookies and milk all over me. And I liked it. That was the beginning."

BEHIND THE SCENES: Born in Brooklyn and raised "happily" in Massapequa, Seinfeld credits his parent's sense of humor as a major influence. One night when he was eight, the family was watching a comedian on television. "My parents were telling me, 'This man's job is to come out and be funny for people.' I couldn't believe it. 'That's his whole job?' I asked. 'Are you kidding me?' And they said, 'No, he's kidding us.'" Seinfeld, who has an older sister, Carolyn, is still single and lives in New York. When asked what's next for him, he answers patly, "Nothing."

PRAYER STARTERS:

- Pray that Seinfeld would seek God's will for his life and creative talents.
- Pray that his personal relationships would bring him clarity and comfort.
- Pray that Seinfeld's honesty and insight about human nature would encourage viewers to respond to God's grace.

Love must be sincere. Hate what is evil; cling to what is good. Romans 12:9

CONTACT: 9830 Wilshire Blvd., Beverly Hills, CA 90212

Courtesy of Cold Spring Harbor Laboratory

James Watson, Francis Crick, and Maurice Wilkins
Nobel Prize-winning Researchers

POINT OF IMPACT: In 1950 James Watson (shown) joined the race to determine the structure of DNA. Maurice Wilkins and another scientist had shown that DNA was a molecule in which two "strands" formed a tightly linked pair. Then in 1953, Francis Crick joined Watson in proposing that the structure of DNA was a winding helix. Watson was only 25 years old. But his discovery of DNA is one of the century's greatest; in 1962 Watson, Crick, and Wilkins won the Nobel Prize for Medicine. At that point, no one knew that their discovery would lead to infertility solutions, cures for cancer, conviction of murderers and rapists (and release of those wrongly convicted), and treatments for diseases such as cystic fibrosis—much less the cloning of sheep! Watson once worked on the Human Genome Project and is still on the Harvard faculty. Dr. Crick turned his attention to embryology, and has since studied consciousness and REM dream sleep at the Salk Institute. As the "gene wars" continue at a white heat, Watson's opinions are still sought at every turn.

Their scientific discoveries still reap breakthroughs.

QUOTABLE: "Francis Crick and I made the discovery of the century, that was pretty clear. I guess time has justified people paying all this respect to me in spite of my bad manners."—James Watson

BEHIND THE SCENES: Crick, 84, and his wife live in a house called The Golden Helix. Wilkins, 84, is retired and lives in England with his wife. Watson, at 72, is still known as the *enfant terrible* of molecular biology.

PRAYER STARTERS:

- Thank God for the Crick/Watson/Wilkins discovery of DNA and its uses in solving serious health problems. Pray for their well-being today.

- Pray that all research scientists will go about their work humbly, acknowledging God's sovereignty, and applying their discoveries responsibly. Ask God to bless them with spiritual truth and insight.

> *Who among the gods is like you, O LORD? Who is like you—majestic in holiness, awesome in glory, working wonders? Exodus 15:11*

CONTACT: Dr. Francis Crick, Salk Institute, P.O. Box 85800, San Diego, CA 92186-5800; Dr. James Watson, Harvard University, Cambridge, MA 02138; no address available for Maurice Wilkins

Kay Arthur

Cofounder and Executive Vice President,
Precept Ministries

Cansler Photography, Chattanooga, TN

POINT OF IMPACT: It began as a Bible study for teenagers in her living room. Before long the group grew and began meeting in a barn. Today Precept Ministries, founded by Kay Arthur and her husband, Jack (who is president), has grown into an international adult Bible study ministry (emphasizing an inductive method of study) with 12,000 study groups in 114 countries. "Many women first come to Precept for the fellowship of other women," explains one participant. "But once they're exposed to what they can learn from the Word of God, they begin to respond and obey." Arthur is the author of Precept upon Precept Inductive Bible studies and more than 36 books, including *Israel My Beloved* and *As Silver Refined.* She has more than 4 million books in print. She hosts the national television program, "How Can I Live?", a daily radio program, "Precept with Kay Arthur," and a weekly call-in program, "Precept LIVE with Kay and Jan."

Her worldwide Bible studies began in a barn.

QUOTABLE: When her first marriage ended in divorce: "Disillusioned and lonely, I shook my fist in the face of God and said, 'To hell with You, God. I'm going to find someone to love me.' Little did I realize that before the foundation of the world, God had said, 'To heaven with you, Kay.' His Son would take my hell so I could have His heaven."

BEHIND THE SCENES: Kay Arthur, 66, first trained as a nurse and has been a businesswoman and a missionary. She has always had a special interest in Israel, where she spends time studying every year. Kay writes and teaches with a rare combination of authority and compassion. She and Jack live in Tennessee. They are the parents of three sons and have nine grandchildren.

PRAYER STARTERS:

- Praise God for the impact of Precept Bible studies on thousands of lives—for the new passion for Bible study and biblical living, and for the Christian fellowship, and encouragement.
- Pray for the continued impact of Kay Arthur's ministries around the world, especially among believers who have grown complacent, and nonbelievers who want to meet God in a personal way.
- Ask the Lord to bless Jack and Kay Arthur with health, love, and joy.

My heart trembles at your word. Psalm 119:161

CONTACT: P.O. Box 182218, Chattanooga, TN 37422; www.precept.org

AP/Wide World Photos

Ehud Barak
Prime Minister of Israel

POINT OF IMPACT: After three years of fueding, economic downturn and an impasse in the peace process under Benjamin Netanyahu, Israeli voters turned in mid-1999 to General Ehud Barak for deliverance. As the nation's most decorated soldier and head of its moderate Labor Party, Barak brings fresh hope for this divided nation. "We are together as one people," he says. "Whatever the disputes we are brothers, and brothers walk together." Barak's election was welcomed by both President Clinton and Palestinian leader Yasser Arafat. But only time will tell what Barak can accomplish. He's distinguished himself as a commando, intelligence chief, and general. Yet he sees himself as a disciple of the pragmatic but peace-oriented Yitzhak Rabin, the assassinated former Israeli leader.

He's a soldier with peace on his mind.

QUOTABLE: "We know that it is incumbent on us, on our generation that fought Israel's wars, to do everything possible to strengthen the nation's security by advancing in the direction of peace agreements."

BEHIND THE SCENES: Barak, 57, was born on a kibbutz (or Israeli work commune) and has degrees from Hebrew University in Jerusalem and Stanford. He's also a trained classical pianist. As a commando leader, Barak once posed as a woman in a secret military raid in Beirut in which three PLO guerrillas were killed. He and his wife, Nava, have three children.

PRAYER STARTERS:

- Pray for peace in Israel. Pray for a turning away from hatred and violence.
- Pray that Prime Minister Barak will seek and obey the Lord's guidance in all his decisions. Pray that he will surround himself with wise, just, and courageous counselors.
- Ask God to keep Barak and his family safe. Pray that they would personally seek the God of Abraham and honor Him in their lives.

> *Give me wisdom and knowledge, that I may lead this people, for who is able to govern this great people of yours? 2 Chronicles 1:10*

CONTACT: 3 Kaplan Street, P.O. Box 187, 91919 Jerusalem, Israel; pm@pmo.gov.il

Deion Sanders
Football Player

Courtesy of Dallas Cowboys

POINT OF IMPACT: They call him "Prime Time" and "Neon" because few sports personalities over the past decade have so courted national media attention as Deion Sanders, whom ESPN named one of the greatest 100 athletes of the past century. One of those ultrarare athletes who played two professional sports—baseball and football—he's the only man in history to play in both a World Series and Super Bowl. Sanders currently plays only football, for the Dallas Cowboys, and is considered by some to be the best cornerback ever. But his impact off the field has been just as great. Since becoming a Christian in 1997, he's now a much-publicized evangelist among fellow football players, youth, and in the city of Dallas.

He intercepted the truth just in time.

QUOTABLE: "I was reading the headlines last week about Don King. And then I started reading a book about Martin Luther King. And I thought to myself, there isn't but one king. That's my king! Only one king that is truly a king."

BEHIND THE SCENES: Despite all Sanders' flash, flamboyance, and success, in 1997 he was a broken man. While fans celebrated his exploits on the field, his marriage was falling apart, he was addicted to sex, and his emptiness frequently reduced him to tears. Then his attorney, a Christian, started talking to Sanders about Jesus Christ and passed along some Christian books. A few days after his second suicide attempt, alone in his apartment, Sanders felt the presence of God and gave his life to Christ. Shortly after his conversion, he started hosting a weekly Bible study for teammates. Now 33, Sanders is divorced and the father of two, daughter Diondra and son Deion Luwynn, Jr.

PRAYER STARTERS:

- Give thanks for Sanders' conversion. Pray that his personal and family life will continue to benefit from the Lord's healing, strength, and wisdom.
- Pray that Sanders' high profile among football fans will bring him many opportunities to accomplish significant and eternal good.
- Ask for safety and success in his professional career.

> *Some trust in chariots and some in horses, but we trust in the name of the* LORD *our God. Psalm 20:7*

CONTACT: Dallas Cowboys, One Cowboys Parkway, Irving, TX 75063

Ellen Johnson
President, American Atheists

POINT OF IMPACT: Now in its fourth decade, the organization Ellen Johnson leads is dedicated to "working for the civil rights of Atheists, promoting separation of church and state, and providing information about atheism." The group was originally founded by Madalyn Murray O'Hair, the noted atheist activist who successfully battled against mandatory prayer in public schools. AA holds an annual convention, publishes a newsletter, a magazine, and also boasts cable TV outreach and web sites, which continue to find larger audiences. The atheists now have headquarters "inside the beltway" in Washington, DC, which will help their lobbying efforts.

She doesn't want her children to believe in God.

QUOTABLE: "I am one of the fortunate few who grew up in an atheist home, and today I'm rearing my two young children in an atheist environment."

BEHIND THE SCENES: In 1995 Mrs. O'Hair, her son, and her daughter vanished. There were accusations that they took more than $600,000 from the AA organization. An ABC *Nightline* program in 1998 strongly suggested that Johnson had prior knowledge of the transfer of money from an AA Trust Fund in Boonton, New Jersey to San Antonio, Texas (where the O'Hairs disappeared). Johnson denies any such knowledge.

PRAYER STARTERS:

- Johnson is using the internet to connect with young people questioning their beliefs. Pray that internet seekers would stumble on convincing Christian websites that can introduce them to Christ.

- Pray that Ellen Johnson would experience a radical spiritual awakening. Pray that all her intellectual arguments would suddenly seem pointless in the light of God's radiant and transforming love and truth.

- Pray for a young person you know who may be struggling with doubt.

- Give thanks that O'Hair's surviving son, Bill, converted to Christianity. Pray for his physical, mental and spiritual growth.

> *You will seek me and find me when you seek me with all your heart.*
> *Jeremiah 29:13*

CONTACT: P.O. Box 5733, Parsippany, NJ 07054-6733; info@atheists.org

Jesse L. Jackson
Baptist Minister,
President, Rainbow
Coalition/Operation PUSH

Photo by Rick Reinhard, Washington, D.C.

POINT OF IMPACT: Maybe his fearlessness traces back to that stain on his shirt in 1968—it was the blood of the dying Martin Luther King, Jr. Jesse Jackson, a young civil rights worker at the time, had been standing by his side when an assassin's bullet struck Dr. King down. Ever since, Jackson has had some of his most public moments in the crosshairs of violent situations: in the Persian Gulf war, he talked Saddam Hussein into releasing 227 hostages; in 1999, he repeated his feat with three prisoners in Yugoslavia. But Jackson's greatest 30-year legacy is fighting for the needs and rights of minorities at home. Through his Operation PUSH and several runs for president as head of a multiracial "Rainbow Coalition," Jackson has touched both the heart and institutions of America with his eloquent appeals for fairness and economic advancement for all.

He's the eloquent voice of the minority rainbow.

QUOTABLE: "Cultural distortion is a form of violence. The media projects African-Americans and other people of color in five deadly ways: we are portrayed as less intelligent, less hard working, less universal, less patriotic, and more violent than we are. We bear this burden every day. . . ."

BEHIND THE SCENES: Jackson, 56, was born in Greenville, South Carolina and attended North Carolina A&T College, where he met his wife of 34 years, Jackie. After graduation, Jackson became a civil rights activist with King's Southern Christian Leadership Conference. Jackson is an ordained Baptist minister. The Jacksons have raised five children and live in Chicago.

PRAYER STARTERS:

- Give thanks for Jackson's passion to inspire and help the downtrodden.
- Jesse Jackson may be responsible for registering more new voters than any other living American. Pray for a growing commitment to participate in the political process among voters, especially among the poor.
- Pray the Jackson would seek God's wisdom in all his decisions today.
- Ask God to protect Jackson from danger and bless his home and marriage.

> *If you show special attention to the man wearing fine clothes . . . have you not discriminated among yourselves and become judges with evil thoughts? James 2:3-4*

CONTACT: www.rainbowpush.org

289

M. Scott Peck
Psychiatrist, Bestselling Author

Courtesy of Simon & Schuster

POINT OF IMPACT: In November 1983, a book entitled *The Road Less Traveled,* written by an unknown Connecticut psychiatrist, first appeared on the paperback bestseller list of the *New York Times Book Review.* It stayed there for 13 years, one month, and two weeks. In that time, it became the number-one nonfiction bestseller in history and turned Dr. M. Scott Peck into a national institution and guru to an estimated 7 million readers. Over the past 16 years, he's written 11 other bestselling books detailing his thoughts about evil, human love, psychology, personal growth, and the grace of God. His influence has helped pave the way for the popularity of self-help books, 12-step groups, and the current plethora of spiritually oriented titles. He is currently the medical director of the New Milford Hospital Mental Health Clinic and a psychiatrist with a private practice in New Milford, Connecticut.

Millions have traveled his less-traveled road.

QUOTABLE: "Life is difficult."—the oft-quoted opening sentence of *The Road Less Traveled*

BEHIND THE SCENES: M. Scott Peck is a man of many contradictions. The guru of addiction recovery has admitted to being powerless against nicotine and alcohol; the man who writes in *The Road Less Traveled* about how to build a lasting marriage engaged in a string of marital infidelities after fame struck. He and his wife, Lilly, live in Connecticut.

PRAYER STARTERS:

- Give thanks for the guidance and encouragement Scott Peck's books have given to so many, and especially for the Christian themes of grace, the reality of evil, and personal accountability that thread through his work.
- Pray for healing, reconciliation, and joy in the Peck family.
- Pray today for someone you know who struggles against an addiction.

> *I have told you these things, so that in me you may have peace. In this world you will have trouble. But take heart! I have overcome the world.*
> *Jesus, in John 16:33*

CONTACT: c\o Simon & Schuster, www.simonsays.com

Shelly Lazarus

Chairman-CEO, Ogilvy & Mather Worldwide

POINT OF IMPACT: Shelly Lazarus, head of mega-ad agency Ogilvy & Mather, sells the sizzle (and delivers the steak) for some of the world's biggest advertising accounts—Kodak, Shell, Mattel, and GTE, to name a few. She's also one of the most powerful women in business, period—*Fortune* listed her as number four in the United States. Yet she's best known for refusing to compromise her role as wife and mother, and for a leadership style that's "nurturing" and "distinctly feminine." About Lazarus, *USA Today* notes, "Despite the stereotypes, some high-ranking executives are refusing to sacrifice family for career. Management experts say that may be exactly what it takes—for top executives to step forward as role models—to change the career-climbing climate that drives some to quit." Last year, Ogilvy & Mather created ads worth $8.8 billion to their clients.

This advertising whiz sells family first.

QUOTABLE: "When I started out, 25 years ago, I was often the only woman at the table. We'd be talking about what women would buy, and then suddenly everyone would look at me—it was amazing; there I was, suddenly representing all women, everywhere."

BEHIND THE SCENES: Once, when she was asked to forgo a family ski trip to attend an important board meeting in Paris, Lazarus refused. "People were horrified," she says. She ended up with a compromise, but she still kept her family first. Lazarus, 51, and her pediatrician husband, George, like to jog in Central Park and watch videos from a nearby Blockbuster with their youngest of three children, Benjamin, who's ten. They live in Manhattan.

PRAYER STARTERS:

- Give thanks for Shelly Lazarus' example of protecting family priorities.
- Pray that she will experience success today in her work; pray that her influence will be for moral courage in the world of advertising.
- Pray today for a busy working mother you know.
- Ask the Lord to bless the Lazarus family with an awareness of His presence, His providence, and His loving purposes for their lives.

   Praise be to the God and Father of our Lord Jesus Christ, the Father of compassion and the God of all comfort. 2 Corinthians 1:3

CONTACT: www.ogilvy.com

Charles Stanley

Pastor, Author, Broadcaster

POINT OF IMPACT: Dr. Charles Stanley is the pastor of the 13,000-member First Baptist Church of Atlanta and founder of In Touch Ministries. Through his broadcasts, his resonant, familiar voice is beamed around the world on more than 500 radio stations and more than 200 television stations. Twice elected president of the Southern Baptist Convention (America's most influential Protestant denomination), Dr. Stanley is among the preeminent Bible teachers in the world. He is a bestselling author whose numerous books, including *The Reason for My Hope, The Source of My Strength, The Blessings of Brokenness: Why God Allows Us to Go Through Hard Times,* and his latest, *Our Unmet Needs,* have sold millions of copies.

He's the Southern gentleman of Bible preachers.

QUOTABLE: "God's love is the most important thing you can know about God."

BEHIND THE SCENES: There's a scribble in the margin of Stanley's Bible—October 11, 1980, beside Psalm 67:2—"Send us around the world with the news of Your saving power and Your eternal plan for all mankind." It was another decade before his first broadcasts were aired. Today, "In Touch" is available worldwide. "My passion from day one," he says, "has been to get the gospel of Jesus Christ to as many people as possible, as clearly as possible, as quickly as possible, as simply as possible, through the Holy Spirit—all to the glory of God." He and his wife Anna have two grown children, Andy and Becky, and six grandchildren. They live in Atlanta.

PRAYER STARTERS:

- Dr. Stanley asks for prayer that "In Touch" will "ever strive to maintain its passion for God and compassion for people."
- Pray for Dr. Stanley's personal and pastoral challenges. Pray also for all pastors—for wisdom, courage, and strength. Pray for your own minister.
- Give thanks for Charles Stanley's half-century of influential ministry. Ask for God's peace and provisions for Charles and Anna and their family.

> *This is love: not that we loved God, but that he loved us and sent his Son as an atoning sacrifice for our sins. 1 John 4:10*

CONTACT: In Touch, P.O. Box 7900, Atlanta, GA 30357. www.intouch.org

"When you pray for your enemies,
asking God to meet their needs and
manifest Himself to them, you are
overcoming evil with good. Instead of
fighting negative thoughts in your
mind, you are filling your mind with
positive thoughts. You are now on the
side of your enemy; you have a
spiritual stake in his well-being.
If God answers your prayer, which
you want Him to do, the
person prayed for will be blessed,
and you will learn about redemption,
the ultimate form of forgiveness."

—PAT ROBERTSON

Ted Koppel
Journalist, Anchor, Nightline

Archive Photo

POINT OF IMPACT: Regarded as one of the best anchors in journalism, Ted Koppel hosts the widely popular news show *Nightline*. The significance of the broadcast has much to do with how its growth has paralleled the development of satellite broadcasting. For the first time, by linking newsmakers worldwide, the show could not only report on but often become a participant in major news events. Prior to *Nightline* Koppel worked as a Foreign and Domestic Correspondent and Bureau Chief for ABC News. Koppel has received many awards for his work, including 30 Emmys and nine Overseas Press Club Awards. In 1992 the Academy of Television Arts and Sciences inducted him into the TV Hall of Fame. Koppel is highly respected for his fairness and his understanding and representation of his guests' viewpoints. Yet Ted Koppel, interviewer extraordinaire, prepares no questions for his interviews.

Satellites link him to the news he reports.

QUOTABLE: "Fame is only an offshoot of what I've always really wanted: to be one of the best."

BEHIND THE SCENES: Koppel is the only child of Jewish parents who fled Nazi Germany in 1938. Koppel was 13 when he and his parents emigrated to the United States. He now resides in Potomac, Maryland, with his wife, Grace. They have four children: Andrea, Deirdre, Andrew, and Tara.

PRAYER STARTERS:

- Thank God for Koppel's devotion and excellence in informing society about worldwide issues.
- Ask for God to continue to work in the hearts of those in the media whose presentation of the facts help to shape society's attitudes.
- Pray for God's blessings on Koppel, his wife, and his four children today, and ask that they would feel surrounded by His love.

> *The righteous man leads a blameless life; blessed are his children after him.*
> *Proverbs 20:7*

CONTACT: 171 Desales St. N.W., Washington, DC 20039

Will Smith

Rapper, Actor

Archive Photo

POINT OF IMPACT: At the ripe young age of 32, Will Smith has already conquered three entertainment genres. As half of a hip-hop duo, Smith helped create two platinum albums and was a millionaire by age 18. Then Smith won the TV role of a quick-witted-home-boy-turned-guest-of-rich-relatives in *Fresh Prince of Bel-Air.* The show ran for six successful years. That's when Smith graduated to movie roles. His first, in *Six Degrees of Separation*, garnered critical praise; the action films that followed—*Independence Day* and *Men in Black*— were Hollywood blockbusters. Smith's 1999 return to music for the album *Big Willie Style* won him a Grammy. About his film future, the former boy wonder says, "I want to play positive characters—characters that represent really strong, positive black images." His most recent role was in *Enemy of the State.*

He's a boy wonder with a positive image.

QUOTABLE: "I don't know what my calling is, but I want to be here for a reason. I strive to be like the greatest people who ever lived. Like Jesus. When I'm angry or hurt I ask myself, what would Buddha or Gandhi do?"

BEHIND THE SCENES: Born in Philadelphia, Smith actually grew up in a middle class family (his father is an engineer; his mother works for the school board). He turned down a scholarship to MIT to study music, preferring to pursue showbiz. Smith is married to his second wife, actress Jada Pinkett Smith, and is the father of two sons, Trey and Jaden.

PRAYER STARTERS:

- Pray that Will Smith's professional and lifestyle choices would inspire youth to reach for their best.
- Pray that Smith would make wise choices about his career, choosing his roles wisely, and using his platform for a greater good than just his own success.
- Ask God to strengthen him in his roles as husband and father.

> *Who is wise and understanding among you? Let him show it by his good life, by deeds done in the humility that comes from wisdom. James 2:13*

CONTACT: Creative Artists Agency, 9830 Wilshire Blvd., Beverly Hills, CA 90212

Tom Daschle

Senator, South Dakota

Photo by Rick Reinhard, Washington, DC

POINT OF IMPACT: As Senate Minority Leader, 53-year-old Tom Daschle is responsible for establishing the Democratic party's agenda and unifying its efforts against the majority Republicans. By all accounts, Daschle has been one of the Democrats' most effective leaders in recent memory. Through his leadership Democrats have been able to blunt the sharp edges of GOP legislation and even block proposals outright. Daschle also helped Democrats unveil their Families First agenda, which seeks to eliminate the deficit and address the concerns of working families: paycheck, retirement, and health security. Working with moderate Republicans, Daschle also worked hard to protect the Medicare and the education budget, helping to pass the largest education increases in history.

In the Senate, he's defining the future for his party.

QUOTABLE: Senator Robert Byrd, himself a former Senate Democratic leader, says Daschle "has steel in his spine, despite his reasonable and modest demeanor."

BEHIND THE SCENES: Daschle goes home to South Dakota as often as possible. Although he became a licensed pilot several years ago, his favorite way to see his state remains what he calls "unscheduled driving." He gets in his car without staff or schedule and stops at Elks Club meetings, restaurants, cattle auctions, or any-place else he finds South Dakotans gathered, to hear what's on their minds. The visits, he says, remind him why he's in Washington in the first place. He and his wife, Linda, have three children.

PRAYER STARTERS:

- Pray that Daschle and other leaders in the Democratic party will be guided by wisdom and courage as they address the needs of working families.
- Ask God to bless Linda and Tom Daschle in their marriage and family with a growing knowledge of God's love.
- Ask for safety in all of Daschle's travels.

> *What kind of people ought you to be? You ought to live holy and godly lives as you look forward to the day of God. 2 Peter 3:11-12*

CONTACT: 509 HSOB, Washington, DC 20510; tom_daschle@daschle.senate.gov

Pamela Eakes

*President, Mothers Against Violence
in America (MAVIA)*

Courtesy of MAVIA

POINT OF IMPACT: Each year, more than 7,000 violent crimes are committed by children with guns taken from their own homes. Half of all handguns in the U.S. are stored unlocked, while 22 million are stored unlocked and loaded. Such statistics deeply concern Pamela Eakes, founder and president of Mothers Against Violence in America, an organization committed to changing America's violence-happy culture. Eakes began the group in 1994 after reading one too many stories about children killing children. Through community and school programs (including SAVE—Students Against Violence Everywhere) and other services, MAVIA members teach children anger management, conflict resolution, and peer mediation as alternatives to violence.

She's mobilizing moms against youth violence.

QUOTABLE: "Our mission is much more global than gun control. We are trying to change the culture. We are trying to teach people how to have more empathy and respect for each other."

BEHIND THE SCENES: Pamela Eakes left a 20-year career in advertising, marketing, and public relations to become president of MAVIA. Born and raised in Murfreesboro, Tennessee, she now lives with her husband, Kenneth, and their two teenage sons in Newcastle, Washington.

PRAYER STARTERS:

- Give thanks for the positive impact of MAVIA and its founder, Pamela Eakes.
- Each October, Student Pledge, along with MAVIA and other anti-violence groups, sponsors the Day of National Concern about Young People and Gun Violence. So far, a million-plus students have promised in writing not to resort to gun violence. Pray for their success this year.
- Pray for a change in values about violence among children and in media and entertainment programming.
- Ask God to bless the Eakes family today with grace, peace, and safety.

Do not envy a violent man or choose any of his ways. Proverbs 3:31

CONTACT: Pamela Eakes, www.mavia.org (for Student Pledge, www.pledge.org)

Archive Photo

Michael Jordan

Professional Athlete, Retired; Businessman

POINT OF IMPACT: At age 36, Michael Jordan is the most recognizable athlete in the world. In 1997–98 he won a record eighth scoring title and led the Chicago Bulls to their sixth NBA championship of the decade. His unique combination of grace, power, and basketball artistry have made him not only the top NBA player of his era, but a cultural phenomenon. Sports journalist David Halberstam notes Jordan has "singlehandedly transformed the American ideal of beauty from white to black." We buy what Michael Jordan endorses, and kids the world over have made Jordan their hero. Not surprisingly, Jordan is a big supporter of charities that cater to children, including the Boys and Girls Club of America and the Jordan Institute for Families at University of North Carolina. "I believe that everything that can be done should be done," he says, "to preserve the family and to improve the quality of life for all individuals, especially children and the elderly." Though he retired for the second time in January, 1999, Jordan's influence and visibility is expected to remain high.

He's called the century's finest athlete.

QUOTABLE: "This is a business and you get paid well, but you have to earn respect. It doesn't matter whether you're getting paid $2 million or $30 million. It shouldn't change the way you play the game of basketball."

BEHIND THE SCENES: Jordan and his wife, Juanita, live with their three children in Chicago. Jordan says that just watching his kids brings him his greatest joy in life. "If I'm having a bad day, when I see them, it's not a bad day anymore."

PRAYER STARTERS:

- Give thanks for Michael Jordan's positive example to millions of youth and for his commitment to his family.
- Pray for spiritual and physical protection for his marriage and children.
- Pray that Jordan will continue to make being "Dad" a top priority in his life.
- Ask for Jordan's continuing influence for good inside professional sports, especially basketball, and through his work in business and charities.

> *Do you not know that in a race all the runners run, but only one gets the prize? Run in such a way as to get the prize. 1 Corinthians 9:24*

CONTACT: jordan.sportsline.com

Elie Wiesel

Author, Crusader, Nobel Prize Laureate

AP/Wide World Photos

POINT OF IMPACT: Elie Wiesel is best known as an eloquent witness to the systematic destruction of six million Jews during World War II. He was the first to name this horror "the Holocaust." When Wiesel was 15, Nazi troops deported him and his family from their native Romania to Auschwitz, the concentration camp where they endured slave labor, starvation, disease, beatings, and torture. His parents and younger sister died there. After the war, Wiesel wrote about his experiences in *Night,* which has become a classic. Wiesel, 72, has used his influence to plead for the oppressed in the Soviet Union, South Africa, Vietnam, Nigeria, and Bangladesh. He has been awarded the Congressional Medal of Freedom and the Nobel Peace Prize. Today he continues to inspire millions through writing, speaking, and teaching.

He survived the Holocaust
to tell the world about it.

QUOTABLE: "If I could bring back one child, I would give up anything I have. If I could free one prisoner, I would give a lot. Just one child. If I could give a feeling of solidarity to a person who is abandoned, I would still give a lot. So you see, I would like to do things that I cannot do. All I have is a few words, and I will give these words. That's what I'm trying to do."

BEHIND THE SCENES: Wiesel says his childhood was "blessed with love and hope and faith and prayer." As a child, he says, he talked much more to God than to people. "He was my partner, my friend, my teacher, my king, my sovereign." Wiesel and his wife, Marion, live in New York City and have one son, Elisha.

PRAYER STARTERS:

- Give thanks for Elie Wiesel's achievement in sensitizing many to the horrors of ethnic and religious hatred. Ask for joy for him and his family.
- Pray for spiritual and emotional healing for survivors of genocide in Europe, Bosnia, Rwanda, and other places.
- Pray that Christians around the world will lead the way in practicing love, promoting justice for the oppressed, and being servants for healing.

> *I remember my affliction and my wandering. . . . Yet this I call to mind and therefore I have hope: Because of the LORD's great love we are not consumed. Lamentations 3:19,21-22*

CONTACT: Random House, 201 E 50th St., New York, NY 10022-7703

George Carey
Primate of the Anglican Church

POINT OF IMPACT: Dr. George Leonard Carey, Archbishop of Canterbury, is the spiritual head of the entire Anglican Communion. Carey oversees 38 national churches (65 million members around the world), including the American Episcopalians and churches in Kenya, Ireland, Trinidad, Canada, Singapore, India, and the Philippines. Carey is renowned as a preacher and mediator among Christian groups. He has been firm in his opposition to any change in the church's teaching on homosexuality. Carey has addressed the international debt problem of Third World, strengthened relationships with Roman Catholics, and promoted his major interest—evangelism. "The church is always one generation away from extinction," he says. "Handing on our torch of faith to the generations of the third millennium will require all our vigor, faith, and enthusiasm."

He wants Anglicans to pass on the "torch of faith."

QUOTABLE: "The church is described as 'broad.' But the breadth exists because we share a common experience and belief, of God made manifest in Christ."

BEHIND THE SCENES: Carey, 65, was born in London's East End, where his father worked as a hospital porter. After service in the Royal Air Force, Carey underwent a spiritual conversion when a Christian friend took him to church. These days he's a big supporter of the Alpha course—lay-led Bible studies that have mushroomed in Anglican churches worldwide. Carey and his wife, Eileen, have four children and seven grandchildren.

PRAYER STARTERS:

- Thank God for Archbishop Carey's evident pastoral concern for his far-flung and often contentious flock, and for his faithfulness to historic Christianity.
- Pray for a deepening hunger for the Word and the Lord of the Word among Anglicans today.
- Ask God to give Carey the wisdom he needs for every decision; ask for God's grace and sweet presence to be very evident in the Carey home.

> *May God be gracious to us and bless us . . . that your ways may be known on earth, your salvation among all nations. Psalm 67:1-2*

CONTACT: Diocesan Secretary Mr. David Kemp, Diocesan House, Lady Wootton's Green, Canterbury, Kent CT1 1NQ

Aaron Spelling
TV Producer

POINT OF IMPACT: He's the genial 71-year-old producer behind such TV shows as *Melrose Place* and *Beverly Hills 90210*. Currently, Aaron Spelling has eight shows on the air, including the recent and surprisingly wholesome hit *7th Heaven*—a show about a functional family reminiscent of the Waltons. In all, he's produced more than 3,000 hours of television entertainment over his 40-year career. And in 1998 he was voted into the Television Academy Hall of Fame. As executive producer of his shows, he's "so involved it's scary," says *Entertainment Weekly*. "He approves every story concept, makes notes on every script, and has final cut on each episode. . . . He has sickle-sharp instincts about what the masses want to see."

Archive Photo

He's been TV's hallowed hitmaker for decades.

QUOTABLE: About his smash hit, *7th Heaven:* "It's one of the thrills of my long career that my least sexy, least naughty show is getting good ratings."

BEHIND THE SCENES: Spelling grew up poor in Dallas, and his family often dined on stale cookies, cream puffs, and cakes donated by a kindly baker. "To this day I can't eat dessert," he says. Because he was a prime target of neighborhood bullies, he was ashamed that his immigrant Jewish parents spoke mainly Yiddish. "I would beg my folks to speak English, and I later hated myself . . . for having done that to them." Because they couldn't afford a television, Spelling watched one through the front window of a local appliance store, "and I dreamed and I dreamed and I dreamed." He has two children (daughter Tori is an actress), and his wife of 27 years is Candy.

PRAYER STARTERS:

- Spelling has admitted, "I could have 50 shows on the air, but if one show fails, I'm a mess." Pray that he would know how deep and wide is God's love for him. Ask that he would seek God's guidance about how to best use his amazing creative gifts, and that he'd feel a peace about his career.
- Ask God to reveal His Father-heart to many in the TV industry today.
- Pray blessings of comfort and joy for Spelling and his family.

> Don't let the world around you squeeze you into its own mold.
> Romans 12:2 PHILLIPS

Contact: www.fox.com

Kofi Annan

Secretary General of the United Nations

UN/DPI photo by Milton Grant

POINT OF IMPACT: Kofi Annan of Ghana is the first sub-Saharan African to hold the post of Secretary General of the United Nations. He's also first Secretary General to rise from ranks of U.N. bureaucracy. Annan has served the organization for more than 30 years, during which he has focused on organizational and financial management, refugee issues, and peacekeeping missions. In 1990, after Iraq invaded Kuwait, he helped negotiate the release of Western hostages. He later led the first U.N. team to negotiate with Iraq on an "oil-for-food" basis to ease the humanitarian crisis there. He has tried to strengthen the U.N.'s traditional peacekeeping missions and find new approaches to conflict resolution. One of his goals is to get the organization into the black financially (many members, the U.S. included, owe back dues). Says one ambassador of Annan, "People trust him because he is honest."

It's his job to give world peace a chance.

QUOTABLE: "No nation needs to face alone the threats which this organization was established to diffuse. Applaud us when we prevail; correct us when we fail, but do not let this irreplaceable institution wither or perish."

BEHIND THE SCENES: Annan, 62, began his formal education in Africa and completed it in the United States. Living through a Minnesota winter as a student, he vowed never to wear earmuffs (they offended his sense of style). But he changed his mind after a midwinter outing nearly froze his ears off. "Never walk into an environment and assume that you understand it better than the people who live there," he said in a 1994 speech. Annan is married to Nane Lagergren, a Swedish artist and lawyer; they live in New York.

PRAYER STARTERS:

- Give thanks for the work of the U.N. around the world, and for diplomats who are dedicating their lives to the community of nations.
- Pray for wisdom, patience, and courage for Annan and other U.N. leaders. Ask for success in their work for peace, health, and safety worldwide.
- Ask for health, rest, and protection for Annan as he travels the globe.

> *They will beat their swords into plowshares and their spears into pruning hooks. Nation will not take up sword against nation, nor will they train for war anymore. Isaiah 2:4*

CONTACT: United Nations, United Nations Plaza, New York, NY 10017

Gerald Levin

CEO, Time Warner, Inc.

Archive Photo

POINT OF IMPACT: Gerald M. Levin heads the world's largest entertainment and media company. Time Warner's movie, publishing, music, and cable TV portfolio includes such industry giants as Time, Inc. (the country's number-one magazine publisher), Warner Bros., Warner Music Group, Home Box Office, Time Warner Cable (the number-one U.S. cable system), Warner Books, and the Book-of-the-Month Club. Time Warner also owns CNN, TBS, TNT, WB TV, and other companies ranging from *Mad* magazine to the Atlanta Braves. Levin, 60, spoke recently of the need to ensure that the communications revolution doesn't leave the less fortunate behind. Time Warner responded to the summons issued at the 1997 President's Summit on America's Future with two major commitments. One of them, Warner's Time to Read program, is already the country's largest volunteer literacy effort, providing more than one million hours of tutoring in 1998.

His company launched the country's largest volunteer literacy program.

QUOTABLE: On philanthropy: "You just have to stand for something that goes beyond individual financial performance."

BEHIND THE SCENES: Levin grew up in a devout Philadelphia Jewish household and as a child was an aspiring rabbi who actually conducted synagogue services before his bar mitzvah. In May 1997, his son Jonathan, a popular English teacher in New York City, was murdered by one of his students. He was forced to reveal his ATM password, then killed after his assailants used the card to withdraw $88. Levin and his wife, Barbara, have four other children.

PRAYER STARTERS:

- Give thanks for the generosity of Levin and his companies. Pray that God would greatly bless their literacy program, and that through it many would eventually be drawn to read God's Word.
- Pray for wisdom and spiritual guidance for Levin's future as he charts the course of such mammoth, important, and influential companies.
- Pray God's abundant blessings on Levin and his family. Ask that He would bring comfort and love in tangible ways today.

> *"He defended the cause of the poor and needy. . . . Is that not what it means to know me?" declares the* LORD. *Jeremiah 22:16*

CONTACT: Time Warner Companies, Inc., 75 Rockefeller Plaza, New York, NY 10019-6908

Eugene Rivers III

Pastor, Activist, Youth Advisor

POINT OF IMPACT: Reverend Eugene Rivers is an African-American former gang member who left the streets of Philadelphia to attend Harvard University, then returned to try to stop youth violence. After two of Rivers' friends were killed in the violence of 1969, he says, "I promised the Lord that if He would let me survive, I would never turn my back on these kids." When he first moved into his poor Boston neighborhood, the evidence he saw that drugs and violence dominated the life of children and youth helped shaped his mission. Now pastor of the Azusa Christian Community in Boston and director of field operations for the Ten Point Coalition, Rivers also directs the Dorchester District Youth Advocacy Project and teaches at Harvard Divinity School. He has met with the president and been courted by the Christian Coalition. *Newsweek* calls him "the Savior of the Streets." By launching one successful program after another, he's set up a working example for leaders across the country.

He's called "the Savior of the Streets."

QUOTABLE: "We have a generation of *de facto* orphans in our inner cities who are drowning in their own blood."

BEHIND THE SCENES: Rivers, 50, considers the success of nationalists like Louis Farrakhan a sign of the failure of Christians to grapple with real life in urban black America. He and his wife, Jacqueline, live in Boston with their family.

PRAYER STARTERS:

- Pray for young urban blacks in North America today. Rivers has said, "Each day, 1,118 black teenagers are victims of violent crime, 1,451 black children are arrested, and 907 teenage girls get pregnant."
- Thank God that Rivers and others have devoted their lives to at-risk youth. Ask God to send more "saviors" into the streets.
- Ask God to protect him and his family, and reward them for their labors.
- Ask God what you can do to help your own neighborhood.

Remember not the sins of my youth and my rebellious ways; according to your love remember me, for you are good, O LORD. Psalm 25:7

CONTACT: National Ten Point Leadership Foundation, Ella J. Baker Housed N411 Washington St., Boston, MA 02124

Jimmy Smits
Actor

POINT OF IMPACT: Since his star-making and award-winning roles in *L.A. Law* and *NYPD Blue*, Jimmy Smits has fame, fortune, and Hollywood in his back pocket. But what he really wants is opportunity—and not just for himself, but for Hispanic actors in general. Smits created The National Hispanic Foundation for the Arts in 1997 for that very purpose: to supply scholarships and grants to Hispanic graduate students and to extend career opportunities for Hispanic artists. Smits' personal success is the exception; most Hispanic actors have to contend with small or stereotypical roles. Smits' talent won the loyalty of well-placed producers like Steven Bochco, who quickly saw room for Smits when David Caruso abandoned *NYPD Blue* mid-season. On Smits' qualifications he says, "The guy's a Ferrari. No matter how hard you push the pedal, there's always more there." In 1998 Smits left the hit series to pursue other interests, including furthering his foundation's influence.

He wants more opportunities for Hispanic artists.

QUOTABLE: On being a heartthrob (Smits is one of *People* magazine's "50 Most Beautiful People"): "I don't see it in the morning when I look in the mirror. It's amazing what a little hair and makeup on the set can do."

BEHIND THE SCENES: Smits, 45, initially earned a degree in education; when he decided to act for a living, his parents thought he was wasting his degree. So he earned another one: an MFA in theater arts from Cornell. He's won an Emmy and a Golden Globe for his television roles. He lives with longtime companion Wanda de Jesus; he's divorced with two kids, Taina and Joaquin.

PRAYER STARTERS:

- Give thanks for Smits's concern and action on behalf of other Hispanic artists. Pray that he'd be successful in his mission.
- Pray against discrimination and stereotyping in Hollywood. Ask God to reveal Himself to many through the beautiful diversity of humankind.
- Ask God to bless Smits with knowledge of His great love for him.

> *I have no one else like him, who takes a genuine interest in your welfare.*
> Philippians 2:20

CONTACT: Creative Artists Agency, 9830 Wilshire Blvd., Beverly Hills, CA 90212

Christian Women Who Are Leading the Way

"I am honestly convinced that we women hold in our hands
the moral and spiritual well-being of our homes, our
nation and ultimately, the world."
—VONETTE BRIGHT

- Pray today for women in Christian ministry whom you know personally—pastors' wives, Sunday school teachers, Bible study leaders.
- Give thanks and pray for those women whose music, writings, or ministry impact your own Christian experience.
- Pray also for the ministries of these influential women:

Shirley Dobson, Chairman of the National Day of Prayer, which is observed the first Thursday of May each year. Their aim is to be a unifying force among all denominations of Christians, Jews and those sympathetic to the need for God in our culture. **CONTACT:** NDP Task Force, P.O. Box 15616, Colorado Springs, CO 80935-5616.

Barbara Brown Taylor, an Episcopal pastor and preacher in Clarkesville, Georgia. She's often cited among the nation's most effective speakers. She is the author of five books, including *Preaching Life* and *Bread of Angels.* **CONTACT:** c/o Piedmont College, PO. Box 10, Demorest, GA 30535

Vonette Bright, cofounder and executive director of Women Today International and host of a daily radio program by the same name. Her ministry helps women connect with God, with one another, and with opportunities for ministry. **CONTACT:** Women Today International, 100 Sunport Lane, Dept. 2600, Orlando, FL 32809 www@ccci.org

Sister Joan Chittister O.S.B., a Benedictine nun and author who is frequently named as a leading theologian. She's been particularly influential in scholarly work on the role of women in the church.

Janet Parshall, host of "Janet Parshall's America," media commentator, author and family advocate. She frequently represents the conservative viewpoint in debates with the likes of Gloria Steinem and Patricia Ireland. **CONTACT:** 1901 N. Moore St., Ste. 200, Arlington, VA 22209

A woman who fears the LORD is to be praised. Proverbs 31:30

Robert Schuller

Pastor, Motivational Speaker, Author

Courtesy of Crystal Cathedral

POINT OF IMPACT: Robert Schuller started his first church in 1955 with $500 and rental rights to a drive-in movie theater. On the first Sunday, 100 persons attended services seated in their cars; Rev. Schuller preached from the roof of the snack bar. Today he preaches in the Crystal Cathedral, an architectural gem, and broadcasts his church service, *The Hour of Power,* to an estimated 30 million viewers. Schuller has established himself as a leading spokesman for "possibility thinking"—life attitudes that emphasize optimism and self-esteem. He counsels presidents, consorts with the pope, and has served as White House representative at state funerals abroad. Some fundamentalist Christians balk at Schuller's theology, labeling it psychobabble or worse. But *Christianity Today* editor and theologian Kenneth Kanzter concluded that Schuller, "believes all the 'fundamental' doctrines. . . . He adheres to every line of the Apostles' Creed with a tenacity born of deep conviction." Schuller has written more than 30 books, six of them *New York Times* bestsellers.

He preaches possibility thinking from a crystal cathedral.

QUOTABLE: "The classical error of historical Christianity is that we have never started with the value of the person. Rather, we have started from the 'unworthiness of the sinner,' and that starting point has set the stage for the glorification of human shame in Christian theology."

BEHIND THE SCENES: Schuller, 73, grew up an overweight, nonathletic loner in the farming community of Alton, Iowa. Yet he knew from age four that he wanted to become a minister. Robert and Arvella DeHaan Schuller have five children, all active in Christian ministry. Son Robert A. Schuller is also an ordained minister of the Reformed Church in America.

PRAYER STARTERS:

- Give thanks for Schuller's ministry, and for the many who have benefited from his ministry over the years.
- Ask that Schuller would seek and find God's wisdom each time he advises another world-changer. Pray that his influence would be only positive.
- Pray that God would bless Schuller and his family with wholeness, health, and spiritual fulfillment today.

> *Be joyful always; pray continually; give thanks in all circumstances, for this is God's will for you in Christ Jesus. 1 Thessalonians 5:16*

CONTACT: 12141 Lewis St., Garden Grove, CA 92840; drschuller@chrystalcathedral.org

David E. Kelley
Producer, Screenwriter

Photo by Craig T. Mathew

POINT OF IMPACT: David E. Kelley, the powerhouse producer and writer behind the series hits *L.A. Law, Picket Fences, Chicago Hope, The Practice,* and *Ally McBeal,* has a near-perfect record as an arbiter of what people want to see on television. His shows have garnered numerous Emmy awards, critical praise, and high ratings. According to the *Los Angeles Times,* "Studio heads say Kelley is one of the fastest, purest writers in television and that his distinctive vision—with its crackling dialogue and multilayered characters—has raised the bar for dramatic shows." He has a fondness for the quirky side of the human personality—the lawyer who interrupts court proceedings by whistling though his nose, the megalomaniacal surgeon who sings showtunes to relieve stress, the career girl who dances with a hallucination of the baby she hopes she'll have someday. Kelley refuses to fill his shows with pat endings and predictable plots: "The questions fascinate me much more than the answers," he says. "If you're looking for answers, don't come to me."

He's the wizard behind TV trendsetters like *Ally McBeal*.

QUOTABLE: On his colleagues' labeling him "The Wizard of Oz": "They call me 'the wizard' because they think I hide behind the curtain. I guess, on one hand, that's kind of flattering. But at the end of the day, all the wizard was capable of doing was filling a balloon full of hot air."

BEHIND THE SCENES: David Kelley, in his early forties, looks more like an anxious college student than one of television's elite. His first career was as a lawyer. He's married to movie star Michelle Pfeiffer; they have two children.

PRAYER STARTERS:

- Pray that TV writers and producers will strive for quality and believability. Pray for success in mixing entertainment and positive moral messages.

- Ask God to bless Kelley for even greater achievements according to God's will for his life.

- Pray for a joyful, enduring marriage for him and Pfeiffer, and for the well-being of their children.

> *But while he was still a long way off, his father saw him and was filled with compassion for him. Luke 15:20*

CONTACT: Fox, P.O. Box 900, Beverly Hills, CA 90213

R.L. Stine
Author, Children's Books

AP/Wide World Photos

POINT OF IMPACT: Robert Lawrence Stine, the "Stephen King for kids," is the world's bestselling children's author. His three hugely popular series—*Goosebumps* and *Fear Street* (for 7- to 12-year-olds), and *Fear Street Seniors* (for teens)—have sold nearly 300 million copies, launched TV and movie spinoffs, a range of merchandise, and even a theme park in Disneyland. The books are billed as "less scary than young adult thrillers, and with more humor." However, Stine has his critics. One mother called his books "schlocky and shocking," and tried unsuccessfully to have them banned from the school library. A mild-mannered, partly balding dad with a twinkle in his eye, Stine admits, "I've killed off teenagers every way you can kill them." But he also offers reassurance: "I try not to make my books too scary. I never go too far. And that's always my goal—shivers, but not nightmares."

He wants to give your child the shivers.

QUOTABLE: "I think of horror as being funny—like riding a roller coaster that makes you laugh and scream at the same time. When things get too heavy, I throw in a joke."

BEHIND THE SCENES: Stine's grown son and only child, Matthew, inspired Stine's stories while growing up. Jane, wife of the 55-year-old author, continues to act as his editor even though she once got so angry over a plot disagreement that she shoved him in a closet and went for a walk. "Plots are all we ever fight about," says Stine, who never learned to type and uses only one index finger to punch out two books a month. They live in Manhattan.

PRAYER STARTERS:

- Pray that children will be protected from any detrimental influences that might arise from Stine's fiction. Pray that the good qualities of Stine's positive characters would outweigh the influence of horror.
- Pray that Halloween's emphasis on fear would prompt readers to reach for God's love and safety. Ask God to protect the children you know.
- Ask for the Lord's grace and peace to bless Stine and his family. Pray for a growing sensitivity in Stine of his potential for good with young readers.

> *Live as children of light (for the fruit of the light consists in all goodness, righteousness and truth) and find out what pleases the Lord. Ephesians 5:8-10*

CONTACT: Scholastic, Inc., 555 Broadway, New York, NY 10012-3999

Sir Roger Penrose
Mathematician, Physicist

Courtesy of Roger Penrose

POINT OF IMPACT: Sir Roger Penrose of Oxford is one of the world's preeminent mathematicians and physicists. Contrary to proponents of artificial intelligence, he suggests that some aspects of the human mind can never be duplicated by computers (for example, the experience of sudden inspiration or emotionally biased reasoning). He's also noted for his fascination with geometry, which has led to some curious but important discoveries—he demonstrated for the first time that a nonrepeating pattern could exist in nature (they're called the Penrose Pattern or "tessellations"). His recent book, *The Emperor's New Mind,* has been called one of the most important works of the second half of the twentieth century. He's come closer than any scientist, scholars say, to addressing the most intriguing questions of all: *How do we think?* and *What is it that makes us human?*

He explores the nature of human intelligence.

QUOTABLE: "Worrying about things that no one else worries about is where insights come from."

BEHIND THE SCENES: Like his friend and collaborator Stephen Hawking, Roger Penrose, 69, has been pulled into the public spotlight: He's gone to Buckingham Palace in 1994 (to be knighted) and to court more recently (to sue Kimberly Clark for copyright infringement after his wife noticed that a roll of quilted toilet tissue bore a striking resemblance to his unique Penrose Pattern).

PRAYER STARTERS:

- Thank God for Sir Roger Penrose's groundbreaking scholarship and for his rigorous study of the human mind.
- Pray that Penrose and other scientists following in his footsteps will be blessed with God's wisdom in their intellectual explorations, and be drawn into a meaningful personal relationship with Him.
- Ask for God to bless Penrose and his family with health and strength.

> *They saw the works of the* Lord, *his wonderful deeds in the deep. Psalm 107:24*

CONTACT: University of Oxford, Wellington Square, Oxford. OX1 2JD. UK

Harvey and Bob Weinstein

Film Producers; Founders, Miramax

Archive Photo

POINT OF IMPACT: The brothers Weinstein have become known for taking quirky, intelligent movies and making them enormous commercial and critical hits. The success of films like *Pulp Fiction, The English Patient, Good Will Hunting,* and *Shakespeare in Love,* have made Miramax "the envy of all independent movie companies," according to the *Los Angeles Times.* With the Weinsteins' 110 nominations and 30 wins at the Academy Awards in the last five years, small wonder that *Time* named the brothers among its 25 Most Influential People. Harvey (shown) and Bob created Miramax in 1979; in 1993 they sold a big piece of the company to Disney for an estimated $60 million. Described as "shrewd negotiators" and "canny marketers," the Weinsteins reveal their trade secrets in a forthcoming book, *The Art of Miramax: The Inside Story.* All profits from the sale of the book will go to charities.

Their success is changing the face of independent filmmaking.

QUOTABLE: "It's an artistic business. It's about picking scripts, picking the right directors and picking the right casting. Either you're good at it or you're not."—Bob Weinstein

BEHIND THE SCENES: Harvey, 48, and Bob, 46, grew up in Queens, New York, where their parents dropped them off at the local cinema to watch movies as a type of babysitter. One brother's dramatic editing approach has earned him the moniker "Harvey Scissorhands."

PRAYER STARTERS:

- Give thanks for the record of high quality filmmaking that the Weinstein brothers have established. Pray that they will use their gifts and platform to reach beyond success to lasting impact for good in society and culture.
- Pray that they will seek the truth and live by it in their business decisions, and that they won't miss the best that God has for them.
- Ask for protection, health, and peace for the Weinsteins and their families.

How good and pleasant it is when brothers live together in unity! Psalm 133:1

CONTACT: www.miramax.com

Julian Bond

Chairman, National Association for the
Advancement of Colored People (NAACP)

Courtesy of NAACP

POINT OF IMPACT: The son of a distinguished educator, Julian Bond was an early participant in the sit-ins of the sixties and a founder of the Student Nonviolent Coordinating Committee. Today as chairman of the board of the NAACP, America's leading civil rights organization for African-Americans, Bond is working to rejuvenate this not-for-profit organization. Under his leadership, the NAACP has recently recovered from a $4 million deficit to show a $2 million surplus. Vowing in his inaugural speech to bring unity, Bond called for a renewed offensive against racial discrimination. "We are going to build a world where private prejudice doesn't become public policy." He also appears on the syndicated weekly TV show *America's Black Forum*.

He leads the biggest civil rights group in America.

QUOTABLE: "I want to try to help restore the NAACP to the luster it deserves. I want us to be as big, bad, and bold as we can possibly be. And wherever race is talked about in the country—in the White House or at the corner barber shop—I want someone to say, 'Here's what the NAACP thinks.'"

BEHIND THE SCENES: Bond, 59, is a "homebody" who prefers his newspaper, books, and computer to outdoor pursuits. Married since 1990 to Pamela Sue Horowitz, a Washington lawyer, Bond has five children from his first marriage: Phyllis, Horace, Michael, Jeffrey, and Julia.

PRAYER STARTERS:

- Give thanks for Julian Bond's four decades of service to Black Americans.
- Pray that in his highly visible role with the NAACP, Bond will exemplify integrity, vision, courage, and morality.
- Pray for understanding, harmony, and respect between Americans of all racial, ethnic, and cultural backgrounds.
- Ask God to bless Bond and his family with protection, peace, and grace.

Blessed are the peacemakers, for they will be called sons of God. Matthew 5:9

CONTACT: 1025 Vermont Avenue N.W., Suite 1120, Washington, DC 20005; www.naacp.org

E. Brandt Gustavson

*President, National Religous
Broadcasters (NRB)*

Courtesy of National Religious Broadcasters

POINT OF IMPACT: According to Brandt Gustavson, you have a one-in-seven chance of hitting a "holy" spot when you spin the AM or FM dial. He cites the *New York Times,* which reports that religious programming is now the third most-common radio format in the nation behind country and adult contemporary formats, reaching more than 20 million people on 1,648 religious stations, an increase of almost 500 stations in the past five years. Gustavson, who's led the NRB for 11 years, says the numbers attest to the "hunger of the American people for something better." One of NRB's goals since it was formed in 1944, explains Gustavson, has been "to protect access to the airwaves of America for our message. What we try to do is lift up Christ and make Him known."

He welcomes the rising tide of Christian broadcasting.

QUOTABLE: "Whenever you have problems facing families, the nation and the moral and spiritual moorings and underpinnings of the nation, you always have people who are looking for answers. And one of the things people are turning to is the stable kind of help given by Christian radio and television."

BEHIND THE SCENES: Gustavson has been involved in Christian radio since it was just a blip on the dial—a few sermons sandwiched between Top-40 and country-and-western tunes. He and his wife, Mary, have two grown children, Ruth and Tim, and two granddaughters.

PRAYER STARTERS:

- Pray for the ministry of the gospel via Christian radio today, that many listeners will come to know Jesus Christ and be strengthened in their faith.
- Pray that Gustavson and other NRB leaders will be directed by the Holy Spirit in all their decisions.
- Ask for God's blessing, protection, and provision for the Gustavson family.

God will bless us, and all the ends of the earth will fear him. Psalm 67:7

CONTACT: NRB, 7839 Ashton Ave., Manassas, VA 20109; www.nrb.org

Tony Blair

Prime Minister of Great Britain

UN/DPI photo by Greg Kinch

POINT OF IMPACT: Even before his election to Prime Minister in 1997, the Right Honorable Anthony Charles Lynton Blair had proven himself a persuasive leader. As leader of Britain's Labour Party from 1994–97, he reshaped his party to attract middle-class voters. His initiatives included taking a moral stance on crime prevention, abandoning socialist economic rhetoric, and combining the ideals of personal responsibility with the value of community. "The aim is to offer people a deal," he says. "We will help construct a community that is worth living in, but in return you've got to take the chances given to you. Opportunity and responsibility go together." In addition to shaping British influence around the world, he faces strife in Northern Ireland, independence movements in Wales and Scotland, and disagreements about Britain's involvement in the new European Union.

He shapes Britain's influence around the world.

QUOTABLE: On his mother's death at 52: "Your own mortality comes home to you. And you suddenly realize—which often you don't as a young person—that life is finite, so if you want to get things done you had better get a move on."

BEHIND THE SCENES: Blair spent his childhood in Scotland and Australia before his family settled in England. When Blair was ten, his father, who was campaigning for Parliament, suffered a stroke that left him unable to speak for three years. Blair has said that this was "one of the formative events" of his life. Now 46, he and his wife, Cherie, both lawyers, have three children—Euan, Nicholas, and Kathryn.

PRAYER STARTERS:

- Pray for wisdom and discernment for Tony Blair in his leadership role as head of the United Kingdom, especially as he negotiates peace in Ireland.

- Blair is a devout Anglican. Pray that he will continue to pursue a vital spiritual relationship with Christ despite the pressures of office.

- Pray for protection and bounty for his marriage and children; pray that his role as husband and father brings him and his family joy and security.

> *Do you see a man skilled in his work? He will serve before kings.*
> Proverbs 22:29

CONTACT: 10 Downing Street, London, SW1A 2AA, England

B.B. King

Blues Singer and Guitarist

Archive Photo

POINT OF IMPACT: He's been king of the Blues for 50 years. His name is Riley B. King, but since his days performing on Beale Street in Memphis, when he called himself "Blues Boy," he's answered to B.B. He's recorded more than 50 albums, but as with many blues singers, it wasn't until King was discovered by white audiences that he emerged as a star. Sixties rockers like Mick Jagger, Mike Bloomfield, Elvis Presley, and Eric Clapton all pointed to King and other black bluesmen as the source of their anguished, guitar-driven sound. His songs tell the story—classics like "Everyday I Have the Blues" and "The Thrill Is Gone." Many have noted the irony that it took a black bluesman from the Mississippi Delta to express the disillusionment of young, white, mostly urban audiences. King has received the Presidential Medal of Freedom, the Grammy Lifetime Achievement Award, and an honorary doctorate from Yale. And at 75, he and his famous guitar named Lucille still average more than 250 concerts per year around the world.

He's the king of the Blues.

QUOTABLE: "People ask me how I get my sound out of the guitar. I tell them that it is the same way that you get the tone when you talk. It's just me."

BEHIND THE SCENES: Born in a sharecropper's cabin in the Delta, King was raised largely by his maternal grandmother. He learned to sing and play guitar in church; his first group was The Famous St. John's Gospel Singers. He left school at 16 to earn $1 a day as a sharecropper and tractor driver. King is the cofounder of the Foundation for the Advancement of Inmate Recreation and Rehabilitation (FAIRR). He's been married three times.

PRAYER STARTERS:

- Pray that B.B. King's music would help many listeners to confront the grim realities of living without God, and prompt them to seek the joy that the Lord promises (John 16:24).
- Pray that the King of the Blues would meet and embrace the King of Joy.
- Ask God to bless King with strength, health, safety, and contentment.

My servants will sing out of the joy of their hearts. Isaiah 65:14

CONTACT: c/o Sidney A. Seidenberg, Inc., 1414 Avenue of the Americas, New York, NY 10019

Sam Donaldson

ABC Chief White House Correspondent;
Coanchor, ABC's This Week

Archive Photo

POINT OF IMPACT: Sam Donaldson was already a 30-year ABC reporting veteran when he was named Chief White House Correspondent for ABC News in January 1998. But it was a job he had held before— from 1977 until 1989, when he first came to the attention of many Americans with his relentless questioning of Presidents Carter and Reagan. Donaldson is also the coanchor of the Sunday morning broadcast, *This Week.* Donaldson has won many awards for his investigative prowess and a reputation for making interviewees quake. Many conservatives see him as a flamethrower for liberal causes. Donaldson's 1987 autobiography, *Hold On, Mr. President*, was an international bestseller.

His aggressiveness sets the tone for the Capitol press corps.

QUOTABLE: On his first efforts to break into New York broadcasting: "They laughed at me. I couldn't get a job. I went and I made the rounds, I met every news director, and they thought I was awful."

BEHIND THE SCENES: Donaldson, 65, was born in El Paso, Texas. When he was 14, his mother shipped him off to the New Mexico Military Institute hoping for improvements in his behavior. Yet his drive and high spirits have served Donaldson well as a journalist. For example, during 1993–94, he tracked down Nazi war criminal Erich Priebke in Argentina (subsequently, Priebke was extradited to Italy and tried for his crimes). Donaldson lives in Virginia with his wife, TV reporter Jan Smith; he has four children from two previous marriages.

PRAYER STARTERS:

- Give thanks for the American legacy of the free press.
- Pray that the Washington press corps will be motivated to pursue significance and service in their reporting.
- Ask God to bless Sam Donaldson with respected Christian colleagues, and with clear signs of His favor on the Donaldson family.

> *Let justice roll on like a river, righteousness like a never-failing stream!*
> *Amos 5:24*

CONTACT: ABC News, 77 West 66th Street, New York, NY 10023

316

Alan Greenspan
Chairman, Federal Reserve System

POINT OF IMPACT: *Time* magazine recently named Alan Greenspan—along with Treasury Secretary Robert Rubin and Deputy Secretary Larry Summers—as "the committee that saved the world." Why? Their decisions are credited with keeping inflation at bay, domestic growth solid, and the world economy from meltdown. In fact, Greenspan is probably the most influential non-elected officeholder in the United States. His job assignment as the nation's top banker is as clear as it is mind-boggling—invent a twenty-first century financial system. Chairman of the Federal Reserve System under three presidents, his decisions about raising and lowering interest rates affect the prices of everything from lima beans to high-tech stocks. One journalist writes, "If you think of the economy as a Mack truck, think of Greenspan as the driver—with one foot on the brake, the other on the accelerator."

It's his job to keep the nation's economy healthy.

QUOTABLE: "If I seem unduly clear to you, you must have misunderstood what I said."

BEHIND THE SCENES: Greenspan, 74, is a Juilliard-trained saxophonist who played with a swing band before entering economics. Treasury Secretary Rubin says he enjoys working with Greenspan because of "both the power of his intellect and the sweetness of his soul." Greenspan is married to his second wife, journalist Andrea Mitchell.

PRAYER STARTERS:

- Pray for wisdom for Alan Greenspan and his advisers as they make decisions that will affect the world. Pray that biblical principles, not greed or ambition, will guide their choices.
- Ask for well-being, spiritual clarity, and joy for Greenspan in his marriage and personal life today.

> *Blessed is the man who finds wisdom, the man who gains understanding.*
> *Proverbs 3:13*

CONTACT: 20th Street & Constitution Ave. N.W., Washington, DC 20551

Archive Photo

John Irving
Bestselling Author

POINT OF IMPACT: Called the twentieth century's Charles Dickens, author John Irving writes sprawling novels that mix tragedy and comedy. His stories rail against foreign policy, social injustices, and the pro-life movement, while exploring the consequences of breaking social codes. His most popular novel, *The World According to Garp,* was named one of the greatest books of the past 100 years and made into a popular movie. His other highly acclaimed books—which have all sold in the millions and been translated into 22 languages— include *The Cider House Rules, A Prayer for Owen Meany,* and *A Widow for One Year.* The *Los Angeles Times* calls Irving America's most important writer.

He's been called the twentieth century's Charles Dickens.

QUOTABLE: "If you asked me one day, I might say, 'Well, sometimes I feel a little bit religious.' If you asked me another day, I'd just say flat out, 'No.'"

BEHIND THE SCENES: Irving, 58, works eight hours a day, seven days a week to produce one substantial novel every four years. Growing up, he had difficulty in school, especially with reading, and even repeated two grades. It was only later, after he had become a parent, that he discovered that he suffers from dyslexia. "I think in the long run it probably helped me, because it forced me to read very slowly." He lives in Dorset, Vermont, with his wife, Janet, and their son, Everett. He has two sons from a previous marriage.

PRAYER STARTERS:

- Ask for health, stamina, and peace for John Irving and his family.
- Pray that his novels would bring good to readers, prompting them toward spiritual and moral depth.
- Ask God to give John Irving an unfolding, personal experience of His grace and power.

> *Seek the* Lord *while he may be found; call on him while he is near.*
> Isaiah 55:6

CONTACT: Random House, 201 E. 50th St., New York, NY 10022-7703

Charles Winsdor

The Prince of Wales;
Heir to the British throne

Archive Photo

POINT OF IMPACT: As the man who would be king of England, Prince Charles is the living symbol of a glorious past and a hopeful future for the United Kingdom of Great Britain and Northen Ireland. After a career in the Royal Navy, Charles has set about exploring the problems of industry, agriculture, and society in the British Isles. In recent years, he's been a strong proponent of corporate social responsibility. Over 800 business leaders, at his invitation, have visited inner-city schools and community projects as part of his "Seeing Is Believing" program. He's patron or president of 200 organizations serving young people, the unemployed, the disabled, the elderly, the problems of the inner cities, education, medicine, arts, and the environment.

He hopes to put the "Great" back in Great Britain.

QUOTABLE: "For the past 15 years I have been entirely motivated by a desperate desire to put the 'Great' back in Great Britain. Everything I have tried to do—all the projects, speeches, schemes have been with this end in mind."

BEHIND THE SCENES: The eldest son of Queen Elizabeth II and Prince Philip, Duke of Edinburgh, was born Charles Philip Arthur George Windsor in 1948. His 1981 wedding to Diana Spencer at St. Paul's Cathedral, London, mesmerized the world. They divorced in 1996 amid rumors that Charles was having an affair with Camilla Parker Bowles, with whom he continues a relationship. Diana died in a car crash in August 1997 in Paris. Their sons are William, 18, a student at Eton College, and Henry (Harry), 16.

PRAYER STARTERS:

- Pray with Solomon in Psalm 72 for Prince Charles—"Endow the king with your justice, O God, the royal son with your righteousness" (verse 1).
- Give thanks for Prince Charles' work on behalf of worthy social causes. Pray for peace and prosperity for the United Kingdom and its peoples.
- Pray for protection and healing for princes William and Henry, and that they will grow up to love, honor, and serve the King of kings.

By justice a king gives a country stability. Proverbs 29:4

CONTACT: Buckingham Palace, London, England

John Filo/CBS 8/97

Mel Karmazin

President and CEO, CBS

POINT OF IMPACT: Mel Karmazin first joined CBS in 1996 when Westinghouse, which owns CBS, bought his company, Infinity Broadcasting. The merger with CBS made Karmazin the largest individual stockholder of Westinghouse, and moved him from being "the most influential man in radio" to one of the most influential men in television. Before coming to CBS, Karmazin helped launch the careers of shock jocks such as Don Imus and Howard Stern. Pugnacious and blunt, Karmazin is beloved by stockholders because of his focus on shareholder value, driving his people hard, and watching every nickel as if it were his own. But some accuse him of putting profit before taste. Says one TV insider, "If Karmazin thinks he can get ratings and sell it and make money, then it's going on the air."

He carries a big stick on both television and Wall Street.

QUOTABLE: On airing Howard Stern's Saturday night show: "I believe it's a program for adults. We believe that parents should be able to control their kids at 11:30 P.M. If they're not, Howard Stern is not the problem; it's something else."

BEHIND THE SCENES: Karmazin's parents were European immigrants who lived in a housing project in Long Island City. His father drove a taxi, and his mother worked in a curtain-rod factory. "My family had zero money," Karmazin says. "We never had a vacation. We never had a car." Today no paintings, photographs, or trophies adorn his midtown Manhattan office. He lives by himself across the street, often goes to work before breakfast, goes home for lunch to ride a stationary bicycle, and cares not, he says, for such perks as limousines or corporate jets.

PRAYER STARTERS:

- Pray that Mel Karmazin will be positively influenced by Christian workers in his industry.
- Pray that television's slide into sensationalism and pandering would end. Pray for better quality programming that also makes better business sense.
- Ask God to fill Karmazin's office and home with an overwhelming sense of His loving presence and greater purposes for his life.

Godliness with contentment is great gain. 1 Timothy 6:6

CONTACT: CBS, 51 W. 52nd St., New York, NY 10019

John Madden
Sports Broadcaster

Archive Photo

POINT OF IMPACT: Since becoming a broadcaster in 1979, John Madden has won 11 Emmy Awards as television's Outstanding Sports Personality/Analyst and become a household name. Every Sunday, it's not just teams squaring off; "it's Madden against . . . every pastor in town." As one minister put it, "Some mornings I look at the men in my congregation and wonder whose opinion they're scheduling their day around—mine or Madden's? I figure the oddsmakers would put it at 15 to 1, Madden." Madden has also written four best-selling books about football. His rambunctious, blue-collar style has transformed what used to be "serious" game analysis into entertainment, bringing in millions of new viewers who are as interested in Madden as the game. *Newsday* calls him "the NFL's top personality."

He put a new spin on sports broadcasting.

QUOTABLE: On how to recover after the football season ends: "Start in February. Don't worry about relationships. Just get the blood flowing. You've been in hibernation. Walk around a little. Stretch . . . but remember: In July the NFL starts training camp. Then you have to start getting in shape to sit around for six or seven hours at a time again. Doubleheaders are a good place to start."

BEHIND THE SCENES: Madden, 64, was head coach of the Oakland Raiders in the sixties and seventies and took them to seven division titles and a Super Bowl win over Minnesota. He and his wife, Virginia, have two sons and live in Pleasanton, California.

PRAYER STARTERS:

- Ask God to show John Madden how to use his considerable influence to encourage men to reach for their personal best.
- Pray that football fans would invest in and celebrate wins in personal commitments and relationships as much as wins on the playing field.
- Ask for the renewing presence of Christ to be felt in the Madden home.

> *I consider everything a loss compared to the surpassing greatness of knowing Christ Jesus my Lord. Philippians 3:8*

CONTACT: 5746 W. Sunset Blvd., Los Angeles, CA 90028

Agnes Nixon

Writer and Creator of Soap Operas

POINT OF IMPACT: The stories that obsess millions of soap opera viewers start in Nixon's imagination, making hers the greatest single influence on daytime fare. She's the head writer and creator of *All My Children, One Life to Live, The Guiding Light,* and *As the World Turns.* Now 72, she is the first daytime figure inducted into the Academy of Arts and Sciences' Television Hall of Fame. She was already a legend when the *Soap Opera Digest* honored her for having had a serial on television five days a week, 52 weeks a year, for the past 20 years—and that was 23 years ago. She helped introduce social issues to daytime television (for example, *All My Children* was the first soap to tackle the abortion question). Critics lambast the daytime potboilers for pandering to audiences' appetites for illicit sex, drawn-out tragedies, and endless destructive obsessions. But Nixon says the soaps are good at what they do—providing harmless diversions. "We don't condone immorality," says Nixon, a devout Catholic. "We simply mirror life."

She's the legendary diva of daytime soaps.

QUOTABLE: "It was fun then and it's fun now. I have never regretted it and never thought I wanted to do any other kind of writing."

BEHIND THE SCENES: She married Robert Nixon, an automobile executive, in 1951 and they settled in a Philadelphia suburb. Recently widowed, she still lives in the same house where she and Robert raised their four children.

PRAYER STARTERS:

- Pray for the millions of daytime TV viewers today who are looking for encouragement and meaning. Pray that programs will—either by positive or negative example—lead them to seek the Lord and make wise choices.
- Pray for Agnes Nixon and other TV writers who shape daytime melodramas, that the "God of all truth" will permeate their scripts and characterizations.
- Ask God to bless Agnes Nixon with health and happiness.

> *Be very careful, then, how you live—not as unwise but as wise, making the most of every opportunity, because the days are evil. Ephesians 5:15*

CONTACT: 77 W. 66th St., New York, NY 10023-6298

Scott MacNealy

CEO, Sun Microsystems, Inc.

CI Photography, Sunnyvale, CA

POINT OF IMPACT: Scott MacNealy doesn't believe in slow and steady progress. Since 1982 he's seen his company, the maker of technical computer workstations and creator of Java programming software, explode. Sun Microsystems was the quickest of computer companies to achieve $1 billion in revenue. And analysts see no end in sight. Even Bill Gates of Microsoft laments that Sun is "out to undo everything we've done." Not many would take on Microsoft, but the 43-year-old MacNealy was a key force in getting the government to file its antitrust case against Gates. Commenting on survival in the computer industry, MacNealy quips, "Have lunch or be lunch." So far his strategy is working. In addition to his shrewd business savvy, he manages to keep "personality" in the company, encouraging a casual atmosphere for employees and even getting Network, his dog, to help promote it. With the company's many international expansions, *Business Week* says, "Sun's mantra has begun to resonate around the globe. . . ."

He's not about to let Bill Gates have all the fun (or money).

QUOTABLE: "If we succeed, we'll change the fundamentals of the computer business the same way Henry Ford changed the fundamentals of the automobile industry."

BEHIND THE SCENES: MacNealy and his wife, Susan, have two young sons, as well as Network the dog. MacNealy spends as much time as possible with his family; he arrived late for an important Sun event because of son Maverick's birth.

PRAYER STARTERS:

- Pray that Scott MacNealy will continue to place importance on his role as a husband and father. Ask for health and peace in his home today.

- Give thanks for the technology that allows science and education to enrich our lives.

- Pray for the new generation of computer system developers—that they will seek the Creator's best in all they do.

> *Commit to the LORD whatever you do, and your plans will succeed.*
> *Proverbs 16:3*

CONTACT: 901 San Antonio Blvd., Palo Alto, CA 94303; www.sun.com

Courtesy of Jewish Defense League

Irv Rubin

*National Chairman, Jewish
Defense League (JDL)*

POINT OF IMPACT: Irv Rubin is one of the world's best-known radical defenders of Jews and Zionism. His Jewish Defense League, though small in numbers (about 7,500 members), stays in the public eye through strident tactics and expert use of media coverage. The group's aim is to combat bigotry aimed at Jews and to promote the interests of Judaism and Israel. Young JDL members are trained to use rifles and karate and organized into civilian patrols. "We've slept on the floors with baseball bats," Rubin says. "There comes a time to take off the kid gloves and tell people, 'If you're getting down in the gutter, we'll get down there too.'" Not surprisingly, Rubin has been arrested (at least 40 times) and in 1978 faced an assassination attempt by the Ku Klux Klan. Rubin's name is allegedly at the top of several neo-Nazi hit lists. But he often says one of the main enemies of Jewish interests is Jewish complacency.

He's a radical defender of Jews and Zionism.

QUOTABLE: "America is a graveyard for Jews. I want to awaken the Jewish lion out there."

BEHIND THE SCENES: Irv Rubin, 54, experienced anti-Semitism firsthand growing up in Montreal (some businesses posted signs reading "No Dogs or Jews Allowed"). His family emigrated to Los Angeles in 1961. He has been married for 17 years and has two sons.

PRAYER STARTERS:

- Pray that Irv Rubin would seek and live by the wisdom of Scripture in all his decisions today. Pray that God will bring him hope and healing today, and bless his marriage, family, and friends.

- Pray for the spiritual renewal of the Jewish people—"'Return to me, and I will return to you,' says the LORD Almighty" (Malachi 3:7)

- Pray for the peace and safety of Jerusalem, Israel, and all Jews worldwide. Ask God what you can do to understand and combat anti-Semitism today.

Remember these things, O Jacob, for you are my servant, O Israel. I have made you, you are my servant; O Israel, I will not forget you. Isaiah 44:21

CONTACT: P.O. Box 480370, Los Angeles, CA 90048

Patrick Reynolds

*Founder, The Foundation for a
Smokefree America*

Courtesy of Foundation for a Smokefree America

POINT OF IMPACT: The Foundation for a Smokefree America is a nonprofit, charitable organization whose mission is to help bring about a smokefree society. And its founder has a name that rattles tobacco magnates everywhere. In 1985, Patrick Reynolds, the grandson of the founder of R.J. Reynolds Tobacco Co., turned his back on his family business and began a personal war against tobacco. Since then he has taken his campaign before Congress, state legislatures, corporations, universities, medical conferences, teenagers, and schoolchildren. Former Surgeon General C. Everett Koop says, "Patrick Reynolds is one of the nation's most influential advocates of a smokefree America" and has called his testimony "invaluable to our society." Recently Reynolds has devoted a greater amount of his attention to educating youth, and in 1998 he produced the educational video, *Straight Talk About Tobacco.*

He's the grandson of R.J. Reynolds, but he campaigns against tobacco.

QUOTABLE: "Am I biting the hand that feeds me? If the hand that once fed me is the tobacco industry, then that hand has killed millions of people and may kill millions more. And I intend to wake people up to that fact."

BEHIND THE SCENES: Reynolds, 51, watched his father and his brother die lingering and painful smoking-related deaths. He often tries to reach younger children with satire. For example, he turns the cigarette cartoon mascot Joe Camel into Joe Chemo, sitting in a hospital bed with an intravenous chemotherapy tube sticking in his arm. "This is a childhood disease," he says. He lives in Beverly Hills.

PRAYER STARTERS:

- Most smokers start before the age of 14 and become addicted before age 19. Pray for a dramatic shift in smoking patterns among the young.
- Give thanks for the impact and courage of Patrick Reynolds' campaign against tobacco. Ask God to give him and his family health in body and spirit today.
- Pray for someone you love today who needs to stop smoking.

> *They cried out to the LORD in their trouble, and he delivered them from their distress. . . . He sent forth his word and healed them; he rescued them from the grave. Psalm 107:6,20*

CONTACT: info@tobaccofree.org

AP/Wide World Photos

Andrew Lloyd Webber
Composer

POINT OF IMPACT: Andrew Lloyd Webber, the reigning king of musicals, penned his first hit musical at age 19 when he teamed with Tim Rice to produce *Joseph and the Amazing Technicolor Dreamcoat.* His second success followed at age 23 with *Jesus Christ Superstar.* Webber's subsequent hits—*Cats, Phantom of the Opera, Starlight Express,* and *Evita* —broke all industry records and, in 1996, the London production of *Cats* became the longest-running musical in history. Webber has won six Tony awards, three Grammys, and one Oscar. In 1992 Queen Elizabeth knighted him for his service to the arts and five years later elevated him to Lord Lloyd Webber with a life peerage in the House of Lords. His current projects include a continuation of *Phantom.*

His *Cats* is the longest-running musical in history

QUOTABLE: "I love musicals, you know. They're my lifeblood."

BEHIND THE SCENES: Musical talent runs in Webber's family. His father was a composer and director of the London College of Music; his mother was a piano teacher; and his brother, Julian, is a world-renowned cellist. Webber, 52, is an art collector who favors Picasso and Canaletto; he's also a food critic for London's *Daily Telegraph.* His autobiography is *Matters of Taste.* He's married to his third wife, Madeleine. Webber has three sons and two daughters.

PRAYER STARTERS:

- Give thanks for Andrew Lloyd Webber's talent, which brings enjoyment to thousands of audiences.
- Pray for the positive impact of Christians in theatre, dance, and music.
- Ask for the well-being of Lloyd Webber's marriage and family.

> *Let us draw near to God with a sincere heart in full assurance of faith.*
> Hebrews 10:22

CONTACT: The Really Useful Company, One Rockefeller Plaza, Suite 1528, New York, NY 10020

Jeffrey Katzenberg
Movie Mogul, Cofounder of DreamWorks

Archive Photo

POINT OF IMPACT: Jeffrey Katzenberg is the man who brought you Moses—in cartoon form, that is. *The Prince of Egypt* was Katzenberg's brainchild and burden. To create a fully fledged biblical hero, Katzenberg met with nearly 700 clerics and scholars, traveled to the Vatican, and studied with Harvard's divinity school faculty. The film is the product of DreamWorks, a company headed by superdirector Steven Spielberg, record mogul David Geffen, and Katzenberg, who joined its ranks after spending a decade at Disney. To create the company, each man invested $33 million of his own money. It's been a worthy investment; the company has scored with hits like *Deep Impact, Antz,* and *Saving Private Ryan. The Prince of Egypt* made a hefty $100 million. Screenwriter Terry Rossio describes Katzenberg's role in his new venture: "He was the guiding force at Disney. He's the driving force at DreamWorks."

He brought the Bible to life for moviegoers.

QUOTABLE: "When I look at certain characters—either in history or in movies—it's their journey as people that interests me. Moses was young and unassuming, a man with no sense of leadership. Suddenly, he's thrown into this mission. He becomes a great, heroic and compassionate leader."

BEHIND THE SCENES: Katzenberg gained the nickname "the golden retriever" because of his uncanny knack for finding promising scripts or concepts. He and Spielberg own a restaurant in Century City called Dive.

PRAYER STARTERS:

- Pray that Jeffrey Katzenberg and other DreamWorks colleagues would continue to strive to bring imaginative, high-quality films to theaters.
- Pray that enduring redemption stories, including those told in Scripture, would continue to fire the imagination of Hollywood.
- Ask God to surround Katzenberg and his family with an indelible sense of His presence and purposes today.

> *In your unfailing love you will lead the people you have redeemed. In your strength you will guide them to your holy dwelling. Exodus 15:13*

CONTACT: DreamWorks SKG, P.O. Box 8520, Universal City, CA 91608

Courtesy of NavPress

Eugene Peterson
Pastor, Author, Bible Translator

POINT OF IMPACT: The contemporary Bible paraphrase that's winning this generation of readers is Eugene Peterson's *The Message: The New Testament in Contemporary English* (NavPress). His translation from the original Greek and Hebrew breathes freshness and clarity into the biblical texts, and what Frederich Buechner calls "the ring of authentic human speech and feeling." The reliability of his translations has won them acclaim from Bible scholars as well. For 29 years Peterson was a Presbyterian pastor. Then in 1991 he became professor of spiritual theology at Regent College, Vancouver, Canada. Known as "the pastor to pastors," he's the author of 18 books, including *The Contemplative Pastor*, and recently, *Leap Over a Wall: Earthy Spirituality for Everyday Christians*. He continues to influence clergy from both mainline and evangelical streams of Christianity.

His paraphrase of Scripture sounds right to modern ears.

QUOTABLE: "The pastorate is one of the few places where you can live a truly creative life."

BEHIND THE SCENES: Peterson says his translation is an effort to put the New Testament "in the street language of the day, the idiom of the playground and marketplace"—because, he says, that's exactly how it was originally written. Peterson and his wife, Jan, live in British Columbia. They have three grown children: Karen, Eric, and Leif.

PRAYER STARTERS:

- Praise God for women and men who make the Bible accessible for everyday use and understanding.
- Ask God to guide Bible translators at work today around the world.
- Ask God to bless Eugene and Jan Peterson with peace and favor. Pray that *The Message* would find new readers among the unchurched.

> *God means what he says. What he says goes. His powerful Word is sharp as a surgeon's scalpel, cutting through everything, whether doubt or defense, laying us open to listen and obey. Hebrews 4:12* THE MESSAGE

CONTACT: NavPress, Box 35001, Colorado Springs, CO 80935

Mohammad Khatami
President of the Islamic Republic of Iran

UN/DPI Photo by Greg Kinch

POINT OF IMPACT: Soon after taking office as President of Iran in 1997, Mohammad Khatami said he respected the "great people of the United States." That one phrase was the single most dramatic shift in Iranian rhetoric since the days of the U.S. hostage crisis in 1980. He's also expressed admiration for the Puritans, the Declaration of Independence, and Abraham Lincoln, and suggested that Iran and the United States begin cultural exchanges among scholars, artists, and tourists. Many Iranians view him as a symbol of hope for the future; others, especially among religious fundamentalists, oppose his liberal policies. Iran, once called Persia, is a nation of 75 million trying to balance the demands of Islamic fundamentalists and the need for stability and progress.

He's changing the way Iranians think about America.

QUOTABLE: "Mr. Khatami is going against nearly the whole establishment, and there are powerful forces who may try to stop what he is doing at any cost."—an Iranian civil servant

BEHIND THE SCENES: Khatami, 57, campaigned for his office on the web (Iran's use of cyberspace is second only to Israel's in the Middle East), and won many female and younger voters when he admitted (in this culture of veiled women) that he liked it when his wife drove him around. Khatami and his wife live simply with their three children in Tehran.

PRAYER STARTERS:

- Give thanks for Khatami's overtures of friendship with America and for the potential for an improved relationship between the two nations.
- When Khatami ran for president, he called for a "civil society." Pray for peace: between Iran and Iraq, and between all Islamic nations and Israel.
- Pray for the safety, health, and protection of Khatami and his family.

The heart of the discerning acquires knowledge; the ears of the wise seek it out. Proverbs 18:15

CONTACT: Islamic Republican Party, Dr. Ali Shariati Avenue, Tehran, Iran

John Ashcroft

Senator, Missouri

POINT OF IMPACT: This Missouri Republican is arguably the leading social conservative in the Senate, taking center stage in opposition to programs and issues that, in his words, "assault" the values of Americans. John Ashcroft, an evangelical Christian, has fought liberal activist judges as well as projects sponsored by the National Endowment for the Arts. He authored the landmark Charitable Choice provision of the new welfare reform law, which allows states to work directly with charities and faith-based organizations to move people from dependence to work. Dr. James Dobson recently devoted two segments of his national radio program to an interview with Ashcroft, describing the senator as "a ray of light in Washington."

He's been called "a ray of light" in Washington.

QUOTABLE: "I think it's time for us to reassert the principle that the values of the people should be imposed on government, rather than the values of government imposed on the people."

BEHIND THE SCENES: Active in the Assemblies of God church, Ashcroft meets with a small devotional group every morning in his office. In addition, Ashcroft enjoys singing and songwriting. He is the baritone voice of the Singing Senators, a gospel quartet including Senators Trent Lott, Larry Craig, and James Jeffords. Ashcroft, 58, and his wife, Janet, have two sons and a daughter.

PRAYER STARTERS:

- Pray for Christians with a high profile in Washington politics—for their integrity, humility, wisdom, and compassion.
- Ask God to protect John Ashcroft's family from harm.
- Pray for groups in Washington who are ministering to the spiritual needs of congressional leaders and government workers.

It is for freedom that Christ has set us free. Stand firm, then. Galatians 5:1

CONTACT: 505 Capitol Court N.E., Suite 100, Washington, DC 20002; john@johnashcroft.org

John F. Kennedy, Jr.

Publisher, Lawyer

Archive Photo

POINT OF IMPACT: He's young. He's beautiful. He's successful. But what really makes John-John Kennedy noteworthy is his name. The most visible and photogenic member of America's royal and foible-afflicted family, Kennedy has a powerful mantle to carry. Though he's been pushed almost since birth to follow his father's footsteps into the Oval Office, the 40-year-old publisher and president of *George* magazine has so far responded with nothing firmer than "maybe." Says an actor acquaintance, "John would rather be Tom Cruise than Bill Clinton." Kennedy studied at Brown University and New York University Law School, finally passing his bar exams (after several well-publicized failures) and becoming an assistant district attorney. He left law to create *George*, considered the political handbook for the "wired generation."

He's the heir apparent of America's "royal family."

QUOTABLE: "Once you run for office, you're in it—sort of like going into the military. You'd better be sure it is what you want to do and that the rest of your life is set up to accommodate that. It takes a certain toll on your personality and on your family life. I've seen it personally."

BEHIND THE SCENES: Kennedy loves sports of all kinds—frisbee, skiing, kayaking, volleyball, snorkeling, softball, and biking, among others. In his single days he was known for dropping in at three or four discos and clubs in an evening. Since 1996, he's been married to Carolyn Bessette.

PRAYER STARTERS:

- Pray that John Kennedy, Jr. will seek and follow the Lord's will in his public and private life. Pray that he will have success in bringing disaffected voters back into the political process.
- Pray for the safety of Kennedy and his wife.
- Ask God to bless the Kennedys—and their extended families—with His peace and grace.

> *The power of the wicked will be broken, but the LORD upholds the righteous.*
> Psalm 37:17

CONTACT: www.george.com

Extraordinary Bounties

"The year that is drawing toward its close has been filled with the blessings of fruitful fields and healthful skies. To these bounties, others have been added which are of so extraordinary a nature that they cannot fail to penetrate and soften even the heart which is habitually insensible to the ever-watchful providence of Almighty God."

ABRAHAM LINCOLN,
Thanksgiving Day Proclamation,
October 3, 1863

On this day of thanksgiving, remember those who are in your personal gallery of "most influential people." Give thanks for those whose love, time, effort, and example—"bounties . . . of so extraordinary a nature"—have most blessed your life.

- **My most influential people then:**

- **My most influential people now:**

- **My gift of influence:** Ask God to show you those for whom your life's impact could be most decisive. Give thanks for this ministry of influence. Ask the Lord to show you how to touch each person for their enduring good and for His glory.

Enter his gates with thanksgiving and his courts with praise;
give thanks to him and praise his name.

For the LORD is good and his love endures forever;
his faithfulness continues through all generations.

Psalm 100:4-5

Marian Wright Edelman

Founder and President,
Children's Defense Fund

Photo by Michael Collopy

POINT OF IMPACT: From an early age, Marian Wright Edelman knew she wanted to change the world—and the part she wanted to affect most was the world of impoverished children. Today, as founder and president of the Children's Defense Fund (CDF), her mission is to ensure every child gets a "Healthy Start, a Head Start, a Fair Start, a Safe Start, and a Moral Start in life." CDF, with a privately funded budget of $18 million, lobbies Congress in areas like foster care, adoption services, curtailing teen pregnancies, and insurance coverage for children. In 1998 alone, Edelman's Black Community Crusade for Children and the Stand for Children campaign brought 300,000 people to the Capitol to fight for children's needs.

She crusades for helpless children.

QUOTABLE: "America is being paralyzed by can't-doers with puny vision and punier will. If the Soviet people could dismantle communism, can't we wage an end to child neglect, poverty and family disintegration, which are graver threats to our national future than nuclear weapons?"

BEHIND THE SCENES: Edelman, 60, was born in South Carolina into a family of Baptist ministers. When she was nine, her parents decided she was old enough to help them clean a sick woman's bedsores. After graduating from Yale Law School, she became the first black woman admitted to the Mississippi Bar. She and her husband, Peter, have three grown sons: Joshua, Jonah, and Ezra.

PRAYER STARTERS:

- Give thanks for Marian Edelman's example of Christian love in action; pray for greater impact in her endeavors on the national scene.
- Writes Edelman, "Every day in America 81 babies die needlessly, six children commit suicide, 13 children are murdered, 1,827 babies are born without health insurance." Ask God to show you what your response should be today for disadvantaged kids.
- Ask for God's grace and protection on the Edelmans and all CDF workers.

Defend the cause of the weak and fatherless. Psalm 82:3

CONTACT: 25 E. Street N.W., Washington, DC 20001; cdfinfo@childrens defense.org

Credit: Steve Fenn/ABC

Patricia Fili-Krushel
President, ABC Television Network

POINT OF IMPACT: Patricia Fili-Krushel, 46, is the highest-ranking woman in network television. Prior to her 1998 appointment as ABC's president, she kept ABC's daytime programming at number one among women ages 18-49, the most coveted demographic group. She was also instrumental in developing Barbara Walters' talk show, *The View.* These days she's not only in charge of the network's business operations, she also oversees all of ABC's entertainment programming, news, and sports. Although her rise to network president was hailed as a milestone for women in the industry, she says, "I haven't run into a glass ceiling or had those kinds of issues. But I feel a certain responsibility as a role model for other women. I'm looking forward to meeting the challenge."

She's the highest-ranking woman in network television.

QUOTABLE: "I'm particular about what I want my children to watch. They can only watch one half-hour during the weekday, and that happens to be a Disney show called *Bill Nye, The Science Guy.* Because they get up so early on Saturday, they can watch ABC, Disney or Nickelodeon. I do not let them watch other, violent cartoons."

BEHIND THE SCENES: According to *Forbes,* Fili-Krushel thinks nothing of stepping out of meetings to take calls from her six- and eight-year-olds about playdates and fruit roll-ups. She says being a mother has made her a better manager—"It's perfected my negotiating skills." She lives in New York.

PRAYER STARTERS:

- Give thanks for the meaningful contributions women are now able to make in top corporation positions.
- Ask God to give Patricia Fili-Krushel wisdom and confidence in her work. Pray that she and her peers will make programming decisions that contribute positively to society, and that such choices bring financial success.
- Pray that God would bless Fili-Krushel in her parenting and in her own personal life. Ask Him to daily reveal to her His abundant love and mercy.

Above all else, guard your heart, for it is the wellspring of life. Proverbs 4:23

CONTACT: ABC, 77 W. 66th St., New York, NY 10023-6298

Frank Tracy Griswold III

*Presiding Bishop, the Episcopal Church
in America*

POINT OF IMPACT: Pledging to be "a presiding bishop who belongs to all," Frank Griswold was installed as the Episcopalians' twenty-fifth Presiding Bishop in 1998. He comes into a church painfully divided over sexual tolerance (for example, ordination of celibate homosexuals and recognition of same-sex unions) and biblical interpretation, and struggling with defections among traditionally minded members. Considered a reconciling influence, Griswold says "the ministry of the presiding bishop is to stand at the center." He's known for his skills as a liturgist and spiritual director, and for overseeing dialogues between Anglicans and Roman Catholics. At 2.5 million members, Episcopalians are in the middle of the pack among Protestants but have historically wielded great influence in government, education, and culture.

He "stands in the center" of a church in conflict.

QUOTABLE: "The church is destined always to contain diametrically opposing views. Part of my task is to help the different voices hear one another through continuing conversation."

BEHIND THE SCENES: Griswold and his wife, Phoebe, live in New York and have two grown daughters who live nearby. Mrs. Griswold has been active in relief work, including the Heifer Project International, which provides farm animals to underdeveloped countries.

PRAYER STARTERS:

- Thank God for church leaders like Griswold, who are committed to reconciliation and unity in the church.
- Most Anglican growth is happening in non-western countries (there are 75 million Anglicans worldwide). Ask God to bless and renew Episcopalian and Anglican fellowships today around the world.
- Ask God to surround Bishop Griswold and his family with the peace of His presence, and to grant him divine wisdom for the tasks at hand.

> [An overseer] must be hospitable, one who loves what is good, who is self-controlled, upright, holy and disciplined. Titus 1:8

CONTACT: Episcopal Church Center, 815 Second Avenue, New York, NY 10017

Credit: Allison Shirreefs

Tom Peters
Bestselling Author

POINT OF IMPACT: Zillion-dollar-a-day management consultant Tom Peters is the bestselling business author in history. His 1982 megaseller, *In Search of Excellence,* coauthored with Robert Waterman, launched a new genre of business books and "business speak." Peters went on to write more bestsellers, including *Thriving on Chaos* and *The Pursuit of Wow!* Harriet Rubin, executive editor of Doubleday's Currency Books, declares that Peters "created a whole new audience of readers—men. [He was the first] to bring men into bookstores in big numbers." Often compared with prophets and evangelists, Peters asserts that the world is full of chaos and threat; the old way of doing business is dead. He's originated current business practices like "downsizing," "empowerment," and "deconstructing bureaucracy." Each year, he delivers hundreds of seminars worldwide.

He's the architect of the modern business environment.

QUOTABLE: "Economic progress, whether it is a two-person coffee shop or whether it is Netscape, is about people with brave ideas. Because it is brave to mortgage the house when you've got two kids to start a coffee shop."

BEHIND THE SCENES: Peters, 58, spent two tours of duty in Vietnam. He made the largest single private donation ever given to the American Civil Liberties Union. Peters and his wife, Susan, and their children live in Vermont.

PRAYER STARTERS:

- Give thanks for the fresh perspectives and dynamism Tom Peters has brought to modern business.
- Ask God to bring to mind one promising businessperson you know. Pray that he or she will pursue excellence—fiscally, relationally, and ethically.
- Ask for health and contentment for the Peters family, and a growing awareness of the person of Jesus Christ.

Whatever is admirable—if anything is excellent or praiseworthy—think about such things. Philippians 4:8

CONTACT: 555 Hamilton Ave., Palo Alto, CA 94301; e-mail: tompeters@businessedge.net

Eugene Lang
Founder and President,
I Have a Dream Foundation

Credit: Swarthmore College/Deng-Jeng Lee

POINT OF IMPACT: It all began in 1981 when businessman and millionaire Eugene Lang was asked to deliver a speech at his old public school in East Harlem. On an impulse, he promised his audience of sixth graders that he would provide college scholarships to anyone who finished high school. Of the 61 children who heard him that day, 90 percent graduated, and two-thirds went on to college. Today, the I Have a Dream Foundation is the nation's leading sponsor-based scholarship program for inner-city youth, with projects in 63 U.S. cities—and expanding. Best of all, Lang's success has become a model for scores of similar programs. In 1996 he was awarded the Presidential Medal of Freedom. Lang has donated millions to other causes, but regards the sixth-grade Class of '81 as special. "I think it's the most significant thing I've done," he says, "because it's caused others to act too."

His dream makes dreams possible for thousands.

QUOTABLE: "If there's one less kid peddling drugs or walking the streets, we've done what needs to be done."

BEHIND THE SCENES: Eugene Lang, 80, grew up poor in New York City. He made his millions by licensing American technology overseas. *Forbes* magazine has called Lang the "quintessential entrepreneur." Lang and his wife, the former Theresa Volmar, raised their three children in Queens.

PRAYER STARTERS:

- Give thanks for Eugene Lang's example of vision, charity, and humility.
- Lang says his initial idea was not to change the world, but to improve the odds for one small group. Ask God to show you one person or group you could influence for good today.
- Pray for schoolchildren in your community, and for their parents and teachers. Pray that together we can nurture a society that champions learning, excellence, and strong character.
- Ask God to give the Langs health, safety, peace, and a sense of His presence.

Where there is no vision, the people perish. Proverbs 29:18 KJV

CONTACT: www.ihad.org

Archive Photo

Kim Jong-il
"Great Leader" of North Korea

POINT OF IMPACT: Kim Jong-il, 58, is one of the world's most mysterious leaders: reclusive, erratic, all-powerful. Within North Korea, Jong-il is worshiped as an omniscient, omnipresent god. He is an avid supporter of nuclear weapons and terrorism, making Stalinist North Korea one of the most dangerous hot spots in the world. Satellite photos have revealed signs of a nuclear weapons program, and recent missile tests in Asia have added to growing international concern. Many worry that food shortages which have caused widespread deaths, could push the country into war with South Korea. "The threat is growing," says U.S. Defense Secretary William S. Cohen. "It poses a danger not only to our troops overseas but to Americans at home."

He's one of the globe's most mysterious dictators.

QUOTABLE: Says one North Korean diplomat: "[Jong-il's] father, whom I have met, was very sharp. He was charming and had great charisma. But the son, he is so strange, he must either be mad or on drugs."

BEHIND THE SCENES: Kim Jong-il was born in the Soviet Union, where his father was training under Joseph Stalin. CIA reports depict Jong-il as a binge drinker with a taste for imported prostitutes and reckless driving. Jong-il lives in Pyongyang, the capital; he is married and the father of two children.

PRAYER STARTERS:

- Pray for all those who suffer at the government's hands in North Korea today. Pray for a turnaround in Kim Jong-il's priorities and politics.
- Pray that God's mercies to Kim Jong-il and his family will be persuasive today, bringing him to seek the one true God.
- Pray for persecuted North Korean believers, who must worship in private.
- Youth of both North and South Korea increasingly wish for a unified Korea. Ask God to bring wise leaders to the forefront in this movement.

> *You, O Lord, reign forever; your throne endures from generation to generation. Lamentations 5:19*

CONTACT: Korea Press International, 2400 Pennsylvania Avenue N.W., Washington, DC 20037

Bill Moyers
TV Journalist

POINT OF IMPACT: Over the last ten years of his impressive 30-year career, Bill Moyers has produced a series of documentaries that have set a new standard in TV journalism. "No journalist has done more than Bill Moyers to make television and its viewers smarter and more thoughtful," writes the *Los Angeles Times*. And Columbia University president Michael Sovern has called Moyers "a unique voice, still seeking new frontiers in television, daring to assume that viewing audiences are willing to think and learn." Since establishing his own company, Public Affairs Television, in 1986, he's produced more than 240 programming hours exploring topics like the men's movement, constitutional democracy, small-town life, the human mind and spirit, the book of Genesis, and the problem of addiction. Media critics consistently place Moyers in the top ten of those who most influence TV news. He's written five bestsellers and been awarded 30 Emmys.

He dares to assume TV viewers want to learn.

QUOTABLE: "After all of the zigzagging and intrigue, I finally wound up exactly where I've had the opportunity to do all the things that interest me."

BEHIND THE SCENES: Moyers and his wife, Judith, have been married more than 40 years. Brought up Southern Baptist in Texas, Moyers attended seminary before eventually turning to politics and then journalism. His oldest son, William Cope Moyers, now 39, experienced many painful years as a drug addict and made a brief appearance on his father's addiction series, "Moyers on Addiction: Close to Home."

PRAYERS STARTERS:

- Give thanks for Bill Moyers' intelligent and revealing TV journalism, and for his appreciation for the power of the deeper realms of art and spirit.
- Pray for success in Moyers' current ventures, and for his continued influence on TV programming.
- Ask God to bless, strengthen, and protect the Moyers family.

A wise man has great power. Proverbs 24:5

CONTACT: Public Affairs Television, 356 West 58th St., New York, NY 10019

Archive Photo

Elizabeth Taylor with Mathilda Krim

Mathilda Krim

Cofounder and Chairman, American Foundation for AIDS Research (amfAR)

POINT OF IMPACT: Mathilda Krim, a biologist, didn't set out to hobnob with celebrities. But as amfAR, the group she cofounded with Elizabeth Taylor, developed into the nation's leading nonprofit organization dedicated to the support of AIDS research, Krim has signed on stars like Madonna, Tom Hanks, Lauryn Hill, Chris Rock, and Sharon Stone as spokespersons and fundraisers. Since 1985, amfAR has granted nearly $155 million to more than 1,750 research teams, to AIDS prevention programs, and to efforts to shape AIDS-related public policy. In 1999 Krim's group developed a campaign to address the country's growing complacency concerning AIDS.

This biologist helps lead the fight against AIDS.

QUOTABLE: "While deaths from AIDS are slowing down in the United States because of more effective drug treatments, the incidence of AIDS and of new cases of HIV infection is rising. Around the world, the HIV-AIDS situation is getting grimmer every day."

BEHIND THE SCENES: Born in Italy and raised in Switzerland, Krim has traveled the world, moving in lofty circles. She and her late husband, Arthur, had their own room at the White House during the Johnson administration. She lives in Manhattan.

PRAYER STARTERS:

- Of an estimated 33 million who live with HIV/AIDS today, two-thirds are in sub-Saharan Africa. Pray for their care, comfort, and healing. Pray for children who are infected or who are orphaned when infected parents die.

- Give thanks to the vigorous work of Mathilda Krim and amfAR. Pray for new medical breakthroughs and for better availability of care.

- Pray for changing attitudes toward sexuality that will preserve health and families, and inhibit the spread of AIDS. Pray that Christians will lead by example in medical and hospice care and family support.

- Ask God to bless Krim and her family with grace and peace.

Blessed are the merciful, for they will be shown mercy. Matthew 5:7

CONTACT: amfAR, 120 Wall Street, Thirteenth Floor, New York, NY 10005; www.amfar.org

J.C. Watts

U.S. Congressman

Photo by Rick Reinhard, Washington, DC

POINT OF IMPACT: J.C. Watts of Oklahoma is the GOP's only black member of Congress and the first black representative from the South since the Reconstruction. Often described as one of the party's most valuable assets, Watts, 43, speaks out against government handouts (which he says "enslave" the poor, including African-Americans) while building bridges for Republicans to the black community. The *Economist* calls Watts one of the most powerful people in the House of Representatives (he is currently Chairman of the Republican Conference, the number-four position in the House). Watts is part of an alliance of conservative lawmakers hoping to harness the energy of community, business, and religious groups to tackle an array of urban family problems.

He's the only black Republican in Congress.

QUOTABLE: "To me 'conservative' doesn't mean Republican or Democrat. It means the way my Mama and Daddy raised me. That meant you were going to work and be in church on Sunday. You were going to go to school and act civilized."

BEHIND THE SCENES: As a teenager Watts fathered two children, later marrying the mother of one. Today he travels widely as a preacher and is a pastor at Sunnylane Southern Baptist Church, Del City, Oklahoma. Watts defends his role as a family champion: "If you had a child out of wedlock, does that mean you can never be involved in a pro-family movement? Redemption is a farce if you can't be forgiven for your mistakes." Watts and his wife, Frankie, have five children.

PRAYER STARTERS:

- J.C. Watts is a spokesman for the Fellowship of Christian Athletes, the Orphan Foundation of America, the March of Dimes, and several antidrug campaigns. Pray for his strength, protection, and integrity.
- Pray for the Watts family and marriage today, that they will be preserved and blessed despite the heavy pressures of Watts' public service.
- Pray for a teenage parent you know today. Ask God to show you how you could lighten his or her load.

We are God's workmanship, created in Christ Jesus to do good works, which God prepared in advance for us to do. Ephesians 2:10

CONTACT: 1210 Longworth House Office Building, Washington, DC 20515-3604

Joni Eareckson Tada

Author, Speaker

Courtesy of JAF Ministries

POINT OF IMPACT: "I'd rather be in this chair knowing God, than on my feet without Him," says Joni Eareckson Tada, a quadriplegic since a diving accident in 1967. She admits the transition from devoted athlete to dependent paralytic was rough. But since she came to terms with her injury and with God, Tada has become an internationally known advocate for the disabled. She founded JAF (formerly Joni and Friends), a worldwide outreach to assist and train others in disability ministry. In 1998, JAF's Wheels program sent 2,165 refurbished wheelchairs to 23 countries. She served on the National Council on Disability for three-and-a-half years, during which time the Americans with Disabilities Act became law. Her *Joni and Friends* daily radio program is heard on more than 700 stations, she speaks widely, and has written *When God Weeps: Why Our Sufferings Matter to the Almighty* (with Steve Estes), and *Heaven: Your Real Home,* among other books.

She's an internationally known friend of the disabled.

QUOTABLE: "Sometimes I think that people whose lives are unscathed by suffering have a less energetic hope. But suffering . . . turns our hearts toward the future. And once heaven has our attention, a fervent anticipation for Christ begins to glow, making everything earthly pale in comparison. Earth's pain keeps crushing our hopes, reminding us that this world can never satisfy, only heaven can."

BEHIND THE SCENES: A feature film about her life, *Joni,* has been translated into many languages and viewed around the world. Eareckson, 50, is a prolific painter—holding the brush between her teeth. She's married to Ken Tada.

PRAYER STARTERS:

- Give thanks for Tada's faithful life. Pray that God would continue to use her to lead many to a deeper understanding of God's love and grace.
- Remember to pray for all who suffer with a physical disability.
- Ask God to bless Joni's personal life and marriage with joy and peace.

    My grace is sufficient for you, for my power is made perfect in weakness.
    2 Corinthians 12:9

CONTACT: JAF Ministries, P.O. Box 3333, Agoura Hills, CA 91301

Dan Rather

Anchorman, CBS Evening News

CBS News 1999 Larry Busacca

POINT OF IMPACT: In 1981, when Dan Rather stepped into Walter Cronkite's sizable shoes as anchor of *CBS Evening News,* few believed he could replace the legendary journalist. But not only has Rather proven his mettle, in 1999 he tied Cronkite's term as anchor (18 years) and has in the process won every accolade known to American journalism. He joined CBS in 1961 and ascended the ranks until settling at last into the anchor chair. He's won multiple Emmys as both a reporter and as host of *48 Hours.* His books include his memoir, *The Camera Never Blinks Twice: The Further Adventures of a Television Journalist.* Rather, 69, has interviewed every president from Eisenhower to Clinton and international leaders from Mandela to Hussein. He speaks widely on journalistic ethics.

He thrives on the rush of reporting.

QUOTABLE: On his job: "I've liked it from the beginning. I do it because I really have a passion for it. Turns out that I really like daily news best. Everything from the adrenaline rush . . . to the fact that you play every day. The scoreboard lights up every day but then the next day, you play again."

BEHIND THE SCENES: In 1995, when Rather reported on Hurricane Opal in Florida, two of his producers "anchored the anchor," clinging to his arms and legs in the fierce winds. He is married to Jean and is the father of two grown children, Robin and Danjack. He has homes in New York and Texas.

PRAYER STARTERS:

- Give thanks for the dedication of journalists like Rather, who risk personal convenience and safety to report the news with fairness, completeness, and accuracy.
- Pray that Rather will seek God's guidance and will for his professional work.
- Ask God to grant the Rathers His favor, protection, and peace.

    He will have no fear of bad news; his heart is steadfast, trusting in the Lord. Psalm 112:7

CONTACT: CBS, 51 W. 52nd St., New York, NY 10019

Keizo Obuchi

Prime Minister of Japan

UN/DPI Photo by Milton Grant

POINT OF IMPACT: Keizo Obuchi became Japan's new prime minister in 1998. He is the sixth to hold that position since President Clinton took office in 1992. (Since 1991 successive Japanese governments have lasted an average of only 16 months.) His Liberal Democratic Party has led Japan more or less continuously since World War II. Obuchi has his work cut out for him: With an economy about half the size of the American economy, Japan is suffering a banking crisis several times more serious than the U.S. savings and loan crisis of the eighties. Obuchi has endured the lackluster opinion of his countrymen with good humor. After being compared to a cold pizza, he pointed out that even cold pizza can be reheated. Supporters say that he's smart and funny and willing to do whatever it takes to turn the economy around.

He's trying to rescue Japan's economy.

QUOTABLE: "Maybe some say it's too late, but [finance minister Kiichi] Miyazawa and I are sacrificing ourselves to get the Japanese policy back on track," he says.

BEHIND THE SCENES: Obuchi, 62, and his wife, Chizuko, have one son and two daughters.

PRAYER STARTERS:

- Pray for wisdom and courage for Obuchi as he leads Japan through difficult economic decisions and plays a vital role in Asia's future.
- Pray for government and business persons around the world who are working to repair Asia's economies and financial institutions.
- Pray for rest, good health, and protection for Obuchi and his marriage.

Wisdom is more precious than rubies, and nothing you desire can compare with her. Proverbs 8:11

CONTACT: 2520 Massachusetts Ave. N.W., Washington, DC 20008

Drew Barrymore

Actress, Producer

Archive Photos

POINT OF IMPACT: Drew Barrymore has a blue-blood Hollywood name, cheeky good looks, and the full attention of millions of teens. She started her career as a precocious seven-year-old in Spielberg's classic, *E.T.* But at age nine she began a long and widely publicized slide into drug and alcohol dependence. She was 21 when, after several rehab stays and a suicide attempt, she finally bounced back. Today at 25, she's known for her sunny disposition, brazen sensuality, and huge box-office appeal. Since 1998, she's starred in *The Wedding Singer, Ever After, Home Fries,* and *Never Been Kissed* (which also marked her debut as an executive producer). Among teens around the world, she's idolized for her sass and well as her success.

She's got Hollywood flower power.

QUOTABLE: "I never realized what a decent companion I am to myself. I like to eat dinners and go to movies by myself—this has been an amazing revelation that I never thought could be true, but it is."

BEHIND THE SCENES: Drew was born in Los Angeles just months after her actor parents divorced. During her teen years, Steven Spielberg, who is her godfather, described Barrymore as "13 going on 29." She recently reconciled with her father, John Barrymore, Jr., whom she grew up hardly knowing.

PRAYER STARTERS:

- Barrymore grew up around substance abuse (her famous grandfather, actor John Barrymore, was an alcoholic, and Drew remembers her drunken father throwing her against a wall). Pray that she will continue to choose a healthy lifestyle for herself.
- Pray that the Lord would bring her strong and supportive Christian friends. Pray that she'll choose to promote positive, moral life choices.
- Ask God to bless Drew with a powerful sense of His sacrificial love for her.

May all who seek to take my life be put to shame and confusion. Psalm 40:14

CONTACT: Creative Artists Agency, 9830 Wilshire Blvd., Beverly Hills, CA 90212

Photo credit: Brian Lanker

Toni Morrison
Author

POINT OF IMPACT: Toni Morrison, 69, is black America's leading novelist and one of the world's most celebrated authors. Her bestselling novels about gender conflicts and the African-American experience include *The Bluest Eye, Sula, Song of Solomon,* and *Beloved* (which won the Pulitzer Prize in 1988). In 1993 she became the first African-American to win the Nobel Prize in Literature and the first American woman to win it since Pearl Buck in 1938. In 1998 *Time* magazine said that Morrison is responsible for "almost single-handedly giving African-American women their rightful place in American literature," inspiring a generation of black artists such as Bebe Moore Campbell and Terry McMillan. *Vanity Fair* has listed Morrison as one of the most powerful women in the United States.

Her celebrated novels have changed the literary landscape.

QUOTABLE: "Recently two close cousins died, both of my brothers died, my mother died, my house burned down. Sometimes things are in disarray. My faith is always being challenged, but that is good: You discover of what you are made."

BEHIND THE SCENES: Granddaughter of a slave, Toni Morrison was born into a family of sharecroppers during the Depression. When Morrison was two, her parents fell short of their four-dollars-a-month rent, and the furious landlord tried to torch the house—with the family inside. Thereafter, Morrison says her father nurtured an angry disbelief in "every word and every gesture of every white man on earth." Divorced, with two grown sons, Morrison lives in Princeton, New Jersey.

PRAYER STARTERS:

- Give thanks for Toni Morrison's humane impact on world understanding of the African-American experience.
- Ask for "the God of all comfort" to touch her life, and through her, the lives of many others; pray for healing between the races.
- Ask for humility among those who exert power by reason of position or circumstance. Ask God to teach you this truth in your own relationships today.

> *I will walk about in freedom, for I have sought out your precepts.*
> *Psalm 119:45*

CONTACT: Alfred A. Knopf, Inc., 201 E. 50th St., New York, NY 10022-7703

Gerhard Schroeder

Chancellor of Germany

Archive Photo

POINT OF IMPACT: In September 1998, Chancellor Gerhard Schroeder became the first German opposition leader to defeat an incumbent chancellor in a federal election. He came into office trumpeting the "New Middle," something like Bill Clinton's New Democrats in 1992 and Tony Blair's New Labour in 1996. Schroeder faces serious challenges: a deeply entrenched welfare state, a combative labor movement, rising unemployment, and a widening rift between the "rich West" and the former communist East Germany. But Schroeder brings fresh ideas and vigorous leadership to the new, united Europe.

He imagines a new kind of Europe.

QUOTABLE: "We can learn from the enormous dynamism of the American system, the willingness to try something new. With new technologies, for example, first to consider the possibilities and then the risks, and to act accordingly."

BEHIND THE SCENES: Schroeder's father was killed while he served with the German Army in Romania in 1944, the year Schroeder was born. His mother cleaned homes to feed her five children. He earned a law degree at night school while working several part-time jobs. Schroeder gained notoriety—and advanced his political career—during the seventies when he defended left-wing terrorists in court. Photogenic and a fan of cigars, Schroeder, 55, and his wife, Hiltrud, have two daughters.

PRAYER STARTERS:

- Pray that Gerhard Schroeder will seek divine leading and wise counsel as he guides Germany into its future. Pray that peace, reconciliation, and healing will prevail as Germany forges a new cultural identity.
- Pray for Schroeder and others who are playing key roles in the European Union—that wisdom and justice will prevail.
- Pray for the Schroeders' marriage and family—for health, rest, and safety.

He who seeks good finds goodwill. Proverbs 11:27

CONTACT: Staatskanzlei, Planckstrasse 2, 30169 Hanover, Germany

Courtesy of FamilyLife

Dennis & Barbara Rainey

Marriage and Parenting Mentors

POINT OF IMPACT: Twenty five years ago, Campus Crusade for Christ, a burgeoning college evangelism ministry, realized they had a new concern: this time it wasn't about saving the lost but saving their own staff members' marriages. Under the leadership of Dennis (shown) and Barbara Rainey, an outgoing Crusade couple with strong teaching gifts, Campus Crusade began to provide premarital and marriage enhancement seminars for its workers. Two years later, the Raineys took their seminars public. This year FamilyLife Marriage Conferences will be held in almost every major North American city. To date, more than 500,000 people have attended FamilyLife's marriage and parenting conferences. *FamilyLife Today*, the Raineys' radio talk show co-hosted with Bob Lepine, now reaches over 2 million listeners each week. A volunteer network of more than 10,000 couples help sponsor regional conferences and lead couples' Bible studies. The Raineys have collaborated on bestsellers including the HomeBuilders Couples series, *Moments Together for Couples,* and *Building Your Mate's Self-Esteem.*

They help keep marriages and families together.

QUOTABLE: "The most important battle being fought today is for the soul of America. And the battle for the soul of our nation begins at home. That's why we urgently need a family reformation."

BEHIND THE SCENES: Dennis Rainey, 51, traces his concerns for the family in part to experiences working with high school students in the 1970s. "I saw that my ministry to students was often undercut by the influence of parents," he says. "I realized that so many families were being torn apart by divorce that we were losing a generation of children." He is an honors graduate of Dallas Theological Seminary. The Raineys have six children.

PRAYER STARTERS:

- Give thanks for the many marriage and parenting relationships that have been helped through the Raineys' ministries.
- Nearly 50 percent of all U.S. marriages end up in divorce. Pray that God will bless the work of FamilyLife with hurting couples and parents. Ask God to strengthen FamilyLife teachers and volunteers.
- Ask God to favor the Rainey family with health, harmony, and love.

Marriage should be honored by all. Hebrews 13:4

CONTACT: P.O. Box 23840, Little Rock, AR 72221-3840; www.familylife.com

H. George Anderson
Presiding Bishop, The Evangelical Lutheran Church in America

Courtesy of Bishop George Anderson

POINT OF IMPACT: In 1978, George Anderson was leading in the balloting to head the Evangelical Lutheran Church in America (ELCA). But he had trouble visualizing himself in the role. "I interpreted that as the lack of an inner call to that task," he said, and withdrew his name. Four years later, when his wife succumbed to cancer, he assumed the role of single parent to two teenagers. "If I had been elected then [in 1978], I would have been pulled away from home at a terrible time," he says. "I had precious time to be with her during those days." But in 1995, Anderson was installed as bishop of the world's largest Lutheran body (over 5 million members). He leads at a time when his church is trying to reach beyond its traditional northern European roots for new members. Beloved for both his pastor's heart and his scholarship, Anderson, 68, is the author of many works on Lutheran history.

He leads the world's largest Lutheran body.

QUOTABLE: "In His life and death Jesus showed how to overcome evil. His life demonstrated that the world does not immediately embrace the good or even tolerate it. But He proved that violence can finally be defeated by love, and that God's purpose will ultimately triumph."

BEHIND THE SCENES: Anderson, an honors graduate from Yale, was born in Los Angeles and adopted by Reuben and Frances Anderson. On the day he was elected bishop, he said, "Adoption by those parents and adoption as a child of God has been a gift with me all my life." Married to Jutta Fischer, he's adopted her two sons, giving him four children and two grandchildren.

PRAYER STARTERS:

- Give thanks for the gifts of faith, scholarship, and culture the world has received from Lutheran believers.
- Pray for spiritual renewal in the ELCA and all Lutheran denominations.
- Praise God for loving adoptive parents; pray for good placements for children waiting for homes today.
- Ask God to bless George Anderson with wisdom and joy in his ministry and family.

> *[An elder] must hold firmly to the trustworthy message as it has been taught, so that he can encourage others by sound doctrine. Titus 1:9*

CONTACT: ELCA, 8765 W. Higgins Road, Chicago, IL 60631

Larry Flynt

Publisher, Hustler *Magazine*

Archive Photo

POINT OF IMPACT: Larry Flynt is different things to different people. To a *New York Times* writer, he is "the era's last crusader." To his adult daughter, Tonya Flynt-Vega, he's a child molester. When the movie about his life, *The People vs. Larry Flynt,* hit theaters in 1996, Flynt-Vega declared that she'd been repeatedly sexually abused as a teenager by her father. Larry Flynt Publications, a 10-story office building in Los Angeles, is home to Flynt's magazine empire (19 titles), his video, CD-Rom, cable and online businesses, and 200-plus employees. That's a long way from the first issue of *Hustler,* which he published in 1974 with the help of his fourth wife, Althea (a heroin addict who later died of AIDS complications) and one employee. Circulation is down, but online profits are skyrocketing. Experts say history will remember Flynt more for his Supreme Court win against a libel suit brought by preacher Jerry Falwell than for his photos.

He's a one-man crusade for hard-core pornography.

QUOTABLE: "When I started in this business, I hadn't even read the First Amendment. I just wanted to have fun and make money."

BEHIND THE SCENES: In 1978 outside a Georgia courthouse, Larry Flynt was gunned down and has been confined to a wheelchair since. He once ran for president, and has appeared in court wearing the American flag as a diaper. Flynt, 58, has four grown children and lives with his former nurse in Los Angeles.

PRAYER STARTER:

- "Pornography and prostitution turned my father's heart stone cold," says his daughter, Tonya. Pray that the Holy Spirit would bring Flynt to a clear and life-changing encounter with Jesus Christ and the abundant life He promises.

- Internet porn accounts for a significant part of the 500 percent growth in online commerce. Pray for lawmakers who are working on new controls. Pray that a new American consensus would turn against sexual exploitation and addiction.

- Ask God to bless Larry Flynt with love and healing.

> *I tell you that anyone who looks at a woman lustfully has already committed adultery with her in his heart. Jesus in Matthew 5:28*

CONTACT: Larry Flynt Publishing, Inc., 8484 Wilshire Blvd., Suite 900, Beverly Hills, CA 90211

Susan Sarandon
Actress, Activist

Archive Photo

POINT OF IMPACT: As one writer put it, "Susan Sarandon has given better performances and been hired for better roles as she's gotten older; in the process, she has come to personify the strong, sexy older woman—a type scarcely known in Tinseltown." She was 45 when she gave her Oscar-nominated performance in *Thelma & Louise*, and 50 when she won Best Actress from the Academy in 1996 for *Dead Man Walking*. Known for her liberal politics, she's also one of Hollywood's most visible activists, lending her name, money, and time to many political, cultural, and health organizations. In 1998 she won the ShoWest Humanitarian Award for "her passion and tireless efforts for numerous causes and charitable endeavors." Recent films include Miramax's *Illuminata* and *Earthly Possessions* for HBO.

On-screen, she plays outspoken, gutsy women; off-screen, she lives like one.

QUOTABLE: On love: "It's a risk. And it doesn't conquer all—an incredibly upsetting lesson."

BEHIND THE SCENES: Sarandon grew up in New Jersey and attended a Catholic school (the nuns declared she had an "overabundance of original sin"). The eldest of nine children, she was arrested for her involvement in Vietnam protests while still in high school. Actor Tim Robbins is her common-law husband and the father of her two late-in-life sons, Jack and Miles. She also has a daughter, Eva Marie, and a reputation as a devoted mother.

PRAYER STARTERS:

- Give thanks for Sarandon's humanitarian passion; pray that she would seek God's direction in her political and social causes.
- Pray that her choice of film roles would influence others for good.
- Pray that she would respond to the Spirit, and grow in faith.
- Ask God to give Sarandon and her family love, protection, and fulfillment.

> *Each of you should look not only to your own interests, but also to the interests of others. Philippians 2:4*

CONTACT: ICM, 8942 Wilshire Blvd., Beverly Hills, CA 90211

Wayne Gretzky
Hockey Player

NHL Photo

POINT OF IMPACT: Ask any ice hockey fan about the dominant figure in the sport today, and you'll get a rush of praise for Wayne Gretzky. Even after his retirement (April '99), he's still "The Great One." Gretzky has affected the hockey world like no skater before him. Over the past two decades he's scored more goals and made more assists than any player in history (the hockey equivalent of Hank Aaron surpassing Babe Ruth's home-run record). He's been named Most Valuable Player nine times, and owns or shares more than 60 other NHL records. He's been one of the few stars who could fill an arena with fans, much the way that Michael Jordan affected NBA attendance. Hockey's explosion in U.S. popularity "is directly attributed to Gretzky," says *Sports Illustrated.* "Well-spoken and unfailingly polite, always respectful of the men whose records he eclipsed, Gretzky has been a treasure to his often-troubled sport. When he leaves, he'll be the man to whom all others are compared."

He's still hockey's greatest asset.

QUOTABLE: "You miss 100 percent of the shots you never take."

BEHIND THE SCENES: Gretzky grew up in Brantford, Ontario, Canada. His father, Walter, used to drag out the garden hose to make a frozen pond so his sons could practice. They called it "Wally Coliseum." Just before breaking Gordie Howe's all-time scoring record, Wayne turned down an offer to make an "I'm going to Disneyland" commercial to celebrate his achievement. He said he didn't want to cheapen the moment. He resides in New York City with his wife, Janet, and children, Paulina, Ty, and Trevor.

PRAYER STARTERS:

- Gretzky is a spokesperson for Youthvision, a multimillion-dollar Canadian youth employment initiative. Pray for young persons who can benefit by Gretzky's example, or who are touched by Youthvision's programs.

- Ask for spiritual refreshment and physical provisions for Wayne's family today.

- Pray for a father you know who, like Walter Gretzky, could make a difference in his children's future today through initiative and faith.

Blessed are those whose strength is in you. Psalm 84:5

CONTACT: c/o 2 Penn Plaza, 14th Floor, New York, NY 10121

David Geffen

Music Mogul, DreamWorks Partner

Photo by Herb Ritts, copyright The David Geffen Company

POINT OF IMPACT: David Geffen's multifaceted influence is hard to pack into a paragraph. Let's start with music: Without a college degree, Geffen became a music legend and a millionaire at 26 (he's a billionaire today). He's had a knack for launching big stars (Jackson Browne, the Eagles and Nirvana, among many others). Always able to inspire tremendous loyalty among his artists, his other music business ventures include Asylum and Geffen Records. Then there are the movies: Along with partners Steven Spielberg and Jeffrey Katzenberg, Geffen created DreamWorks, the first major new Hollywood studio in 60 years—and put together $2 billion worth of investment capital to make it happen. In its first year, DreamWorks released *Deep Impact, Antz, Saving Private Ryan,* and *The Prince of Egypt.* The studio's approach to movies and movie making is already seen as a major influence in Hollywood's future. Geffen, who is openly gay, has contributed millions to fight AIDS.

He makes music—and money—for a dream team.

QUOTABLE: About DreamWorks' achievements so far: "Were our dreams bigger than our ability to accomplish them? Maybe. But what we've accomplished, as far as I'm concerned, is a dream. Anyone who wants to bet against us is going to be wrong."

BEHIND THE SCENES: Geffen, 54, grew up Jewish in a blue-collar neighborhood in Brooklyn. He's the subject of the 1997 biography *The Rise and Rise of David Geffen* by Stephen Singular. He's single and lives in Los Angeles.

PRAYER STARTERS:

- Pray that the DreamWorks team will continue to set high standards for entertainment that also reaches for the viewer's heart, mind, and spirit.
- Pray that David Geffen will experience God's best for his life; pray that wisdom and integrity will shape his business and personal choices.
- Ask God to grant Geffen health, safety, and a growing awareness of His love and mercies.

> *Call to me and I will answer you and tell you great and unsearchable things you do not know. Jeremiah 33:3*

CONTACT: www.geffen.com

Nadine Strossen

President,
American Civil Liberties Union (ACLU)

AP/Wide World Photos

POINT OF IMPACT: When the U.S. pornography industry met recently, featured speaker Nadine Strossen hailed them as human rights champions. "I want to underscore how extremely essential your efforts are. I want to thank and applaud you for your fight and contribution for First Amendment freedom." Since 1991, she's been president of the American Civil Liberties Union, the largest, highest-profile, and most controversial legal organization in the country. Her 1995 book, *Defending Pornography*, set up the ACLU to become an influential watchdog for the interests of pornographers. The major battlefield of this decade is in cyberspace—for example, the ACLU is currently fighting the new Child Online Protection Act in the courts. Many note that because Strossen professes to be a feminist, she wields much more clout than a man could in the same role. Strossen makes more than 200 public presentations a year around the world and writes a monthly column for the online magazine *Intellectual Capital.*

She's a feminist who defends pornography.

QUOTABLE: "I am constantly asked why I continue to defend pornography on so many levels. The answer is I have to keep defending free speech for pornography because so many other people keep attacking it, especially here in the United States with our puritanical heritage."

BEHIND THE SCENES: Strossen, 50, grew up in Minneapolis. She graduated from Harvard Law School, where she edited the *Harvard Law Review*. She's married to Eli Noam, and they have residences in Manhattan and Carmel, New York.

PRAYER STARTERS:

- Strossen calls efforts to restrict online porn as "innumerable, persistent and nasty attacks on sexual expression." Pray that those who seek to restrict pornography will proceed in ways that honor God, meet constitutional requirements, and protect society.

- Pray that Strossen's passion for protecting civil liberties will lead her to desire the spiritual freedom that can be found only in Christ.

- Ask God to bless Strossen and to fill her with a hunger for His love.

> *Now the Lord is the Spirit, and where the Spirit of the Lord is, there is freedom. 2 Corinthians 3:17*

CONTACT: nadinestrossen@intellectualcapital.com.

Luciano Pavarotti
Opera Singer

Archive Photo

POINT OF IMPACT: Italian tenor Luciano Pavarotti has a name that is a household word in upscale neighborhoods and trailer parks, Andean villages and Chinese markets. His purity of tone gives him a signature sound and his musical range has earned him the title, "the King of High Cs." His concerts and recordings with Placido Domingo and Jose Carerras have been phenomenally successful. And his public performances in open spaces have drawn the biggest audiences for a classical musician in history (a crowd of 500,000 in New York's Central Park, for example). In 1990, only Madonna and Elton John sold more recordings worldwide. As the century's most successful promoter for operatic music, he brings untold numbers of new fans to his demanding art. He's passionate about training opportunities for young singers and has organized a series of charity concerts to benefit needy kids.

He's the century's greatest promoter of operatic music.

QUOTABLE: "I want to be famous everywhere."

BEHIND THE SCENES: Luciano Pavarotti, 65, grew up poor in Modena, Italy. His father was a baker and his mother worked in a cigar factory. By the age of 19, he was teaching elementary school for eight dollars a month. Then in 1963 he substituted for an ailing tenor in *La Bohème* at the Royal Opera House, Covent Garden. The London audiences went wild with enthusiasm, and his career was launched. He has three children by his ex-wife Adua Veroni, and lives in New York and Italy with a companion, Nicoletta Mantovani.

PRAYER STARTERS:

- Give thanks for the great talent of Pavarotti; pray that he will strive to use his musical gifts to inspire listeners and to bring honor to God.
- Pray for the upcoming generation of opera singers who—led by stars such as Italian tenor Andrea Bocelli—are finding success bringing opera to new audiences.
- Ask God to shower Pavarotti and his family with His love and mercies, and pray that Pavarotti would recognize the source of his blessings.

> *Sing to the Lord, for he has done glorious things; let this be known to all the world. Isaiah 12:5*

CONTACT: www.lucianopavarotti.it

Archbishop Desmond Tutu

Churchman, Author, Activist

Photo by Rick Reinhard, Washington, DC

POINT OF IMPACT: Anglican Bishop (and later Archbishop) Desmond Tutu is famous around the world as the Christian who successfully led South African churches in opposition to apartheid. The race-segregation policy was introduced by the government's Nationalist party in order to maintain the control of 4.5 million whites over the 23 million blacks in the country. Laws included limited education for blacks, segregation to squalid "homelands," detention without trial, as well as the introduction of "the pass," which blacks were required to carry at all times. Tutu refused to carry "the pass" and spoke out against the policies while following a strict commitment to nonviolence. In 1984 he was awarded the Nobel Peace Prize for his efforts. Now retired, he is also the recipient of many honorary degrees and is the author of a number of books, including *An African Prayer Book* and *The Rainbow People of God*.

His righteous opposition to apartheid still echoes around the world.

QUOTABLE: "Goodness is stronger than evil; love is stronger than hate; light is stronger than darkness; life is stronger than death; victory is ours through Him who loves us."—*African Prayer Book*

BEHIND THE SCENES: Tutu's first jobs were selling peanuts at railroad stations and caddying on a golf course. He wanted to be a doctor but lacked the funds, so he studied to be a schoolteacher like his father. When he contracted tuberculosis and was hospitalized as a teen, he was visited by an Anglican priest who had a profound influence on him. Tutu, 69, lives in Cape Town.

PRAYER STARTERS:

- Give thanks for Tutu's faithfulness and perseverence. Ask God to continue to protect the Archbishop from harm.
- Pray that God will continue to speak truth through Tutu's life to the whole of Africa.
- Ask God to bless Tutu and his family with health, joy, and prosperity.
- Pray for the African continent today—for physical provisions, for peace, and for increasing love and tolerance among its peoples.

> *Be on your guard; stand firm in the faith; be men of courage; be strong. Do everything in love. 1 Corinthians 16:13-14*

CONTACT: Bishopscourt Claremont Cape 7700, South Africa; upallen@emory.edu.com

Heidi G. Miller

CFO, Citigroup

POINT OF IMPACT: "I'm a Jewish girl from Queens," she says. But to powerbrokers in banking and insurance, she's Heidi G. Miller, keeper of the bank. At 46, she's ranked third most powerful woman in business by *Fortune*. In October 1998, when Travelers Group merged with Citicorp, Miller was appointed the executive vice president and CFO of the new Citigroup. With $700 billion in assets, the company was at the time the largest financial institution in the world. "There are no shrinking violets in this company," she says. "Being a CFO in a place where everyone acts like a CFO is a tough job. It's not like a manufacturing company. Everybody here has an opinion on liquidity and can read a balance sheet." Miller's responsibilities include keeping the company's credit ratings high. "I like report cards," she says, "and those are my grades."

She plays with $700 billion—and it's not play money.

QUOTABLE: Miller is fond of the axiom: "Man plans, God laughs."

BEHIND THE SCENES: Miller graduated from Princeton and earned a Ph.D. in history from Yale. In order to make the most of her drive time between Manhattan and her home in Greenwich, Connecticut, she listens to taped lectures on subjects like philosophy and religion. Her husband, Brian, also works in finance. They have two sons, Jonathan and Matthew, ages 14 and 9. Miller also serves on the board of the Children's Defense Fund.

PRAYER STARTERS:

- Pray that Heidi Miller would seek and follow God's wisdom in her financial recommendations and decisions; pray that her legacy would be of integrity, farsightedness, and courage.
- Pray that investors on the world money markets would practice integrity and prudence.
- Ask God to protect the Miller family from danger. Pray that they will seek Him and His best for them today.

Dishonest money dwindles away, but he who gathers money little by little makes it grow. Proverbs 13:11

CONTACT: Citigroup, 153 E. 53rd St., New York, NY 10043

Stanley Prusiner

1997 Nobel Laureate in Medicine

POINT OF IMPACT: Next time you visit an aging family member in a care center, thank God for Dr. Stanley Prusiner. His research has revealed a class of infectious "rogue proteins" called *prions* that wreak havoc on the brains of humans and other mammals. His work has been linked with understanding Alzheimer's and other dementia-related illnesses, including "mad cow disease." For his achievements, he was awarded the Nobel Prize for Medicine in 1997. When he proposed his ideas about prions in 1982, they were considered heretical by most scientists, but many of those doubters now sing a different tune. "It's terrific," said former skeptic David Baltimore of the Massachusetts Institute of Technology. "These are the mythological stories of science—people who have really kept their own faith and lived through a period of disgrace and finally are discovered to be right." Prusiner says his next goal is a cure for prion-based diseases.

He endured mockery—until research proved him right.

QUOTABLE: "Awards do not vindicate a piece of science. Only data does that."

BEHIND THE SCENES: Prusiner, 58, endured decades of criticism, and says the press was especially cruel. He refused all interviews after an article in a national magazine mocked his work and him personally. Prusiner and his wife, Sandy, have two daughters, 13 and 20. He lives in San Francisco.

PRAYER STARTERS:

- Thank God for new medical knowledge that promises to help overcome human suffering. Ask the Lord to reveal His love and His truths to the Prusiner family today. Pray that He will bless them with love and health.

- Pray for the ongoing work of Prusiner and other medical researchers. Pray for their strength and courage as well as their success.

- Ten percent of those over 65 and almost half of those over age 85 suffer from Alzheimer's disease. Pray for a person or a family you know today who is facing this health challenge.

> *Even when I am old and gray, do not forsake me, O God, till I declare your power to the next generation. Psalm 71:18*

CONTACT: Department of Neurology, University of California, School of Medicine, San Francisco, CA 94143

Cokie Roberts

News Analyst, National Public Radio;
Coanchor, ABC's This Week

ABC Photo

POINT OF IMPACT: Colleagues say Cokie—Mary Martha Corinne Morrison Claiborne Boggs Roberts— excels at what she does because she understands the political process and isn't daunted by it. National Public Radio listeners have long been familiar with her pithy comments; she was the NPR Congressional Correspondent for more than ten years. In that time, she won numerous awards, including the highest honor in public radio, the Edward R. Murrow Award. She was named cosuccessor to Brinkley on *This Week with David Brinkley* when she and Sam Donaldson became coanchors of the program in November 1996. Her consistent ability to make sense of the news has won her a wide and influential audience.

Millions rely on her to make sense of the news.

QUOTABLE: "I was raised to be skeptical of the media—and right they were. But here I am, a reporter, telling sometimes 'vicious truths.'"

BEHIND THE SCENES: The daughter of late Congressman Hale Boggs and his wife, Lindy, Cokie Roberts was reared in Louisiana and loves spicy Cajun food. She once admitted that she carries a bottle of Tabasco sauce in her purse so she can pep up dull Washington dinners.

PRAYER STARTERS:

- Thank God for all journalists who love the truth. Pray that more news analysts and editorial writers will humbly seek God's leading in their work.
- Praise God for the freedom of the press in America.
- Ask God to bless and protect Cokie and Steven Roberts today.

> *Wisdom makes one wise man more powerful than ten rulers in a city.*
> *Ecclesiastes 7:19*

CONTACT: Nightline/This Week, 1717 DeSales St. N.W., Washington, DC 20036

C. Peter Wagner

Founder, Global Harvest Ministries;
President, World Prayer Center

Courtesy of Global Harvest Ministries

POINT OF IMPACT: Peter Wagner is clearly a man who likes to spread the Word. In 1992, after a career as a church growth expert, he created Global Harvest Ministries in Colorado to join prayer networks in intercession for global evangelism, among other goals. With the launch in 1998 of the World Prayer Center, Wagner is attempting to link pray-ers and needs on all continents. At the World Prayer Center, individual prayer requests arrive via e-mail and fax and are passed to volunteers who pray for each. "The world has never seen a prayer movement matching what God has been doing during the decade of the 1990s," he says. Wagner hopes to coordinate some 50 million pray-ers eventually, and has plans to establish other prayer centers in England, Japan, and elsewhere. Center director Chuck Pierce says simply, "We want to make it hard for people to go to hell."

He's making it hard for people to go to hell.

QUOTABLE: "I'd suspect that the one who's most aware of the power of this prayer movement is the devil himself. He's never lost so much territory in such a short time. He has great wrath because he knows his time is short. But there's little he can do about the advance of the kingdom of God."

BEHIND THE SCENES: Wagner, 69 was for many years a professor of church growth at Fuller Theological Seminary, and is the author of more than 50 books. He and his wife, Doris, have three grown children and seven grandkids.

PRAYER STARTERS:

- Praise God for the growing worldwide prayer movement. Pray that the Spirit would continue to bring revival and renewal to His church. Pray for the success of the World Prayer Center, which Doris Wagner directs.

- Give thanks for Peter Wagner's years of faithful ministry; pray for the impact of his many former students around the world, and for those now being trained at the Wagner Leadership Institute.

- Ask the Lord to favor the Wagners and their family with physical and spiritual protection, and a sweet sense of His presence.

Pray in the Spirit on all occasions with all kinds of prayers and requests.
Ephesians 6:18

CONTACT: P.O. Box 63060, Colorado Springs, CO 80962-3060; pwagner@wpccs.org

Harold Kushner

Rabbi, Author

Courtesy of Leigh Bureau

POINT OF IMPACT: Rabbi Harold S. Kushner, rabbi laureate of Temple Israel in Natick, Massachusetts, is best known as the author of *When Bad Things Happen to Good People*, an international bestseller published in 1981 that has been named one of the ten most influential books in recent history by Book-of-the-Month Club members. Over the past 20 years, Kushner's books have given voice to the spiritual, ethical, and emotional struggles of Baby Boomers; he's explored the problem of evil, guilt and forgiveness, and holding on to faith in the face of suffering. His other books include *How Good Do We Have to Be? When All You've Ever Wanted Isn't Enough* (which won the 1995 Christopher Medal), and *Who Needs God?* Kushner's advice is unfailingly down-to-earth, candid, probing, and redemptive.

He's "rabbi" to the baby boomers.

QUOTABLE: "I believe in a God who does not send the tragedy but who sends the incredible grace to deal with the tragedy."

BEHIND THE SCENES: Kushner's faith was severely tested when his three-year-old son was diagnosed with a fatal genetic disorder. "I did not want to worship a God who would do this to my son," Kushner says. Watching his son slowly die by age 14 shattered Kushner's assumption that if he were good, everything would be okay. The crisis led ultimately to the writing of *When Bad Things Happen*. . . . Now Kushner, 64, says he and his wife, Suzette, "could not have loved and mourned our son without the help of God." People sometimes lose faith when bad things happen, he says, but just as often that is when they truly find God. The Kushners have one daughter.

PRAYER POINTS:

- Give thanks for the hope and guidance Rabbi Kushner has given millions who wouldn't approach a pastor or rabbi, or attend religious services.
- Pray that an ongoing spiritual awakening among Baby Boomers will lead many to embrace enduring truths and the personal God of the Bible.
- Pray for God's best for the Kushners, and for Kushner's continued writing success.

The LORD is good, a refuge in times of trouble. Nahum 1:7

CONTACT: 145 Hartford St., Natick, MA 01760-3199

Betty Stanley Beene

President and CEO,
The United Way of America

Courtesy of United Way

POINT OF IMPACT: When she became United Way president in 1996, Beene inherited an organization that was trying to recover from a scandal involving its former president. To accelerate the healing process, Beene traveled to United Way programs in every state to listen and learn—and to spread her zeal about the power of community-based compassion. By nearly every measure, her evangelistic approach has paid off. Giving and volunteer numbers are up, and new projects are proliferating. Founded in 1918, United Way is the nation's largest source of private support for health and human services. Today the national office supports nearly 1,400 autonomous regional United Ways, and through them, 45,000 local agencies and services that touch millions of lives. In 1997–98 alone, campaigns raised $3.4 billion.

She helps communities help their own.

QUOTABLE: "We must never stop believing that we can make a change in the lives of our friends, relatives and neighbors. I have seen it and know in my heart that it is real."

BEHIND THE SCENES: With degrees in journalism and business, Betty Beene got her start in volunteer work on the local Girl Scouts Council in Houston. But she's quick to attribute any personal success to God's leadership, saying she tries to root her busy life in prayer, Bible study, and deep reflection. "I've been blessed by parents who taught me that God never leaves us alone," she says. Other blessings she points to: "my husband, Bill, extraordinarily dedicated volunteers—and plenty of energy."

PRAYER STARTERS:

- Pray for United Way's success in its efforts to "increase the organized capacity of people to care for one another."
- Betty Beene asks for prayer that she'll be granted the leadership capabilities and direction she needs each day.
- Pray for community-helping efforts in your area—for staff and volunteers, and for generous givers.
- Ask God to bless Beene and her family with peace and well-being.

He who is kind to the poor lends to the LORD. Proverbs 19:17

CONTACT: 701 North Fairfax Street, Alexandria, VA 22314; www.unitedway.org

"Evil would want us to think the worst about who we are, so we would have that behind our eyes as we look at our neighbor, and we would see the worst in our neighbor. Jesus would want us to see the best of who we are, so we would have that behind our eyes as we looked at our neighbor, and we would be able to see the best in him or her. You can be an accuser or an advocate. Evil would have you be an accuser in this life. Jesus would have you be an advocate for your neighbor."

—FRED ("MISTER") ROGERS
in *Christian Parenting Today*,
quoting his seminary mentor, William Orr

Franklin Graham
Evangelist; President, Samaritan's Purse

Courtesy of Samaritan's Purse

POINT OF IMPACT: At age 22, after traveling the world and avoiding his father Billy's ministry, Franklin Graham committed his life to Christ while alone in a Jerusalem hotel. Dr. Bob Pierce, founder of the relief assistance organizations Samaritan's Purse and World Vision, invited Graham to join him on a mission to Asia. There, he felt a calling to work in areas affected by war, famine, disease, and natural disasters. Since 1979 Franklin has been president of Samaritan's Purse, and in 1989 he conducted his first evangelistic crusade. He now conducts ten a year with the Billy Graham Evangelistic Association (BGEA). Since 1995 he's served as the first vice-chairman of BGEA and is in line to succeed his father. His autobiography is *Rebel with a Cause*, "He thinks big, he's a driver," says a friend. "When he sees a need, he jumps in with both feet believing God will make things happen."

He's a rebel with a Christian cause.

QUOTABLE: "You may be guilty of adultery. You may be guilty of stealing. You may be guilty of lying. I don't care what your sin is, God will forgive you. What I'm asking you to do is to humble yourself before God."

BEHIND THE SCENES: Franklin, 48, has always had a passion for speed—in the air (where he is a pilot) and on the ground. At a recent youth crusade, both he and Billy Graham wore motorcycle jackets. He and his wife, Jane Austin Cunningham, have three sons and one daughter; they live in North Carolina.

PRAYER STARTERS:

- Give thanks for the Lord's faithfulness in Graham's life, and for the vigor and dedication he brings to his ministries.
- Ask God to bless and protect the Grahams' family and marriage in the midst of enormous pressures.
- Pray for protection for the spiritual lives and integrity of everyone at Samaritan's Purse and BGEA. Pray for disaster relief efforts worldwide.

> *With your help I can advance against a troop; with my God I can scale a wall. Psalm 18:29*

CONTACT: P.O. Box 3000, Boone, NC 28607; usa@samaritan.org

Tony Hall

U.S. Congressman

POINT OF IMPACT: According to President Clinton, "There may be no one in Congress who is as admired as Tony Hall, a man who lives his faith every day . . . and still has enough left in his mind, in his heart, to care for the children who are hungry and homeless and dispossessed all across the world." Hall (D., Ohio) has spent most of his tenure in Congress championing federal efforts to deal with global hunger. He is chairman of the House Democratic Caucus Task Force on Hunger and is founder and chairman of the Congressional Hunger Center. In a party known for its support of abortion, Hall is an outspoken opponent. He's called on Congress to apologize for slavery, authored a measure to promote teaching character education in schools, and worked actively to improve human rights around the world. Hall was nominated for the 1998 Nobel Peace Prize.

He's the conscience of Congress about hunger.

QUOTABLE: "Congress is afflicted with famine. We are hungry for heart—heart for the needy, the powerless, and the forgotten."

BEHIND THE SCENES: Early in his career, Hall, an evangelical Presbyterian, visited Mother Teresa in India. When he asked her how he could better serve people, she walked over to a little child, picked him up, and held him. She looked at Tony and told him to do the work that was in front of him. In April 1993 Hall went on a three-week hunger strike to protest the demise of the House Select Committee on Hunger and to draw attention to the plight of the starving. Congressman Hall, 58, is married to Jane Dick; they have two children.

PRAYER STARTERS:

- Give thanks for Tony Hall's courage on behalf of needy children around the world. Pray that his Christian testimony will continue undiminished.

- Pray that Congress will respond to Hall's example, taking measures to deal with famine—of the hungry around the world, and of their own "famine of the heart" that Hall warns against.

- Ask God to meet the physical and emotional needs of the Hall family today.

> *He will defend the afflicted among the people and save the children of the needy; he will crush the oppressor. Psalm 72:4*

CONTACT: 432 Longworth, Washington, DC 20515-3303

Nobuyuki Idei
Co-CEO, Sony

POINT OF IMPACT: Nobuyuki Idei is the president and co-CEO for Sony Corp., one of the most highly recognized brand names in the world. Japan, however, sees Idei as more than a CEO of a great company. He is considered one of the only men capable of leading the country out of its economic mess. In 1998 *Fortune* magazine named him Asia's Man of the Year. Sony, best known as the leading manufacturer worldwide of audio, video, communications, and information technology, is also a leader in motion pictures, television, and computer entertainment. Now Idei is leading Sony's drive to be a central player on the information highway. He wants to merge every home's consumer electronics with everything from satellites to the internet, creating a global wireless network. He calls it *convergence.*

He's Asia's favorite CEO and their hope for economic recovery.

QUOTABLE: "Convergence is happening not only between audio and video but between computers and communication. There is a fundamental change in society, and this is our opportunity."

BEHIND THE SCENES: A new grandfather in his early sixties, Idei drives a Porsche, favors Italian suits, and appears at opening night concerts by such Sony stars as Celine Dion. In the span of a week in early March, he attended both the Grammy Awards in Los Angeles and a Rolling Stones concert in Tokyo. As a youth, Idei dreamed of becoming a violinist but gave that up to major in economics. He lives in Tokyo with his wife, Teruyo, and a daughter.

PRAYER STARTERS:

- Give thanks for the positive economic impact of Sony Corporation, for families and communities worldwide who benefit from its prosperity.
- Ask God to bless Nobuyuki and Teruyo Idei today with eternal life through Jesus Christ. Ask for health and joy for their family.
- In the first eight months of 1998, 22,000 Japanese businessmen were reported to have committed suicide because of financial failures. Pray that Idei will make decisions today for Japan that bring hope and economic recovery.

> *[Christ] is the image of the invisible God. . . . by him all things were created. . . . He is before all things, and in him all things hold together. Colossians 1:15-17*

CONTACT: Sony Corporation of America, 550 Madison Ave., New York, NY 10022

William Rehnquist
Chief Justice of the Supreme Court

Archive Photo

POINT OF IMPACT: For 27 years, the Honorable William Rehnquist has played a key role in deciding the final word on what constitutes the law of the land. As Chief Justice since 1986, he's the country's top judicial officer, overseeing and managing the nine-judge court. Early in his career, Rehnquist earned a reputation as an ultraconservative (he wrote the dissenting opinion in the landmark case legalizing abortion). Since then he's been responsible more than anyone else for turning the court away from decades of liberal judicial activism to a more reserved, interpretive approach. *All Politics,* an online magazine, says he "has amassed what is perhaps the court's most conservative record of the last 25 years." Yet to win the votes of less-conservative colleagues, Rehnquist has been willing to moderate his views.

His word is law.

QUOTABLE: "I'm a strong believer in pluralism: don't concentrate all the power in one place. You don't want all the power in the government as opposed to the people. You don't want all the power in the federal government as opposed to the states."

BEHIND THE SCENES: Rehnquist, 76, was the presiding judge over President Clinton's Senate impeachment trial in 1999. He was active in civic and church work in Arizona and continues to be an active member of Emmanuel Lutheran Church, Bethesda, Maryland. A widower, he has three children.

PRAYER STARTERS:

- Give thanks for our heritage of the rule of law, and for the civil liberties guaranteed by the Constitution.

- Pray that William Rehnquist will seek God's wisdom in all his decisions today; pray that his leadership of the other eight justices will promote fairness, thoroughness, mutual respect, and justice.

- Ask the Lord to protect Judge Rehnquist's health and well-being, and grant him a clear sense of His pleasure and purposes in his life.

> *Judge carefully, for with the LORD our God there is no injustice or partiality or bribery. 2 Chronicles 19:7*

CONTACT: 1 First St. N.E., Washington, DC 20543

Nora Ephron

Screenwriter, Author, Director

POINT OF IMPACT: Nora Ephron has taken parental advice all the way to the bank. Once told: "Take notes, everything is copy," the successful writer has turned real-life foibles and lessons into funny, poignant movies. Says Columbia President Amy Pascal, "Her wonderful sense of humor is only matched by her terrific insight into human nature." Described as "without a doubt one of the most talented and respected names in Hollywood," Ephron is the brain behind such hits as *When Harry Met Sally* and *Sleepless in Seattle*. Three of her screenplays have been nominated for Academy Awards. In recent years, she added directing to her résumé, including the recent *You've Got Mail* (which she also wrote). In her new project, *Red Tails in Love: A Wildlife Drama in Central Park,* she writes, produces, and directs.

Her romantic comedies portray modern life and love.

QUOTABLE: "I love that movies have a way of being autobiographical for all of us even though they aren't at all autobiographical."

BEHIND THE SCENES: Born in New York City, Ephron, 59, comes by her talents naturally—her parents, Phoebe and Henry Ephron, are authors and screenwriters as well. Ephron was educated at Wellesley and started her career as a general assignment reporter for the *New York Post*. She is married to writer Nicholas Pileggi and has two children.

PRAYER STARTERS:

- Pray that Nora Ephron will seek and follow God's leading in her creative and personal life.
- Pray that her influence in Hollywood will promote respect between the sexes, fidelity in marriage, insight into human nature—and wholesome fun.
- Ask the Lord to shower Ephron and her family with His best for their lives.

> *Things that are too amazing for me . . . the way of an eagle in the sky, the way of a snake on a rock, the way of a ship on the high seas, and the way of a man with a maiden. Proverbs 30:18-19*

CONTACT: c/o Warner Bros., 4000 Warner Blvd., Burbank, CA 91522

Martin Lee

Chairman of the Democratic Party,
Hong Kong

Courtesy of Martin Lee

POINT OF IMPACT: Hong Kong's most prominent democratic politician is a prim, bookish lawyer. Yet, "perhaps more than any other person in Hong Kong, this man scares China," writes the *San Jose Mercury News*. While friends and colleagues were acquiring foreign passports in anticipation of "the Handover" of the former British colony to mainland China, Lee said his "little worm of a conscience made me ask what I had done for the community, having taken so much out of it." He decided to stay. Overwhelmingly voted back onto the governing council in 1998, Lee represents Hong Kong's largest political party and a key hope for a democratic future. "Martin Lee will be the man to watch," said one analyst. "I think of him as the canary that the miners used to send down into the mine to breathe the air to tell whether it was safe for them to go down. Will they survive? He is in that role."

In Hong Kong, he speaks for a democratic future.

QUOTABLE: "Few people in the world understand and treasure liberty as Hong Kong people do. We are committed to using our mandate to advance freedom and democracy for the people of Hong Kong."

BEHIND THE SCENES: Martin Lee has received international recognition for his extraordinary contributions to human rights and his efforts to defend Hong Kong freedoms. Lee, 62, a devout Catholic, is married and has one son.

PRAYER STARTERS:

- Pray that Martin Lee will be gifted with discretion, knowledge and courage as he leads his people at this critical juncture in Hong Kong's history.
- Pray for peace and stability for the 6.5 million people of Hong Kong. Pray for the impact of Christians in this economic hub of Southeast Asia.
- Ask God to strengthen and encourage Lee in his Christian faith and to protect his family.

Who knows but that you have come ... for such a time as this? Esther 4:14

CONTACT: 704A Admiralty Center, Tower I, 18 Harcourt Rd., Hong Kong; www.martinlee.org

Photo by Micah Marty

Robert Coles
Child Psychiatrist

POINT OF IMPACT: Pulitzer Prize-winner Robert Coles has accomplished through observation, insight, and persistence what stadiums full of preachers could never do—convinced scores of Ivy League academics that children have a spiritual life that matters. Since the seventies, he's been a research scientist at Harvard University and a professor of psychiatry and medical humanities. The author of 60 books, he still teaches one of the university's most popular literature courses (nicknamed "Guilt 105" because of his emphasis on personal moral reflection). In his best-known book, *The Spiritual Life of Children,* he looks at how children from various backgrounds acquire religious values and how these impact their lives. He accuses contemporary culture of raising morally abandoned children.

He teaches the world about the spiritual lives of children.

QUOTABLE: "We live out what we presumably want taught to our children. And our children are taking constant notice, and they're measuring us not by what we say but what we do."

BEHIND THE SCENES: A turning point for Coles, 71, came in the early sixties when he witnessed six-year-old Ruby Bridges facing racist mobs alone in New Orleans. Coles joined the civil rights movement and decided to make the inner world of children his life study. His research team for *The Spiritual Life of Children* included his wife, Jane, and their three grown sons (all also trained physicians).

PRAYER STARTERS:

- Give thanks for Coles' positive spiritual impact in academic circles, where many aren't otherwise receptive.
- Coles was raised Episcopalian. Ask God to nurture a spiritual intimacy with Himself in every member of the Coles family. Pray for health and peace for Robert and his wife.
- Pray that educators and parents worldwide will have a growing commitment to incorporating biblical truths in everyday life.

From the lips of children and infants you have ordained praise. Psalm 8:2

CONTACT: 1350 Massachusetts Avenue, Cambridge, MA 02138

Karolyn Nunnallee

National President, MADD

Courtesy of M.A.D.D.

POINT OF IMPACT: Karolyn Nunnallee leads the most influential organization fighting drunk driving today. Mothers Against Drunk Drivers (MADD) is a nonprofit grassroots organization with more than three million members and 600 chapters nationwide. The group's goal is "to find effective solutions to the drunk driving and underage drinking problems, while supporting those who have already experienced the pain of these senseless crimes." Nunnallee, who lost a daughter to a drunk driver, is lobbying to get Congress to set a national standard for legal intoxication at .08 blood alcohol concentration. This is now law in 16 states (32 fix the line at .10). About her impact as a lobbyist, Rep. Charles Canady (R-Fla.) says she's very effective. "It's difficult to ignore the powerful personal experience she speaks from."

She turned personal tragedy into public gain.

QUOTABLE: "Unfortunately, as Americans have seen progress in the war against drunk driving, they have grown complacent, even lethargic."

BEHIND THE SCENES: The Nunnallees lost their daughter, Patty, in one of the most deadly alcohol-related crashes in the nation's history. On May 14, 1988, in Carrollton, Kentucky, a drunk driver (and repeat offender) with a .24 percent blood-alcohol concentration slammed head-on into a bus carrying 68 people returning from a church outing. His pickup punctured the bus's gas tank, setting it afire. Twenty-four children and three adults were killed, and 30 others injured. Patty Nunnallee, age ten, was the youngest victim. Karolyn, 49, and her husband, Jim, have another daughter, Jeanne. They live in Fort Meade, Florida.

PRAYER STARTERS:

- Give thanks for Nunnallee's willingness to turn her loss into public good. Pray for her continued strength, blessing, and influence.
- Pray for countless other families who've lost loved ones to drunk drivers.
- Give thanks and pray for MADD volunteers across the country. Pray for success in their lobbying, education, and community awareness efforts.

Let us be self-controlled, putting on faith and love. 1 Thessalonians 5:8

CONTACT: MADD, P.O. Box 541688, Dallas, TX 75354-1688; www.madd.org

INDEX OF NAMES

INDEX OF NAMES

INDEX OF NAMES

PRAYER & RENEWAL
RESOURCES APPENDIX

If my people who are called by my name will humble themselves
and pray and seek my face and turn from their wicked ways,
then will I hear from heaven and will forgive their sin
and will heal their land.
2 Chronicles 7:14

AD2000 and Beyond Movemement: Prayer Track/C. Peter Wagner, director, 2860 S. Circle Dr., Suite 2112, Colorado Springs, CO 80906; (719) 576-2000; fax: (719) 576-2685; e-mail: info@ad2000.org; online: www.ad2000.org

Bethany World Prayer Center: Unreached Peoples Project, 13855 Plank Rd., Baker, LA 70714; (504) 664-2000; fax: (504) 774-2001; e-mail: 102132.52@compuserve.com; online: www.goshen.net

Campus Crusade International: William R. Bright, president, 100 Sunport Lane, Orlando, FL 32809; (407) 826-2000; fax: (407) 826-2187; online: www.ccci.org

Children's Global Prayer Movement, Esther Network International: 854 Conniston Road, West Palm Beach, FL 33405-2131; (561) 832-6490; fax: (561) 832-8043; e-mail: lcci-eni@flinet.com

Christian Solidarity International: Zelgistrasse 64, PO Box 70 CH-8122, Binz by Zurich, Switzerland; 41-1-980-47-00; e-mail: csi-int@csi-int.ch.; online: www.csi-int.ch

Concerts of Prayer International: David Bryant, president, P.O. Box 770, New Providence, NJ 07974; (908) 771-0146; fax: (908) 665-4199; e-mail: copinj@aol.com

Every Home for Christ: Dick Eastman, president, P.O. Box 35930, Colorado Springs, CO 80935-3593; (719) 260-8888; fax: (719) 260-7505; e-mail: info@ehc.org; online: www.sni.net/ehc

Global Harvest Ministries/World Prayer Center: C. Peter and Doris Wagner, directors, P.O. Box 63060, Colorado Springs, CO 80962-3060; (719) 262-9922; fax: (719) 262-9920; e-mail: info@globalharvest.org; online: www.globalharvest.org

Houses of Prayer Ministries: Alvin Vander Griend, director, P.O. Box 141312, Grand Rapids, MI 49514; (800) 217-5200; fax: (616) 791-9926; e-mail: hope@missionindia.org; online: www.missionindia.org/hope

Great Commissionary Kids: 1445 Boonville Ave., Springfield, MO 65802; (417) 862-2781; fax: (417) 862-0503; e-mail: The-Greath-Commissionary-Kids@ag.org

Intercessors for America: Gary Bergel, director, P.O. Box 4477, Leesburg, VA 20177-8155; (703) 777-0003; fax: (703) 777-2324; e-mail: usapray@aol.com; online: www.ifa-usapray.org

International Reconciliation Coalition for Indigenous People: P.O. Box 1417, Castle Rock, CO 80104; (303) 660-9258; fax: (303) 660-0621; e-mail: ircoal@aol.com

International Reconciliation Coalition: P.O. Box 296, Sunland, CA 91041-0296; (818) 896-1589; fax: (818) 896-2077; e-mail: 75717.777@compuserve.com; online: www.reconcile.org

International Renewal Ministries: Terry Dirks, executive director, 8435 N.E. Glisan Street, Portland, OR 97220; (503) 251-6455; fax: (503) 251-6454; e-mail: irm@multnomah.edu; online: www.multnomah.edu

Mission America Coalition: Paul Cedar, executive director, 901 East 78th Street, Minneapolis, MN 55420; 1-800-995-8572; fax: (612) 853-1745; e-mail: missionamerica@compuserve.com; online: www.missionamerica.org

Moms in Touch International: Fern Nichols, president, P.O. Box 1120, Poway, CA 92074-1120; (619) 486-4065; fax: (619) 486-5132; e-mail: mitihqtrs@ compuserve.com

National Day of Prayer: Jim Weidmann, executive director, P.O. Box 15616, Colorado Springs, CO 80935-5616; (800) 444-8828 or (719) 531-3379; fax: (719) 548-4520

Pray Down at High Noon: Terry Teykl, director, P.O. Box 278, Spring, TX 77383; (281) 355-7475

Pray Hollywood 2000: Rick Clark, founder, 1610 Elizabeth Street, Pasadena CA 91104; (626) 296-7600; fax: (626) 963-6587

Pray! Magazine: Jon Graf, editor, P.O. Box 35004, Colorado Springs, CO 80935; (800) 691-7729; fax: (719) 598-7128; e-mail: pray.mag@navpress.com online: www.praymag.com

PrayerNet Weekly E-mail Newsletter: e-mail: 75711.2501@Compuserve.com

Praying Through the Windows Project: Beverly Pegues, executive director, 11005 Highway 83 N., Suite 159, Colorado Springs, CO 80921; (719) 522-1040; fax: (719) 277-7148); e-mail: cin@cin1040.net; online: www.christian-info.com

Promise Keepers: Bill McCartney, founder, P.O. Box 103001, Denver, CO 80250-3001; (303) 964-7600; fax: (303) 433-1036; online: www.promisekeepers.org

US Prayer Track/Pray USA: Eddie Smith, director, (888) Pray-USA or (713) 466-4009; online: www.usprayertrack.org

Worldwide Day of Prayer for Children at Risk: PO Box 633, Oxford, OX2 OXZ U.K.; 44-1865-450800; fax: 44-1865-203567; e-mail: prayer@viva.org

Youth with a Mission International: PO Box 26479, Colorado Springs, CO 80936; (719) 380-0505; fax: (719) 380-0936

You Can Help Us
Make The Pray 365 Project
Even Better!

- Do you have updated information you'd like to pass along?
- Would you like to nominate a person or persons for our next edition of *Praying for the World's 365 Most Influential People?*
- Would you like to share answers to prayers that have been prompted by using this book?
- Do you want to make suggestions for making this book more effective for you, your church, or your ministry?

We'd love to hear from you. Please contact:

The Pray 365 Project
P.O. Box 723
Sisters, OR 97759
USA

(541) 549-4246; Fax: (541) 549-0824
www.pray365.com
e-mail: pray365prj@aol.com

About the Editors

David Kopp, a free-lance writer and editor, is co-author of *Love Stories God Told* and *Unquenchable Love* (Harvest House). His most recent book is *Praying the Bible for Your Life*. He is currently a senior editor with *Christian Parenting Today* magazine, which he helped found in 1988. Kopp was born in Zambia to missionary parents.

Heather Harpham Kopp is the author of seven books including *Love Stories God Told* and *Unquenchable Love* (which she co-authored with her husband), *Daddy, Where Were You?* and *Praying the Bible for Your Children*. The Kopps have five children and live in Oregon.

Larry Wilson is a free-lance writer and editor living in Los Angeles. He is the former senior editor of *World Vision* magazine, for which he co-wrote with John Robb the report, "You Can Change the World Through Prayer." Prior to that, Wilson served as an editor with *Moody*. Currently he works extensively as a journalist with international aid organizations.